Mosses Lichens & Ferns

of Northwest North America

DALE H. VITT
JANET E. MARSH
ROBIN B. BOVEY

Mosses Lichens & Ferns

of Northwest North America

First printed 1988 5 4 3 2

Printed in Canada

The Publisher: **Lone Pine Publishing**

206, 10426 - 81 Ave.
Edmonton, Alberta
Canada T6E 1X5

202A, 1110 Seymour Street
Vancouver, British Columbia
Canada V6B 3N3

#180, 16149 Redmond Way
Redmond, Washington
USA 98052

Canadian Cataloguing in Publication Data

Vitt, Dale H. (Dale Hadley), 1944–
A photographic field guide to the mosses, lichens and ferns of northwest North America

Includes index.
ISBN 0-919433-41-3

1. Cryptogams—Canada, Western—Indentification.
2. Cryptogams—Canada, Northern—Identification.
3. Cryptogams—Northwest, Pacific—Indentification.
I. Marsh, Janet E. II. Bovey, Robin B. (Robin Bruce), 1947– . I. Title.
QK509.V48 1988 586.097 C88-090246-9

U.S. ISBN 0-295-96666-1

Typesetting by Pièce de Résistance Ltée, Edmonton, Alberta.
Printing by Quality Color Press Ltd., Edmonton, Alberta.

Cover Photograph: *Conocephalum conicum*

The publisher gratefully acknowledges the assistance of Alberta Community Development, the Department of Canadian Heritage and the Recreation, Parks and Wildlife Foundation of Alberta, the support of the Canada/Alberta Agreement on the cultural industries, and the financial support provided by the Alberta Foundation for the Arts.

Table of Contents

Preface

What follows is an introduction to the small, yet beautiful world of mosses, liverworts, lichens and ferns for those interested in understanding more about their surroundings. All of the plants dealt with here are small, but nonetheless, the characters that distinguish the species are mostly as clear as those that differentiate species of trees. It is just a matter of practice in looking and thinking small. The greatest difficulty is in seeing and understanding these small characters, the coloured photographs and discussions of the differences between species will overcome this. Additionally, we have provided distribution maps that indicate where individual species have been found. These small plants are especially particular as to where they grow, and as a result, their habitats are often quite specific. We have described these in detail and have included descriptions of the major vegetation zones of northwestern North America. For those wishing to use keys, we have included these for each of the groups.

This book deals with about 15% of the species found in our area and these along with other common species are found in our keys. In all, there are about 900 mosses, 1200 lichens, 250 liverworts and 100 ferns and allies found in northwestern North America, of these we have included 170 mosses, 20 liverworts, 156 lichens and 28 ferns. These species are representative of the northwestern portion of North America, from the Saskatchewan-Manitoba border in the east to coastal British Columbia and Alaska in the west. The treatment includes Oregon, Idaho and northern Wyoming to the south and arctic Alaska and subarctic western Canada to the north. Special attention is paid to species occurring in the Canadian Rocky Mountains and to those found in the lowland west coast rain forests.

Mosses, liverworts, lichens and ferns and their allies are known collectively as terrestrial green cryptogams and are of significance to boreal, montane and northern ecosystems. This is especially true of forests in the northwestern part of North America where the ground in the temperate rain forest and the boreal forest is usually completely covered by mosses and lichens hang from the tree branches. It has been suggested that as much as half of the material produced in these forests can be mosses and lichens. Ferns and their allies (*Lycopodium, Equisetum* and *Selaginella*) are often called vascular cryptogams and are most abundant in the temperate rain forest of the west coast.

These relatively inconspicuous plants play a vital role in nutrient cycling and water drainage control. Lichens have been utilized for the past few decades as indicators of air pollution, while in peat mosses there is a permanent long term record of past climatic and pollution events. The dead stems of the peat moss *Sphagnum* contain the elemental records of the first atomic explosions in the 1940's as well as the first use of leaded automobile fuel. With about 15% of northwestern North America covered by muskeg and peat, the future economic importance of the peat mosses cannot be underestimated. These small plants are also critical indicators of nutrient conditions in aquatic habitats. The change of nutrient levels of lakes, marshes and swamps can often be predicted by the cryptogamic flora of an area. In addition to the biological and potentially economic roles these plants play, they also represent an attractive portion of the forest and tundra which frequently escapes attention.

This is the first book to be published in North America that includes coloured photographs of all these plants. Although technical floras exist, they can functionally be used only with the aid of a microscope and in the case of lichens, with the use of complex microchemical tests. We would like this book to introduce these organisms to you.

Dale Vitt
Janet Marsh
Robin Bovey

June 1988

During the six years since this book was first published, we have received many comments—mostly good, but a few with constructive criticisms. And to our dismay, even after diligent proofing originally, we have been able to discover a few mistakes. We hope we have remedied these. Over the past six years several name changes have occurred, especially in the lichenized fungi. These and the corresponding names used in this book are listed at the end of the sections on mosses (p. 138) and lichens (p. 254). We are grateful to both Grant Kennedy and Glenn Rollans of Lone Pine Publishing for their interest in our book which provided the stimulus for us to compile this revision. Bernard Goffinet and Trevor Goward contributed significantly to our revision of the lichen portion. And finally we hope to see many more tattered-edged copies of this book indicating that it is being used to recognize and to identify these small, yet important plants and fungi.

Dale H. Vitt
July 27, 1994.
Edmonton, AB.

Acknowledgements

We are much indebted to many people and especially families and friends who have made this book possible. Much of the work was done under a Government of Canada Unemployment Insurance Job Creation Program funded by Employment and Immigration, Canada. We have also been supported by research grants, especially from the Natural Sciences and Engineering Research Council of Canada (NSERC) Grant A6390 to D.H. Vitt. This work was made possible because of facilities provided by the Department of Botany at the University of Alberta and in particular the Cryptogamic Herbarium was of importance to us. Cynthia Marsh's efficiency made life much easier.

Our distribution maps were prepared after much tedious work by Terry Friedrich and John Sisson, and through the computer skills of William Boyd. The diligent correcting, editing, proof reading and typing of our manuscript was largely done by Sandra Vitt. The word processing skills of Rosaleen Campbell, Brenda Lovas and Elaine Maloney-Gignac were greatly appreciated.

We have made liberal use of work done by colleagues and former students, and in particular we wish to gratefully acknowledge Irwin Brodo, Diana G. Horton, Jan Janssens, Paul Marino, Barbara Murray, Wilbur Peterson, Wilfred Schofield and Jon Shaw. Our field work in coastal British Columbia was greatly facilitated by Wilfred Schofield and René Belland, both good friends and great bryologists. Our manuscript was much improved by suggestions made by Irwin Brodo (lichens), Donald Farrar (ferns), Diana Horton (mosses and liverworts), Elizabeth John (lichens) and Wilfred Schofield (mosses and liverworts); to these botanists we are grateful.

Our illustrations were done by John Maywood and Sandra (Scott) Davis, both of whom are skilled illustrators, we appreciate their expertise. George Braybrook's usual elegance at manipulating the scanning electron microscope is, as always, appreciated. The background each of us has gained from previous experiences was of much significance in completing this work. It is only through many years of collecting, observing and loving these plants that a synthesis of their biology and ecology can be made. We wish to thank Natural Sciences and Engineering Research Council of Canada (DHV), Environment Canada, Banff-Jasper Biophysical Land Classification (JEM) and the Nature Conservancy Council, United Kingdom (RBB) for supporting much of our previous field and photographic experiences.

And last, but by no means least, we would like to thank Grant Kennedy for his advice, encouragement and continued support.

A Key To Symbols Used

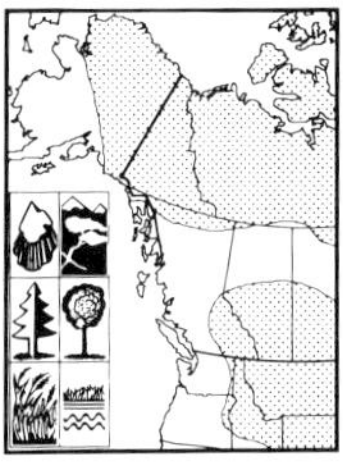

The shaded areas on the map indicates the known distribution for that species.

The symbols in the left hand corner of the map indicate the typical habitat for that species.

Habitat symbols

Arctic-alpine Tundra

Subarctic-subalpine Forest Tundra

Coniferous Forest

Wet Coniferous Forest

Dry Coniferous Forest

Deciduous Woodland

Grassland-savannah

Peatlands

The species in this book are classified into the following broad groupings.

Sphagnum mosses

Acrocarpous mosses

Pleurocarpous mosses

Leafy liverworts

Thalloid liverworts

Crustose lichens

Foliose lichens

Fruticose lichens

Horsetails

Club mosses

Ferns

Introduction

History of Collectors

Although Georg Steller collected a few specimens of vascular plants in 1741, during a brief stop on Kayak Island in the Gulf of Alaska while on Bering's voyage, few botanists visited northwestern North America until the late 1700's. In April 1791, Captain George Vancouver began his voyage to survey the west coast of North America. His surgeon and naturalist, Archibald Menzies made the first collections of mosses, liverworts and lichens in 1792 as they explored the coast between California and Alaska. In 1825-1827, the Scottish botanist, Thomas Drummond, who served as assistant on the Second Land Arctic Expedition under the command of Captain John Franklin, collected cryptogamic plants between Ontario and the Rocky Mountains. He spent the winter of 1825-1826 near Jasper, Alberta. In 1826, David Douglas explored the eastern slopes of the Rockies and climbed Mt. Hooker in the Canadian Rockies. Between 1858 and 1861, David Lyall collected extensively during the survey of the 49th parallel, conducted by the British Oregon Boundary Commission. All of these early collectors are commemorated in scientific names, including the mosses *Leucolepis menziesii*, *Metaneckera menziesii*, *Pohlia drummondii*, *Neckera douglasii*, *Polytrichum lyallii* and the lichen *Ramalina menziesii*.

Beginning in 1872, as botanist to the Natural History Survey of Canada, and continuing until his retirement in 1916 on Vancouver Island, John Macoun made many collections throughout western Canada. His Catalogue of Canadian Plants summarized much of our knowledge of cryptogamic plants when published between 1892 and 1902.

During the late 1800's, R.S. Williams made significant collections as he travelled from Skagway, Alaska to Dawson City, Yukon during the Klondyke Gold Rush of 1898-1899. The Harriman Expedition into Alaska also took place in 1899 and in 1902, J. Cardot and I. Thériot published the first major treatise of Alaskan mosses based on these collections, while in 1904, Clara Cummings published on the Alaskan lichens.

In the early part of the twentieth century, significant collections were made by a number of botanists, many of whom were amateurs. Among the most noteworthy are A.H. Brinkman in Alberta and interior British Columbia, Faye MacFadden in Idaho and southeastern British Columbia, T.C. Frye in Alaska and Washington, J.B. Leiberg in Idaho, L.F. Henderson in Oregon, R.S. Williams in Montana and J.W. Bailey in Washington. In 1928, Lois Clark and T.C. Frye published their book on liverworts of the Northwest, while between 1928 and 1940, A.J. Grout's *Moss Flora of North America* contributed much to our knowledge of the group in northwestern North

America. Early work on ferns included W.R. Maxon's contribution of the ferns to Abrams *Illustrated Flora of the Pacific States* in 1923 and T.C. Frye's 1934 publication of *Ferns of the Northwest*.

Since the 1940's the number of collections of these plant groups has increased dramatically. Particularly important are collections made by Kjeld Holmen in the western Arctic; William C. Steere in northern Alaska; Charles Bird in Alberta; Howard Crum and Henry Imshaug in the Rocky Mountains; Fred Hermann in Montana; Wilfred Schofield, George Otto, Teuvo Ahti and Irwin Brodo in British Columbia and Elva Lawton in Washington. Herman Persson of Stockholm wrote much about the Alaska-Yukon mosses and liverworts but only saw the area once. Collectors of ferns include T.C. Frye, A. Kruckeberg, D.M. Britton and T.M.C. Taylor. Our knowledge has been synthesized in the 1960's, '70's and '80's by several excellent technical books. These include Rudoph M. Schuster's *The Hepaticae and Anthocerotae of North America*, Volumes 1-4 (1966-1980); Hildur Krog's *Macrolichens of Alaska* (1968); Wilfred B. Schofield's *Some Common Mosses of British Columbia* (1969); T.M.C. Taylor's *Pacific Northwest Ferns and Allies* (1970); Elva Lawton's *Moss Flora of the Pacific Northwest* (1971); Seville Flowers' *Mosses of Utah and the West* (1973); John Thompson's *American Arctic Lichens* (1984); and D.B. Lellinger's *A Field Manual of the Ferns and Fern-Allies of the United States and Canada* (1985).

Currently, cryptogamic plants are being studied by researchers in several universities in western North America. These universities maintain excellent collections in their herbaria and these can be consulted if help is needed in identifying specimens of these plants. Important herbaria are those at the University of Alaska, Fairbanks; the University of Alberta, Edmonton; the University of British Columbia, Vancouver; the University of Calgary and the University of Washington, Seattle.

Names used in this book

Unlike many ferns and flowering plants, most mosses, liverworts and lichens do not have popular English names. As a result, the only name available is the scientific one. This is not as bad as it seems, as these names are often no longer than the English name (compare lodgepole pine with *Pinus contorta*) and they have the advantage that each species of plant has its unique name. Here are a few rules to remember:

1) The system of names (the nomenclature) is hierarchial, that is, a family contains one to several genera, in turn each genus contains from one to many species.

2) The names are all in Latin or latinized Greek, so it does not matter if you are French, Chinese or Russian; everyone can write and speak about plants in the same language throughout the world.

3) When Linnaeus began this system in 1753, he considered the correct name of each organism to be a descriptive phrase of three to many words. Since he felt everyone probably could not remember all these phrases, he printed in the margin "a trivial epithet", so that each organism had two names, its genus name and secondly, its specific or trivial epithet. This became known as the binomial system, with each organism having its unique combination of genus and species names. Thus *Sphagnum* is the genus for peat mosses while *S. magellanicum* is one of about 40 species in the area covered by this book. If several species of a single genus are discussed

in a single paragraph, the genus can be abbreviated by the first letter of its name, for example, *S. fuscum* or *S. angustifolium*.

4) The author who first described a species is also part of the technically complete botanical name. If an author's name is in parentheses it means that the author treated that species in a separate genus (or at a different rank, e.g., variety). The author whose name follows the parentheses is the one who transferred the species to its present genus (or rank). For example, in 1801, Hedwig described a moss *Dicranum cirrata* Hedw. In 1874, S.O. Lindberg transferred the name to the genus *Dicranoweisia* and the full name would be *Dicranoweisia cirrata* (Hedw.) Lindb.

We list in the index the full name of all species treated in this book, but in the individual treatments, we have written only the genus and species name. Common English names are given if available, but it should be noted that in many cases, common names refer to a genus and not a species. For example, "witches hair lichen" refers to any species of *Bryoria*, "reindeer lichens" refer to species of *Cladina* and some Cladonias, whereas "knights plume moss" is a common name for a single species *Ptilium crista-castrensis*. "Feather mosses" in Alberta would include *Hylocomium splendens* and *Pleurozium schreberi*, but along coastal British Columbia they would also include *Rhytidiadelphus loreus* and perhaps *R. triquetrus*.

Climatic and Vegetation Zones of Northwest North America

Climate

Distributions of mosses, liverworts, lichens and ferns are largely controlled by two climatic factors, temperature and precipitation. Together, these two

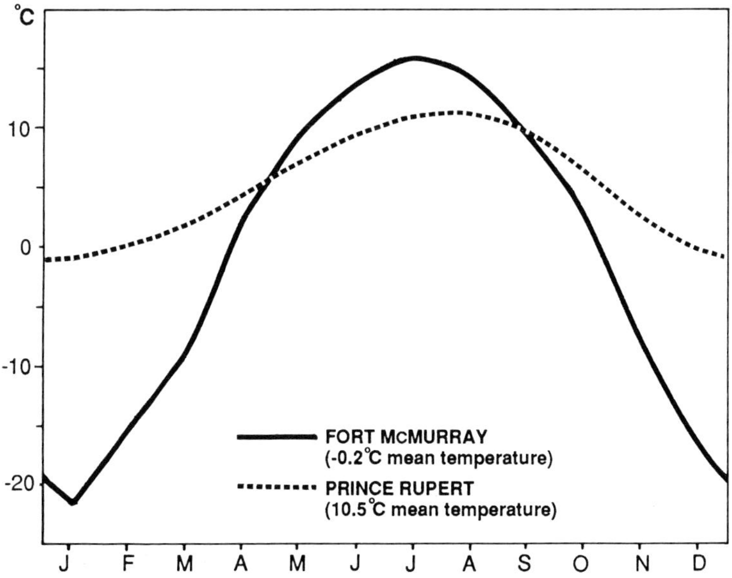

Fig. 1a Annual temperature Fort McMurray, Alberta; Prince Rupert, British Columbia.

parameters determine the potential evapotranspiration of an area. East of the continental divide, at the crest of the Rocky Mountains, precipitation is limited and temperatures are low, whereas west of the divide, precipitation increases and temperatures are more moderate. A decided oceanic influence is present along the coast, whereas the climate farther inland is markedly continental. Extremes of precipitation and temperature patterns along this gradient differ considerably and are shown in Figures 1a and 1b for Fort McMurray in Alberta and Prince Rupert in British Columbia. The former typifies the climate

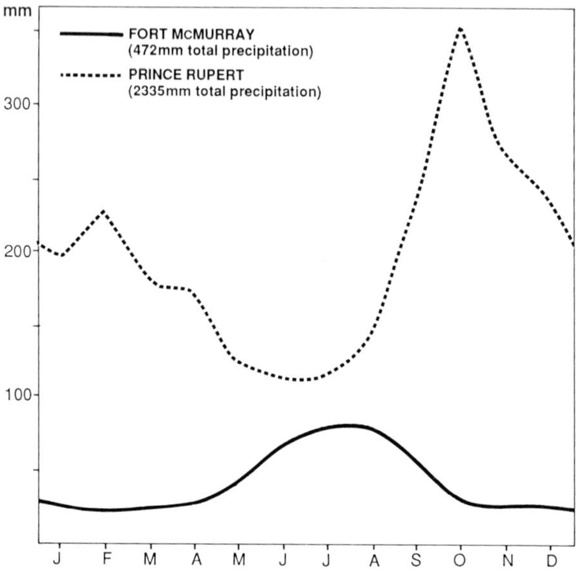

Fig. 1b Annual rainfall Fort McMurray, Alberta; Prince Rupert, British Columbia.

of the boreal forest east of the Rockies, whereas the latter is illustrative of the lowland temperate rain forest of coastal western North America.

These broad climatic gradients influence the overall vegetation of an area and many cryptogamic species are largely restricted to one or a few of these vegetation types.

Vegetation Zones

In northwestern North America, seven broad vegetation types can be delimited (Figs. 2-3), based on the dominant plant growth forms and landscape physiography. These are 1) arctic-alpine tundra, 2) subarctic-subalpine forest-tundra, 3) dry coniferous forest, 4) wet coniferous forest, 5) deciduous woodland, 6) grassland-savannah and 7) peatlands. Additionally, aquatic habitats including numerous lakes, ponds, wetlands and streams are present and a small amount of cold desert is present in southern Oregon and Idaho. A synopsis of each of the vegetation types is given below as an aid to ecological situations in which cryptogamic plants occur. The general habitat preferences of each cryptogamic species is also shown graphically on distribution maps accompanying the species treatment. These have been prepared with the following symbols, which relate directly to the following vegetation zones.

The symbols used are:

Arctic-Alpine Tundra

Subalpine-Subarctic Forest-Tundra

Wet Coniferous Forest

Dry Coniferous Forest

Deciduous Woodland

Grassland-Savannah

Peatlands

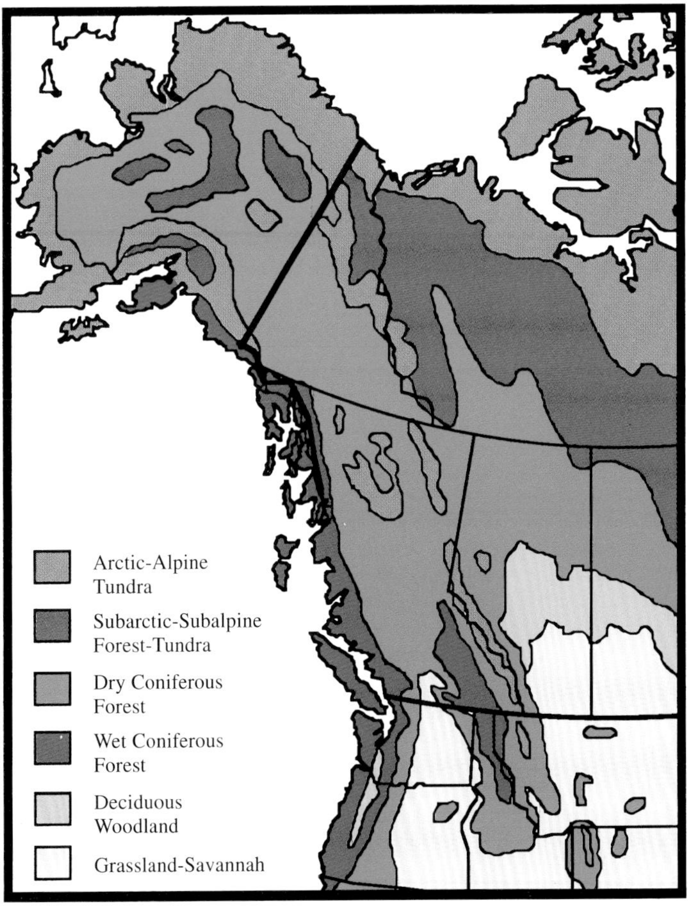

Fig. 2 Vegetation zones of northwest North America.

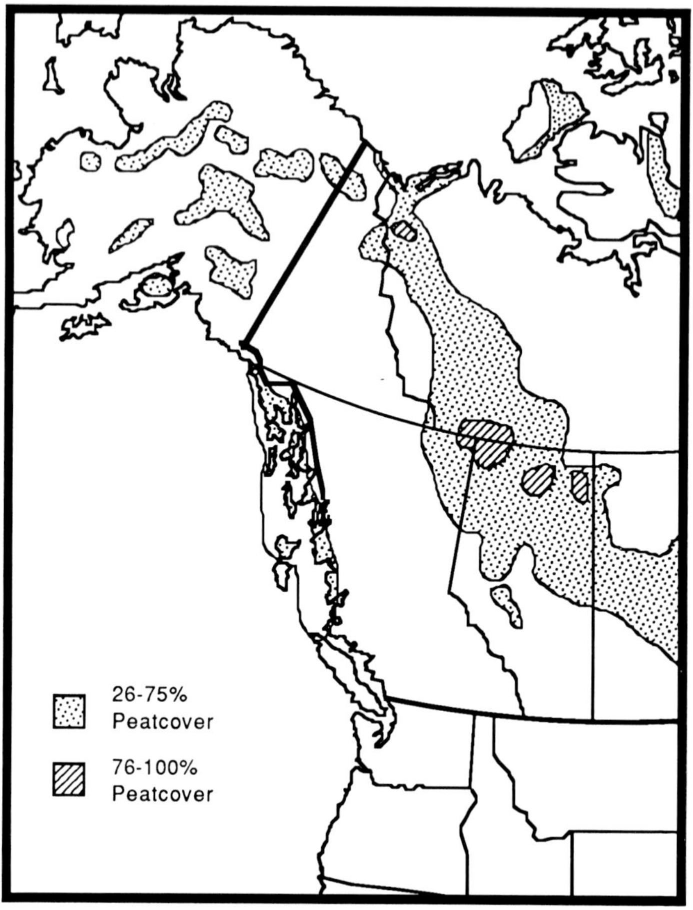

Fig. 3 Peatlands of northwest North America.

Arctic-Alpine Tundra

This vegetation is confined to high elevations and latitudes north of tree-line. Tundra vegetation is characterized by dwarf shrubs, cushion plants, sedges and grasses. The climatic conditions are harsh and include low temperatures, generally little precipitation, high winds and short growing seasons. Mosses, liverworts and lichens constitute a large portion of the vegetation. At still higher elevations and latitudes, semi-desert conditions may exist, where plant cover is discontinuous and here, lichens are the most conspicuous plants. Perhaps they are most abundant here due to their ability to drastically slow physiological functions for an almost indefinite period, only revitalizing when conditions permit their resumption of photosynthesis. Distributions of moss and lichen species within the tundra are mostly controlled by the substrate type, especially acidic and basic rock types, as well as by moisture patterns. The Canadian Rockies are particularly noted for beautiful alpine landscapes, whereas northern Alaska, the northern portion of the Yukon and much of the Northwest Territories, especially the Canadian Arctic Islands have considerable arctic tundra.

Lush alpine tundra in the Kananaskis area, Rocky Mountains southwest Alberta.

Subalpine-Subarctic Forest-Tundra

Subalpine-Subarctic forest-tundra forms a transition between tundra at higher elevations and latitudes, and evergreen coniferous forests at lower elevations and latitudes. The zone consists of treed areas where the trees are sometimes widely, sometimes densely spaced. Generally as elevation

Subalpine-alpine transition; krummholz on higher slopes. Banff National Park.

or latitude increases, the trees are reduced in stature and number. In the alpine, this thinning-out process takes the form of krummholz, where groves of stunted trees interfinger with lush, shrub tundra. At higher latitudes, a broad zone of subarctic forest tundra exists. This subarctic transition has as its dominant tree species *Picea mariana* (black spruce). The subalpine zone of the eastern slopes of the Rockies consists of moist forests of *Abies lasiocarpa* (alpine fir) and *Picea engelmannii* (engelmann spruce). In western British Columbia, Washington and Oregon, *Tsuga mertensiana* (mountain hemlock), *Abies amabilis* (pacific silver fir) or *Abies lasiocarpa* (alpine fir) may be dominant, whereas *Larix lyallii* (subalpine larch) is sometimes abundant from southern Alberta southward. In general, the climate of the subalpine is cool and moist, with greater snow accumulation than either the tundra or lower elevation forests. Drier areas often have dominant tree species similar to those of lower elevations; this is particularly true of such species as *Pseudotsuga menziesii* (douglas fir) west of the Rockies and *Pinus contorta* (lodgepole pine) and *Picea glauca* (white spruce) east of the continental divide. Epiphytic lichens are abundant in the subalpine-subarctic forest zone.

Wet Coniferous Forest

As interpreted here, the wet coniferous forest encompasses the temperate rain forests of the western coast of North America as well as the relict rain forests of interior British Columbia and Idaho. It is defined by the presence of *Thuja plicata* (western red cedar) or *Picea sitchensis* (sitka spruce).

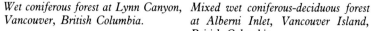

Wet coniferous forest at Lynn Canyon, Vancouver, British Columbia.

Mixed wet coniferous-deciduous forest at Alberni Inlet, Vancouver Island, British Columbia.

Tsuga heterophylla (western hemlock), *Abies grandis* (grand fir), *Chamaecyparis nootkatensis* (yellow cedar) and *Pseudotsuga menziesii* (douglas fir) are often abundant components of these forests. The forest floor is normally covered by the mosses *Rhytidiadelphus* (especially *R. loreus*) and *Hylocomium splendens*. Ferns as well as epiphytic mosses, liverworts and lichens are conspicuous, probably due to the abundant precipitation and mild temperatures.

Dry Coniferous Forest

Physiographically, the boreal forest east of the Rocky Mountains, the montane forests of the Rockies, especially those of the eastern slopes, and the forests of central Alaska and northern British Columbia can generally all be included in dry coniferous forest vegetation. Floristically, this vegetation is considerably influenced by geography. In northern Canadian boreal areas,

Dry coniferous forest on banks of Sunwapta River, below Sunwapta Falls, Jasper National Park, Alberta.

Picea glauca and *Pinus banksiana* (jack pine) dominate, whereas along the eastern slopes of the Canadian Rockies *Pinus contorta* and *Picea glauca* are dominant. In interior Alaska, *Picea glauca* and *Betula papyrifera* are dominant, the latter more important in western Alaska. Reindeer lichens (mostly of the genus *Cladina*) cover the ground in the open, dry forests. Farther south, *Picea pungens* (colorado blue spruce) and *Pseudotsuga menziesii* are abundant and west of the continental divide, *Pseudotsuga menziesii* is the most conspicuous tree. Much of the ground in these forests is covered by the feather mosses *Hylocomium splendens* and *Pleurozium schreberi*.

Deciduous Woodland

This vegetation type is primarily restricted to the transition between boreal montane forests and grassland and is dominated by *Populus tremuloides* (aspen). Also included in this zone are riverine forests of *Populus balsamifera* (balsam poplar) and *P. trichocarpa* (black cottonwood). In montane zones, aspen forests often occur on alluvial fans, or form an early successional stage after fire. Other sites are dominated by *Betula papyrifera* (paper birch) and along the western coast, *Acer* (maple), *Sambucus* (elderberry) and *Alnus* (alder) species often occur as isolated stands. In the intermountain and coastal valleys of Washington and Oregon *Quercus garryana* (oregon white oak) can occur in pure stands or in association with *Arbutus menziesii* (madrona). As drier conditions prevail, especially south of the boreal forest, the woodlands become

Deciduous woodland of small aspen at Kootenay Plains, western Alberta.

discontinuous, gradually becoming restricted to small patches which form what is often called the "aspen parkland zone". In central Yukon and Alaska, northern Alberta and southern Northwest Territories, often dry conditions, calcareous soils and high fire frequency allow deciduous woodlands to dominate the landscape. Here aspen occurs as the most prevalent tree, interspersed sporadically with white spruce.

Grassland - Savannah

The grasslands (or prairie), cover large expanses of the southeastern and southwestern area, extending northward to south-central British Columbia in the west and to east-central Alberta east to central Saskatchewan. A discontinuous belt of grassland and parkland continues northward to the

Short-grass prairie-aspen parkland transition in central Saskatchewan.

southern Yukon Territory. West of the Rocky Mountains, the grasslands of the Columbia and Snake River basins are often called the Palouse Prairie and here the summers are hot and dry. This area is characterized by the bunch grass *Agropyron spicatum*. A savannah of *Pinus ponderosa* (ponderosa pine) and *Pseudotsuga menziesii* forms a sharp transition to the montane forests of the north, east and west.

East of the Rockies, the grasslands of the Great Plains are prevalent. The southwestern part of Alberta, the Cypress Hills, west central Saskatchewan and the Wood Mountains (southern Saskatchewan), are all of relatively high elevations (submontane) and have prairies dominated by *Festuca scabrella* (rough fescue). Otherwise, the main prairie area east of the Rocky Mountain foothills and south of the aspen parkland is dominated by *Stipa comata* (spear grass) and *Bouteloua gracilis* (blue grama).

Grasslands of this latter type occupy close to 50% of the total native prairie area of the Canadian prairie provinces, as well as a large part of the Great Plains in the USA, as far south as northern Nebraska. Along the eastern slopes of the Rockies, a transitional savannah is present, and includes scattered individuals of *Pinus contorta* or *Pseudotsuga menziesii* and the grasses *Koeleria cristata* (june grass), *Elymus innovatus* (hairy wild rye) and *Calamagrostis canadensis* (reed grass).

Peatlands

Wetlands, consisting of marshes and swamps, as well as peatlands composed of bogs and fens, make up about 15% of the landscape of western Canada.

Peatland: rich fen at McClelland Lake, northeast of Fort McMurray, Alberta.

Peatland: raised bog near Prince Rupert, coastal British Columbia.

Marshes, often dominated by Typha latifolia (cattail) and swamps often with *Alnus* sp. (alder) and *Salix* spp. (willows) occur sporadically throughout our region, but they are particularly abundant in the prairie and deciduous woodland areas. In these wetlands, significant deposits of peat are not formed, due to the rapid decomposition rate of dead plant material.

Peatlands are formed when there is decreased decomposition of dead plant material, which in turn allows large accumulations of peat to form. If the peatlands are influenced by ground water, they are minerotrophic and termed fens. On the other hand, if peat build-up is sufficient to raise the living surface above the soil water limit, then the area is influenced only by water received from precipitation; these are termed bogs and are ombrotrophic. Bogs are more common in coastal areas, whereas fens are common under continental climatic regimes. Poor fens are characterized by relatively low pH and are dominated by peat mosses (*Sphagnum* spp.), as are bogs that have even lower pH; while rich fens have relatively high pH and are dominated by brown mosses (true mosses). As used here, extreme rich fens are those with the moss *Scorpidium scorpioides*, while transitional rich fens are dominated by one of several species of the brown moss *Drepanocladus*.

Except on the exposed coast of British Columbia, where the peatlands are dominated by a mixture of *Thuja plicata*, *Chamaecyparis nootkatensis* and *Pinus contorta* (a different subspecies from the montane one), peatlands are dominated by *Picea mariana* (black spruce) and *Larix laricina* (eastern larch). Larch is more common in minerotrophic peatlands, while black spruce occurs in those with less soil-water influence and sometimes in drier peatlands. Peatlands also are formed in tundra habitats, where a variety of sedges are the predominant vascular plants.

Collection, Preservation, and Study of Mosses, Liverworts and Lichens

Recommended for field use are 1) a canvas side sack, 2) a hand lens of 10X or 14X secured on a strong cord, 3) number 2 light or heavy duty paper bags, or a supply of newspapers cut to suitable size and folded to about 4 x 5 inches, 4) a water-proof pen or pencil, 5) a knife and 6) a cold chisel and hammer for rock lichens.

Recommended for home or laboratory use are 1) a dissecting microscope, 2) a compound microscope, 3) forceps, 4) container with hot water, 5) razor blades and 6) dropper bottle with water.

The following advice on collecting is extracted from S. Flowers' book on mosses of Utah and is excellent for both bryophytes and lichens. These plants can be collected at any time of the year but certain small mosses are best gathered in the spring while there are capsules. A specimen is simply lifted from the substratum by hand. The excess soil, leaf litter, conifer needles or twigs can be removed by a knife. The specimen is placed in a paper bag (do not use plastic bags as the material will mold quickly) or paper envelope previously labeled with the date and place of the collection. Data included may be any of the following: moisture, substrate, exposure, associated vegetation and elevation. All the specimens from the same locality may be placed in a larger paper bag and labeled with: state or province, county, mountain, valley, or canyon, distance and direction from the nearest town or landmark, longitude and latitude, date and elevation.

At home, the specimens may be further cleaned and trimmed to convenient size. Damp or wet specimens are spread out to dry; thick cushions or sods may be cut vertically into thin slices to be placed in envelopes. Some thick mats may be flattened between several thicknesses of newspapers or herbarium blotters under light pressure for several hours, then removed and dried in the air. It is essential that each specimen be kept with the original sack or envelope upon which the data are recorded.

Some lichens require special attention. Many lichens growing on rocks must be removed with the rock by use of a cold chisel (about 1/2 inch wide) and geologic hammer; others can be removed with a knife. To prepare lichen specimens for your collection special care should be used for the following types of lichens. Dried foliose and fruticose lichens that are bulky need to be moistened with distilled (or rain) water as alkaline tap water may cause changes in lichen colours. These specimens can then be placed between sheets of newspaper layered with corrugated cardboard, lightly pressed and placed in a well ventilated area until dry (do not use heat as it may discolour lichens containing cyanobacteria). The soil attached to crustose lichens should be moistened with a dilute solution of white glue and water and air dried to prevent the lichen crust from breaking apart. Lichens, in general are very brittle when completely dry and one can help protect the specimens by placing some soft tissue over the lichen material once it is in proper herbarium packets.

Permanent collection envelopes (packets) should be folded from a good quality paper (preferably 100% cotton stock of 20 or 24 pound substance). A standard size of about 10 x 14 cm can be made from 21.5 x 28 cm sheets as follows. Bring the lower edge upward about 3/4 the length of the sheet and crease. Next, fold the upper 1/4 down and over the first fold, crease. Finally, fold the outer 3 cm of both sides back. Small envelopes made similarly for very small specimens or loose pieces should be made of thinner paper and placed in those of standard size. A 7.5 x 12.5 cm file card placed in the packet serves to strengthen it and also can be used to lift delicate and brittle specimens from the packet in future study.

It is best to assign a number to each specimen when it is collected in the field or at least when identified. A comprehensive field notebook of localities and species identification can then be maintained for future reference. Labels may be written on the flap of the packet or better on specially cut labels to be pasted on the flap.

A sample label:

PLANTS OF CANADA

Calliergon trifarium (Web. & Mohr) Kindb.
Alberta: Hinton Area, eastern foothills of the Rocky Mountains, 12.2 km south of Hinton junction of Hwy 40.
53° 20'N, 117° 30'W 1135 m
Extreme rich fen surrounding small body of water.
Scorpidium scorpioides and *Drepanocladus revolvens* are dominant mosses.
Dale H. Vitt 33834 May 31, 1987

Another label, slightly different, might be as follows:

PLANTS OF THE YUKON TERRITORY

Sphagnum girgensohnii Russ.
KEELE PEAK: About 3.5 km SE of Keele Lake, 0.75 km north of the toe of glacier 101.
63° 27'N, 130° 23'W Elev. 1500 m
On east facing granitic cliffs and associated alpine tundra. *Racomitrium* spp. dominating acidic alpine tundra.
Dale H. Vitt 32173 July 16, 1985

For beginners, shoe boxes are ideal for storage and can usually be obtained free. Boxes 15 x 45 cm by 13 cm deep with tight lids will accommodate 30 to 60 specimens filed in card fashion. Beginners may file specimens according to families, but as a collection increases in size and variety, it becomes more convenient to file them alphabetically by genus. There is less chance of misplacing specimens, and expansion is easier.

Microscopic Techniques in the Study of Mosses, Liverworts and Lichens

The detailed examination of moss leaves is best done under a compound microscope. Prepare the leaves by picking one stem from your specimen with a forceps, moisten it in hot water (temperature just below boiling), place it on a microscope slide and scrape the leaves off the stem by running a blunt edged utensil (small knife, dull razor blade, edge of forceps or flattened needle) from the tip down the stem. The leaves will be scraped off backwards and remain on the slide when the stem is removed. Also, this technique will remove any outgrowths from the stem and assure that the alar cells are removed intact with the leaves. Hepatics are often best observed with leaves and stem intact, unless the stem is too thick, then the leaves are best picked off the stem individually.

Details of the peristome and capsule are best seen after a similar procedure of moistening the material and then the capsules are cut first longitudinally and then horizontally just below the mouth with a razor blade. Spores are carefully teased away and a cover slip is added for compound microscope observation. Always use moist material (either fresh or after moistening in hot water) and always do your dissections on a glass microscope slide under a dissecting microscope. A cover slip is essential in all cases.

Microscopic examination of lichen fruiting bodies proceeds best by first wetting the fruiting body with a drop of water. Then under a dissecting microscope, take a single edged razor blade and cut two or three very thin slices of the fruiting body. Using the corner of the razor blade, transfer these slices to a drop of water on a glass microscope slide. Cover with a glass cover slip. Observe the mount under the compound microscope; at first at low power (10X) to observe the orientation of the hymenium, asci and spores, and then at high power (40X) to observe individual spores. To help release the spores from the ascus, tap the cover slip with the eraser end of a pencil. Note observations on a file card to keep with the specimen.

Microchemistry as an Aid to Lichen Identification

Lichens contain many substances, some of which are pigments and these give the lichens their characteristic colours. Phenolic acids in the form of despides, and despidones are also included in this group. Lichen substances are normally formed only in the symbiotic state and not when the fungus is grown in isolated culture. The ecological roles of the lichen substances include light screening agents, chemical weathering of substrates, allelopathic effects and anti-herbivore defence mechanisms. What is particularly important to us is that these lichen substances are used in the classification of lichens. In most cases, closely related species have similar substances.

Microchemical colour tests are useful aids in lichen identification. Certain chemicals produce distinctive colours when they react with the chemical compounds of lichens. These microchemical tests are usually applied to the cortex or medulla. Use a razor blade to expose the medulla of a small piece of lichen that has been broken from the thallus. Using a thin glass pipette or a toothpick, apply the chemical reagent to the cortex or medulla and observe the reaction using a hand lens or dissecting microscope. After observing thc results, discard the tested piece and record the results on the packet or file card so the tests will not be needed again.

Chemical reagents referred to in this book are:

C Calcium hypochlorite or household bleach, such as Javex or Chlorox (make sure it is fresh).

KOH Potassium hydroxide solution (about 10-20%). Dissolve about 20 household lye pellets in 20 ml of water.

PD Paraphenylenediamine (available from a scientific supply house). Dissolve a few grains in ethyl alcohol (the solution must be fresh each time it is used). This must be handled very carefully as it is toxic and permanently stains books, clothing, or furniture. Mix it on a microscope slide or in a small vial, rinse thoroughly afterwards.

I Aqueous potassium iodide, available from drug stores as iodine tincture.

Long wave ultra violet light (UV) will fluoresce with such lichen acids as squamatic acid. In several *Cladonia* species it emits a bluish-white colour. The use of the UV test is an easy and rapid method for identification of lichens which contain fluorescent substances. A small hand held long-wave UV source, available from scientific supply companies is a useful tool for this purpose. Be careful not to look directly into the UV light source. Short-wave UV lights are not recommended, as they do not fluoresce many lichen substances and are very dangerous.

The following is a list of common microchemical spot tests as applied to the *lichen* medulla, together with the major lichen substance that produces the resulting colour.*

Microchemical Test	Lichen Substance	Lichen Example
KOH+ yellow to pale-yellow	atranorin	*Cladonia ecmocyna* and ***Physcia adscendens*
KOH+ yellow	stictic acid	*Baeomyces rufus*
KOH+ yellow to blood-red	salazinic acid	*Parmelia sulcata*
KOH+ yellow to red	norstictic acid	*Aspicilia cinerea*
KOH+ purple	parietin	*Xanthoria elegans*
PD+ yellow to orange	thamnolic acid	*Icmadophila ericetorum*
PD+ deep yellow to orange	salazinic acid	*Parmelia omphalodes*
PD+ yellow to orange	norstictic acid	*Lobaria pulmonaria*
PD+ red-orange	stictic acid	*Cetraria hepatizon*
PD+ red	fumarprotocetraric acid	*Cetraria islandica* and *Cladonia gracilis*
C+ red or pink	gyrophoric acid	*Umbilicaria vellea*
C+ red	lecanoric acid	*Flavopunctelia flaventior*
I+ blue	isolichenen	*Sphaerophorus globosus*
UV+ bright blue-white	squamatic acid	*Cladonia squamosa*

*Other lichen substances may be present to contribute to the microchemical colour reactions.
**microchemical spot test on the upper cortex.

Lichen Thallus Colours

The following is a reference list of lichen thallus colours.

Colour	Species	Page Number
Yellow-green	*Evernia mesomorpha*	252
	Xanthoparmelia taractica	223
	Dactylina arctica	245
	Lobaria pulmonaria	235
Yellow	*Cetraria canadensis*	212
	Parmeliopsis ambigua	222
Grey-green	*Parmeliopsis hyperopta*	222
	Hypogymnia physodes	225
	Parmelia sulcata	220
Brown-grey	*Rhizocarpon geminatum*	184
	Physconia muscigena	237
	Peltigera canina	230

Collection, Preservation and Study of Ferns

Ferns, being much larger than bryophytes and lichens, require somewhat different methods in order to study them. Dried specimens can be collected and preserved for permanent study. However, never collect a fern specimen unless at least ten plants of the species are in the immediate area. Never collect without permission and then be sure the fern you are about to collect is not a rare or endangered species. Almost all ferns can be identified based on characters of the frond; there is no need to kill the plant by digging up the rhizome and underground parts. Restrict your collecting to one or several entire fronds. Plastic bags are the best way to store your collections while in the field, but they must be pressed as soon as possible.

Ferns need to be pressed in order to be preserved as specimens. This is best not done in telephone books or Sears catalogues, but in a plant press. A plant press consists of a series of corrugated cardboards or blotters or both to dry the plants, sheets of newspaper to hold the plants and a sturdy top and bottom frame or two pieces of plywood 30 X 45 cm. Ropes or belts around the press are used to pull it tight.

Once a press is in hand, proceed as follows. Open the press and lay the first corrugate on the bottom frame. Open a single sheet of newspaper and lay the fern on half the paper. Be sure all of the plant parts are spread flat so there is little overlap. Turn over one frond or frond part so the finished specimen will show both top and bottom surfaces. It is best if the frond is fertile, since that is the basis of most identification. If the frond is longer than the newspaper, fold it in a V or N, with as little overlap as possible, or cut the frond into parts and press them separately. Close the newspaper, put a corrugate on top and you are ready to press the next specimen. Make notes on the margin of the newspaper on details not shown by the specimen alone, such as locality, collector, date, habitat, abundance, size, variation and colour.

When finished placing your ferns in the press, add the top frame and tighten as tightly as you can by pulling the straps (stand on it if you can). The drying process takes a few days, and if you have especially large or wet specimens it may be necessary to change the newspapers. Once dry and removed from the press the ferns can be stored in the newspaper (called flimsies) or mounted on a heavy white paper. Standard sized herbarium sheets are 29 X 49 cm. Attach the specimen to its herbarium sheet by dribbling white glue on the one side of the frond (be sure they are mounted with at least part of the sporangia up). Do not completely cover the back surface, but use streaks of glue. Then place the specimen in an aesthetically pleasing position on the sheet, pressing it lightly. Add small weights to the specimen to hold it down while the glue dries. Add an extra dribble of glue as a strap over the larger axes. Never use cellophane tape since this discolours, dries out and comes off after a few years.

A label (as shown before) should be attached to the lower right corner. Remember in collecting specimens it is important that you take only species that are in no way rare or endangered. When in doubt, leave the plant alone or carefully remove only an individual frond (if the plant is robust), but even this must be done with utmost care and a sharp knife, since pulling off a leaf usually results in disturbing the whole plant.

Notes on Photography

Photographing mosses and lichens will be a new and interesting challenge to anyone who has never tried his hand at it before. The basic principles of lighting and composition apply, but the size and inaccessability of many mosses and lichens bring a new dimension of photography to many people, that of field macro-photography.

The photographs for this book were taken during two field seasons and all of them were taken within the geographic range of the book. With only a couple of exceptions, all the photographs were taken in the field and although this provided some interesting and awkward challenges, hopefully it has added to the "natural" quality of the illustrations, as well as giving readers a feeling for the macro habitats within which the specimens were growing.

The photographs were taken on Kodachrome 64 film (ASA 64), which helped to keep grain to a minimum and to ensure an even colour reproduction. However the problem with using this slower speed film is the need for correspondingly more light during exposure. The problem is compounded in macro-photography by the continual need for more depth of field when illustrating three dimensional objects. A solution is to use as small an aperture as possible.

The basic equipment needed for moss and lichen photography is a good 35 mm single lens reflex camera and a macro lens. The photography for this book was done using a Nikon FM2 camera and a Micro-Nikkor 55 mm f/2.8 lens. Another essential piece of equipment for taking photographs of mosses and lichens is a versatile tripod. By far the most versatile tripod available is the Benbo Tripod (manufactured and marketed by Kennett Engineering, U.K.), which was used for all the photographs in the book. The use of a tripod ensures good composition, allows the photographer to maintain critical focus and permits the use of slower shutter speeds to overcome lack of light. It also gives welcome relief from the many uncomfortable body contortions that seem to be a part of photographing mosses and lichens.

Even with the use of a tripod there were still many occasions when the lack of natural light was a real problem and on these occasions a Nikon Macro Ringlight Unit SM2 with a Nikon SR-2 Battery Pack was used. This is an excellent flash unit for reproduction ratios higher than 1:1. For reproduction

ratios lower than 1:1, a pair of small flash heads was used, to give as balanced a lighting effect as possible.

With the use of a good tripod and the relevant flash system, it is possible to overcome nearly all the problems of depth of field associated with all but the few flat, two dimensional species. It is usually important to work at the smallest possible aperture (f/16 to f/32) when judicial focusing should ensure the required depth of field.

For reproduction ratios greater than 1:1, Nikon auto extension rings were used. These are a cheap and effective way to give higher reproduction ratios. For reproduction ratios up to 1:12, a Nikon PB-6 Bellows Unit was also used.

Great care should be exercised in selecting subjects for photography. By selecting specimens growing on a tree stump or a bank, it is often possible to avoid or at least minimise problems with depth of field. Careful selection of the correct and most effective angle of shot, will also help considerably to accentuate features and ensure critical focus.

Voucher specimens were collected for the photographs in the book, which helped ensure correct identification. While this will not be necessary for personal collections, care should be taken to make a note of the name of the species, where this is important, as the microscopic features may well not show up later in the photograph.

MOSSES

Mosses

Their Structure and Biology

Definition

Flowering plants, conifers, ferns, club mosses and horsetails all belong to one of two large, general groups of green land plants, the Tracheophytes. This group can be defined by having well-developed water and food conducting systems and by having the sporophyte or diploid generation independent from and dominant over the gametophyte or haploid generation. This alternation of generations is characteristic of all plants, and in tracheophytes the gametophyte is very small (e.g., pollen grains and ovules), or consists of separate, small, thalloid structures (e.g., fern prothallia). Mosses, liverworts and hornworts all belong to the second group of green land plants, the bryophytes. These plants all have poorly developed water and food conducting systems and most importantly, have the sporophyte attached to and largely dependent on the gametophyte for the entire life cycle.

Since the main biological function of the sporophyte is to disperse spores once meiosis has taken place, while the function of the gametophyte generation is to affect fertilization (via water movement of sperm), sporophytes tend to be large and erect, while gametophytes are often small and flattened. This, of course, is particularly true in land plants, where water is not so readily available.

Evolutionarily, the biological features of the two generations have resulted in tracheophytes being generally tall plants with large independent sporophytes (and a conducting system to facilitate this large size), while bryophytes are small plants with the sporophyte dependent on a generally small gametophyte (hence a poorly developed conducting system). Whereas tracheophytes have developed numerous structural features that allow them to maintain a correct water balance, bryophytes have not. Rather, the bryophytes have solved the problem of keeping sufficient water for growth by either growing only in moist places or by physiological drought tolerance termed "poikilohydry". During dry periods, these poikilohydrous plants do not maintain water in their plant bodies, but they merely dry up, turnoff and become dormant. Upon rewetting, they almost immediately begin to photosynthesize and resume biological activity. So, when bryophytes seem dry and crusty, they are not dead, just resting; their way of living in areas where they cannot keep all the water from evaporating. Whereas mosses and lichens are similar in this respect, most liverworts have only limited abilities to be physiologically drought-tolerant.

Mosses comprise the largest of the three groups of Bryophytes. There are about 8,000-9,000 species in the world. Scientifically, they are classified as the class Bryopsida or some books use the class name Musci.

All mosses have a leafy gametophyte that, when mature produces sex organs, the antheridia (male) and archegonia (female). If fertilization occurs, an erect sporophyte develops and is permanently attached to the gametophyte. This sporophyte contains a capsule in which meiosis occurs and spores are produced. The new gametophytes of the following generation develop from these spores.

Technically, mosses are those bryophytes in which capsule enlargement and maturity take place after seta elongation. This sporophyte developmental pattern can easily be seen in the field in young developing sporophytes.

Life Cycle and Structural Features

A moss plant begins life as a spore, a single celled green sphere, usually with an ornamented and thickened outer wall that resists drought and decay for an extended period of time. Germination of this spore on a suitable substrate results in the development of a filamentous (or rarely thalloid), branched, green structure termed a protonema. Eventually, this mat of alga-like filaments may reach a centimetre across. Some of the branches penetrate the substrate and differentiate into rhizoids. These lack chlorophyll, and are several cells long, with oblique crosswalls. In time, small knots of cells appear at various places on the protonema; these enlarge and produce small leaves arranged spirally around a short central stem. The young plants (the gametophores) grow rapidly by the division of a four-sided apical cell. When mature, the gametophore will consist of a stem, leaves and gametangia (Figs. 4 - 5).

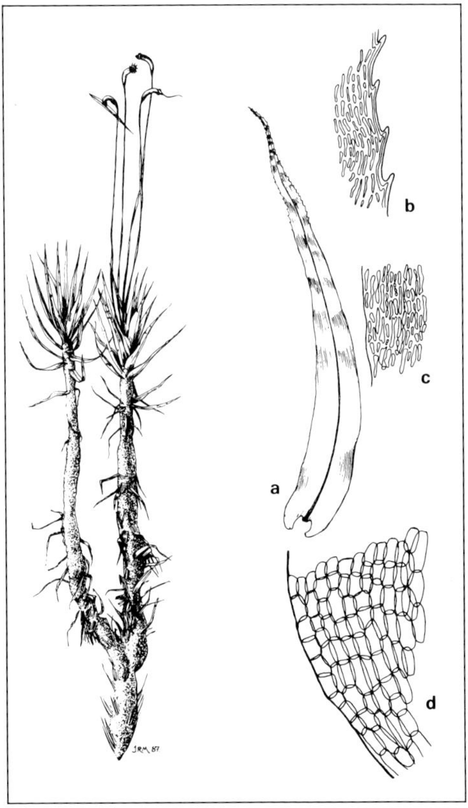

Fig. 4. Plant of *Dicranum polysetum*, with a - leaf; b - upper leaf cells at margin; c - medial leaf cells near costa; and d - alar cells.

The Stem

The stem, when viewed in transverse section, consists of a central strand of narrow, elongate cells. Sometimes these are not present, whereas in other mosses they are well-developed and form a distinct central zone. They are dead cells and serve to conduct water. These hydroids are similar to the xylem of tracheophytes, but they contain no secondary walls and have no lignin. Surrounding the central strand are broader, shorter, living cells of the cortex.

These generally become thicker walled and smaller as the stem surface is approached and most mosses have two to four layers of thick-walled epidermis. A few mosses have a hyalodermis that is formed when the outermost layer is enlarged and hyaline.

The stems of many mosses have branches arising along the stem, from buds or from just beneath the terminal sex organs. If they arise from buds, then in most cases the buds are surrounded by scale-like structures called pseudoparaphyllia. Some mosses produce green, filamentous (and often branched) structures along the stem, which are photosynthetic and termed paraphyllia. Sometimes these are produced in sufficient quantity to cover the stem in a felty fuzz called tomentum. Other mosses have tomentum consisting of rhizoids, which are non-chlorophyllose and generally have longer cells. Thus, pseudoparaphyllia are constantly associated with branch buds, while paraphyllia are produced along the stem.

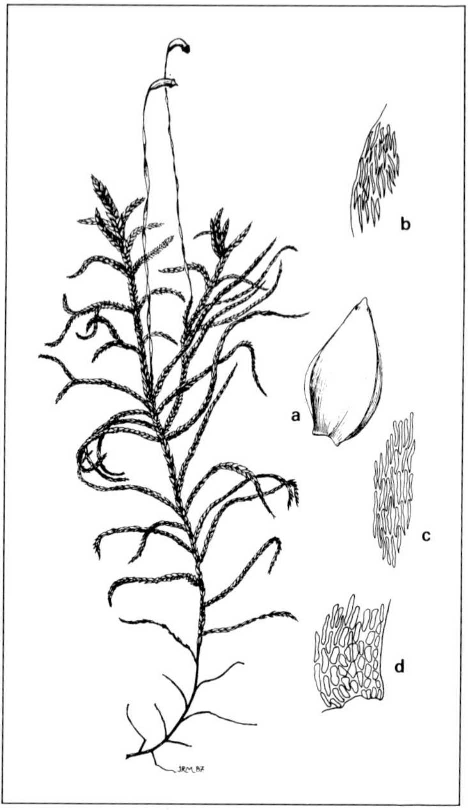

Fig. 5. Plant of *Pleurozium schreberi*, with a - leaf; b - upper leaf cells at margin; c - medial leaf cells near centre of leaf; and d - alar cells.

The Leaf

Leaves consist of a lamina that is almost always one layer of cells thick and a costa, a central vein of several layers of differentiated cells. The leaf is attached to the stem by alar cells, which may or may not be different from the lower leaf cells. These, in turn, may or may not be different from the upper leaf cells. These latter cells are always chlorophyllose, while the basal cells are often reddish, hyaline or brown. Leaf cells may be smooth, or have one to several small bumps (papillae - Fig. 6); likewise, they may be flat or have bulging walls. Cells that are both bulging and papillose are sometimes called mamillose. The two leaf surfaces, the back (or dorsal = abaxial) and the front or inner (or ventral = adaxial) may be different in surface structure or, as in most cases, they may be similar. Some mosses have leaves that are bordered by differentiated cells that are usually longer and thicker-walled cells; other species have margins on the leaves with a variety of teeth or dentations, or the margins can be variously reflexed or revolute. Leaf cell shapes vary from round to elongate-linear and include rhombic, rectangular and hexagonal shapes. The costa usually consists of a central layer of large cells, the guide cells and one to several layers of thick-walled fiber-like cells

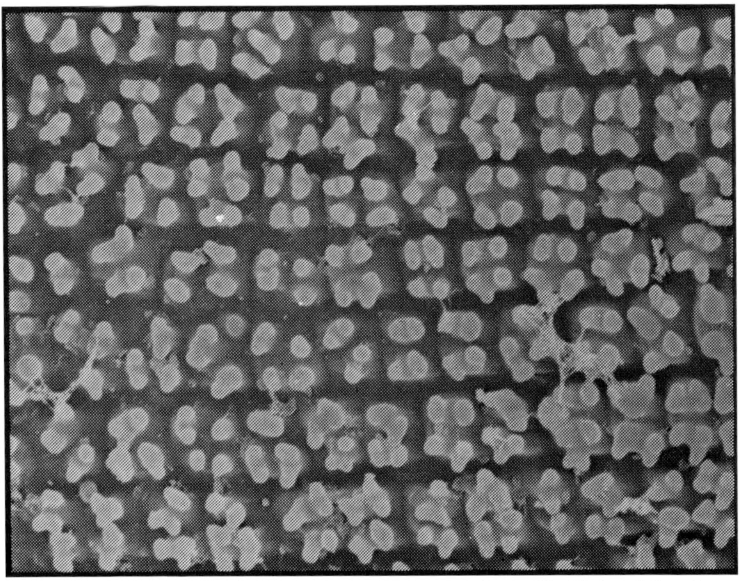

Fig. 6. Papillae of the upper leaf cells of the moss *Tortula ruralis*. Each cell has three-four, forked papillae. Micrograph courtesy of SEM Laboratory, Department of Entomology, University of Alberta.

calledstereids, that form stereid bands on one or both sides of the guide cells. The costa is lacking, very short and double, or double and long in some mosses; in others it is expanded to compose all or nearly all of the leaf. Occasionally green lamellae are produced on the ventral costal surface, making the leaf many cells thick. The costa usually ends just below the leaf apex, but sometimes it extends beyond the lamina as a stout cusp or as a long hyaline awn. Some leaves are subulate, with the upper portion composed mostly of costa.

Gametangia

Sperm are produced in the antheridia which are multi-cellular, usually ovoid sacs produced either terminally on stems or laterally along the stems and surrounded by differentiated leaves in structures called perigonia. Each perigonium contains three to six antheridia and some sterile hairs, the paraphyses. Sperm are released through a terminal cap upon stimulus of water. The sperm have two flagella and are highly active while surrounded by a water film.

Eggs are produced in archegonia which are multicellular, flask shaped structures produced terminally or laterally in perichaetia. Each perichaetium contains several archegonia and some paraphyses. If the apical cell of the stem is used in production of the perichaetium, the moss is acrocarpous and rarely has many branches (Fig. 4); if the apical cell is not used, then the moss is pleurocarpous and mostly has several to numerous branches produced from lateral buds (Fig. 5). The archegonia have a long neck; each has an egg in the enlarged base (the venter). Fertilization is accomplished when a sperm fuses with an egg by swimming down the archegonial neck canal. A zygote, the first sporophytic cell, results. Development proceeds in the venter, differentiating into a foot embedded in the gametophyte, a stalk (seta) and a capsule. Later, as the seta elongates, the enlarged venter (epigonium) splits and the young capsule carries the apical part aloft as a cap (calyptra). The lower part remains around the foot as a small cup, the vaginula. Usually, one sporophyte is produced from each perichaetium.

The Seta

The stalk upon which the capsule is elevated usually contains some water conducting cells (hydroids) and/or food conducting cells (leptoids) in the central area. Often the seta is hygroscopic, due to the pattern of cells on the outer seta surface. In mosses occurring under xeric conditions, the seta is often shortened, so that the capsule is immersed or emergent from the perichaetial leaves when mature. Except in very rare abnormal situations, the seta of mosses is never branched.

The Capsule

The developing capsule differentiates into several regions, especially a basal (proximal) neck (apophysis) which has stomata, an urn or area where the spores are produced, and an apical (distal) part that forms the operculum. The capsule, until dehiscence of the spores, is photosynthetic and supplements the supply of carbohydrates provided by the leafy gametophore.

In longitudinal section, the capsule shows an outer layer of non-chlorophyllose, usually thick-walled, cutinized cells (the exothecium). Inside are several layers of thin-walled chlorophyll-containing cells and then a layer of spongy sporogenous cells. Next, there is a space, then a second layer of sporogenous cells attached to a central column of sterile cells (the columella). The two layers of archesporial cells undergo meiosis and produce four spores for each mother cell. The operculum eventually detaches by splitting at a ring of differentiated cells (annulus) and the capsule is open for potential dispersal of the spores. However, spore dispersal is regulated by the differentiation and presence of specialized layers of cells located at the capsule mouth, the peristome (Fig. 7). (Note: peat mosses, granite mosses and some very specialized true mosses do not have a peristome; granite mosses open by four vertical slits and have no operculum.

The Peristome

Moss peristomes are of two types. Firstly, there are those composed of bundles of whole cells (Nematodontous - Fig. 8). These generally have 64 blunt, short teeth that do not move. In these mosses, the columella is expanded at the apex to form a plate-shaped epiphragm. Expansion and contraction of this epiphragm opens and closes the spaces between the 64 teeth, and spore regulation is similar to that of a salt shaker (Fig. 9).

Secondly, there are those composed of articulated parts of cells, that is, of fused cell walls (Arthrodontous - Fig. 7). These generally have 16, lanceolate, acute teeth in either one or two rows. In these mosses, the columella does not expand at its apex. Spore dispersal is regulated by hygroscopic movements of the one or two layers of teeth. The Diplolepideous Peristome is one where the outer ring of teeth (exostome) is composed of two concentrically fused layers of cell walls, the outermost of which has two tiers of cells per tooth (Fig. 10). Generally, there is also an inner layer of teeth (called endostome segments - Fig. 11). These usually alternate with the exostome teeth, with the latter hygroscopically interfingering between the segments (see Fig. 7).

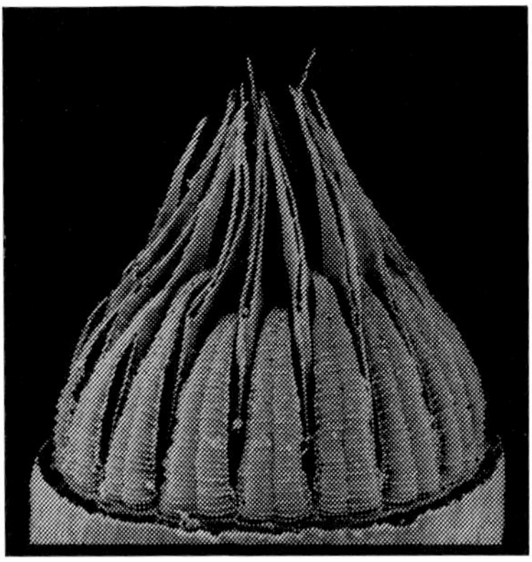

Fig. 7. Peristome of *Brachythecium asperrimum.*

The Haplolepideous Peristome is always of one layer (Fig. 12). The outer surface of each of the 16 teeth has a single tier of cells, while the inner surface has 1.5 cells per tooth. Remember that each tooth is composed of two concentric layers of fused cell walls. Thus, the Haplolepideous peristome has one ring of 16 teeth (sometimes partially split to 32); the inner surface composed of 24 cells, the outer of 16 cells, without any vertical cells walls visible on the outer tooth surface (Fig. 13). The Diplolepideous Peristome has two (or sometimes reduced to one) rings of 16 (or fused to eight) teeth; the outermost layer (exostome) has the inner surface composed of 16 cells, the outer of 32 cells, with each tooth having a vertical cell wall running vertically on the outer surface.

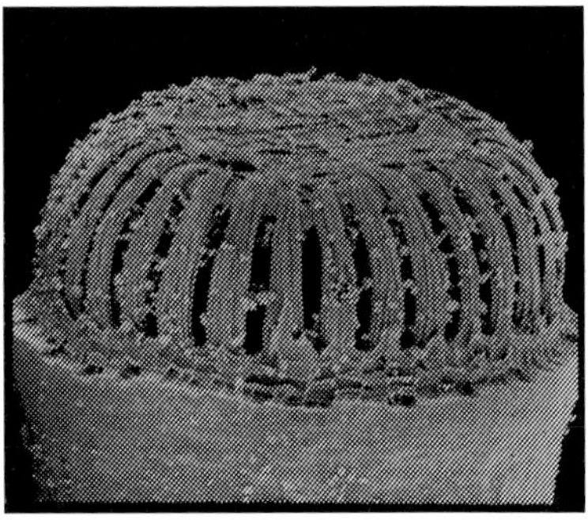

Fig. 8. Peristome of *Atrichum undulatum* – the 64 teeth are each composed of bundles of whole cells.

Classification

The class Bryopsida (Musci) is here divided into three groups: 1) the peat mosses (Sphagnidae with about 150 species worldwide) with unique leaf structure, capsules elevated on gametophytic stalks, no peristome and capsule opening by an operculum; 2) the granite mosses (Andreaeidae with about 100 species worldwide) with black plants, capsules opening via four-longitudinal slits and no peristome or operculum (both of these groups have thalloid protonema); and 3) true mosses (Bryidae with about 8000 species worldwide) with a sporophytic seta, operculum, peristome and filamentous protonema.

The true mosses can be further divided into those with nematodontous peristomes (mainly those placed in the Polytrichaceae). These generally are large mosses with relatively well developed conducting tissues. *Dawsonia* of

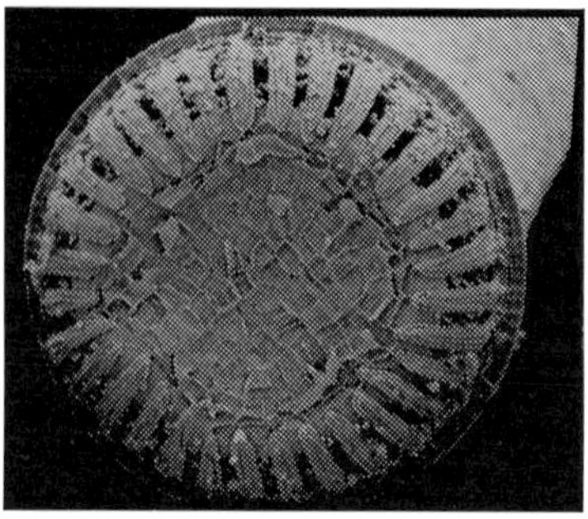

Fig. 9. Epiphragm and 64 peristome teeth of *Atrichum undulatum*. Spaces between the teeth with spores just beneath act as a salt shaker in spore dispersal.

Fig. 10. Diplolepideous peristome, with an outer exostome and an inner endostome of *Leucolepis menziesii*.

Fig. 11. Endostome of a diplolepidous moss (*Leucolepis menziesii*). The exostome has been removed in order to expose the pleated lower membrane of the endostome.

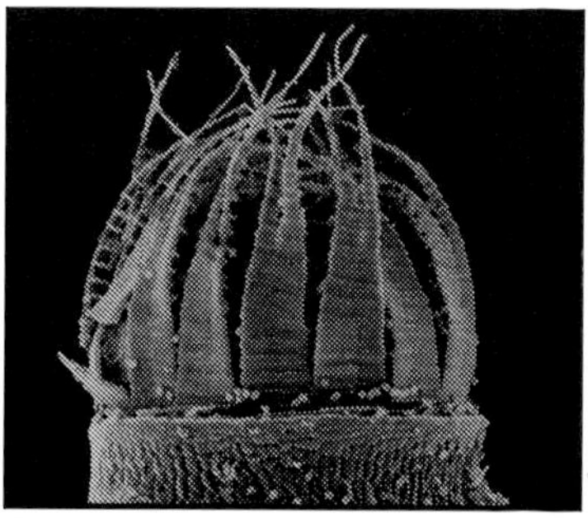

Fig. 12. Haplolepideous peristome with one layer of teeth (*Dicranella heteromalla*).

Australasia is the largest terrestrial moss reaching a maximum of nearly one metre in height. Other mosses are those with arthrodontous peristomes. Two groups are recognized: haplolepideous and diplolepideous. Whereas all haplolepideous mosses are acrocarpous, diplolepideous groups are either acrocarpous or pleurocarpous. The book contains numerous species in all three groups and the text is arranged according to this broad classification. It stresses similarities used in classifying these plants based on their phylogenetic relationships; accordingly, mosses that look similar to each other are placed close to one another in the text. Derived species are placed last, those that have more primitive features are placed first.

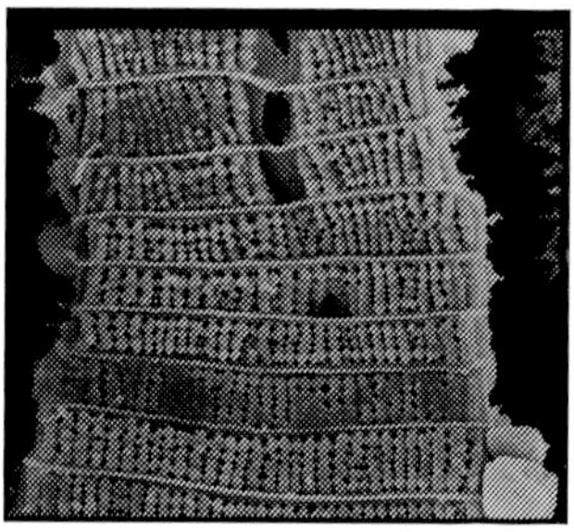

Fig. 13. Close up of outer surface of peristome tooth (haplolepideous) of *Dicranella heteromalla*.

Key to the Recognition of Species*

* *Names in parentheses are additional, common species not included in this book.*

1. Plants with clusters of branches along a single, erect stem; leaf cells of 2 kinds - long narrow chlorophyllose cells separating large hyaline cells containing more or less spirally arranged thickenings (fibrils) and pores 2

1. Plants not branched or with branches arising singly along a prostrate to erect stem; leaf cells of 1 kind - all cells green, no spirally arranged thickenings (fibrils) or pores present 7

2. Leaves spoon-shaped, ovate, with inrolled margins; the apex forming a hood. Turgid, fat plants with swollen branches 3

2. Leaves spear-shaped, lanceolate, with erect to incurved margins, the apex open and forming a channel. Slender plants with skinny branches 4

3. Plants red; green cells of leaves smooth, in transverse section oval. Found mostly in the boreal forest . . . . *Sphagnum magellanicum* (pg. 53)

3. Plants brown; green cells of leaves with papillae where they contact hyaline cells, in transverse section trapezoidal. Found in coastal peatlands . . . . *Sphagnum papillosum* (pg. 53)

4. Plants yellow-green to green, never with any red or brown 5

4. Plants brown (at least the stem) or purple-red 6

5. Stem leaves flat and erose across the top (as cut with "pinking shears"); plants green, with one pendent branch between groups of spreading ones (seen only in the apical portion when viewed from the side). Found in forested habitats . . . . *Sphagnum girgensohnii* (pg. 54)

5. Stem leaves rounded and entire at the apex; plants yellow-green, with two pendent branches between groups of spreading ones. Found in open peatlands . . . . *Sphagnum angustifolium* (pg. 54)

6. Plants brown, forming hummocks in open or shrubby, acid peatlands . . . . *Sphagnum fuscum* (pg. 55)

6. Plants purple-red, forming lawns or low hummocks in forested, shrubby or open boreal peatlands . . . . *Sphagnum warnstorfii* (pg. 55)

7. Gametophyte seemingly absent (consisting only of protonema); sporophyte of an asymmetric capsule, bone-white peristome and papillose seta; plants gregarious or isolated . . . . *Buxbaumia aphylla* (pg. 116)

7. Gametophyte present (with leaves and stems); sporophyte with symmetric to asymmetric capsules, coloured peristome (or absent) and smooth to papillose seta; plants in mats 8

8. Leaves attached in two rows on opposite sides of the stem (distichous) 9

8. Leaves attached all around the stem (the stems may be flattened [complanate] but the leaves are not distichous in these cases) 12

9. Leaves equitant (each clasping the one above by an extra flap lying in the same plane as the leaf), lanceolate to oblong; upper leaf cells smooth, clear 10

9. Leaves not equitant (not having an extra flap and clasping the one above, rather leaves with expanded bases), subulate; upper leaf cells papillose, obscure 11

10. Plants large (2-5 cm long), found in flowing water; leaves ligulate-lanceolate . . . . *Fissidens grandifrons* (pg. 132)

10. Plants small (< 1 cm long), found on moist soil and peat; leaves oblong to ovate-oblong . . . . (*Fissidens osmundoides*)

11. Capsules erect. Common on calcareous rock outcrops . . . . *Distichium capillaceum* (pg. 131)

11. Capsules inclined (to 90°). Infrequent on calcareous soil banks and on peat... .... *Distichium inclinatum* (pg. 131)

12. Plants 2 to 3 pinnate, each year forming a flattened frond; the fronds arranged in a stair-step, ascending pattern. Common feather moss of boreal and coastal forests .... *Hylocomium splendens* (pg. 107)

12. Plants various, never with an ascending stair-step frond pattern 13

13. Leaves with vertical tiers of cells (lamellae) or filaments extending upward on inner (adaxial) side of leaf 14

13. Leaves without vertical tiers or filaments of cells on adaxial side 23

14. Plants bulbiform; leaves with numerous, erect filaments hidden by overlapping leaf laminae. Found on prairie soils and dry, calcareous rock outcrops .... (*Aloina brevirostris*)

14. Plants elongated; leaves with numerous lamellae. Found in mesic to dry forests, prairie and tundra 15

15. Lamellae covered by overlapping leaf laminae; margins entire 16

15. Lamellae exposed; the leaf laminae plane to erect; margins serrate 18

16. Leaves ending in a short to ± long, hyaline awn .... *Polytrichum piliferum* (pg. 58)

16. Leaves ending in a short, reddish awn 17

17. Stems without, or with only a few, whitish rhizoids. Found on inorganic soils .... *Polytrichum juniperinum* (pg. 57)

17. Stems matted with whitish rhizoids. Found on organic soils, especially common on *Sphagnum fuscum* hummocks .... *Polytrichum strictum* (pg. 57)

18. Leaves bordered by elongate cells; lamellae occurring only on narrow costa, 2-5 in number .... *Atrichum undulatum* and *A. selwynii* (pg. 60)

18. Leaves without differentiated border of elongate cells; lamellae occurring on expanded costa across much of leaf surface, 10-50 in number 19

19. Leaves with lamellae on both the inner and outer leaf surfaces; lamellae of inner surfaces few (10-15), undulating .... *Oligotrichum aligerum* (pg. 60)

19. Leaves with lamellae only on inner leaf surface; lamellae numerous (30-50), straight 20

20. Capsules 4-angled in transverse section; apical cells of lamellae notched in transverse section. Common in the boreal forest . *Polytrichum commune* (pg. 56)

20. Capsules round in transverse section; apical cells of lamellae rounded or flat in transverse section. Common at higher elevation and along the coast 21

21. Leaves strongly contorted and much twisted when dry. Found in coastal forests *Pogonatum contortum* (pg. 58)

21. Leaves erect, imbricate and ± straight when dry. Found in montane habitats 22

22. Plants olive-green, with narrow leaves; apical cells of lamellae about as wide as those below, finely papillose and ovate; the lumen pyriform. Common in alpine-montane habitats .... *Pogonatum alpinum* (pg. 59)

22. Plants bluish-green, with broad leaves; apical cells of lamellae broader than those below, coarsely papillose and round, the lumen rectangular-rounded. Infrequent, mostly in acidic alpine tundra .... *Pogonatum urnigerum* (pg. 59)

23. Plants dendroid 24

23. Plants not branched or with few to numerous lateral branches 25

24. Stem leaves green, heart-shaped, with entire margins; capsules erect. Widespread, usually in swampy or peaty habitats .... *Climacium dendroides* (pg. 113)

24. Stem leaves pale, nearly white, triangular, with sharp marginal teeth; capsules nodding. Common in coastal forests .... *Leucolepis menziesii* (pg. 72)

25. Leaves without a costa or costa short and double, double, or single with 2-3 lateral spurs 26

25. Leaves with a single costa (to at least mid leaf) 55

26. Leaves ending in hyaline points; capsules immersed in the perichaetial leaves .... *Hedwigia ciliata* (pg. 111)

26. Leaves ending in green, reddish-brown or black points; capsules exserted above the perichaetial leaves 27

27. Small, blackish plants with papillose, rounded, upper leaf cells; capsules opening by 4 longitudinal slits. Found on exposed, acidic rocks . *Andreaea rupestris* (pg. 56)

27. Small to mostly large, greenish plants with smooth (rarely slightly papillose), longer than wide upper leaf cells; capsules opening by an operculum. Found in montane, coastal or boreal forest areas 28

28. Leaves plicate, at least in lower half.............................. 29

28. Leaves smooth, transversely undulate or with revolute margins 33

29. Plants golden-red; stems not or infrequently branched; leaf apices reflexed. Found in calcareous seeps and wet tundra, occasional in peatlands .... *Orthothecium chryseum* (pg. 110)

29. Plants green; stems irregularly branched; leaf apices erect. Found terrestrial or epiphytic in upland, coastal or mesic boreal forests 30

30. Plants regularly and closely pinnate, feather-like; fronds flat, erect to ascending, triangular; leaves strongly falcate-secund ...... *Ptilium crista-castrensis* (pg. 106)

30. Plants irregularly pinnate or not branched, not feather-like; stems prostrate to loosely ascending, coarse; leaves erect to loosely and irregularly falcate-secund 31

31. Plants large, prostrate, not or little branched; leaves indistinctly plicate and rugose, falcate-secund.................................. *Rhytidiopsis robusta* (pg. 109)

31. Plants very large, ascending, irregularly and abundantly branched; leaves plicate, loosely falcate to spreading 32

32. Costa double, weak, not obvious; stem tips with leaves loosely & slightly falcate, plicate below. Common in lowland coastal forests......................... .... *Rhytidiadelphus loreus* (pg. 108)

32. Costa double, strong and apparent; stem tips with leaves untidy, sticking out in all directions, regularly plicate throughout. Widespread in coastal and mesic boreal forests .... *Rhytidiadelphus triquetrus* (pg. 108)

33. Mature branches erect, producing abundant, conspicuous propagula in their upper leaf axils .... *Platygyrium repens* (pg. 105)

33. Mature branches prostrate to erect, without propagula in upper leaf axils...34

34. Plants harsh, aquatic, occurring in swiftly flowing streams .... *Hygrohypnum bestii* (pg. 92)

34. Plants soft, terrestrial, or if emergent or aquatic, then found in fens and ponds 35

35. Leaves falcate-secund (if thread-like, then only slightly so) 36

35. Leaves spreading, imbricate, complanate or squarrose-recurved 43

36. Leaf margins revolute; golden plants of dry, calcareous rocks .... *Hypnum revolutum* (pg. 104)

36. Leaf margins plane; yellow-green to red-brown plants of various habitats 37

37. Plants found around bases of aspen trees in boreal forest habitats; leaves pointed upward; capsules erect, straight .... *Pylaisiella polyantha* (pg. 105)

37. Plants found on rocks, tree trunks, in fens or marshes. Leaves pointed to one side or downward; capsules curved, horizontal 38

38. Plants swollen, turgid, with wide, broadly pointed leaves. Found aquatic or emergent in calcareous water or in fen pools . . . . *Scorpidium scorpioides* (pg. 87)

38. Plants slender, with narrow, acuminate leaves. Found on rocks, trees or in swamps, never submerged 39

39. Alar cells not differentiated from basal cells; plants dull-green, filiform. Found on calcareous rock crevices . . . . *Platydictya jungermannioides* (pg. 106)

39. Alar cells differentiated from basal cells; plants lustrous, greenish. Found on fens, swamps, dry rock surfaces or tree trunks 40

40. Stems with an outer layer of enlarged hyaline cells 41

40. Stems with outer layer of small cells, similar to those of the cortex 42

41. Leaves often somewhat complanate, never circinate; alar cells hyaline and inflated. Found in fens, swamps and along gravelly or sandy stream banks throughout the area . . . . *Hypnum lindbergii* (pg. 102)

41. Leaves falcate-secund to circinate; alar cells small, quadrate. Found epiphytic on branches and trunks west of the Rockies . . . . *Hypnum subimponens* (pg. 103)

42. Leaves strongly falcate-secund to circinate, long acuminate, serrulate in upper portion, often whitish-green. Common in coastal forests . . . . *Hypnum circinale* (pg. 103)

42. Leaves slightly falcate-secund, not circinate, short acuminate to acute, entire or nearly so in upper portion, yellow-green. Common on dry, calcareous rocks . . . . *Hypnum vaucheri* (pg. 104)

43. Leaves complanate 44

43. Leaves spreading, imbricate or squarrose-recurved 48

44. Leaves undulate 45

44. Leaves not undulate (smooth) 46

45. Leaves broadly ovate, acute, decurrent at insertion, entire to serrulate at apex; capsules horizontal, on long setae arising perpendicular from upper surface of plant; plants found on logs, stumps and soil . . . . *Plagiothecium undulatum* (pg. 101)

45. Leaves ovate-lanceolate, acuminate, not decurrent at insertion, serrate to mid-leaf; capsules erect, emergent on short setae arising at an angle from the underside of the plant; plants growing on tree trunks . . . . *Neckera douglasii* (pg. 115)

46. Costa none; leaf cells large, flaccid, hexagonal; leaf apex obtuse; leaves ovate . . . . *Hookeria lucens* (pg. 116)

46. Costa short and double; leaf cells elongate, narrow, linear; leaf apex acute to acuminate; leaves lanceolate to ovate-lanceolate 47

47. Leaves decurrent at insertion, without elongate gemmae on stem. Widespread in coastal & boreal forests, often in peatlands . . . *Plagiothecium denticulatum* (pg. 101)

47. Leaves not decurrent at insertion, often with elongate gemmae on stem. Coastal forests, rare inland . . . . *Isopterygium elegans* (pg. 102)

48. Leaves markedly squarrose-recurved 49

48. Leaves imbricate to wide-spreading, recurved 50

49. Plants large, erect, forming green carpets among grasses in lawns. Found along roadsides & on subalpine, herbaceous slopes . . *Rhytidiadelphus squarrosus* (pg. 109)

49. Plants small, prostrate, forming red-brown, spreading mats on calcareous rock surfaces . . . . *Campylium halleri* (pg. 93)

50. Leaves tightly imbricate, ovate; plants small, worm or hair-like 51

50. Leaves spreading to loosely erect, oblong to lanceolate; plants large, bushy 52

51. Plants forming long, filiform strands on acidic rock surfaces (more rarely on bark); leaves serrulate in upper half . . . . *Pterigynandrum filiforme* (pg. 112)
51. Plants forming short, worm-like strands, either individually among other mosses or in loose mats on calcareous peat or soil ledges on rock outcrops; leaves entire in upper half . . . . *Myurella julacea* (pg. 111)

52. Rough, epiphytic plants (occasionally on rock) with 3 or more costae, 2 lateral and 1 central one about half the leaf length . . . *Antitrichia curtipendula* (pg. 114)
52. Smooth, terrestrial plants with no costa (or double and very short) 53

53. Leaves spreading with reflexed upper portions; plants bristly in appearance; leaf apices channelled and long acuminate . . . . *Campylium stellatum* (pg. 93)
53. Leaves erect; plants never bristly in appearance; leaf apices flat or with an apiculus, obtuse to acute 54

54. Stems red; stem apices falcate, round in cross-section; alar cells quadrate; plants erect. Forming extensive lawns & hummocks in upland boreal forests, more infrequent in upland coastal forests & forest-tundra . . *Pleurozium schreberi* (pg. 107)
54. Stems green; stem apices erect, flat in cross-section; alar cells inflated and hyaline. Plants of lawns, roadside ditches, rich fens and calcareous seeps, never in upland forests in extensive mats . . . . *Calliergonella cuspidata* (pg. 87)

55. Leaves brittle, tips readily break, mostly found with all leaf tips broken . . . 56
55. Leaves not brittle, tips remain attached. Found with all leaf tips intact 57

56. Found on rock or soil covered ledges; upper cells densely papillose; hyaline lower cells extending up leaf as a V . . . . *Tortella fragilis* (pg. 123)
56. Found on tree trunks, stumps and logs; upper cells smooth or with low papillae; yellow lower cells grading to upper cells along a straight line. . . . . *Dicranum tauricum* and *D. fragilifolium* (pg. 126)

57. All leaf cells with markedly wavy and sinuose walls 58
57. All leaf cells with straight walls, sometimes pitted 60

58. Leaves oblong to lingulate, broadly rounded-obtuse, coarsely blunt-toothed . . . . *Racomitrium aciculare* (pg. 133)
58. Leaves lanceolate, acuminate to awned, the awn serrate or entire 59

59. All leaf cells papillose, plants yellow- to whitish-green. Common roadside plants west of the Rockies . . . . *Racomitrium canescens* (pg. 134)
59. Laminal (green) leaf cells smooth; cells of hyaline awn papillose; plants hoary. Infrequent arctic or alpine (or exposed lower elevations) plants . . . . *Racomitrium lanuginosum* (pg. 134)

60. Black, aquatic or emergent plants of fast-flowing streams; never with hyaline pointed leaves; often coarse and rough in texture 61
60. Green, brown, yellow or reddish plants of various habitats; with or without hyaline pointed leaves; usually soft in texture 62

61. Leaf margins plane, irregularly serrate to mid leaf; leaves 3-5 mm long; capsules subspherical with a persistent operculum; peristome inconspicuous. . . . . *Scouleria aquatica* (pg. 137)
61. Leaf margins revolute, entire or irregular at apex; leaves 1-3 mm long; capsules elliptic with a deciduous operculum; peristome well-developed and conspicuous . . . . *Schistidium rivulare* (pg. 137)

62. Leaves ending in a hyaline awn or hyaline point 63
62. Leaves acute, blunt, subulate or ending in a reddish or yellow awn 68

63. Upper leaf cells (excluding awn) densely papillose 64
63. Upper leaf cells smooth or with low papillae 65

64. Plants dioicous, leaves conspicuously squarrose when wet; margin recurved from base nearly to apex . . . . *Tortula ruralis* (pg. 120)

64. Plants synoicous, leaves erect spreading when wet, margins recurved 1/3 to 2/3 of the length .... *Tortula princeps* (pg. 120)

65. Capsules shortly exserted above perichaetial leaves 66

65. Capsules immersed in perichaetial leaves 67

66. Setae arched, hyaline awn 1/2 length of leaf, abruptly tapering from main body of leaf .... *Grimmia pulvinata* (pg. 135)

66. Setae straight; hyaline awn less than 1/4 length of leaf, gradually tapering from main body of leaf .... *Grimmia affinis* (pg. 135)

67. Peristome lacking; capsules spherical; opercula flat. Small hoary plants on very dry calcareous cliffs. Infrequent .... *Grimmia anodon* (pg. 136)

67. Peristome well-developed; capsules oblong; opercula rostrate. Medium-sized, reddish plants on dry rock surfaces. Common .... *Schistidium apocarpum* (pg. 136)

68. Plants forming dark-green tufts on tree bark; calyptrae hairy, large, covering nearly all of immersed to shortly exserted capsules 69

68. Plants not tufted on tree trunks; if epiphytic, then loosely branched and trailing or forming mats; calyptrae never hairy; capsules various 75

69. Leaves ovate, obtuse, with abundant gemmae on the leaf surfaces. Common, found on aspen trunks .... *Orthotrichum obtusifolium* (pg. 65)

69. Leaves lanceolate, acute to acuminate; gemmae absent or if present; leaves never obtuse. Found on deciduous tree trunks (rarely on conifers and rocks if coastal) 70

70. Propagula produced terminally on the shortly excurrent costa; plants found exclusively in areas subject to salt spray .... (*Ulota phyllantha*)

70. Propagula not present or if present, then on the leaf laminae; plants found in areas not subject to salt spray 71

71. Capsules immersed or emergent in the perichaetial leaves 72

71. Capsules shortly exserted above the perichaetial leaves 73

72. Capsules smooth, ovate-oblong; autoicous; perigonia not conspicuous .... *Orthotrichum striatum* (pg. 64)

72. Capsules lightly 8-ribbed, cylindric; dioicous; male plants often forming separate tufts with bulging, conspicuous perigonia .... *Orthotrichum lyellii* (pg. 64)

73. Plants tufted with spreading, prostrate stems; spores very large ($\pm$ 50 um); leaf apices filiform .... *Ulota megalospora* (pg. 66)

73. Plants tufted without spreading, prostrate stems (all stems ascending); spores smaller (20-30 μm); leaf apices acute to acuminate 74

74. Leaves loosely erect, flexuose to straight when dry; basal area of uniform cells .... *Orthotrichum speciosum* (pg. 65)

74. Leaves markedly crisped when dry; basal area expanded with the outer basal cells forming a differentiated, hyaline margin .... (*Ulota obtusiuscula*)

75. Large, showy epiphytic plants forming dark green, descending or perpendicular fronds; the lower stems unbranched, the upper stems pinnately branched and frondose. Common in coastal forests - when dry with downcurled fronds, when wet with spreading ones .... *Dendroalsia abietina* (pg. 113)

75. Plants various, not frondose; stems never downcurled 76

76. Plants pleurocarpous (sporophyte lateral); stems mostly prostrate, with numerous lateral branches; upper cells (2) 3-10 times longer than broad, rhombic to rectangular 77

76. Plants acrocarpous (sporophytes terminal); stems erect, not branched or occasionally branched beneath perichaetia; upper cells mostly as broad as long, isodiametric, rounded, hexagonal or quadrate; a few species with cells 2-5 (10) to 1, rectangular to rhombic 115

77. Leaves conspicuously rugose (as crumpled paper); plants of exposed calcareous sites .... *Rhytidium rugosum* (pg. 110)
77. Leaves smooth, plicate or undulate; plants of various habitats 78

78. Leaves undulate, asymmetric .... *Metaneckera menziesii* (pg. 115)
78. Leaves smooth or plicate, usually symmetric 79

79. Upper leaf cells papillose, at least on the back side of leaf; papillae sometimes formed by projecting cell ends 80
79. Upper leaf cells smooth 87

80. Plants finely and delicately twice pinnately branched .... *Thuidium recognitum* (pg. 84)
80. Plants evenly or irregularly pinnately (once) branched 81

81. Leaves with short, flexuose, yellowish to hyaline hair points .... *Claopodium crispifolium* (pg. 86)
81. Leaves acuminate to acute, not ending in hair points 82

82. Stems without paraphyllia; leaf cells sometimes smooth or nearly so .... *Isothecium myosuroides* (pg. 94)
82. Stems with paraphyllia; leaf cells mostly conspicuously papillose 83

83. Upper leaf cells 3-6:1; paraphyllia filiform, numerous on stems and leaf bases; stems regularly pinnate. Plants of fens and swamps .... *Helodium blandowii* (pg. 85)
83. Upper leaf cells 2-4:1; paraphyllia polymorphous, mostly compactly branched, fairly abundant on stems; stems irregularly to regularly pinnate. Plants of mesic to dry habitats 84

84. Costa ending about mid-leaf .... *Heterocladium dimorphum* (pg. 83)
84. Costa ending in or just below apex of leaf 85

85. Leaf margins revolute from base to below apex; upper leaf cells papillose; laminal cells often nearly smooth .... *Lescuraea radicosa* (pg. 112)
85. Leaf margins plane or revolute only near base; upper leaf cells papillose by single central projections; laminal cells papillose 86

86. Plants moderately-sized; stems regularly pinnately branched. Found on dry, calcareous soil and rock outcrops, common in the Rockies .... *Thuidium abietinum* (pg. 84)
86. Plants small; stems irregularly branched. On logs in mesic aspen woodlands. Rare except in the boreal forest .... *Haplocladium microphyllum* (pg. 85)

87. Plants large, robust, aquatic, harsh; occurring in streams; up to 30 cm long; without paraphyllia .... *Hygrohypnum bestii* (pg. 92)
87. Plants small to large, slender to moderate, soft; occurring terrestrially or aquatically; mostly less than 10 cm long, with or without paraphyllia 88

88. Leaves very complanate, ovate to broadly oblong. Plant appearing to have 2-ranked leaves .... *Homalia trichomanoides* (pg. 114)
88. Leaves spreading, falcate-secund to erect, lanceolate to oblong. Plants having spirally arranged leaves 89

89. Leaves falcate-secund 90
89. Leaves erect to spreading, straight 95

90. Stems with numerous paraphyllia; costa shortly excurrent, strong .... *Cratoneuron commutatum* (pg. 91)
90. Stems without paraphyllia; costa ending below apex, weak to strong 91

91. Leaves conspicuously plicate. Found in moist, terrestrial habitats .... *Drepanocladus uncinatus* (pg. 90)
91. Leaves smooth or striate. Found aquatic, emergent or in peatlands 92

92. Stems with uniform cells throughout the cortex, (no central strand present). Yellow-green, frequently branched plants of shrubby fens .... (*Drepanocladus vernicosus*)

92. Stems with a few small, thick-walled cells in centre of cortex (central strand present). Green to reddish-brown, irregularly branched plants of fens 93

93. Stems with one layer of enlarged cells surrounding cortex (hyalodermis present). Found in fens. .... (*Drepanocladus revolvens*)

93. Stems with outer layer of cells of similar size to those of cortex (hyalodermis not present). Found in poor fens or eutrophic areas 94

94. Leaf margins entire; alar cells inflated. Found in eutrophic ditches .... *Drepanocladus aduncus* (pg. 90)

94. Leaf margins serrulate at apex; alar cells enlarged. Found in disturbed and oligotrophic peatlands .... (*Drepanocladus fluitans*)

95. Leaves rounded at apex, obtuse or with a tiny apiculus 96

95. Leaves acute to acuminate, or narrowed to a filiform apex 99

96. Plants reddish, young leaves ending in a tiny apiculus. Found in acidic alpine seeps and poor fens .... *Calliergon sarmentosum* (pg. 89)

96. Plants brown or green, young leaves obtuse. Found in calcareous seeps and rich fens 97

97. Costa strong, ending at the apex; stems loosely pinnately branched; alar cells abruptly inflated. Robust plants often emergent in rich fens... *Calliergon giganteum* (pg. 88)

97. Costa narrow, ending well below apex; stems unbranched or sparsely branched; alar cells enlarged. Slender plants of fens and peatland forests 98

98. Plants dark brown; leaves ovate; alar cells not particularly differentiated; stems with noticeable spiral leaf arrangement. Found in stringy mats or among other mosses in extreme rich fens .... *Calliergon trifarium* (pg. 88)

98. Plants yellow-green; leaves oblong; alar cells gradually enlarged and hyaline; stems without noticeable spiral leaf arrangement. Found in loose mats or occasionally among other mosses in transitional rich fens .... *Calliergon stramineum* (pg. 89)

99. Leaves abruptly contracted to filiform point.... *Cirriphyllum cirrosum* (pg. 100)

99. Leaves acute to acuminate 100

100. Leaves with conspicuous plications 101

100. Leaves smooth or at most delicately striate 103

101. Plants erect; stems with abundant red tomentum. Found in fens .... *Tomenthypnum nitens* (pg. 97)

101. Plants prostrate; stems without red tomentum. Found on tree trunks, logs & rocks 102

102. Leaves broadly acute; cilia of peristome well-developed. Plants of xeric rock surfaces, common in the Rockies .... *Homalothecium aeneum* (pg. 96)

102. Leaves slenderly acute; cilia of peristome rudimentary. Plants of tree trunks & logs west of the Rockies, rarely on rock ... *Homalothecium fulgescens* (pg. 96)

103. Leaves with a strong costa ending in or just beyond apex; paraphyllia present (but sometimes few) on stems; alar cells inflated and hyaline .... *Cratoneuron filicinum* (pg. 91)

103. Leaves with a narrow costa ending well below apex; paraphyllia absent from stems; alar cells quadrate and coloured 104

104. Leaves obtuse to very broadly acute, imbricate. Found on moist rocks along streams west of the Rockies .... *Scleropodium obtusifolium* (pg. 100)

104. Leaves slenderly acute to acuminate, erect to spreading. Found in various habitats 105

105. Alar cells usually numerous, 15-50 cells, subquadrate, thick-walled; leaves coarsely serrate in upper 1/3, not decurrent. Often whitish-green. Common epiphytic plants of coastal forests, not found east of the Rockies .... *Isothecium myosuroides* (pg. 94)

105. Alar cells less numerous (10-20 cells), rectangular to quadrate, thin-walled; leaves entire to serrulate, decurrent or not. Usually yellow-green to green. Common, widespread plants 106

106. Stem and branch leaves markedly different in size and shape 107

106. Stem and branch leaves essentially similar in size and shape 108

107. Plants robust; stems evenly and closely pinnately branched, rarely arched; the branches in one plane .... *Kindbergia oregana* (pg. 95)

107. Plants medium-sized; stems irregularly pinnately to twice pinnately branched, often arching .... *Kindbergia praelonga* (pg. 95)

108. Leaf margins entire, inflexed just below apex. Plants of wet rocks in swiftly flowing water, often found in splash zone of streams and in waterfalls (sometimes ± falcate-secund) .... *Hygrohypnum luridum* (pg. 92)

108. Leaf margins serrulate, at least at apex, plane. Plants of fens, seeps and drier terrestrial and epiphytic habitats 109

109. Leaf apices bluntly acute, with short cells (rhomboid-hexagonal) in apex; costa ending as a spine; branch leaves often slightly complanate and spreading .... *Eurhynchium pulchellum* (pg. 94)

109. Leaf apices sharply acute to acuminate, with long cells (elongate) in apex; costa not ending as a spine; branch leaves erect 110

110. Stems ± erect-ascending, not much branched; leaf margins nearly entire (or serrulate at leaf apex). Plants of rich fens, calcareous seeps and alpine-arctic tundra .... (*Brachythecium turgidum*)

110. Stems prostrate or nearly so, with numerous branches; leaf margins serrulate. Plants of seeps and drier, terrestrial habitats 111

111. Leaves noticeably decurrent. Found on wet rocks and emergent in calcareous seeps *Brachythecium rivulare* (pg. 97)

111. Leaves not or slightly decurrent. Terrestrial or epiphytic 112

112. Plants of subalpine-arctic late snow areas. (Common in the Rockies northward) .... *Brachythecium groenlandicum* (pg. 98)

112. Plants of logs, tree trunks and soil at low elevations 113

113. Leaves smooth, not striolate-plicate, somewhat decurrent; setae conspicuously rough (papillose). Common west of Rockies .... *Brachythecium asperrimum* (pg. 99)

113. Leaves somewhat striolate-plicate, not decurrent; setae smooth or with a few papillae. Common east of the Rockies 114

114. Capsules erect; alar cells small, dense.. *Brachythecium acuminatum* (pg. 99)

114. Capsules inclined; alar cells large, lax... *Brachythecium salebrosum* (pg. 98)

115. Capsules showy, erect, with a skirt-like expansion, ± 0.5-1.0 cm wide, bright red or yellow. Exclusively on dung 116

115. Capsules not especially conspicuous, erect or inclined, lacking a skirt-like expansion, <5 mm wide, green or black, or capsules not present. On various substrates (including dung) 117

116. Capsules yellow .... *Splachnum luteum* (pg. 63)

116. Capsules bright red .... *Splachnum rubrum* (pg. 63)

117. Plants white-silvery; the upper 1/3-1/2 of each leaf without chlorophyll. Found in disturbed areas .... *Bryum argenteum* (pg. 68)

117. Plants green, yellow, pink, red or brownish-green; the upper 1/3-1/2 of each leaf with chlorophyll. Found in various habitats 118

118. Leaves markedly squarrose-recurved wet or dry. Found in fens .... *Paludella squarrosa* (pg. 81)

118. Leaves erect to spreading, wide-spreading only when wet............119

119. Leaves in conspicuous ranks, in 3 spiralled ranks or 5 star-shaped ones .. 120

119. Leaves evenly and spirally inserted around stem, not in 3 ranks (when viewed from the side) or in 5 ranks (when viewed from above) 121

120. Leaves in 5 ranks; plants star-shaped (from above). On acidic alpine soil .... *Conostomum tetragonum* (pg. 80)

120. Leaves in 3 ranks (especially evident from the side and when the plant is damp). In rich fens.................................*Meesia triquetra* (pg. 82)

121. Leaves multi-stratose, consisting of an expanded costa of large, dead, porose, hyaline cells sandwiching smaller, living, non-porose, green cells; laminae not evident. Plants whitish-green, at higher elevations *Paraleucobryum enerve* (pg. 129)

121. Leaves uni- to bistratose; costa narrow and confined to centre of leaf; laminae evident. Plants green to black, found at all elevations 122

122. Capsules with 4 peristome teeth; sterile plants usually terminating in a cup-shaped cluster of leaves enclosing gemmae......... *Tetraphis pellucida* (pg. 61)

122. Capsules with 16 peristome teeth or peristome lacking; sterile plants terminating in a leafy apex or rarely in a nonleafy propaguliferous axis...............123

123. Leaves with thickened cuticular ridges, each extending for 2-5 cells along 1 row of cells. On acidic alpine-arctic rocks .... *Dicranoweisia crispula* (pg. 128)

123. Leaves with papillae or with smooth cells. Habitats various.............124

124. Plants in bright red cushions; leaves obtuse. Found on exposed perennially wet rocks along the coast .... *Bryum miniatum* (pg. 68)

124. Plants of shades of green; leaves obtuse to subulate. Habitat various..125

125. Leaves bordered by elongate cells in 2-5 rows 126

125. Leaves bordered by cells similar to those toward costa.................136

126. Leaf cells 3-6:1, long-hexagonal, border gradually differentiated; margin entire or singly toothed near apex; leaves ovate-lanceolate to lanceolate..........127

126. Leaf cells 1-3:1, hexagonal, border usually abruptly differentiated; margin entire, singly or doubly toothed; leaves elliptic, ovate or oblong 128

127. Leaves long decurrent. In wet habitats ...... *Bryum pseudotriquetrum* (pg. 67)

127. Leaves not decurrent. Found in dry habitats ..... *Bryum caespiticium (pg. 67)*

128. Margins entire 129

128. Margins toothed...131

129. Plants blackish-red, especially in older parts; leaf cells longer than wide; leaves with reflexed margins; apiculus strong. Found exclusively in extreme rich fens ... . *Cinclidium stygium*

129. Plants green; most leaf cells as long as wide (isodiametric); leaves with plane margins; apiculus weak or lacking. Found in coastal forests and boreal fens...130

130. Leaf border very strong and conspicuous. Plants of coastal forests....... .... *Rhizomnium glabrescens* (pg. 76)

130. Leaf border weak, not conspicuous. Plants of boreal and montane fens .. ..*Rhizomnium gracile* (pg. 76)

131. Leaf teeth in pairs (doubly serrate).................................132

131. Leaf teeth set singly (serrate).......................................133

132. Synoicous; leaf cells 1-2:1, with smooth walls. Frequent west of the Rockies.....................................*Mnium marginatum* (pg. 73)

132. Dioicous; leaf cells 2-3:1, with pitted walls. Rare, found in the subalpine zone of the Rockies ....*Mnium arizonicum* (pg. 73)

133. Leaves toothed to about the middle. Common east of the Rockies, rare westward .... *Plagiomnium cuspidatum* (pg. 74)

133. Leaves toothed to the base or nearly so. Found throughout 134

133. Leaves toothed to the base or nearly so. Found throughout 134

134. Dioicous. Leaves 3-10 mm long, strongly decurrent; 3-7 sporophytes per perichaetium. Found west of the Rockies .... *Plagiomnium insigne* (pg. 75)

134. Synoicous. Leaves 3-6 mm long, not to moderately decurrent; 1-4 sporophytes per perichaetium. Found throughout 135

135. Leaves not decurrent; plagiotropic stems absent. Found west of the Rockies .... *Plagiomnium venustum* (pg. 75)

135. Leaves moderately decurrent; plagiotropic stems present. Found throughout .... *Plagiomnium medium* (pg. 74)

136. Upper and median leaf cells papillose, at least on the back side of leaf or costa (though sometimes obscure and difficult to see), mamillose or with cuticular ridges 137

136. All leaf cells smooth (including bulging cells) 164

137. Leaves sharply contracted from a hyaline or orange, sheathing base to an elongate upper portion 138

137. Leaves gradually narrowed from base to apex 139

138. Leaf base hyaline; leaves in upper portion bistratose; upper leaf cells rectangular 2-4:1; capsules round. Found in acidic tundra and rock crevices of higher elevations .... *Bartramia ithyphylla* (pg. 79)

138. Leaf base orange; leaves in upper portion unistratose; upper leaf cells quadrate 1:1; capsules cylindric. In coniferous forests. .... *Timmia austriaca* (pg. 77)

139. Leaves with minute cuticular bumps covering all of leaf, otherwise cells smooth, obscurely 3-ranked; capsules round. Found on neutral to basic cliff faces .... *Plagiopus oederiana* (pg. 80)

139. Leaves with cells papillose (from 1 to several papillae per cell), never 3-ranked; capsules various. Found in various habitats 140

140. Upper leaf cells densely papillose, with several c-shaped papillae, 2-3 irregularly bulging papillae or 1-2 large, forked papillae 141

140. Upper leaf cells bulging or with one central conical papilla per cell, or cell ends projecting as papillae, some species papillose only on back of costa ... 153

141. Leaves ligulate to slenderly lanceolate, generally slender throughout; often gradually narrowed from base to apex 142

141. Leaves oblong, ovate, ovate-lanceolate or lingulate, generally wide at base, often as wide (or nearly so) near apex as at base 145

142. Leaves strongly crisped-tortuose when dry; hyaline basal cells extending upward as a V .... *Tortella tortuosa* (pg. 123)

142. Leaves flexuose to somewhat twisted when dry; hyaline or coloured basal cells grading evenly to upper cells 143

143. Leaf margins revolute to at least the upper 1/4; plants reddish; peristome present. Found on calcareous soil or rarely on rock (*Bryoerythrophyllum recurvirostrum*)

143. Leaf margins plane or narrowly recurved below; plants green; peristome lacking. Found in rock crevices 144

144. Capsules smooth; papillae conic, confined to cell lumens; lower cells smooth .... *Gymnostomum recurvirostrum* (pg. 122)

144. Capsules strongly 8-ribbed; papillae clavate, covering lumens and crosswalls; lower cells with numerous (8-12) small, elliptic, cuticular papillae............ .... *Amphidium lapponicum* (pg. 133)

145. Plants butter-yellow to chartreuse, leaves narrowly oblong. Found on disturbed, calcareous soil, roadbanks and prairies east of the Rockies; an urban weed in Vancouver .... *Barbula convoluta* (pg. 122)

145. Plants green to dark brown, leaves ovate-lanceolate to lingulate. Found on subalpine and montane soil and rock crevices 146

146. Numerous, filiform propagula present in upper leaf axils; sterile plants with muticous leaves; capsules spirally ribbed; peristome double .... *Encalypta procera* (pg. 117)

146. Numerous filiform propagula never present in upper leaf axils; sterile plants muticous or piliferous; capsules ribbed or smooth; peristome single or lacking 147

147. Leaf margins strongly revolute; costa increasing in width upward, convex ventrally; capsules exserted well above leaves .... *Desmatodon obtusifolius* (pg. 121)

147. Leaf margins plane to recurved, if revolute then capsules emergent; costa decreasing in width upward, concave ventrally; capsules exserted to immersed 148

148. Plants tufted on dry calcareous rock surfaces, glaucous; capsules emergent in perichaetial leaves; calyptrae hairy; papillae forked .... *Orthotrichum pellucidum* (pg. 66)

148. Plants forming cushions or turfs on mesic calcareous or acidic rock outcrops or on tundra soil; capsules exserted on long setae; calyptrae naked; papillae c-shaped 149

149. Calyptrae large, sheathing all of capsule, mitrate, shaped as a candle snuffer; basal leaf cells with thickened crosswalls 150

149. Calyptrae small, sheathing only operculum and part of the length of the capsule, cucullate; basal leaf cells with unthickened crosswalls 152

150. Leaves ovate-lanceolate; peristome none .... *Encalypta alpina* (pg. 119)

150. Leaves ovate, broadly oblong or lingulate; peristome single, reduced or none 151

151. Calyptrae fringed below; capsules smooth. On neutral to acidic rock .... *Encalypta brevicolla* (pg. 118)

151. Calyptrae erose below; capsules often 8-ribbed. On all substrates, but preferring calcareous ones .... *Encalypta rhaptocarpa* (pg. 118)

152. Leaves muticous or ending in a short yellowish awn; peristome reddish, short, straight; upper leaf cells clear, with small, widely spaced papillae .... *Desmatodon latifolius* (pg. 121)

152. Leaves ending in a long red awn; peristome white, long, spirally twisted; upper leaf cells obscure, densely papillose .... *Tortula norvegica* (pg. 119)

153. Upper leaf cells longer than broad, about 3-5:1 154

153. Upper leaf cells as long as broad, 1-2:1 157

154. Alar cells not differentiated; capsules round. Found in calcareous seeps and on wet soil .... *Philonotis fontana* (pg. 81)

154. Alar cells differentiated, forming conspicuous groups; capsules cylindric. Found on tree bases, inorganic soil and logs 155

155. Leaves markedly undulate .... *Dicranum polysetum* (pg. 124)

155. Leaves not undulate 156

156. Common plants; leaves with 2-4 dorsal ridges (lamellae) in upper 1/4; costa with one row of guide cells; setae usually 1 per perichaetium .... *Dicranum scoparium* (pg. 124)

156. Rare plants; leaves without ridges in upper dorsal 1/4; costa with 2 rows of guide cells; setae 2-4 per perichaetium .... (*Dicranum majus*)

157. Leaves undulate. Found in peatlands .... *Dicranum undulatum* (pg. 125)

157. Leaves not undulate. Found in various habitats 158

158. Leaves broadly ovate, obtuse, imbricate. Arctic-alpine .... *Aulacomnium turgidum* (pg. 78)

158. Leaves lanceolate, acute to narrowly obtuse. Boreal, coastal or arctic-alpine 159

159. Alar cells well differentiated 160

159. Alar cells not or poorly differentiated 161

160. Small, slender arctic-alpine plants, forming dense cushions in open tundra and in peatlands . . . . (*Dicranum elongatum*)

160. Medium-sized boreal and montane plants forming cushions on rotting logs and on tree bases . . . . *Dicranum fuscescens* (pg. 125)

161. Stems with abundant reddish tomentum; upper leaf cells each with one central papilla; plants often terminating in a leaf-less axis covered by propagula . . . . *Aulacomnium palustre* (pg. 78)

161. Stems without reddish tomentum; upper leaf cells with irregularly bulging, mamillose or projecting cell ends; plants not terminating in a leafy axis 162

162. Upper cells mamillose-bulging; leaves bluntly acute. Small plants of wet to damp habitats . . . . *Dichodontium pellucidum* (pg. 127)

162. Upper cells irregularly papillose; leaves sharply acute. Larger plants of mesic habitats 163

163. Capsules round, erect-inclined, symmetric; leaves linear-lanceolate, 4-8 mm long . . . . *Bartramia pomiformis* (pg. 79)

163. Capsules oblong, horizontal-curved, strumose; leaves lanceolate, 3-4 mm long . . . . (*Cynodontium strumiferum*)

164. Minute plants (< 3 mm high) with ovate-hemispheric capsules. On calcareous rock surfaces of the Rockies and northward . . . . *Seligeria donniana* (pg. 132)

164. Small to large plants 5 mm high with cylindric to hemispheric capsules. Found in various habitats 165

165. Leaves consisting mainly of costa, about 1/2 to 2/3 leaf width at base; sometimes ending in short hyaline awns. In coastal peatlands and forests . . . . *Campylopus atrovirens* (pg. 129)

165. Leaves consisting mainly of lamina, the costa 1/10 to 1/3 the leaf width at base; never with hyaline awns. Habitat various 166

166. Leaves falcate-secund; alar cells well differentiated 167

166. Leaves erect-imbricate to twisted-contorted; alar cells not differentiated 169

167. Plants of acidic seepages, sometimes submerged in streams or along waterfall courses; capsules hemispheric; always with a dark red or black colouration; alar cells red . . . . (*Blindia acuta*)

167. Plants of earthen banks and peaty soils; capsules oblong-cylindric; always green in colouration; alar cells hyaline 168

168. Capsules smooth when dry; setae red; leaf margins recurved in part; mouths of capsules not oblique when dry. Widespread . . . . . . *Dicranella varia* (pg. 126)

168. Capsules plainly ridged when dry; setae yellow; leaf margins plane; mouths of capsules oblique when dry. West of Rockies . . . . (*Dicranella heteromalla*)

169. Leaf cells strongly bulging; plants glistening golden-yellow; leaves elliptic to ovate-oblong, or obtuse . . . . *Bryobrittonia longipes* (pg. 117)

169. Leaf cells flat; plants variously dark-green to yellow-green; leaves ovate to linear-lanceolate, mostly acute 170

170. Leaf cells quadrate, rounded-hexagonal or short rhombic-rectangular, moderately thick-walled; leaves ligulate, lanceolate or subulate from a sheathing base 171

170. Leaf cells hexagonal, rectangular or elongate-rectangular, thin-walled; leaves mostly oblong-ovate, some species lanceolate or ligulate 176

171. Leaves ligulate, rounded at apex; the costa about 1/2 the width at base . . . . *Meesia uliginosa* (pg. 82)

171. Leaves lanceolate to subulate-sheathing, acute; the costa about 1/6 to 1/3 the width at base 172

172. Leaf margins revolute to below apex; capsules curved, abruptly horizontal, ribbed; setae purple. Common weed of open soil.. *Ceratodon purpureus* (p. 130)
172. Leaf margins plane or only reflexed below; capsules erect or horizontal, symmetric or strumose, smooth; setae brown to yellow. Habitat various....... 173

173. Leaves strongly crisped-contorted when dry 174
173. Leaves erect-spreading to flexuose when dry.......................... 175

174. Small yellow-green plants of tree trunks and logs in coastal forests; leaves lanceolate; capsules erect, symmetric........... *Dicranoweisia cirrata* (pg. 128)
174. Medium-sized, dark green plants of wet banks and logs in boreal-coastal forests and wet tundra; leaves abruptly narrowed to a slender subula; capsules curved, strumose .... *Oncophorus virens* (pg. 127)

175. Blackish-green plants of rich fens; leaves lanceolate, straight; capsules ovoid, curved.................................... *Catoscopium nigritum* (pg. 83)
175. Golden-green plants of calcareous rock crevices, occasionally in fens; leaves subulate, flexuose-twisted; capsules erect, cylindric........... *Ditrichum flexicaule* (pg. 130)

176. Plants with conspicuous axillary propagula in upper leaf axes .... *Pohlia filum* (pg. 71)
176. Plants never with axillary propagula.............................. 177

177. Leaves rounded-obtuse .... *Tayloria lingulata* (pg. 62)
177. Leaves acute to acuminate 178

178. Leaves irregularly serrate; capsules greenish-black, erect, with sticky, yellow spores. Forming conic tufts on dung .... *Tetraplodon angustatus* (pg. 62)
178. Leaves entire or denticulate; capsules nodding, green, with nonsticky, green spores. On substrate other than dung 179

179. Plants whitish-green, with large, thin-walled leaf cells. On wet, calcareous soil and seepages .... *Pohlia wahlenbergii* (pg. 69)
179. Plants green to reddish-green, with thicker-walled leaf cells. Not common in calcareous seeps... 180

180. Leaves linear; capsules pyriform; upper leaf cells 5-10:1 .... *Leptobryum pyriforme* (pg. 72)
180. Leaves ovate to lanceolate; capsules cylindric to pyriform; upper leaf cells 3-7:1 181

181. Leaves concave, ovate, ending in a reflexed apiculus; plants pink to whitish-green. In alpine-arctic rock crevices .... (*Plagiobryum zierii*)
181. Leaves flat, lanceolate to ovate-lanceolate, ending in an acute apex; plants golden to olive-green. In various habitats 182

182. Plants very glossy, with an opalescent sheen; leaves ovate-lanceolate .... *Pohlia cruda* (pg. 69)
182. Plants dull to somewhat shiny (but not opalescent); leaves lanceolate or ovate-lanceolate 183

183. Leaf cells rectangular; leaves ovate-lanceolate; setae strongly hygroscopic; capsules ribbed .... *Funaria hygrometrica* (pg. 61)
183. Leaf cells elongate-hexagonal to pentagonal-hexagonal; leaves lanceolate; setae straight, stiff; capsules smooth 184

184. Rare, plants of wet calcareous cliff faces; capsules with endostome only .. .. *Mielichhoferia macrocarpa* (pg. 71)
184. Common, plants of boreal and coastal forests; capsules with well-developed exostome.. 185

185. Monoicous, fertile leaves same size as vegetative leaves; capsules cylindric. Widespread, expecially common on rotting logs of montane and boreal forests.... .... *Pohlia nutans* (pg. 70)
185. Dioicous, fertile leaves greatly enlarged; capsules short, + ovate. Found on mineral soil banks in coastal forests...................... *Pohlia longibracteata* (pg. 70)

x 3.5

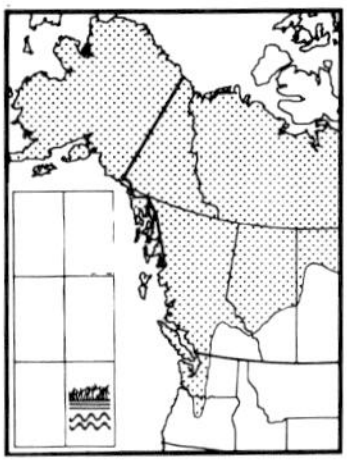

Sphagnum magellanicum. Peat mosses all belong to the genus *Sphagnum*. They have the ability to acidify their surroundings and can hold 20 times or more their dry weight in water. The leaves consist of a single layer of alternating small, living green cells with large, dead hyaline cells. Branches are attached to the stem in groups (or fascicles) and are either pendent along the stem or spread outward. Capsules are often produced, but persist only briefly. Colour is an important character in differentiating the 40 or more species in western North America. *Sphagnum magellanicum* is characterized by fat, turgid plants that are red. It forms moderate-sized hummocks or lawns in minerotrophic and ombrotrophic peatlands. A sequence of species from *S. angustifolium* (yellow-green) in the hollows to *S. magellanicum* (red) at mid-hummock to *S. fuscum* (brown) on the hummock top is normally present throughout the western boreal region.

Sphagnum papillosum is a robust, fat species that forms hummocks only in oceanic British Columbia and Alaska. The plants are light brown and all branches are thick and turgid. This species has wide moisture tolerances and can be found in damp depressions as well as on hummocks. Other fat Sphagna include the coastal *S. imbricatum*, which has slender branchlets mixed with thick spreading branches and is also brown, and the widespread *S. magellanicum* that is usually bright red.

x 2.5

x 3.5

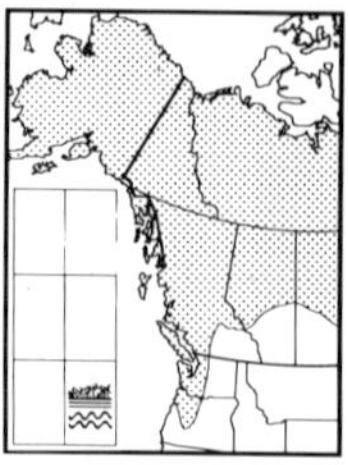

Sphagnum angustifolium is a slender yellow-green species that forms lawns and fills hollows, always above the water level. It has two pendent branches between the radiating arms of spreading branches (observe the side of the head of the plant). The stem leaves are small and blunt. It is never red or brown, and it occurs in weakly ionic peatlands (poor fens).

x 2.5

Sphagnum girgensohnii. A species similar in appearance to *S. fuscum*, *S. nemoreum* and *S. warnstorfii*, that occurs almost exclusively in forested habitats on shallow peat or on cliff shelves. It is an "acutifolia", thus it is slender, with one pendent branch between young fascicles. It is green - never red or brown. The capitula are flat-topped and the plants usually larger than others in the section Acutifolia. Microscopically, it is distinguished by having stem leaves resorbed across their upper portion; they are flat on top and look as if someone cut them with "pinking shears". It forms loose lawns throughout the boreal forest. Along the coast, it is common in higher elevation forests and it rarely occurs with other Sphagna, except *S. nemoreum*. Farther north, in Alaska, Yukon and N.W.T., it is one of the most common species, forming low hummocks in shrubby tundra.

x 3.5

Sphagnum warnstorfii is one of several common, slender, small, red Sphagna. It is a species of more calcareous habitats, often found with *Tomenthypnum nitens*, forming small hummocks or lawns in rich fens. It often occurs below *S. fuscum* on hummocks in boreal muskegs. The leaves are spirally five-ranked along the branches (use a hand lens to see this) and the plants are more or less flat-topped. The colour often has a purple tone. *S. nemoreum* has rounded "pom-pom" shaped heads, is "pinky" red, and forms isolated hummocks in black spruce forests (never in open fens associated with *Tomenthypnum*). Towards the coast, *S. rubellum* becomes a dominating component of lawns in ionically poor peatlands. It would never occur with *S. warnstorfii*. These three *Sphagnum* species can be identified with certainty only by observing stem leaf shape and branch leaf pore pattern under the compound microscope. Microscopically, *S. warnstorfii* has minute, strongly ringed pores in the upper half of young leaves, these contrast with much larger pores in the lower half of the leaves. The stem leaves are tongue-shaped and entire. This is the most common species of *Sphagnum* in Alberta, becoming increasingly rare coastward and northward.

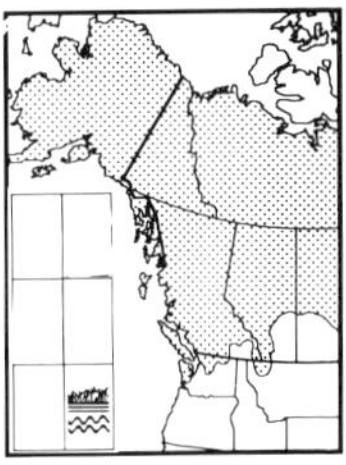

Sphagnum fuscum is a hummock-forming species. It is slender and brown, with dark brown stems and has one pendent branch between radiating arms of the capitulum (head). The stem leaves are tongue-shaped and without fibrils in the hyaline cells. *Sphagnum fuscum*, like *S. warnstorfii*, belongs to the section Acutifolia, characterized by having one pendent branch between each tier of spreading branches (best seen in the lower portion of the head or capitulum). This is a species of ombrotrophic hummocks, either in true bogs or on isolated hummocks in ionically rich fens. It is common in Alberta, becoming rare on the coast where it is replaced by *S. imbricatum*.

x 2

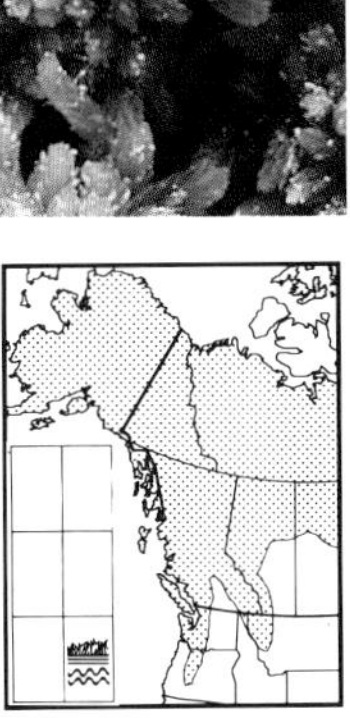

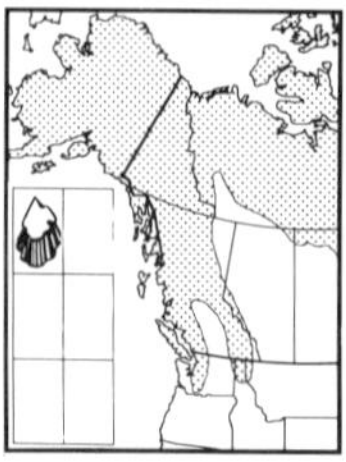

x 3

Andreaea rupestris. The small, tufted, black plants with leaves that are strongly divergent, incurved and reddish-black when wet and tightly appressed when dry, characterize *Andreaea*. When capsules are present, they are split longitudinally into four valves and lack an operculum and peristome. They are shortly exserted on a pseudopodium, which is usually sheathed by the perichaetial leaves. *Andreaea rupestris* lacks a costa and has papillose, thick-walled cells in slightly asymmetric leaves. About ten species of this genus occur in western North America, all confined to acidic rock surfaces and seeps at high elevations. The small, compact tufts of *A. rupestris* are difficult to remove from the rock surface, and when scraped off, come apart as individual plants. *Andreaea rupestris* is the only common species inland from the coastal mountains and south of northern Alaska and Yukon.

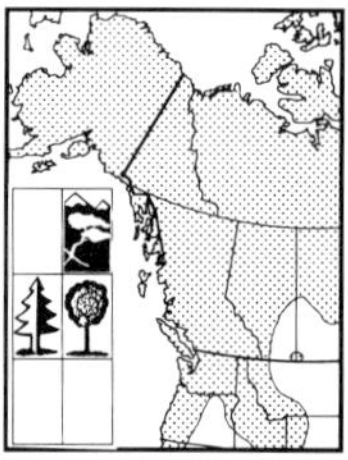

x 1

Polytrichum commune is the largest unbranched moss in western Canada with stems 10-20 cm long. The plants occur in loose mats and they often have capsules that are square in cross section and are borne on wiry setae up to 10 cms long. The leaves diverge when moist and are twisted when dry. The lamellae cover all the upper leaf surface and the margins are strongly toothed. The apical cells of the lamellae are U-shaped in transverse section and the calyptrae are densely hairy. This species forms loose lawns in shaded, moist forests; it can occasionally be found at higher elevations or in swampy ditches.

x .5

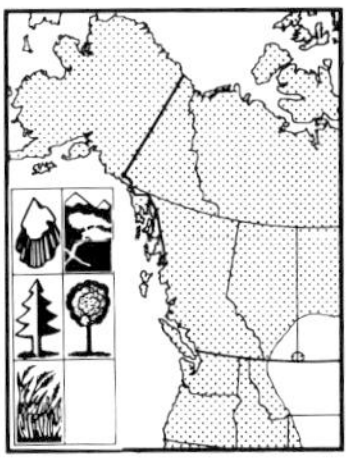

Polytrichum juniperinum. The reddish-brown leaf points and entire leaf lamina (margins), which overlap the lamellae, are characteristic of this species. *Polytrichum juniperinum* is reasonably common in a variety of habitats on inorganic soils. It is frequent on disturbed prairie soil, on soil in boreal and montane forests and on disturbed soil banks at higher elevations. This species lacks any hint of marginal teeth, and has no white tomentum on the stems.

x 1.5

Polytrichum strictum. The stiff, erect plants have leaves with lamellae (and are several to many layers thick) which characterize this species and other members of the Polytrichaceae. Unlike most other mosses, water is conducted internally via a well-developed conduction system. This species is distinguished by reddish-brown leaf points and entire leaf lamina (margins), which overlap the lamellae. When viewed with a hand lens, the upper leaf surface is shiny and blue-green with a single line running the length of each leaf, where the laminae meet and overlap. *Polytrichum strictum* shares these features with *P. juniperinum*. However, *P. strictum* differs as it is smaller, more compact and its stems are matted with whitish-grey rhizoids. It is found on organic soils, as opposed to *P. juniperinum*, which occurs on mineral soils. *Polytrichum strictum* is most commonly found growing as separate, individual plants on *Sphagnum* hummocks in both boreal and montane peatlands. The plants remain about a centimetre above the peat moss surface and indicate the driest of the *Sphagnum* hummocks.

x 2

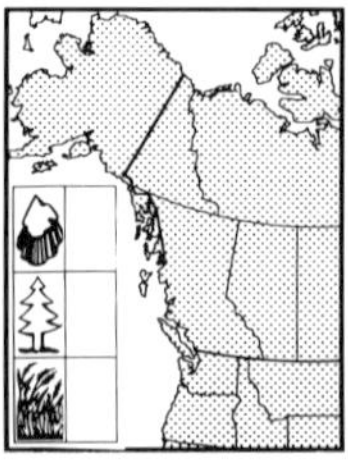

Polytrichum piliferum is characterized by having stout, hyaline leaf points and laminal margins which overlap the lamellae. The hyaline tips are usually spinulose and merge abruptly into the leaf blade. It is the only species of the genus with long awns hyaline to their base. *Polytrichum piliferum* is found on sandy soils. It occurs on drier sites than P. *juniperinum* and the plants are short, stout and rarely branched.

x 1.5

Pogonatum contortum occurs along the west coast. It has lamellae covering nearly all of the upper leaf surface and contorted leaves when dry. These differentiate this species from all local *Polytrichum* species, *Pogonatum alpinum* and other smaller species. Other genera (e.g. *Atrichum* and *Oligotrichum*) have considerably fewer lamellae, which are restricted to the costa or central portion of the leaf and can be seen with a hand lens. The capsules are cylindric and the calyptrae hairy. Be sure and check that the leaf lamellae cover the surface, as *Atrichum undulatum* is very similar but has fewer lamellae and a distinctive leaf border of long cells. This species is found on exposed mineral soil, along roadbanks, stream banks and earth-slides and is common on the sides of hiking trails in low elevation British Columbia forests.

x 2

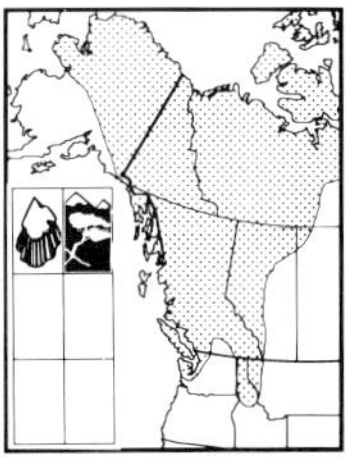

Pogonatum urnigerum is a smaller member of the Polytrichaceae with plants 1-2 cm high and about 0.5-1.0 cm wide. The leaves are broad and coarsely toothed; when wet they are spread 90° from the stem and the plants look like miniature grey-green flowers. *Pogonatum dentatum* differs in its apical cell shape of the lamellae. The plants grow as isolated individuals on disturbed acidic, gravelly or sandy, alpine soil and on humid cliff ledges to sea level. It is common at Mt. Edith Cavell in Jasper National Park, where it occurs with *P. alpinum*. See also under *P. alpinum*.

x 2

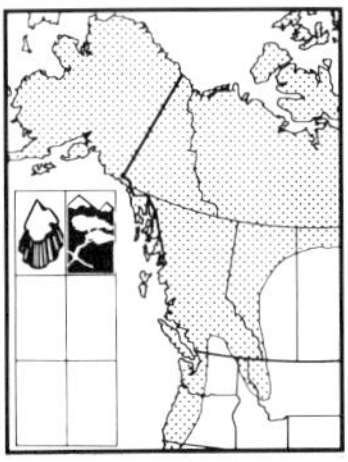

Pogonatum alpinum has its upper leaf surface totally covered by lamellae. This Polytrichaceous moss has conspicuously toothed leaf margins and when the leaves are peeled off the stem, they have a noticeable, clear basal sheath. The plants are generally from 1-10 cm high and do not branch. The capsules are circular in cross-section and erect. Differentiation from other Polytrichaceae in the field can be troublesome, as technical differences in the terminal cell of the lamellae are used to distinguish species. These can be observed only with the compound microscope. Some hints: *P. alpinum* has relatively narrow, toothed leaves that are stiff, it is generally a high elevation species on mineral soils; *P. urnigerum* has broad leaves with coarse teeth and short plants, it occurs in acidic tundra; *Polytrichum commune* is much larger, has curved leaves when moist, and grows on organic soils; and *Polytrichum lyallii*, occurs only along the coast and is not distinguishable in the field.

x 2

Oligotrichum aligerum is a member of the Polytrichaceae and thus has lamellae arising from the upper (ventral) surface of the leaf. This is one of the smaller members of the family, characterized by lanceolate leaves with lamellae confined to the middle portion of the leaf. The lamellae are sinuose and loosely arranged on the upper surface. Additionally, this species has numerous, stubby lamellae on the dorsal surface of the leaf. Unlike *Polytrichum* species that have four-angled capsules, this species has nearly cylindric capsules. The plants are small, rarely over a half centimetre high. The sinuose lamellae differentiate it from nearly all other species, including the common *Pogonatum alpinum*. *Oligotrichum hercynicum* is a second species of the genus that has no lamellae on the back of the leaf and is found at higher elevations. These species are sufficiently delicate that their Polytrichaceous relationship must be carefully ascertained with a hand lens. *Oligotrichum aligerum* is found on exposed soil in mesic, low to mid-elevation situations.

x 1.5

Atrichum selwynii. The lanceolate leaves bordered by elongate cells, serrate margins, and strong, single costa having two to four erect lamellae on its upper surface are features that typify the species of this genus. *Atrichum undulatum* is the largest of the genus and is common west of the cordillera, while *A. selwynii*, with broader, shorter leaves is occasionally found on the eastern slopes. The genus is a member of the Polytrichaceae and has erect-curved, cylindric, smooth capsules that have one ring of 64 blunt peristome teeth (See Fig. 8). This ring of 64 teeth distinguishes this family of mosses from all others. *Atrichum* is among the smaller of these normally large, coarse mosses. It never has lamellae on the leaf laminae, thus these are always one cell thick. *Timmia* somewhat resembles *Atrichum,* but never has lamellae (easily seen with a hand lens). *Atrichum* species occur on acidic soils, mostly in mesic situations. They often occur along moist sandy trail banks, with species of *Dicranella.*

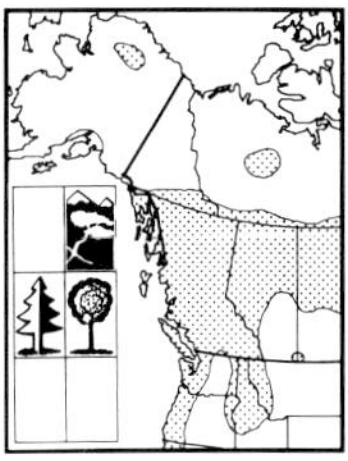

Tetraphis pellucida has perfectly elliptic, acute leaves. When fertile, the narrowly cylindric, smooth, erect capsules with four peristome teeth are definitive. The setae are straight in this species, and abruptly bent below the capsule in *T. geniculata*. The leaves have smooth quadrate cells and a narrow, single costa. Perichaetial leaves are much longer and narrower. Often the stems end in an expanded, cup-like, terminal rosette that contains multi-cellular gemmae. This species occurs in two different habitats: 1) in moist acidic rock crevices where it is constantly sterile and has gemmae cups, and 2) on rotten stumps and logs that are in an advanced state of decay. If you can kick the stump and it collapses, then this species is likely to be there; if it doesn't collapse, you're in pain and you won't find *Tetraphis*!

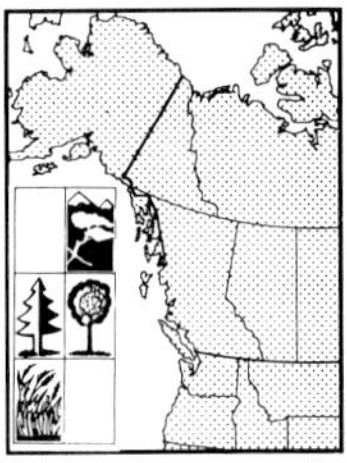

Funaria hygrometrica, with *Bryum argenteum* and *Ceratodon purpureus*, can be classed as a "weed of the world" and is known from locations as diverse as the sidewalks of New York City and the subantarctic. It particularly likes one or two year old campfire sites, where the fire has released large amounts of nutrients. Other sites of nutrient deposition in the vicinity of campsites are also colonized. *Funaria hygrometrica* is the only common species of the genus in western Canada. It has broad (ovate), flaccid leaves with large, rectangular, smooth cells. Although the plants are small, the sporophytes are conspicuous with curved setae 2-5 cm high that when wetted twist and spin. The capsules are horizontal, 16-ribbed, and when old are bright yellow. The sinuose setae are distinctive.

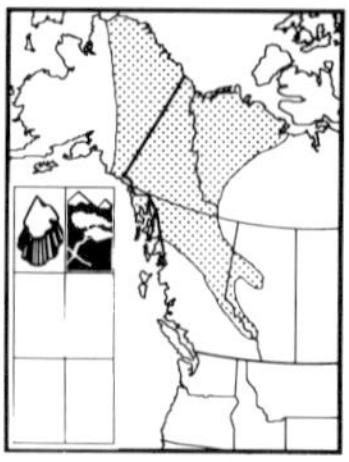

x 2

Tayloria lingulata is a member of the family Splachnaceae (or dung mosses), however this species is not confined to animal dung nor is it as showy as the Splachna. It occurs in alpine and subalpine seepages and fens, preferring acidic substrates. The blunt, tongue-shaped leaves and erect, slender setae, terminated by erect, elliptic, green capsules are distinctive features. The leaves have large, thin-walled cells that look quite different when wet and dry. The *Bryum*- or *Funaria*-like plants, with their erect capsules should identify this rare species.

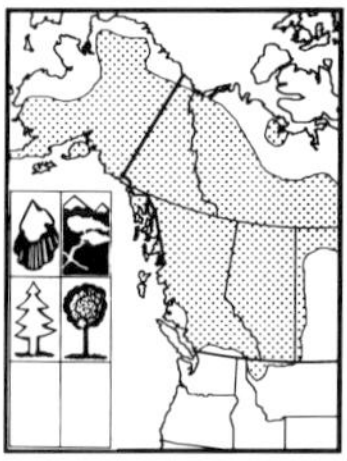

x 1

Tetraplodon angustatus occurs on animal dung, skeletons and carcases of small mammals in drier boreal and montane forests. A second species, *T. mnioides* sometimes occurs with it. *Tetraplodon angustatus* has irregularly dentate leaf margins (easily seen with a hand lens); short setae with capsules that have a hint of yellow or green, but are usually black when they mature in the spring. *Tetraplodon mnioides* has entire leaf margins and totally black capsules with relatively long setae. The capsules mature in late summer and fall. *Tetraplodon* has the lower portion of the capsule only slightly expanded, whereas *Splachnum* has the lower part at least double the width of the upper portion. Both genera have sticky spores that are fly dispersed to nitrogenous substrates. *Tetraplodon* occurs in drier forests than *Splachnum*.

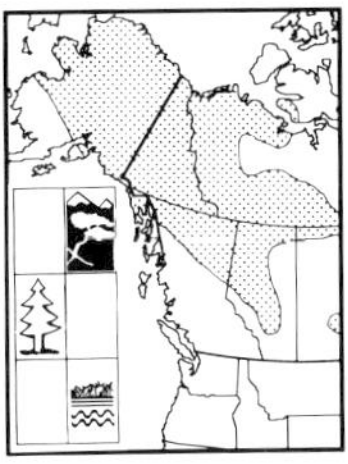

Splachnum luteum and *S. rubrum* are the most spectacular mosses of western North America. The bright yellow or red, expanded, skirt-like capsule bases are often a centimetre across and elevated 5-10 cm above the substrate. The plants grow only on animal dung, mostly on moose dung in fens and bogs across the boreal forest. The yellow *S. luteum* is more common than *S. rubrum* which is red. Both species have spores dispersed by flies and perhaps the expanded capsules are "airports" for the flies to land on, after which they fly to fresh dung to lay their eggs and facilitate dispersal of the *Splachnum*. *Splachnum luteum* often grows with either *S. sphaericum* or *S. ampullaceum*, both having smaller, less showy capsules. Each of those species has distinctive colours (shades of red and pink) and odours.

x 2

Splachnum rubrum is an attractive bryophyte that has brilliant red, inflated capsules on long pink setae. The capsules are 0.5 to over 1 cm across and the setae are from 2-15 cm high. It can only be confused with *S. luteum* which has bright yellow capsules. Both these species are confined to dung (usually that of moose) in muskeg situations. They occur with other, less obvious Splachnaceae such as *S. sphaericum* and *S. ampullaceum*. *Tetraplodon* species are usually found in drier areas and often on rabbit and mouse skeletons and dung. The leaves, although not conspicuous relative to the sporophytes, are broadly ovate, flaccid, yellow-green and shiny when moist, but they dry to a shriveled, difficult to see mass. *Splachnum rubrum* probably occurs scattered throughout mainland western North America, but has not been widely found. It may be more common in the boreal zone and be replaced by *S. luteum* farther north. (See discussion under *S. luteum*.)

x .5

Orthotrichum lyellii is the largest species of the genus. It has slender leaves; cylindric, emergent capsules and large, hairy, bell-shaped calyptrae. The plants are irregularly branched and occur in loose tufts on branches and trunks of deciduous trees in humid rain forests of the west coast. It is the most mesophytic species of the genus. One can find male and female plants growing separately; the males are somewhat smaller than the capsule-bearing females. This is an attractive species that is a dominant component in coastal rain forests, and rare elsewhere. It can reach 20 cm in length, but normal length is about 5 centimetres.

x 3

Orthotrichum striatum is similar to *O. speciosum* and *O. lyellii*. It is distinguished from these by having immersed, oblong-ovate, totally smooth capsules with a peristome of 16 recurved exostome teeth and 16 erose, erect endostome segments. Like *O. speciosum*, it is autoicous and has recurved leaf margins. The plants are slightly smaller than those of either *O. speciosum* or *O. lyellii*, but are difficult to identify without capsules. It is not as common as either of these two species but occurs in similar habitats, in coastal and lowland rain forests. We have not seen *O. striatum* occurring on rock surfaces.

x 2

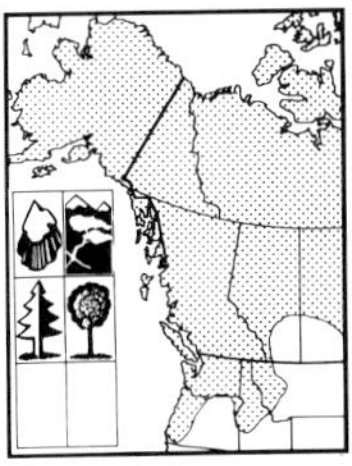

Orthotrichum speciosum has lanceolate, acute leaves, with shortly exserted, cylindric capsules. The peristome is well-developed and the calyptrae have numerous hairs. It is similar to *O. laevigatum* and often these can only be told apart with difficulty by their peristome features. This is a moderate-sized species that occurs on aspen or poplar trunks with *O. obtusifolium*. It also is common on rock outcrops where it can form extensive mats. *Orthotrichum speciosum* also extends to the arctic and alpine tundra, growing on soil in dry situations.

x 3

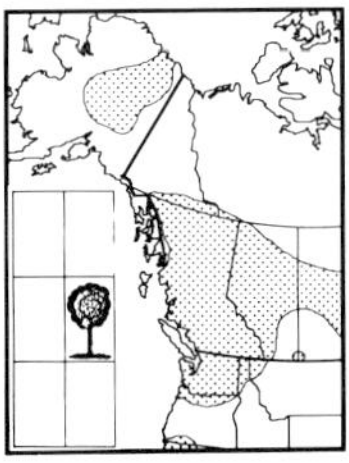

Orthotrichum obtusifolium. The small, unbranched plants have ovate, obtuse leaves, almost always with numerous three to five celled filamentous brood-bodies. The capsules are emergent from the leaves and eight-ribbed. The calyptrae are without hairs. *Orthotrichum speciosum* is much larger, forming loose clumps while *Orthotrichum obtusifolium* has its leaves widely spreading when moist, but they are tightly appressed when dry giving the plants a very different appearance. This is a common species occurring on the trunks of aspen and poplar trees. Along with *O. speciosum*, this is the only species of moss that occurs on aspen trunks between 1 and 2 metres above ground level.

x 1.5

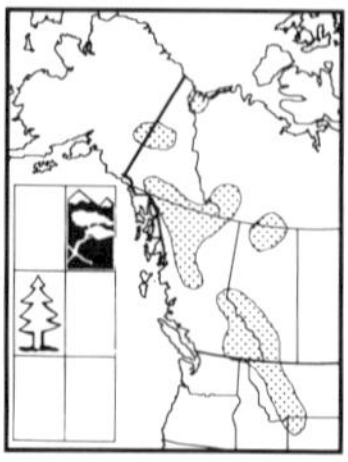

Orthotrichum pellucidum is an extreme xerophyte occurring on dry, exposed, limestone outcrops. It has a distinctive "glaucous" look about it. The short, blunt leaves, dark colour and oblong, emergent, eight-ribbed capsules are characteristic. *Orthotrichum* is a difficult genus, with about 20 species in western North America; most grow on rock. The large, plicate, bell-shaped calyptrae, that usually have abundant hairs, are characteristic of the genus. *Orthotrichum pellucidum* is common on dry calcareous outcrops while other species occur on more mesic rocks or on acidic substrates. *Grimmia* species are smaller, have hair points, and form tight compact cushions.

x 3

Ulota megalospora. This small, infrequent *Ulota* is distinguished from others of its genus by having creeping stems with ascending branches. The plants form small tufts usually on *Acer*, *Betula* and *Alnus* trunks. This species is half the size of other Ulotas and smaller than all coastal Orthotricha except perhaps *O. consimile*. The leaves of this species are flexuose twisted while those of the more common *U. obtusiuscula* are crisped-twisted and the plants do not have creeping stems. Furthermore, as its name suggests, *U. megalospora* has very large spores (about 50 μm vs 20-30 μm in other species). *Ulota megalospora* becomes more common in the north where it is restricted to coastal situations, especially as an epiphyte on deciduous trees. It is also common on the Queen Charlotte Islands on scrubby pine trunks in open peatlands.

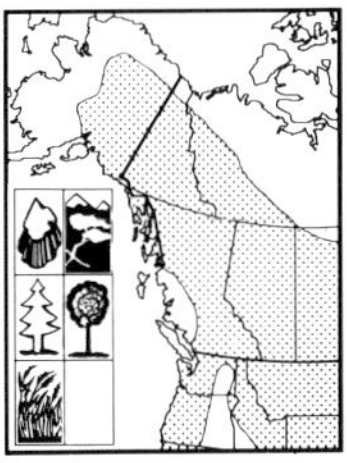

x 3

Bryum caespiticium. The genus *Bryum* is not well understood by bryologists and for many species only specimens with spores and peristomes can be named. About 50 varieties and species are reported from western Canada; of these, *B. caespiticium* is common on dry, calcareous soils, especially in weedy situations. It can be recognized by acuminate leaves with excurrent costae, nondecurrent bases and a multistratose border. The spores are 11-14 μm wide and the peristome has cilia and densely papillose exostome teeth. As in nearly all Brya, the capsules are cylindric, smooth and nodding and are positioned on long, slender setae. Almost all these species have excurrent costae and leaves bordered by elongate cells, which are easily seen with a hand lens. By contrast, species of *Pohlia* have costae ending below the apex and nonbordered leaves.

x 1

x 1

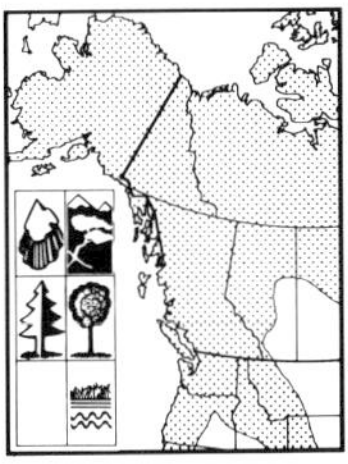

Bryum pseudotriquetrum. This is the most common *Bryum* in western Canada. Its morphology is variable, sometimes it has acuminate, narrow leaves and in other instances it has ovate, blunt leaves. It rarely has capsules and is often found as scattered individuals among other mosses. It is recognized by green colouration, red stems, long decurrent leaf bases and leaves with a distinct, unistratose border. *Bryum pseudotriquetrum* is characteristic of rich fens, where it occurs emergent in pools, but it is also common along streams in drier, boreal and montane forests mostly on soil or humus. It is distinguished from all other Brya by long decurrent leaves and green colour.

x 3

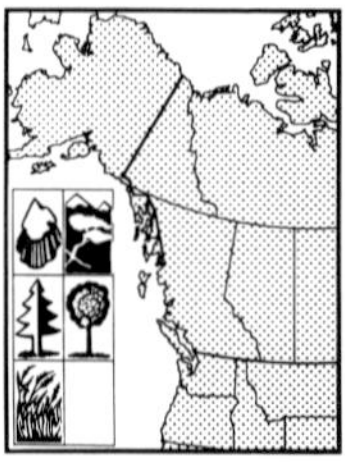

Bryum argenteum. The small, compact, silvery-green plants characterize this easily learned *Bryum*. The silvery colour is due to the lack of chlorophyll in the upper leaf cells. The plants often have a recurved, apiculate leaf apex. Bulbiform brood bodies are often present in the leaf axils. The thin-walled, rectangular (sometimes rhomboidal) leaf cells and a costa extending about two thirds the length of the leaf are helpful characters. This weedy species mostly occurs on sandy soils, however it is also known from cracks of pavement, yards, roofs and building crevices. In its natural habitats it is infrequent and in all situations, capsules are rare. No other moss is silver.

x 2.5

Bryum miniatum. This species forms spectacular glossy, wine-red to golden-brown cushions, often emergent from seeps on exposed rocks. The leaves are oblong to ovate and blunt; they have a strong, single costa that ends in or just below the apex. The leaves are erect, concave and imbricate when wet or dry. It rarely produces capsules. No other moss forms such brilliant red cushions in our area. In western North America, *Bryum miniatum* occurs most frequently along the coast. Although other Brya may be somewhat similar, the combination of blunt, imbricate leaves and reddish colour is usually sufficient to identify this species.

x 2

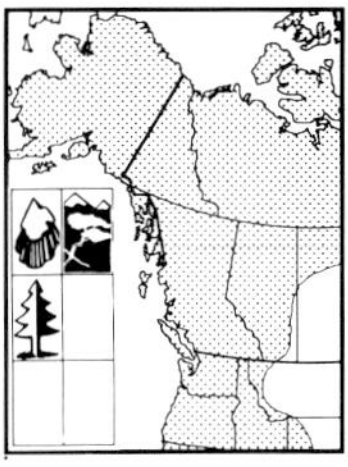

Pohlia cruda can be distinguished by the very shiny, yellow-green leaves which are ovate-lanceolate, serrulate in the upper half and have thin-walled, elongate cells. The bright gold and irridescent, rather broad leaves are distinctive once this "look" is differentiated from the dull, narrow leaves of *P. nutans*, and the whitish-green, broad leaves of *P. wahlenbergii*. The broad leaves (ovate-lanceolate) are excellent field characters. All Brya have bordered, entire leaves. Capsules of these two genera are largely similar - smooth, cylindric and nodding. *Pohlia cruda* is common in our area, frequently occurring in crevices of rock outcrops and cliffs in both acidic and calcareous areas. It is also found on organic soil, on peat banks and in depression areas of rock outcrops. It often grows with *Timmia* species, *Encalypta procera, Tortula ruralis* and *Ditrichum flexicaule*.

x 2

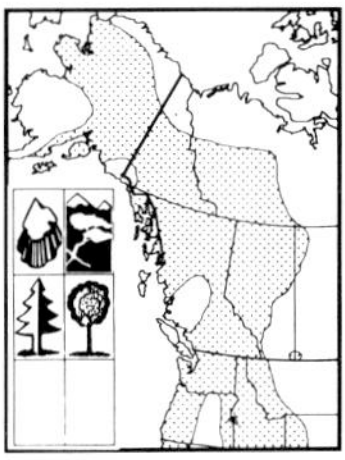

Pohlia wahlenbergii has a distinctive whitish-green cast. The rather broad leaves are similar to those of *P. cruda*, but the whitish cast and red stems serve to differentiate these two species. While *P. cruda* occurs in a variety of habitats, mostly associated with mesic cliffs, *P. wahlenbergii* is characteristic of wet, calcareous seeps and springs. There it grows with *Cratoneuron* species and *Philonotis fontana*. It is distinguished from these by acrocarpous plants, ovate leaves and smooth (nonpapillose) leaf cells. This species occurs in the boreal forest on river banks subject to seasonal flooding; nearer to the coast it can form extensive meadows in late snow melt alpine areas and along subalpine streams.

x 2.5

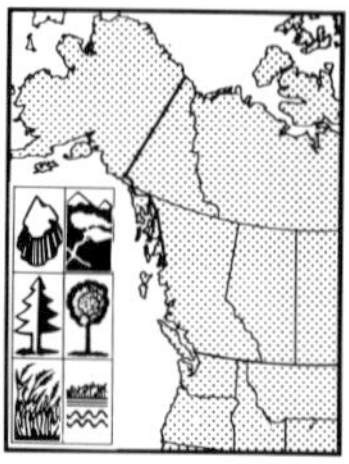

Pohlia nutans is a small moss with little character, but once recognized, it is easily identified. Unlike *P. cruda* it often has capsules. It is characterized superficially by the *Bryum*-like leaves; however, on closer examination the lanceolate leaves have serrulate margins, a costa ending below the apex and long rectangular cells with thick walls. The smaller size, more lanceolate leaves with thick cell walls and a decidedly dull appearance differentiate this species from *Pohlia cruda*. A common name for *Pohlia nutans* is "copper-wire moss", a name derived from the distinctive colour of the setae. This species is a very common component of montane and boreal forests, where it occurs on small patches of exposed soil and on rotting logs. It can be found in small amounts on just about every log in the dry white spruce-pine forests of the Rockies and interior British Columbia areas. It is also common growing as individual plants on *Sphagnum* hummocks where it has been called *P. sphagnicola*.

x 4

Pohlia longibracteata. This coastal species is characterized by having large, showy perigonial bracts surrounding and flaring outward from terminal perigonia. These bracts are often two to three times as long as the vegetative leaves. The capsules are short and ovate, much more so than the cylindric capsules of *P. nutans* and *P. cruda*. As compared with the common *P. nutans*, with which it shares similar leaf shape and colour, this species is larger. It never has propagula and the glossy golden shine of *P. cruda* is lacking. This species is restricted to coastal forests where it is infrequently found on sandy cliffs and banks.

Pohlia filum. Of the 20 or so species of *Pohlia* occurring in our area, about eight have small propagula produced in the axils of the upper leaves. These are normally abundant and easily seen with a hand lens. They may be linear and twisted, rhombic or round, some occur singly, others in groups of 10-20 or more. They are sometimes darkly coloured or others are green. *Pohlia drummondii* has single, large, elliptic or round propagula and is often a shiny, reddish colour; *P. filum* has single, smaller, round, green propagula and is a shiny green colour. The stems are erect, stiff and unbranched in both species. Capsules are rarely produced. Most all of these species occur on exposed mineral soil; most are acidophiles and these should be looked for on gravelly glacial outwash, along sandy streams and on soil of ditches and depressions. They occur in disturbed microhabitats, and rarely are found with *P. cruda*, *P. nutans* or *P. wahlenbergii*.

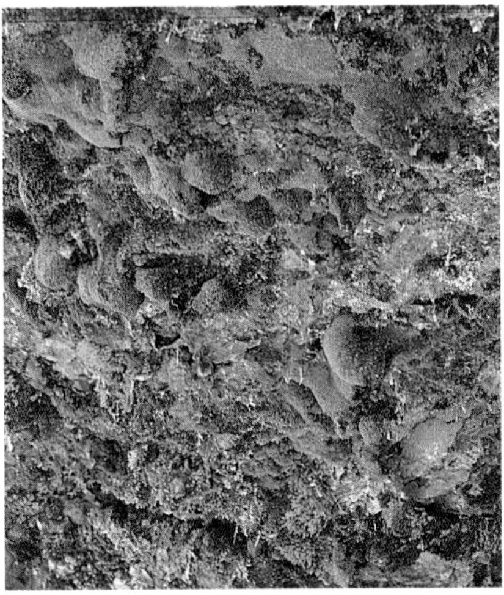

x 2

Mielichhoferia macrocarpa is one of the great rarities of northern hemisphere mosses. It is *Bryum*-like, with typical large, smooth, hexagonal leaf cells, strong costa and plants loosely arranged in mounds on rock surfaces. The peristome is well-developed in *Bryum*, but here in this genus the outer layer is lacking and the inner one consists of 16 filaments. The peristome development is the key to correctly identifying this species; sterile material cannot safely be determined. This moss is so rare that it is known from only five widely separated localities in western North America. It occurs on wet, seeping calcareous rock, often beside or at the back of waterfalls. Any fertile moss appearing Bryaceous that is found on rock surfaces near waterfalls should be looked at closely. Other species of this genus (e.g. *M. mielichhoferi*) are indicators of substrates with abundant copper. These so-called "copper mosses" have been used as indicators by prospectors looking for heavy metals.

x 3

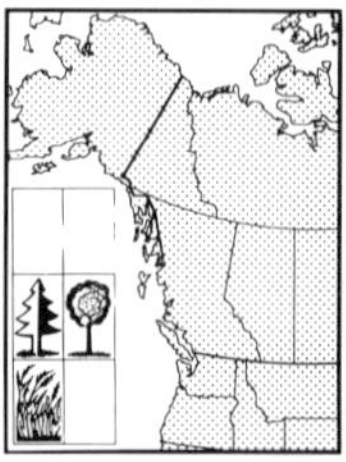

Leptobryum pyriforme is known by the narrow, almost setaceous leaves and pear-shaped nodding capsules. Sporophytically, the species is typically *Bryum*-like but gametophytically it superficially resembles a *Dicranella*. The leaf cells are smooth, thin-walled and usually longer than 6:1. As the name indicates, the glossy capsules are pyriform (or pear shaped) and usually have a pink tone. It is commonly fertile and is characteristic of disturbed soil banks and it is often found on the sides of hiking trails in montane forests.

x 1

x .5

Leucolepis menziesii is an attractive species mostly restricted to humid coastal forests. There, the large, 2-5 cm high, glossy, umbrella-like plants stand out in their unique growth form. The leaves are costate and the capsules ovate-cylindric, smooth and pendent (like those of *Bryum* and *Mnium*). Only *Climacium dendroides* has somewhat similar dendroid plants. However, *Leucolepis* is much more delicate and the branches more umbrella-like rather than tree-like. As well, *Climacium* has erect capsules. This species occurs on logs, boulders and soil in moist situations; occasionally on tree bases extending upward onto the lower portions of the trunks in lush forests; but rare inland.

x 1.5

x 2.5

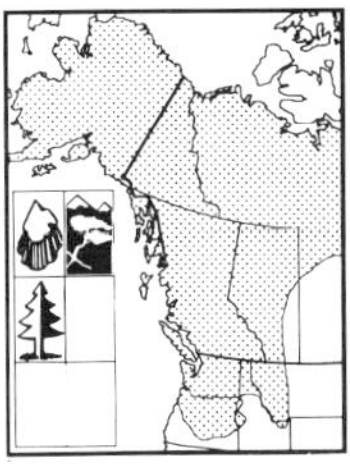

Mnium marginatum. Like *M. arizonicum* (see next species), this species has small, double teeth on the leaf margins. *Mnium arizonicum* has a dark blue-green tone to the leaves, whereas *M. marginatum* is more olive-green. It occurs in crevices of calcareous rocks and is common west of the Rockies. *Mnium thomsonii* and *M. ambiguum* are probably more common in the Rockies and northward, both having double teeth and occurring in similar habitats. These species have no blue tones, but identification of these three species is difficult without a compound microscope to determine leaf cell sizes.

x 2.5

Mnium arizonicum. Most members of the family Mniaceae have rounded-ovate leaves with complete borders. The cells are hexagonal and the leaves "dry up" conspicuously when water is in short supply. Capsules are similar to those of *Bryum*. Recently the Mnia have been divided into three genera, one with entire margins (*Rhizomnium*), one with single teeth (*Plagiomnium*) and one with double teeth set side by side (*Mnium*). In western Canada, *Mnium* has six species. *Mnium spinulosum* has the largest teeth, while *M. arizonicum* and *M. blyttii* have small teeth hardly discernable as double. *Mnium arizonicum* has leaf cells about twice as long as wide as a diagnostic character. The habitat of this species is precise and predictable. It occurs directly beneath spruce and fir trees in heavily shaded subalpine spruce-fir forests. It is sometimes the only moss occurring in this habitat; in the Kananaskis, Alberta area it can be very abundant in just this microhabitat.

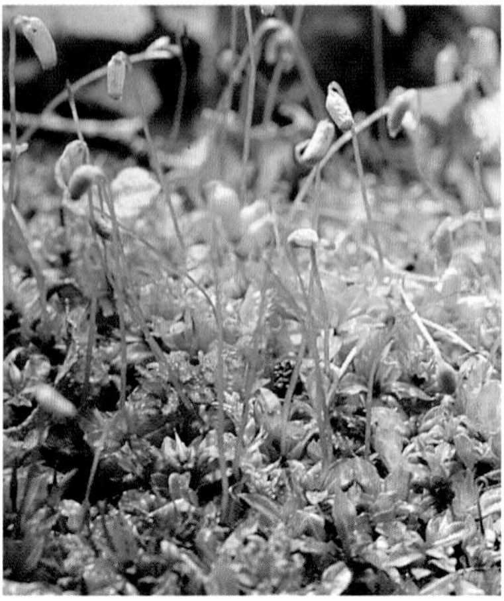

x 1.5

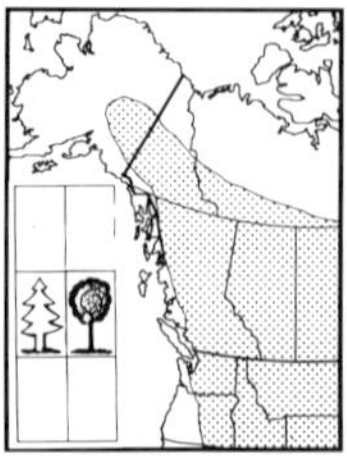

Plagiomnium cuspidatum has leaves with single, marginal teeth. In this species the teeth are restricted to the upper half of the leaf, while in *P. ellipticum* they extend to the leaf base. Both of these are common species throughout the boreal forest; *P. ellipticum* occurs on organic soil in swamps and fens and beside streams on moist banks, while *P. cuspidatum* is found on inorganic soils in upland aspen-spruce forests as well as riverine thickets at lower elevations. In these habitats it occurs at tree bases, on logs, banks, trail sides and exposed soil, often with *Eurhynchium pulchellum*. The prefix "Plagio" is derived from the plagiotropous shoots (as in strawberries), and species of this genus generally have specialized sterile spreading "runners" as well as the erect, fertile shoots as in other Mniaceae.

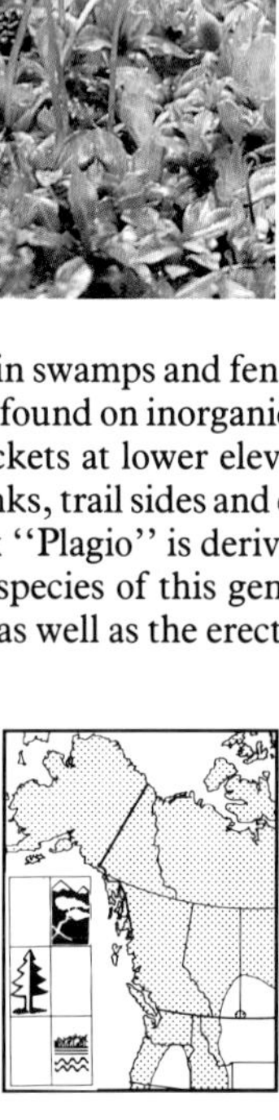

Plagiomnium medium. The marginal teeth of the leaves in this species occur from apex to just above the insertion. The medium-sized plants are similar to those of *P. ellipticum*, but are slightly larger and a darker colour. These two species are best discriminated by sexual condition and decurrency of the leaves of the fertile stems. *Plagiomnium medium* is synoicous, thus often fertile and has long decurrent leaves, while *P. ellipticum* is dioicous, mostly sterile and has short (or no) decurrencies. Both of these species are common in the boreal forest but are largely replaced on the west coast by *P. venustum* and *P. insigne*. The former is synoicous, but without leaf decurrencies, while the latter is dioicous and has long decurrencies. Both are much larger than *P. medium*.

Plagiomnium venustum is a large, showy "*Mnium*" restricted to humid coastal forests of the west coast. It has large, single teeth extending to the leaf base and lacks the arching plagiotropous shoots. It is among the largest of the single toothed Mnia. Also in the coastal forests are two additional, large species: *Rhizomnium glabrescens* which has thickened, conspicuous entire margins and *Plagiomnium insigne* which is more similar to *P. venustum*. The former is larger (3-8 cm high), has strongly decurrent leaves and is dioicous, while *P. venustum* is smaller (3-4 cm high), has nondecurrent leaves and is synoicous (male and female together in the same perichaetium). All of these grow on rotting logs, moist soil and on tree bases in coastal rain forests.

Plagiomnium insigne. The largest *Mnium* of the west coast, this species is characterized by strongly decurrent leaves, dioicous sexual condition and leaves with single teeth to near the insertion. Only *P. venustum* can be confused with this species: it is smaller, has nondecurrent leaves and lacks the plagiotropous shoots common in *P. insigne*. As all Mnia, when wet this species has beautiful, glistening, spreading leaves, often made even prettier by water droplets lying on the large leaves; when dry, the leaves become shriveled and erect and the plants appear dead and ugly. However, when moistened by rain or dew in the early morning, the plants seemingly instantaneously become alive again. This physiological ability of mosses to very quickly take up water and begin photosynthesis in a matter of minutes has enabled many species to live in very dry habitats. *Plagiomnium insigne* is restricted in its distribution to lowland rain forests along the west coast and extends inland in relict cedar forests to southeastern British Columbia.

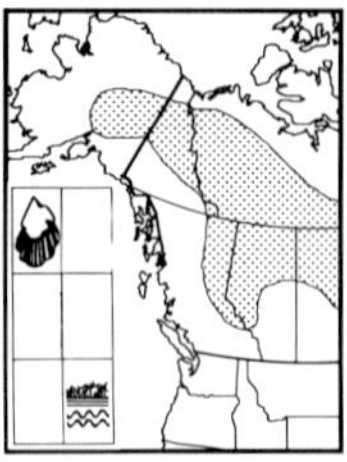

x 3.5

Rhizomnium gracile. Whereas *R. glabrescens* and *R. nudum* have smooth (without fuzz) stems, this rather rare species and the more common *R. pseudopunctatum* have the stems covered by a dense mat of rhizoids. These arise from stem cells and are called micronemata. The leaf margins are entire and the apical apiculus is small. *Cinclidium stygium* has a much stronger apiculus and recurved margins. *Rhizomnium gracile* is dioicous with leaves about 3-4 mm long, while *R. pseudopunctatum* is synoicous with leaves up to 6 or 7 mm long. Both species occur in fens, swampy areas and moist depressions in boreal and montane forests. Usually they grow on organic soil, including alpine and subalpine fen meadows and calcareous seeps. They are rarely on rock outcrops, where species of *Mnium* are more common. Several additional species of *Rhizomnium* occur in western Canada, but these two species are by far the most common, except near the coast where *R. glabrescens* is more dominant.

x 1.5

x 2

Rhizomnium glabrescens is a west coast species with oval leaves (about twice as long as wide) that have a strong border. The leaf margins are entire and the plants have widely spreading upper leaves that often look like small green flowers. It commonly produces sporophytes with nodding, cylindric capsules. Male plants are separate and are recognized by enlarged leafy heads with dark centres (the antheridia). If single teeth are present on the leaves, see *Plagiomnium*; if they are double see *Mnium*. *Rhizomnium nudum* has leaves as wide as long, and *R. pseudopunctatum* is rare on the coast and has male and female on the same plant. This species is common on rotten logs and on other moist substrates in coastal, lowland rain forests. Also close is *R. magnifolium*, it differs in having lower stems covered in rhizoids and a less conspicuous leaf border.

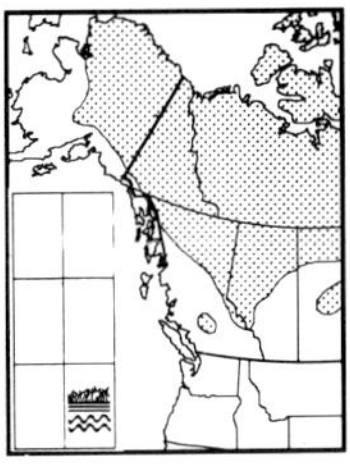

x 2.5

Cinclidium stygium. A genus of four northern species, *Cinclidium* resembles species of *Rhizomnium*, but differs in having a stronger leaf border, leaf cells longer than wide and, in *C. stygium*, a strongly apiculate leaf apex. The plants of this species are a blackish red-silver colour and the leaf margins are recurved backwards. There is some tomentum of rhizoids on the stems. The capsules are nodding, cylindric and smooth, and on long setae. The peristome is a beautiful structure; the inner layer is fused above to form a dome; below, the reduced teeth of the outer layer lie alternate to the spaces of the inner one. This species occurs in rich fens, it is rare but should be sought when such species as *Calliergon trifarium* and *Catoscopium nigritum* are found. *Calliergon stygium* can also be found in calcareous alpine seeps where it grows with *Paludella squarrosa*.

x 1

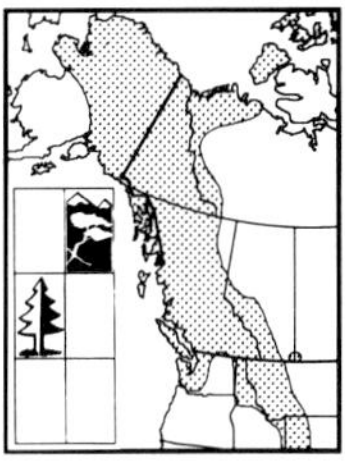

Timmia austriaca. The genus *Timmia* is common in montane forests and is distinguished by large, erect plants with sheathing leaves, which have small, quadrate, papillose-bulging upper leaf cells. *Timmia austriaca* is the commonest species, having orange-brown, smooth leaf sheaths. The leaves are glossy when dry and usually imbricate, with the laminae curling inward. The species is dioicous and capsules are not common. In contrast, *T. megapolitana* is distinguished by hyaline leaf sheaths and an autoicous sexual condition (and hence capsules are more common). *Timmia* species (four in our area) can be mistaken for species of *Polytrichum*, however the latter always have lamellae covering the leaf surface and thus appear opaque, whereas Timmias have leaves one cell thick and are translucent. They occur on calcareous rock shelves, among forest litter or along streams, most commonly in coniferous forests. The genus is not common in the boreal forest and along the coast.

x 1.5

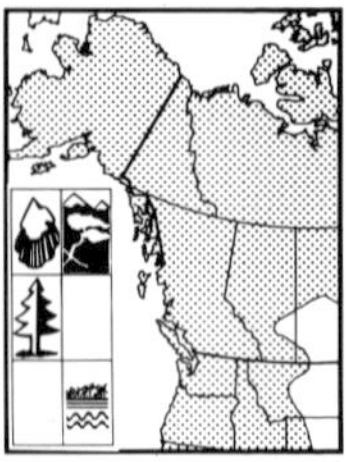

Aulacomnium palustre is distinguished by the yellow-green colour of the leaves, which contrasts sharply with the reddish-brown tomentum of the stems. The leaves are sharply pointed, loosely arranged and twisted when dry, as opposed to the stiffly imbricate leaves of the more northern *A. acuminatum*. In general, *A. palustre* is smaller than *A. acuminatum* and commonly produces triangular, leaf-like brood bodies on terminal stalks. The leaf cells are all isodiametric, thick-walled and unipapillate and a strong, single costa is present. *Aulacomnium palustre* is common in western Canada, occurring on disturbed peat and on organic soil, from calcareous alpine meadows to fens across continental Canada. It is often found with *Tomenthypnum nitens* in boreal mixed mires. Three additional species of the genus are known in the west; two are northern (see below) and the third, *A. androgynum*, is mostly coastal and occurs on rotten or burnt stumps.

x 1.5

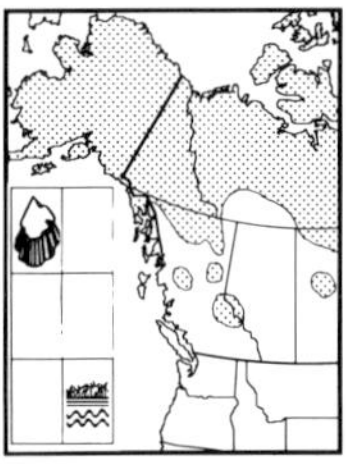

Aulacomnium turgidum. The bright yellow-green colour combined with concave, oblong-ovate leaves with rounded apices, differentiates this species. The leaves are strongly imbricate as in *A. acuminatum* but rounded and concave at the apex. In the arctic, it often grows intermixed with *A. acuminatum* on the larger, drier hummocks in sedge meadows. Farther south, it occurs in open alpine meadows, on organic soil or on rich humus in drier situations. This species prefers a calcareous habitat and is found with *Rhytidium rugosum*, *Thuidium abietinum* and *Hylocomium splendens*.

x 1.4

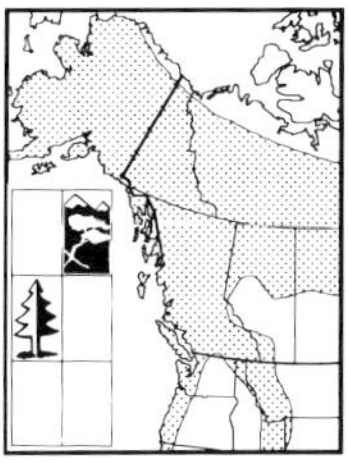

Bartramia pomiformis. Like *Bartramia ithyphylla*, this moss has perfectly globose, 16-ribbed capsules. However, *B. pomiformis* has twisted-flexuose leaves that are gradually narrowed from base to apex. The leaf cells are papillose by means of projecting cell ends. *Plagiopus oederiana* is similar in capsular features, but has spirally-ranked leaves that have numerous minute cuticular bumps, rather than distinct papillae. It is a dark olive-green colour, whereas *B. pomiformis* is usually glaucous light-green or bluish-green. Sometimes this species is called "apple moss" because the young capsules resemble shiny green apples. It occurs on mesic rock outcrops in montane forests and also to near sea level. It is not infrequent in acid rock crevices in coastal forests; but is rare in the Rockies, where it is replaced on the predominantly calcareous substrates by *Plagiopus oederiana*.

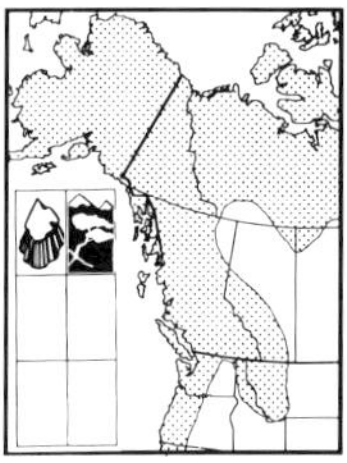

x 1.5

Bartramia ithyphylla. When fertile, this small, arctic-alpine species is recognized by globose, finely ribbed capsules on short setae, about 1 cm high. The papillose leaf cells and stiffly erect, subulate leaves, which have a broadly oblong, sheathing hyaline base (shiny under a hand lens) can also be used to distinguish this species. The leaf cells are rectangular and papillose at their upper ends by means of projecting walls. The upper margins are serrate and bistratose. *Bartramia ithyphylla* is found in moist depressions and exposed organic soil in acidic tundra. The other three species of *Bartramia* are low elevation species, while other genera of the family (e.g. *Philonotis*, *Plagiopus* and *Anacolia*) are much larger plants and rarely have sheathing, subulate leaves. Only *Conostomum tetragonum* occurs in similar habitats, and it has very distinctive, five-ranked leaves.

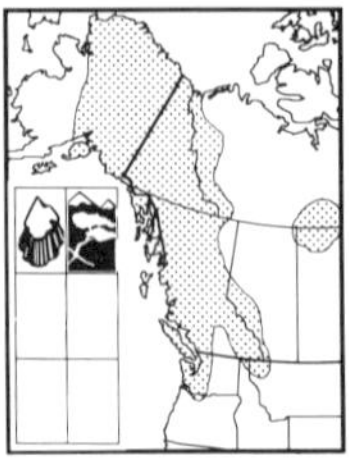

x 2.5

Conostomum tetragonum is easily distinguished in the field by the five, very regular vertical ranks of leaves that are highly papillose, whitish and have an excurrent, yellowish costa forming a short awn. The capsules are round, 16-plicate and characteristic of the Bartramiaceae. Quite specific in its habitat preferences, this species forms small, compact, hard tufts in moist depressions and on soil-covered ledges of acidic cliffs and outcrops. Although it is not common, it occurs at higher elevations with *Bartramia ithyphylla*.

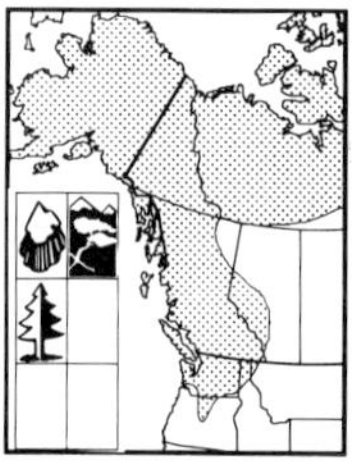

x 2.5

Plagiopus oederiana has rather stiff leaves in three spiralled ranks. The leaves are widely spreading when moist, but are flexuose-appressed when dry. Belonging to the Bartramiaceae, it has the characteristic round, 16-ribbed capsules of the family. Microscopically, *Plagiopus* has minute, cuticular bumps, perhaps as many as 20 or so per cell. These are not confined to the lumen as are papillae, but occur continuously on the outer cell surface as is the case in many hepatics. Perhaps most easily told by its habitat, *Plagiopus* grows on moist calcareous cliffs, often with *Ditrichum flexicaule* and *Metaneckera menziesii*. *Philonotis* occurs in calcareous seepages, while *Bartramia* is found on acidic rocks or in exposed tundra.

Philonotis fontana has erect growing glaucous-green plants with a distinct costa and recurved leaf margins. The papillose leaf cells and red coloured stems characterize this species. Only *Pohlia wahlenbergii* is a similar dull whitish-green colour. When capsules are present they are erect, round, 16-ribbed and have a small mouth; when old they sometimes become horizontal and somewhat asymmetric. The papillae in *Philonotis* occur as projections of the cell ends; in *P. fontana* these projections are at the basal end of each cell. Although variable, this species is by far the most common of the five or so in the genus in our area. The plants often form carpets through which water flows from calcareous seepages or springs, yet the plants themselves shed water and remain "dry". The habitat of calcareous seeps is characteristic.

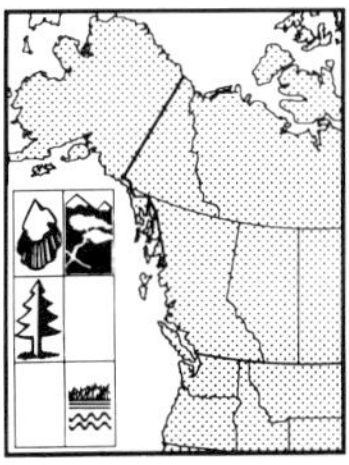

x 1

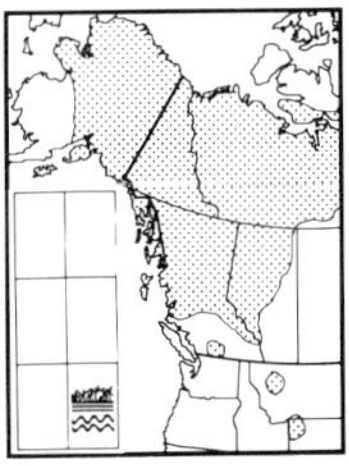

Paludella squarrosa is a truly beautiful species. The largely unbranched plants grow erect and can form extensive lawns in minerotrophic fens. The leaves have a costa and broadly reflexed margins. They arise from a decurrent base, are stiffly spreading upward and become stiffly squarrose-recurved in their upper half. Hence each closely set leaf stands out from the stem and forms a precise pattern. The colour of the plants is best described as dull yellow-green, with a hint of chartreuse. This is a characteristic plant of rich fens. It is most common in the more continental areas of British Columbia and Alberta, but is also found in calcareous alpine springs, meadows and along small tundra streams.

x 2

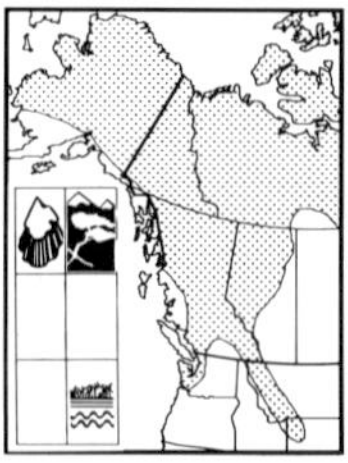

Meesia uliginosa. The erect, ligulate, blunt leaves that contain a costa one third to one half the width of the leaf at the base are characteristic of *M. uliginosa*. The leaf margins are recurved and entire, and the leaves are not decurrent. It is often fertile, with curved, long-necked capsules positioned on long 2-6 cm setae. This species is rare enough to be of particular interest when found. It occurs on calcareous substrates, on peaty soil banks, exposed organic soil and in wet depressions at higher elevations; occasionally it grows in depressions associated with forests surrounding rich fens at lower elevations.

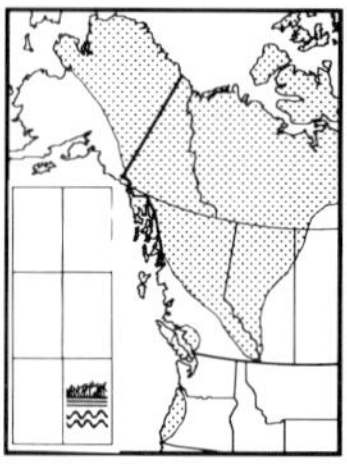

x 3

Meesia triquetra is easily distinguished by the spreading leaves in three obvious ranks. The leaves are decurrent, ovate-lanceolate with sharply serrate margins and sharply pointed apices, and contain a relatively narrow costa. Other species of *Meesia* have blunt leaf apices. When fertile, the capsules have a long neck and are abruptly bent horizontally as they expand to the urn (about half way up). The setae are very long (3-10 cm). This is a rare component of extreme rich fens but relatively abundant when present; it is found in pools and flarks, often with *Scorpidium*, *Drepanocladus revolvens*, *Catoscopium* and *Calliergon trifarium*.

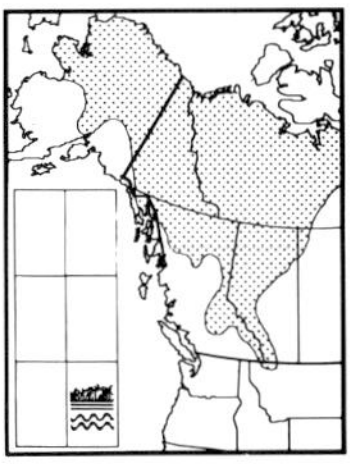

Catoscopium nigritum forms dense, blackish cushions in extreme rich fens, mostly along the edges of pools and flarks. It is easily identified when fertile by the black "golf-club-shaped" capsules. Gametophytically, the small plants have spreading-curved leaves with narrowly recurved leaf margins in the lower portion and leaf cells that are smooth and quadrate above. The leaves are lanceolate-acuminate with a strong costa. Often the plants are reduced in stature, with the younger leaves stiffly spreading and not curved. The youngest branches are tristichous, a characteristic that can be most useful in naming the species. Like *Calliergon trifarium*, this species is exclusive to rich fens, where the black "golf-clubs" are always a delight to find.

x 2.5

Heterocladium dimorphum is a high elevation species only extending inland in south-eastern British Columbia and the Kananaskis-Banff area of Alberta. The small, irregularly branched plants look superficially like those of *Haplocladium microphyllum*. However, the latter species has a strong costa, while *Heterocladium* has only a very short one. *Claopodium* species are somewhat larger and have crisped leaves. *Heterocladium macounii* is a coastal species of humus, soil and more rarely tree trunks in shaded, humid forests, while *H. dimorphum* is found inland. In general, small pleurocarpous plants, ovate leaves with rhombic, papillose cells, paraphyllia on the stems and a short costa distinguish these two species.

x 1.5

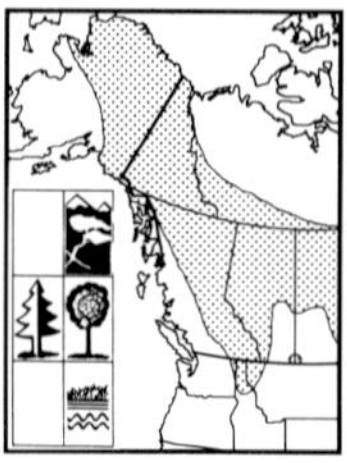

Thuidium recognitum is a delicate looking moss. It is twice pinnately branched, with stem leaves larger than branch leaves. The plants are dull, owing to the pluripapillose leaf cells. Richly branched paraphyllia are common along the stems and all leaves have a strong single costa. Leaf cells are rhombic in shape. *Thuidium abietinum* is once pinnately branched, as is *Helodium blandowii*. *Haplocladium*, *Heterocladium* and *Claopodium* are smaller, more nondescript genera. *Thuidium recognitum* occurs in rich, shaded, boreal forests; in wooded muskegs; and in ecotonal willow and birch zones. It is rare in open fens and at higher elevations and absent near the coast.

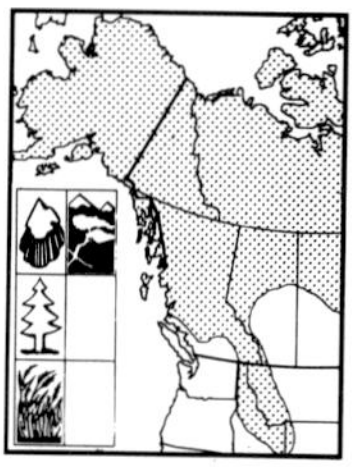

Thuidium abietinum can be distinguished by the regularly pinnately branched stems, numerous paraphyllia, stoutly papillose leaf cells which are more or less rhombic in shape and a well-developed single costa. The plants are large, dull and wiry in appearance and easily identified in the field. When wet they are very different in appearance owing to the widely spreading leaves that are tightly appressed when dry. Other closely related species of the Thuidiaceae are either twice pinnately branched or grow in moist habitats. This species is a xerophyte occurring in calcareous, exposed conditions with *Tortula ruralis* and *Hypnum revolutum*. It is abundant in the drier areas of Alberta and the interior of British Columbia, extending down the Fraser River to Hope.

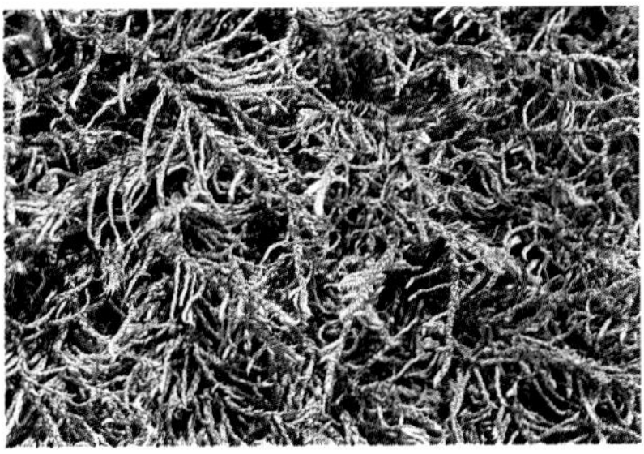

Haplocladium microphyllum is one of the few eastern species that reaches westward along the southern edge of the boreal forest. Although it is seldom collected, it is not uncommon in its special habitat of moist rotting logs in aspen forests. We have not seen it in montane forests. This species is a small straggling *Thuidium*. It is loosely and singly pinnately branched; it has the apical cells of the branch leaves with one papilla, which differentiates it from species of *Thuidium* which have several. The abundant leaf-litter in aspen forests means few bryophytes are found on the ground, but when objects, such as logs, provide a raised substrate above the forest floor they are covered by *Pohlia nutans*, *Brachythecium acuminatum* and *Eurhynchium pulchellum*. On the more moist sites, *Haplocladium microphyllum* also occurs.

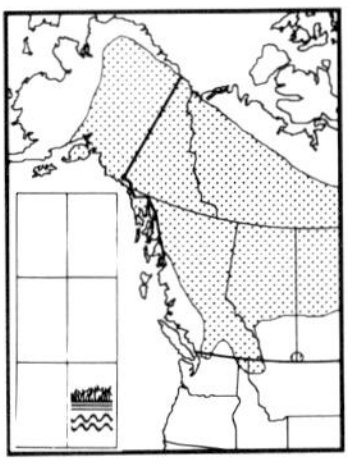

Helodium blandowii is a large, infrequent moss very similar in appearance to *Thuidium abietinum*. It is regularly pinnately branched, with erect leaves and fronds. The stems are covered with unbranched filamentous paraphyllia. The branch leaves are smaller and narrower than the stem leaves. It occurs exclusively in minerotrophic peatlands, often with *Hypnum lindbergii* and *Drepanocladus vernicosus*. These fens are not as ionically rich as those with *Scorpidium* and *Drepanocladus revolvens*. *Helodium* never occurs on dry, calcareous rock outcrops as does *Thuidium abietinum*, thus these two superficially similar species are easily distinguished by habitat alone. The *Thuidium* has densely branched, stubby paraphyllia that are very different than those of *Helodium*. Other *Thuidium* species are twice pinnately branched and are prostrate in habit; *Helodium* always has ascending stems, much like those of *Tomenthypnum nitens*.

x 1.5

Claopodium crispifolium. Related to *Thuidium* and *Heterocladium*, this genus contains three species in western Canada. It is differentiated by a strong, pellucid (clear) costa, rather regularly pinnately branched stems and few paraphyllia. The leaf cells are papillose. *Claopodium bolanderi* and *C. crispifolium* both have short, delicate, yellowish, hair pointed leaves; *Heterocladium, Thuidium* and *C. whippleanum* lack these. This is a west coast species growing on mesic calcareous cliffs and tree trunks at lower elevations. It is a common epiphyte near the coast, but also found in rock crevices in southeastern British Columbia. *Claopodium bolanderi* is somewhat smaller and reaches the eastern slopes of the Rockies.

Claopodium bolanderi resembles a small, irregularly branched *Thuidium* species. Species of both genera have papillose leaf cells and a decidedly dull overall appearance. *Claopodium* has a costa that appears shiny even in the field with a hand lens, while the costa in *Thuidium* is dull and not evident. *Claopodium bolanderi* occurs in thin mats on rock surfaces and soil over rock ledges, more rarely on tree trunks. It differs from *C. crispifolium*, which occurs mostly on tree trunks, by being smaller, less regularly branched and under a compound microscope it has two or more papillae per leaf cell, while *C. crispifolium* has only one per cell. In both species, the costa extends beyond the leaf as a clear, pellucid point. The three species of *Claopodium* are all coastal, whereas species of *Thuidium, Helodium* and *Haplocladium* are abundant members of dry coniferous, transitional aspen parkland and peatland communities. *Claopodium bolanderi* is found at higher elevations, while *C. crispifolium* is more common at lower elevations.

Calliergonella cuspidata. This species is common in the Vancouver area as a yard weed. It occurs on moist roadside banks, in ditches and in wetland areas as well. It is easily determined when found in man-made habitats by the terminal 0.5-1.3 cm of each stem which is flattened and spear-shaped; farther down the stem, branches occur at irregular intervals. It is rare in natural situations, but has recently been found in wet, open fens in the boreal forest of Alberta. It is distinguished from such commonly found fen species of *Drepanocladus*, by the lack of a costa and from *Scorpidium* (which is of similar size and often sometimes strongly resembles *Calliergonella*) by its imbricate, nonfalcate-secund leaves and the flattened stem tips. If still in doubt, *Calliergonella* has a conspicuous stem hyalodermis and inflated alar cells resembling those of *Calliergon giganteum* (with a strong costa). *Pleurozium schreberi* has red stems and occurs in drier habitats.

× 1

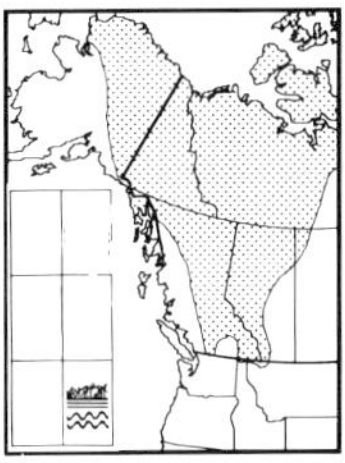

Scorpidium scorpioides. The very large plants, 4-6 mm wide, that are dark reddish-green to nearly black and have falcate-secund, somewhat wrinkled leaves, are characteristic of this species. The leaves do not have a costa and have a few, enlarged, hyaline cells at the insertion. Relative to species of *Drepanocladus* and *Hypnum*, both of which have falcate-secund leaves, *Scorpidium* is more turgid, larger and has broader and shorter leaves. *Scorpidium scorpioides*, one of two species in the genus, is characteristic of calcareous fens throughout the boreal region of western Canada. It occurs submerged in or emergent from pools of water with a high pH and high calcium bicarbonate content. The older portions of the stems are usually coated with marl. In the montane zone it is sometimes replaced by *Cratoneuron commutatum*, which is differentiated by a strong, single costa.

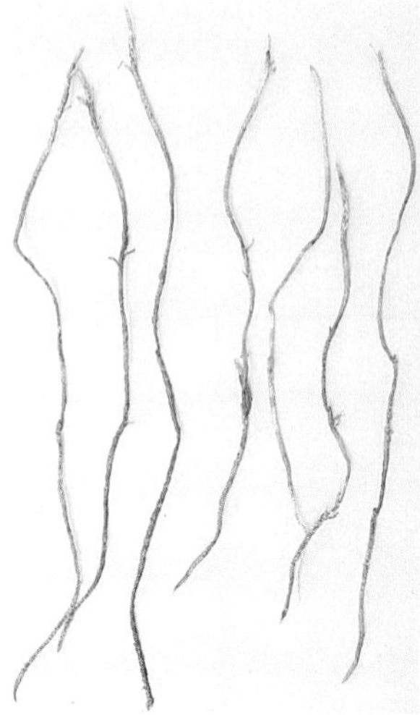

x .5

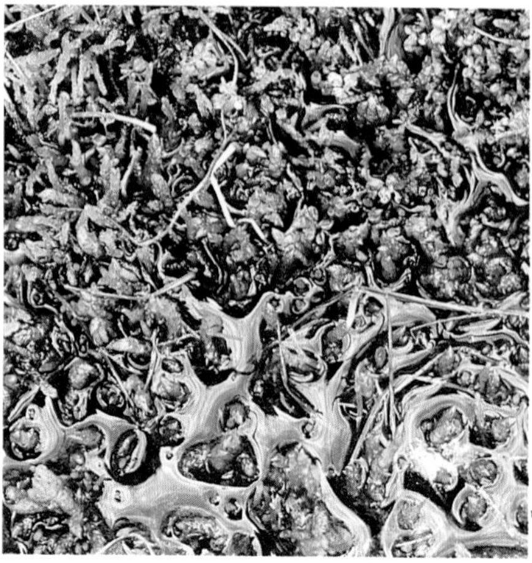

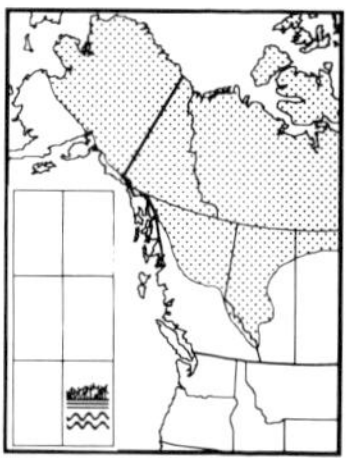

Calliergon trifarium is distinguished by imbricate, ovate leaves that have a costa extending from half to three quarters of its length. The alar cells are enlarged, hyaline or orange and form relatively large, decurrent, but not sharply delimited groups. The stems are slender, unbranched and grow intermixed with other wetland species such as *Drepanocladus revolvens* and *Scorpidium* species. If *Scorpidium scorpioides* is present in large amounts, this species should be looked for as isolated strands. These have a distinctive spiral arrangement of leaves, may be 7-10 cm long and are much smaller than the dominant *Scorpidium*. *Calliergon trifarium* occurs in extreme rich fen pools.

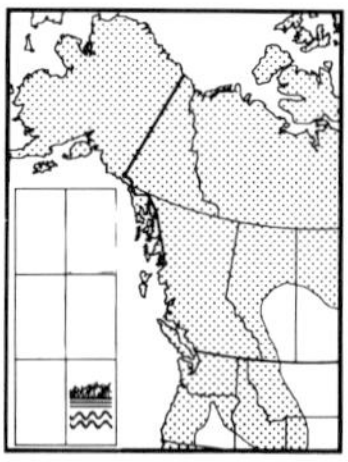

Calliergon giganteum is the largest *Calliergon* and is characterized by ovate, obtuse leaves with a strong, percurrent costa and conspicuous, abruptly differentiated, hyaline, inflated groups of alar cells that form large, decurrent, concave auricles at the leaf angles. The leaves of the lateral branches are usually much narrower and different in shape than the stem leaves (the latter are used for identification purposes). In more southern areas, the plants are always abundantly pinnately branched, but arctic specimens are often unbranched. This species occurs in minerotrophic fen pools. It has a soft texture and is often found floating or just emergent from the water.

Calliergon stramineum is characterized by oblong, blunt leaves that have a costa ending about two thirds the way up the leaf. *Calliergon sarmentosum* is superficially similar, but has upper leaves ending in a small apiculus and a reddish-purple colour. *Calliergon stramineum* is unbranched and usually light or glossy yellow-green. Other species of *Calliergon* have ovate or ovate-oblong leaves. This species is widespread but infrequent in swamps, fens and on peaty ground from sea level to the alpine zone. The species sometimes forms pure, yellow-green, loose mats (the plants are nearly string-like in texture), or other times it occurs as single strands among *Sphagnum* plants. It is rarely found submerged among *Scorpidium* plants in extreme rich fens as is *C. trifarium*.

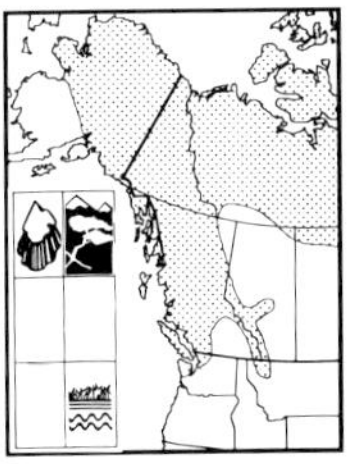

x 2.5

Calliergon sarmentosum can best be distinguished by its purple-red colouration and oblong-ovate leaves, which are narrowed to a cucullate and apiculate tip. The stems are irregularly branched and the costa extends three quarters to five sixths the way up the leaf. The alar cells are inflated and hyaline, often becoming golden-orange and porose toward the costa and form large, decurrent groups. This species is most common on seepy, acidic cliff shelves in alpine and subalpine areas, and is probably more common toward the coast in more humid situations, especially near pools in wetlands of alpine and subalpine sites.

x 1

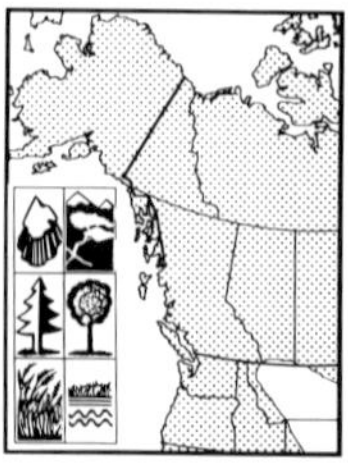

Drepanocladus aduncus. This largely wetland genus of about ten species is characterized by falcate-secund, costate leaves. *Drepanocladus aduncus*, as is typical of *Drepanocladus*, is a variable moss. It has flaccid, slender, widely-spaced leaves. In this species, the leaf margins are entire, even one tooth means it is toothed; the costa is weak; the colour is green and the alar cells are inflated and hyaline. Both *D. revolvens* and *D. vernicosus* have more compact plants, while *D. fluitans* and *D. exannulatus* have toothed leaf margins. *Drepanocladus aduncus* prefers eutrophic water and hence is common in roadside ditches, disturbed pools and marshes.

x 1.5

x 2
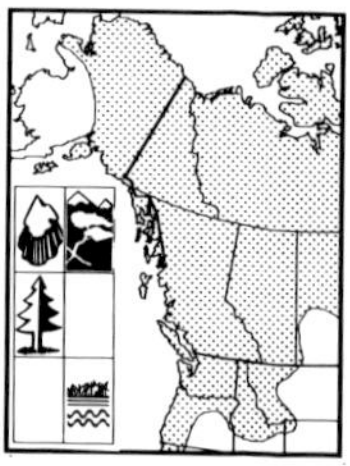

Drepanocladus uncinatus is distinguished by its costate, falcate-secund leaves, which are deeply plicate. The leaves are drawn out to a fine point and the upper margins are irregularly serrulate. The basal cells are more or less thick-walled and short-rectangular. At the insertion there are several enlarged hyaline alar cells that often remain attached to the stem. This species, with *D. revolvens*, has the outer layer of cortical cells enlarged. *Ptilium crista-castrensis* can superficially look like this species, however it has no costa, which can be hard to tell with all the plications. It is profusely and regularly branched, forming a triangle, while *D. uncinatus* is at most irregularly pinnately branched. *Drepanocladus uncinatus* is found in much drier situations than other species of the genus. It often forms large pure mats at the moist bases of large boulders, where it is associated with *Hylocomium splendens* and *Timmia* species. It also occurs on calcareous rock surfaces where it can look like *Hypnum revolutum*, which has no costa.

Cratoneuron commutatum. The rigid, coarse and rough texture of the plants are characteristic. This species has falcate-secund leaves, a strong excurrent costa and inflated alar cells. It tends to grow erect or have ascending stems and often is regularly pinnately branched. Paraphyllia are numerous on the stems and can be seen with a hand lens. This species forms dark, golden-brown mats around calcareous seeps and springs, and along montane streams and alpine seepages. It often grows with *C. filicinum* and *Philonotis fontana*; neither of these has falcate-secund leaves, nor abundant paraphyllia.

x 1

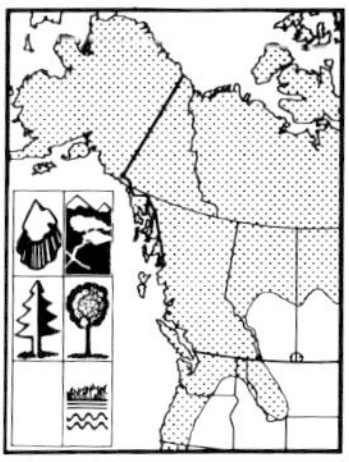

Cratoneuron filicinum is distinguished by ovate-lanceolate leaves with an abruptly acuminate, blunt apex. The strong costa ends in the apex, and the alar cells are enlarged and hyaline (sometimes yellowish) and often form a bulging group. The leaves are stiff and loosely erect or sometimes slightly falcate-secund. Species of *Hygrohypnum* have a shorter, more slender costa, while *C. commutatum* has strongly falcate-secund leaves. *Cratoneuron filicinum* is common on periodically inundated calcareous rocks. It can be common around calcareous seeps and in montane springs, especially along the Rocky Mountains of Alberta-British Columbia.

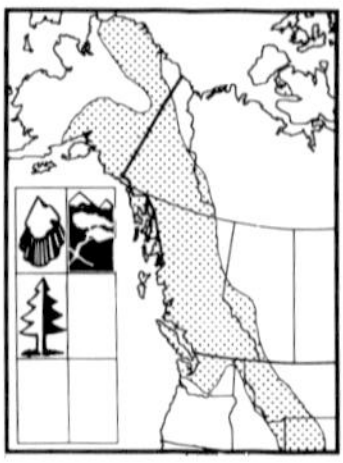

x .5

Hygrohypnum luridum is distinguished by concave, ovate-oblong leaves narrowed to a short, but acute point. The costa ends about midleaf and the upper margins are usually slightly inrolled making the leaf look more slender than it actually is. The alar cells in most *Hygrohypnum* species are not inflated and hyaline, which distinguishes them easily from *Calliergon* species, while the leaves are much shorter and blunter than in species of *Drepanocladus*. The cells are linear-oblong with rounded ends, rather than linear with pointed ends. The leaves are often slightly falcate-secund. Look for this species below Athabasca Falls in Jasper National Park, where it forms carpets in the splash zone below the falls. About 12 additional species are found in our area.

x 3.5

Hygrohypnum bestii is an extremely coarse, rigid, aquatic moss. The leaves have a strong costa and are somewhat falcate-secund. This species is twice the size of other calciphiles with which it can occur. These other smaller species, including *Cratoneuron commutatum*, *Brachythecium* species, *Drepanocladus revolvens* and other Hygrohypna are softer and rarely truly aquatic as is *H. bestii*. The plants of this species are mostly 10-30 cm or more long and have the leaves either missing or represented only by the costa in the lower portions of the stems, torn off by the strong current of the montane streams in which it grows. *Fontinalis* is occasional in our area and either has strongly keeled leaves or occurs in stagnant pools and slowly flowing streams. *Scorpidium scorpioides*, when growing submerged, can be as large but it is found in lakes and fen pools and is very soft in texture.

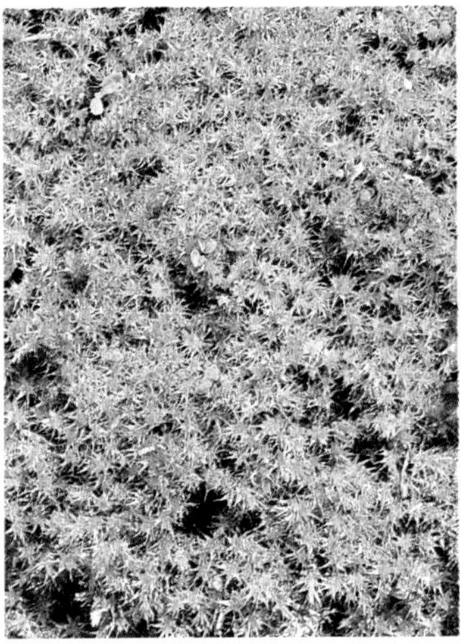

x 1

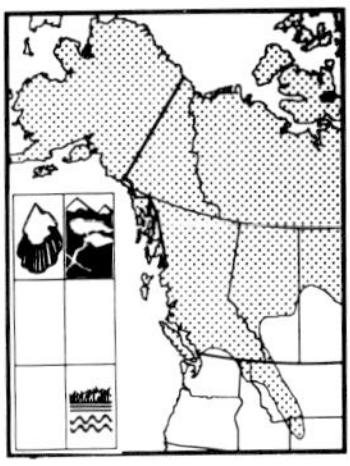

Campylium stellatum. The genus *Campylium* contains species with squarrose-spreading leaves that are broad at their base and narrow to a channelled, slender apex. This structure gives the mats a bristly appearance. The six species of the genus in our area occur in very different habitats. Although pleurocarpous, *C. stellatum* is a moderate-sized moss that grows in an ascending manner. The bristly appearance and widely spreading leaves are characteristic. From above, the plants appear "star-shaped" with many points. There is only a short costa, or in some leaves it is lacking. Sporophytes are very rare. *Campylium polygamum* is similar to *C. stellatum* but occurs in less rich sites and has a costa and less spreading leaves. *Campylium stellatum* is a dominant component of rich fens and occurs in the hollow-hummock sequence typical of these highly calcareous fens. The sequence, from pool to hummock, is *Scorpidium scorpioides - Drepanocladus revolvens - Campylium stellatum - Tomenthypnum nitens*. *Campylium stellatum* forms lawns and mini-hummocks, however expect your feet to get wet when you collect it.

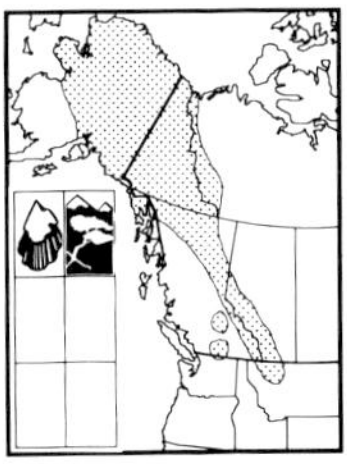

x .5

Campylium halleri forms reddish-brown, spreading mats on calcareous cliff faces. This is one of the few pleurocarpous mosses that attaches directly to a rock face; it is rarely found on soil, debris or in crevices. The leaves are all squarrose-recurved and arranged in a compact, tidy manner. Sporophytes are often present. *Hypnum recurvatum* is somewhat similar, but has falcate-secund leaves. *Campylium halleri* is a rare moss; it has been found occasionally in the calcareous canyons of Jasper-Banff-Kananaskis area of Alberta, but is more common in the Alaska-Yukon region and is widely scattered in British Columbia.

x .5

x 2

Isothecium myosuroides can be described as ''dirt common'' along the coast. It is extremely variable, forming hanging curtains from branches, matted on tree trunks, trailing on boulders or expanding on logs. The mats can be thin with almost filiform stems or robust, branched and loose. The white-green colour; erect, slender, serrate leaves (seen with a hand lens) and the presence of a costa help identify it. Generally in humid coastal rain forests any hanging, trailing, branched, white-green moss with erect leaves could be this species. If you are unsure, your best bet is to name it *Isothecium*, chances are you'll be right. Other names for this moss are *I. spiculiferum* and *I. stoloniferum*.

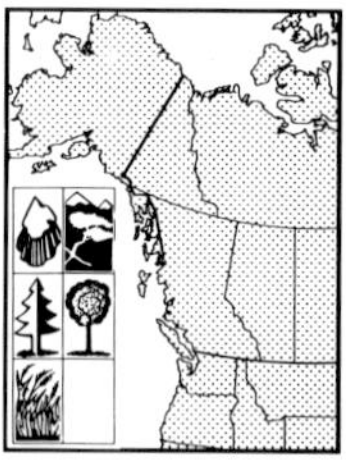

x 1.5

Eurhynchium pulchellum can be distinguished by the pleurocarpous, irregularly branched plants with ovate, usually obtuse, branch leaves that have serrulate margins, short apical cells and a costa ending as a spine about three quarters of the way. The branch leaves are stiffly spreading and when compared with other pleurocarpous, costate taxa (e.g. *Brachythecium*) are much shorter and blunt. This gives the plants a very different appearance. This species is common throughout the area, especially in boreal and montane forests, mostly around tree bases and on logs that are slightly raised above the forest litter. It is common in aspen forests.

x 2

Kindbergia praelonga (=**Eurhynchium praelongum**). This coastal rain forest species is irregularly to regularly pinnately branched. The leaves are cordate and shortly acuminate, with finely serrulate margins and a strong single costa ending just below the apex. The stems grow prostrate with the younger portions arching. The setae are papillose and the operculum is long. There are no paraphyllia and the leaves are not plicate. Stem and branch leaves differ in shape and size. This species occurs on logs, boulders and trees in moist, humid forests; it is especially abundant in swampy forests. Although the endemic *K. oregana* is showier with more robust, evenly pinnate stems and longer pointed leaves; *K. praelonga* is widespread and probably more common. The preciseness of *K. oregana* (a white collar moss) can be contrasted with the irregular roughness of this species (a working man's moss)!

x 1

x .5

Kindbergia oregana (=**Eurhynchium oreganum**). Like its sister species, *K. praelonga*, this species is common in lowland coastal rain forests. It is characterized by regularly branched stems. The plants are much more robust and coarse than those of *K. praelonga* and the leaves are longer. The evenly pinnate stems form beautiful, yellow-green mats. No other moss with nonfalcate-secund leaves forms such evenly pinnate plants. The species does not occur outside the temperate rain forests of the Pacific Northwest (see also under *K. praelonga*).

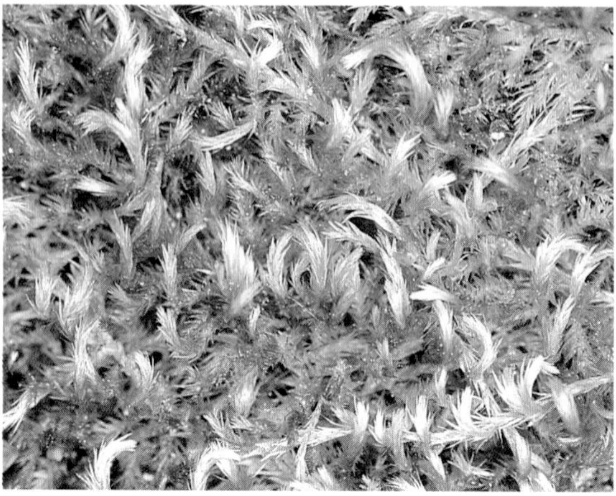

x 2

Homalothecium aeneum is a spectacular bright gold-copper colour. The plants have horizontal stems that give rise to numerous erect branches about 1 cm high. When dry these curl upward, with the entire mat consisting of inrolled and upcurled branches. When wet these become straight. This genus is related to *Brachythecium*; both have lanceolate, costate leaves with long pointed cells. While *Brachythecium* grows on soil, has flattened mats and never has upcurled branches; *Homalothecium* occurs on the trunks and bases of trees along the coast and and inland it is found more commonly on rock faces. All Homalothecia have strongly plicate leaves and the upcurled branches and golden sheen are characteristic. *Dendroalsia* has downcurled branches, and branches that are pinnately branched. *Homalothecium* consists of seven species, all coastal except *H. aeneum*. They are separated most easily by microscopic features.

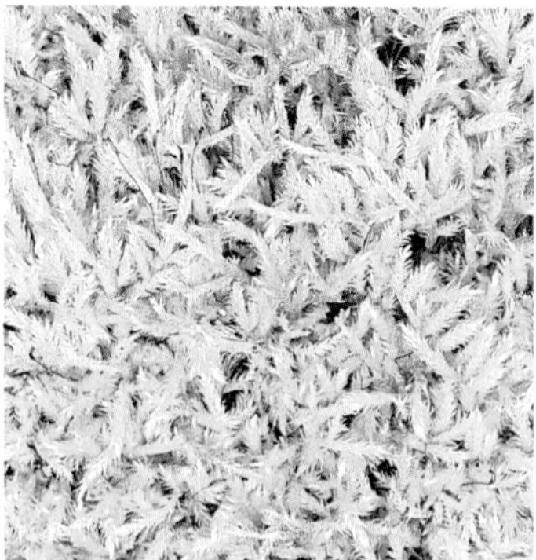

x 1

Homalothecium fulgescens. The most common coastal species, *H. fulgescens* forms large mats on tree trunks, logs and tree bases; more rarely it occurs on rock. When moist, it looks like a plicate *Brachythecium*, with erect-spreading leaves and spreading branches; however, on drying, it takes on the characteristic look of *Homalothecium*, with strongly upcurled branches. In general, this species is replaced by *H. aeneum* on rock in the western cordillera, and by *H. nevadense* on rock and in slightly drier situations in the Pacific Northwest. Some bryologists have considered this western North American endemic to be similar to the Eurasian *H. lutescens*.

x 1.5

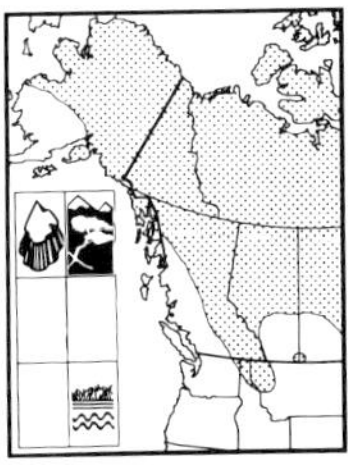

Tomenthypnum nitens is distinguished from other mosses in our area by the golden colour, sharply acuminate stem and leaf apices and strongly plicate leaves, which are costate. The stems are characteristically covered by reddish-brown tomentum. *Orthothecium* has ecostate leaves, while *Tomenthypnum* contains a single, strong costa ending about three quarters the way up the leaf. The plants are pleurocarpous and regularly pinnately branched, they grow erect and form hummocks in fens. In the boreal forest, hummocks in calcareous mires are dominated by this species, replaced below it by *Campylium stellatum* and above by species of *Sphagnum* or if drier conditions prevail - by feather mosses.

x .5

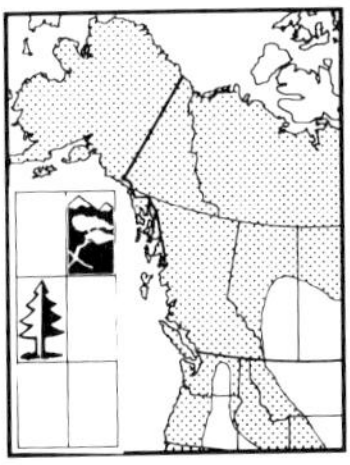

Brachythecium rivulare occurs emergent in streams and along calcareous spring banks. It is often found with *Cratoneuron* species and *Philonotis fontana*. It is usually recognized by broad, nonplicate leaves gradually narrowed to a short, acute apex. *Brachythecium erythrorrhizon* occurs in similar habitats and has strongly plicate leaves with long slender acuminate apices, while *B. nelsonii* has nonplicate leaves with slender apices. These species all have leaves attached to the stem by long, slender groups of cells that run down along the stem. As a result the leaves are somewhat farther apart than other species, giving these species an overall different look.

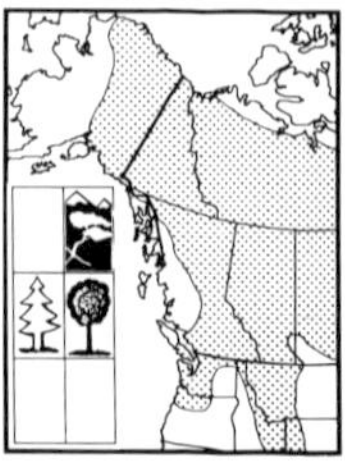

x 2

Brachythecium salebrosum. The genus *Brachythecium* has about 15-20 species in western Canada. Generally, all species are yellow-green in colour, with single costa and lanceolate, acuminate, often somewhat plicate leaves. They branch irregularly and are found in mesic to dry habitats, often on logs, humus and soil in montane-boreal forests. Two species are common in drier low elevation forests: *B. salebrosum* with entire or very finely toothed leaf margins, and *B. campestre* with distinctly serrulate margins, only seen with a hand lens. Both are conspicuously plicate and equally abundant. *Brachythecium starkei* occurs in moist forests and at higher elevations, it is nonplicate and has broader, decurrent leaves. These species often grow with *Eurhynchium pulchellum* and *Plagiomnium cuspidatum*.

x 1.5

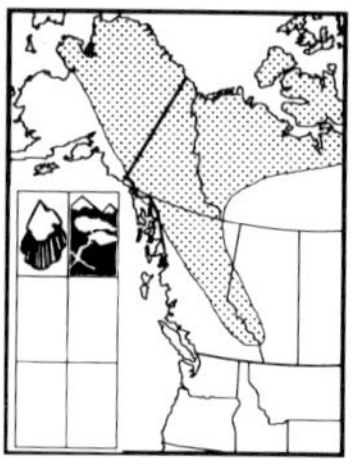

Brachythecium groenlandicum. An alpine-subalpine species, *B. groenlandicum* occurs in late snow areas, often growing with *Lescuraea radicosa* and *Tortula norvegica*. It is best distinguished from *B. campestre* and *B. salebrosum* by habitat. These two species have more plicate leaves and often are ever-so-slightly falcate-secund. Another similar species, *B. turgidum*, has larger, yellow-green, sparsely branched plants which, unlike most other *Brachythecium* species, are ascending to erect. The leaves are costate and narrowly ovate-lanceolate with slenderly acuminate apices. Sometimes *B. groenlandicum* strongly resembles *B. turgidum* and these specimens are puzzling and need to be studied carefully. *Brachythecium turgidum* is common in calcareous alpine meadows and subalpine fens. At lower elevations it occurs infrequently in rich fens, eutrophic meadows, pond shores and streamsides.

x 1

Brachythecium asperrimum is typical of most Brachythecia as it has lanceolate leaves, a strong single costa and yellow-green colouration. It is most common on logs, but also occurs on wet ground and tree bases in lowland coastal forests. The leaves of this species are relatively broad, plicate and sometimes slightly falcate. When with sporophytes, the black, horizontal and curved capsules; setae roughened with papillae (easily seen with a hand lens); and blunt opercula are characteristic of this species. It is profusely branched and often forms loose mats with spreading, arching stems. The correct name for this species may be *B. frigidum*.

x 2.5

Brachythecium acuminatum is similar in gametophytic appearance to *B. salebrosum* and *B. campestre*. The plants are somewhat less branched and the leaves are serrate in the upper part. The capsules are erect and symmetric, and the peristome has no cilia in the endostome. These sporophytic features led some bryologists to recognize the genus *Chamberlainia*, however we are not inclined to do so. When sterile, *B. acuminatum* is difficult to distinguish from other Brachythecia that grow in low elevation boreal forest habitats on rotting wood, logs and stumps. This species is the least common species in the boreal forest and we have not seen it west of the Rockies. It seems to occur most frequently with *Haplocladium microphyllum* in the aspen woodland transition zone.

x 2.5

Scleropodium obtusifolium is a nondescript moss of perennially wet rock surfaces. It is common only in lowland coastal situations, along stream banks, stream side outcrops and boulders that are splashed. The leaves are spoon-shaped (ovate, obtuse and concave). They are tightly imbricate giving this rather large moss a worm-like appearance. The plants are not much branched and form rather stubby, yellow-green mats. The presence of a well-developed, single costa and no hint of falcate-secund leaves helps in identification. *Scleropodium touretei* has more slender leaves and occurs in drier habitats. Whereas *Scouleria* and *Schistidium rivulare* only occur in the splash zone, this species most often occurs slightly higher. In the Rockies, *Hygrohypnum luridum* replaces *Scleropodium* along most streams.

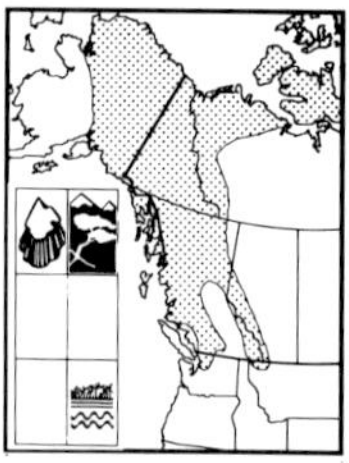

x 2.5

Cirriphyllum cirrosum is a beautiful, large, often golden-coloured pleurocarpous moss of calcareous alpine seeps and wet rock surfaces. It is closely related to *Brachythecium*; however, the leaves are abruptly contracted in their upper portion to a slender flexuose point (but not really an awn). The leaves are concave and have a short single costa. Otherwise it is very similar to *Brachythecium* species, which sometimes grow in similar calcareous habitats. The latter species are less branched and have gradually narrowed (acuminate) leaves. In the high arctic, *Cirriphyllum* is a common component of wet meadows where it is more difficult to tell from *B. turgidum* and *B. groenlandicum. Cirriphyllum cirrosum* is restricted to arctic-alpine or more rarely upper montane zones.

x 3

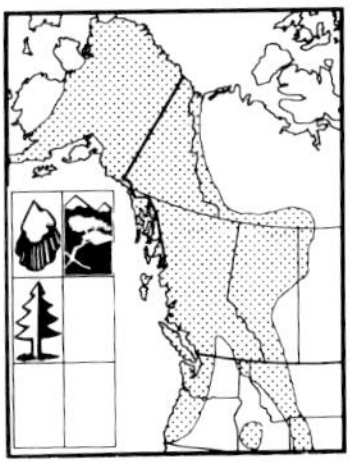

Plagiothecium denticulatum is distinguished by shiny, golden plants with complanate leaves. There is no hint of the leaves being falcate as they are in *Hypnum* species. The leaves have a very short, double costa (or none at all) and the leaf bases are decurrent. This species is much smaller (less than 2 mm across) than *P. undulatum*. It is found on swampy soil, moist humus and in grassy fens (often with *Hypnum lindbergii*). It also occurs on tree bases, inorganic soil, logs and occasionally on moist cliff faces and is rare at high elevations. Another species, *P. laetum*, is very similar, but differs in microscopic cell features.

x 1

Plagiothecium undulatum is a large, showy moss found in humid coastal forests. It is about 4-8 mm wide, has complanate leaves and is a whitish-green colour. The leaves are undulate. Each stem is like a short sword. The plant grows prostrate and rarely branches even though it is pleurocarpous. Its typical habitat is on rotting logs in shaded, low elevation, rain forests. It can sometimes be found growing over boulders, on forest floor humus and on cliffs. There is no other large, terrestial, complanate moss in our area.

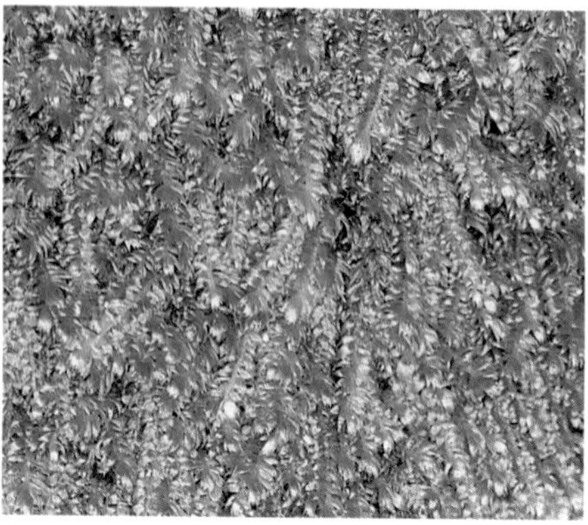

x 2

Isopterygium elegans is a lovely, shiny, yellow-green moss with slender plants and a flat (complanate) leaf arrangement. The lanceolate leaves have no costa. This species is separated from *Hypnum* species by not having falcate-secund leaves and sometimes it produces great numbers of filiform axillary propagula. It is coastal in distribution, where it occurs on earthen banks, thin humus and on boulder faces in humid montane forests. A few inland stations have been reported, but it is rare away from the coast. It has recently been placed in a new genus - *Pseudotaxiphyllum*. *Isopterygium pulchellum* occurs in crevices of calcareous rocks. It is small, ever-so-slightly falcate-secund and bright, shiny yellow-green. Species of *Isoptergyium* have no hint of alar cell differentiation.

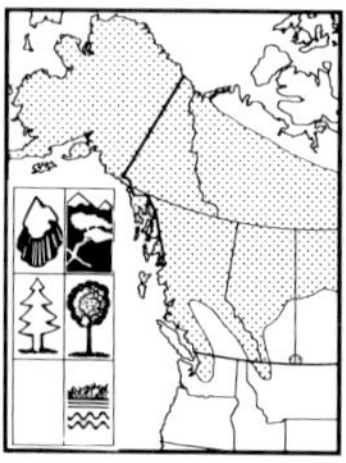

x 2

Hypnum lindbergii is one of two species of the genus that occurs in wet, fen habitats. These are distinguished from *Drepanocladus* species by the near absence of a costa and by the falcate-secund leaves which are more complanate (flat), with only the tips secund. *Hypnum lindbergii* is shiny, yellow-green and is found in minerotrophic peatlands, often as individual strands or forming straggly mats at the bases of sedge clumps. It has a large group of hyaline, inflated alar cells, while the closely related *H. pratense* has poorly developed alar cells and is more complanate. Toward the coast it occurs in swampy situations and also on sandy banks of calcareous streams, often with *Climacium dendroides*. It is typical of transitional rich fens, and forms extensive mats along the lower Fraser River.

x 2.5

Hypnum subimponens. The falcate-secund leaves with an obscure, short, double costa are characteristic of the genus *Hypnum. Hypnum subimponens* is yellow-green, regularly pinnately branched and occurs as a common epiphyte of the west coast forests. *Hypnum circinale* is smaller and a whitish-green colour. Microscopically, *H. subimponens* has an outer layer of enlarged, hyaline cells on the stem cortex and small, quadrate alar cells. It does not occur east of the humid interior of British Columbia. When fertile, it has long, slightly curved capsules; these are much longer than other associated Hypna such as *H. circinale*. It resembles *Drepanocladus uncinatus*, which has a costa and strongly plicate leaves and a similar, long, curved capsule.

x .5

Hypnum circinale has slender, noncostate, falcate-secund leaves. They have a wide base and gradually narrow to a long point. The glossy light green plants are irregularly branched and are common epiphytes of coastal forests. No other *Hypnum* is as slender and produces such a braided appearance from the hanging, closely matted stems. *Isothecium myosuroides* forms similar white-green braided mats, but the costate leaves are never falcate-secund. The capsules of *H. circinale* are inclined and short. This species can be a dominant component of lowland, coastal rain forests. It is infrequent in *Thuja plicata* relict forests of southeastern British Columbia.

x 1.5

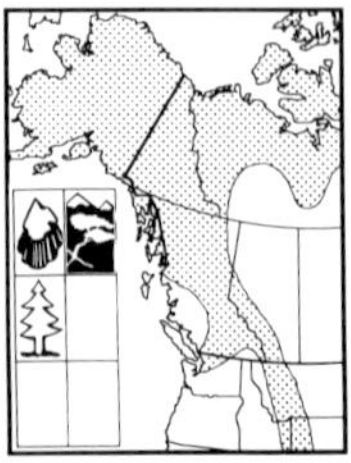

Hypnum revolutum is the easiest species of the genus to recognize. The revolute leaf margins are characteristic. In addition, the plants are golden-green in colour and have a characteristic shine, which once recognized, makes field identification easy. The leaves are ovate-lanceolate with short apices and the more or less quadrate alar cells form a well-defined, opaque area. The genus *Hypnum*, recognized by falcate-secund leaves without a costa, occurs in upland habitats (with *Drepanocladus uncinatus*). The similar, but costate genus *Drepanocladus*, occurs in wetland habitats with *Hypnum lindbergii*. *Hypnum revolutum* is found in xeric habitats and forms thin mats on granitic and calcareous boulders. It is a widespread species, often occurring with *Tortula ruralis* in the drier parts of rock outcrops.

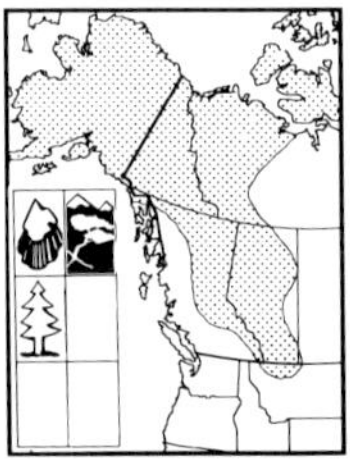

x .5

Hypnum vaucheri. The unbranched or scarcely branched stems with somewhat falcate-secund leaves that are rather quickly narrowed to a sharp apex are characters of this species. The median leaf cells are short for the genus (less than 40 μm) and the alar cells form a large opaque group of subquadrate cells, usually 12-18 cells up the margin. There is no hint of revolute leaf margins (as in *H. revolutum*) and the short, stocky leaves are hardly falcate. It is readily confused with *H. cupressiforme*, from which it is distinguished by microscopic details. *Hypnum vaucheri* is mainly continental in distribution while *H. cupressiforme* is both coastal and continental. *Hypnum vaucheri* is found on dry, calcareous rock outcrops, often in exposed situations.

x 1

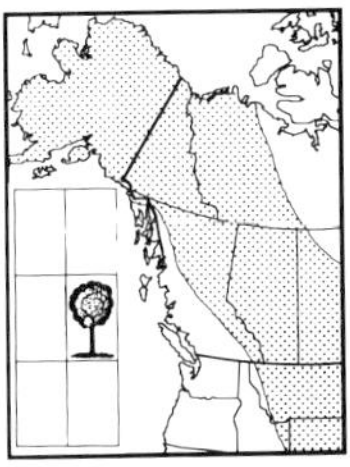

Pylaisiella polyantha forms the stockings that cover the base of most aspen trees in the boreal forest of western Canada. The small pleurocarpous plants have erect capsules (rare for mosses related to the Hypnaceae). The golden-green plants have stiffly falcate-secund leaves, but unlike other mosses which have the leaf tips pointing downward, in *Pylaisiella* they point upward. There is no costa and there are never any propagula produced. Although this moss occasionally grows on rock or on logs, its predominant habitat is at the base of aspen and poplar trees. *Platygyrium repens* is similar, but produces conspicuous clusters of propagula in the upper leaf axils. It grows on rotting logs especially on those from which the bark has fallen off.

x 2

Platygyrium repens has a greasy appearance, with the mat darker toward the centre and the spreading, prostrate, younger branches a light green colour. It resembles *Pylaisiella polyantha* in size, but is darker, has conspicious clusters of propagula and occurs mostly on decorticated logs. The leaves do not have a costa and the propagula are quite evident at the tips of the interior, more erect branches. Only *Pseudoleskeella nervosa*, among the small pleurocarpous mosses, has similar conspicuous axillary propagula; this latter species has leaves with a strong costa and often occurs on calcareous rocks. *Platygyrium repens* is much more common in the east, reaching Alberta and into central British Columbia. In the west it occurs in aspen dominated habitats with *Haplocladium microphyllum*.

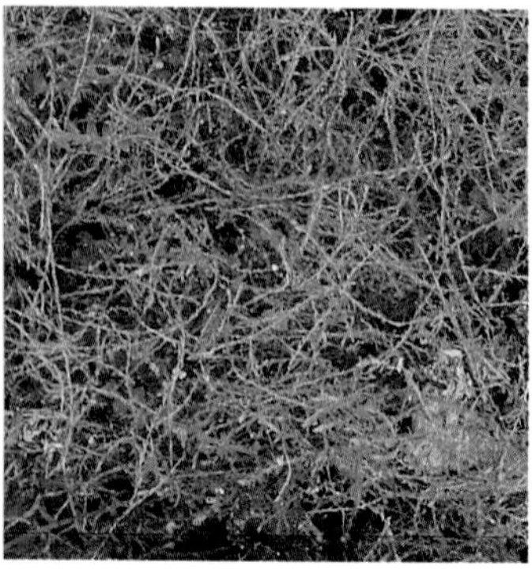

x 2

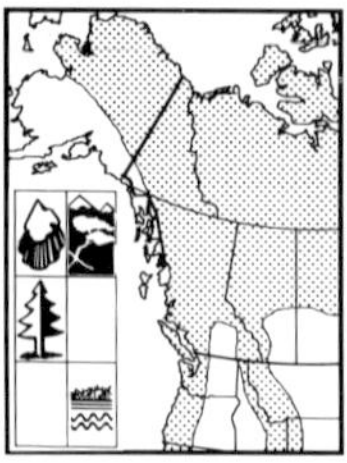

Platydictya jungermannioides can be characterized by the silky, yellow-green leaves that are ecostate and lack strongly differentiated alar cells. The leaves are erect-spreading, often slightly secund, slenderly acuminate and have serrulate margins. Rarely does this species form pure mats; instead it usually occurs as isolated strands among other mosses in calcareous rock crevices or peaty depressions. In the field, the small thread-like, dull-green plants with leaves ever so slightly falcate are distinctive. This is probably the smallest pleurocarpous moss of our area, which grows in slender threads in the field. It occurs in similar habitats to another small nondescript moss - *Isopterygium pulchellum*. This moss can be distinguished from *P. jungermannioides* by its shiny, yellow-green plants, definitely falcate leaves, no alar cells and entire leaf margins.

x.2

x 1

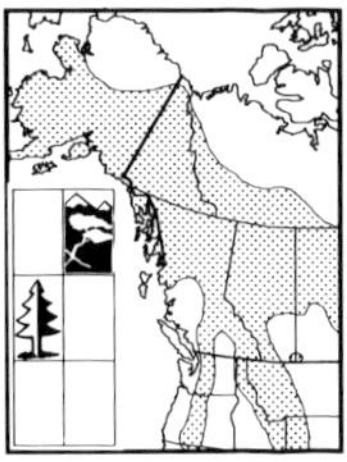

Ptilium crista-castrensis. The prettiest and nicest feather moss, also the least abundant. Sometimes named ''knight's plume'' moss because of the neatly and closely pinnately branched fronds. All leaves are plicate, falcate-secund and there are no obvious costae. These characters indicate relationships to the genus *Hypnum*. Only *Drepanocladus uncinatus* can be mistaken for *Ptilium*; rarely, however, is the *Drepanocladus* as evenly branched. Of course the *Drepanocladus* has a strong single costa, but due to the plicate leaves this is hard to see. *Ptilium* is the most mesophytic of the three feather mosses (see also under *Hylocomium splendens* and *Pleurozium schreberi*). The rich golden-green patches growing in low areas of mesic boreal and montane forests are a pleasure to come across. It becomes rare along the coast, largely replaced by *Rhytidiadelphus loreus*.

x 1.5

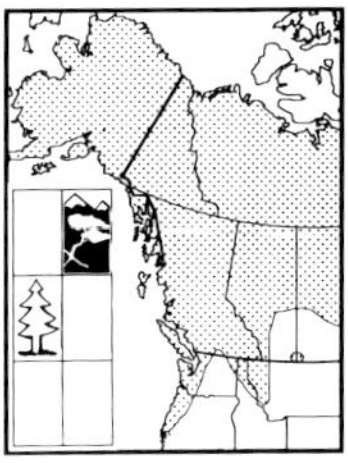

Pleurozium schreberi has been called "big red stem" by forest ecologists in western Canada, as this common feather moss has conspicuous red stems without any paraphyllia. The plants are coarse and robust, irregularly once pinnately branched, with shiny yellow-green, bluntish, noncostate leaves. Together with *Hylocomium splendens* these two mosses can form a continuous ground cover in boreal and low elevation, drier, montane forests. *Pleurozium schreberi* often appears to occur on hummock tops, while *H. splendens* occurs either on smaller hummocks or below *Pleurozium* on the larger ones. *Ptilium crista-castrensis*, the third feather moss, occupies the moist depressions and is not as common. *Pleurozium* is not common outside the forest, thus is not to be expected in tundra habitats.

x .5

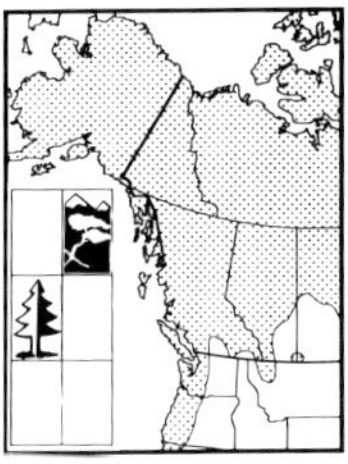

Hylocomium splendens is the most common moss of the boreal forest, and is often called a feather moss as it can be feather-like in appearance. No other moss has the stair-step configuration of the branches which are formed from annual growth increments. The fronds are twice pinnately branched and there are numerous paraphyllia on the stems. The costa is double and not readily evident. Along the coast each increment may be 3-5 cm long, while in the continental boreal forest east of the continental divide each increment is only 2-3 cm long. It commonly grows in abundance with *Pleurozium schreberi* which is once pinnately branched and has a smooth red stem. These two mosses often form a continuous mat in coniferous boreal and montane forests. They are largely replaced by *Rhytidiadelphus loreus* in coastal forests and by *R. triquetrus* in mesic interior British Columbia forests. *Hylocomium* extends into the alpine and arctic; here it does not have the stair-step increments and is merely irregularly, twice pinnate.

x 1

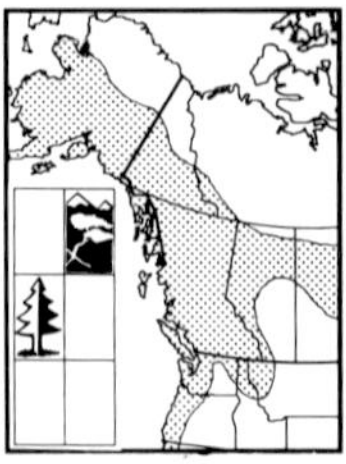

Rhytidiadelphus triquetrus is commonly called the "goose neck moss" due to the curved or secund apical portion of the main stem. Another whimsical name for this moss is "frightened cat-tail moss". The robust, coarse, irregularly branched plants with divergent, spreading leaves are characteristic. The leaves have a double costa and there are no paraphyllia. The apical tuft of leaves is often quite noticeably more ruffled than those below. This species forms small turfs on the most mesic upland white spruce forests east of the Rockies. West of the divide, it becomes more common and occasionally it covers considerable area, but it never is a dominant component of the forest floor vegetation as is *R. loreus* or *Hylocomium splendens*. It is the largest of the three species of the genus (see also under *R. loreus*, for further comparisons).

x 1

Rhytidiadelphus loreus. This large moss forms the dominant ground cover of lowland and montane forests near the west coast. Elsewhere it is rare. The plants are characterized by pinnate branching with some of the branches tapering to fine points. The leaves are irregularly spreading and secund, but are never squarrose. There are obscure costae and the leaves are conspicuously plicate. *Rhytidiopsis robusta* has numerous paraphyllia, *Rhytidium rugosum* has rugose leaves and a single costa, while *Rhytidiadelphus triquetrus* has a double costa and a "rough" appearance and *R. squarrosus* has neatly squarrose nonplicate leaves.

x 3.5

Rhytidiadelphus squarrosus is a common weed in yards of the Seattle-Vancouver areas. Its large, erect plants with nearly squarrose, nonplicate leaves make it easily recognized. Other mosses of this habitat (*Pseudoscleropodium*, *Calliergonella* and *Brachythecium* species) have erect, imbricate leaves. *Campylium stellatum* has squarrose leaves, however it is smaller, occurs in dense mats in fens and has conspicuous alar cells. Other species of the genus are identified by plicate leaves and occurrences in forested habitats. Farther inland, in natural situations, *R. squarrosus* occurs on wet grassy slopes and in swampy areas, sometimes with *Climacium dendroides*. It is not common in the boreal forest or in the Rockies.

x 1.5

Rhytidiopsis robusta grows prostrate on forest litter in montane and subalpine forests. This is a very pretty moss which is usually found by itself, without other feather mosses present. Extensive mats can occur, especially in southern British Columbia and northern Idaho. In this area, a large, endemic *Brachythecium*, *B. hylotapetum*, often is found in association with this species. The plants are robust (much larger than any other falcate-secund species), have few branches and are longitudinally plicate with falcate-secund leaves. There are numerous paraphyllia on the stems and the costa is double and ends at mid-leaf. *Rhytidiadelphus* species grow erect, while *Rhytidium rugosum* has wrinkled (rugose) leaves with revolute margins and a single costa.

x 4

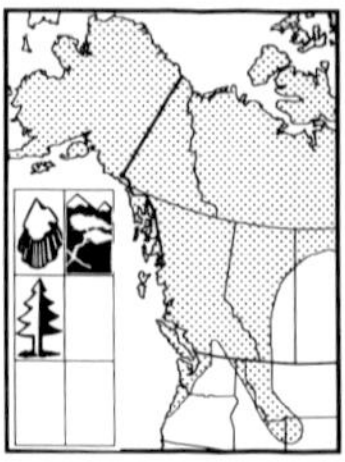

Rhytidium rugosum is distinguished by robust plants with falcate-secund, wide leaves which are conspicuously rugose, like crumpled paper and have revolute margins. No other terrestrial moss in our area has rugose leaves, but several have longitudinally striate leaves. The smaller *Hypnum revolutum* has revolute leaf margins, but the leaves are much narrower and never rugose. A xerophytic calciphile, this species prefers exposed, high elevation sites, however, it occasionally occurs at low elevations (including boreal forest and prairie) in sunny microhabitats. *Thuidium abietinum* and *Aulacomnium turgidum* are often found in association with it.

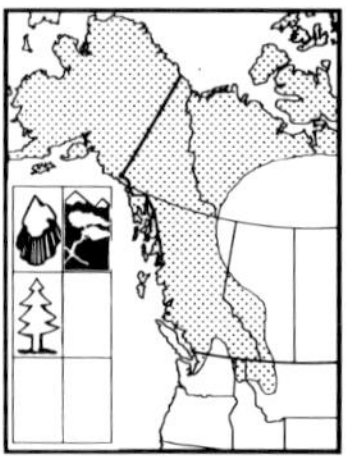

x .5

Orthothecium chryseum. The large, shiny, reddish-golden, iridescent plants are attractive and distinctive. The leaves are strongly plicate and ecostate and have recurved margins. The leaf shape is variable; when well developed, the leaves are ovate-lanceolate and abruptly narrowed to a shortly acuminate tip; however, in much of the alpine material the leaves are gradually narrowed to an acuminate point. The lack of a costa helps in distinguishing this species from *Tomenthypnum nitens*, when the latter species lacks tomentum. This species is confined to calcareous substrates. It commonly occurs in seepages and in other constantly wet situations; it is more common in the interior mountains and at higher elevations in alpine meadows and along calcareous springs and streams.

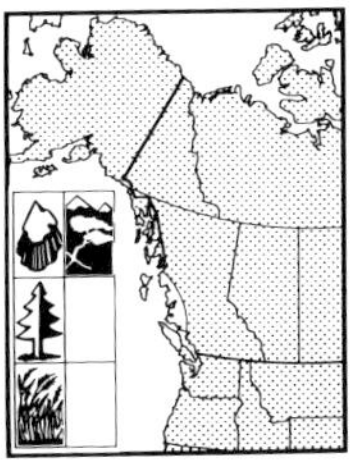

X 1

Hedwigia ciliata is easily recognized in the field when dry by grey-green, spreading mats on dry acidic rock surfaces. This is a large moss that has the apical portion of each leaf white and the lower two thirds light green. When dry, the leaves are appressed, but when wet the leaves stand out 90° from the stem. This change takes place in a matter of minutes. There is no costa, and the capsules are buried in specialized leaves. These perichaetial leaves are quite pretty, with their upper portions fringed with marginal cilia. *Orthotrichum* and *Grimmia* form cushions, while *Racomitrium* species have a strong costa (seen with a hand lens). *Racomitrium lanuginosum* and *R. canescens* superficially resemble this species; both have conspicuously keeled leaves due to the strong, single costa. The one species of *Hedwigia* is a common moss on dry acidic boulders, cliffs and rock surfaces. It is most frequent in the montane zone of the western cordillera and is much less common at higher elevations.

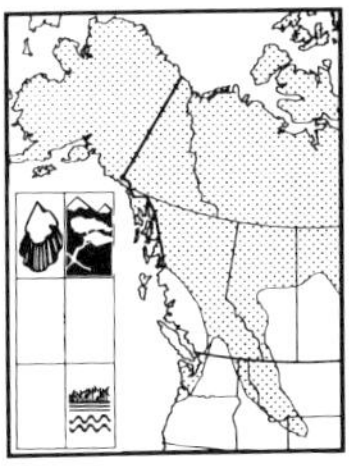

Myurella julacea. The very small, usually light-green "worm-like" plants characterize the genus *Myurella*. The leaves are ecostate and very concave and ovate, and the leaf cells are papillose by means of projecting cell walls on the abaxial side. In *Myurella julacea* the papillae are sometimes obscure and not well-developed. It is distinguished from *M. tenerrima* by julaceous stems, with more closely imbricate, rounded-obtuse leaves. In *M. tenerrima* the leaves are sharply pointed and more distant along the stem. A species of calcareous rock crevices, or more rarely forested fen depressions, it often occurs with *Encalypta* species, *Ditrichum flexicaule*, or intermixed with *Distichium capillaceum*.

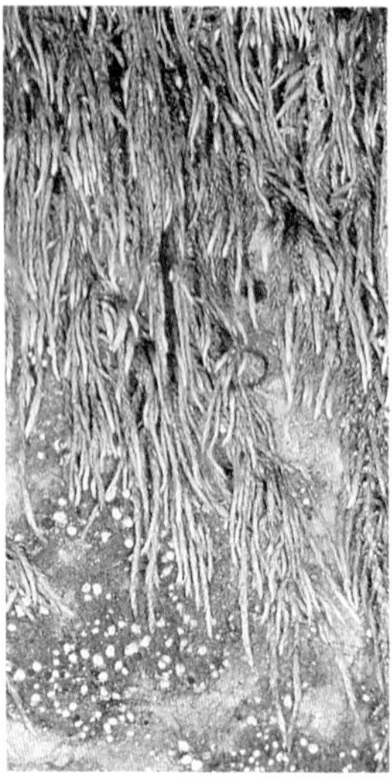

x 2

Pterigynandrum filiforme. This moss is characteristic of acidic rock outcrops in montane forests. Nearer the coast it can be found on trunks and branches of *Thuja* and *Acer*. The delicate, trailing, light-green mats are nicely distinctive. The small, blunt leaves are without a costa, and the upper leaf cells are indistinctly papillose. The growth habit of silky hair is typical. Few, if any other mosses have this look, perhaps *Isothecium* or *Hypnum circinale* when on tree trunks, but *Pterigynandrum* is somewhat more coarse.

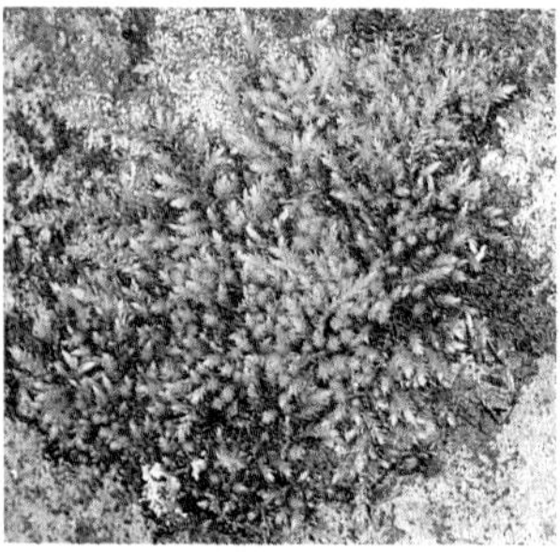

x .5

x 1

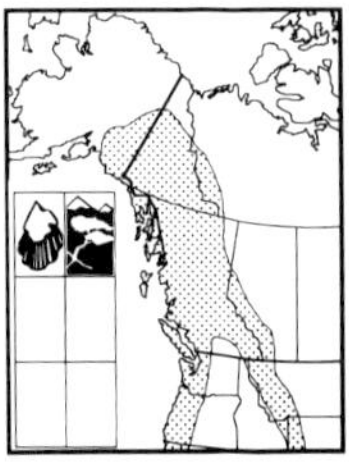

Lescuraea radicosa is characterized by rather coarse plants that are irregularly branched and dull. The leaf cells are short and without papillae. Most distinctive, however is the strong, excurrent costa and revolute leaf margins. Like the genus *Homalothecium*, *Lescuraea* is represented by several species near the coast, but only one reaches very far inland. Near the coast, species of both genera occur commonly on logs, tree trunks and branches, but inland they are more restricted to rocks and soil. Typically the species occurs in late snow areas growing on boulders or on humus in mesic grassy depressions, where it is associated with *Tortula norvegica*. Nearer the coast, this species also occurs as an epiphyte; but it is difficult to distinguish from other species of *Lescuraea* without microscopic examination. It is the only common *Lescuraea* east of the Rockies.

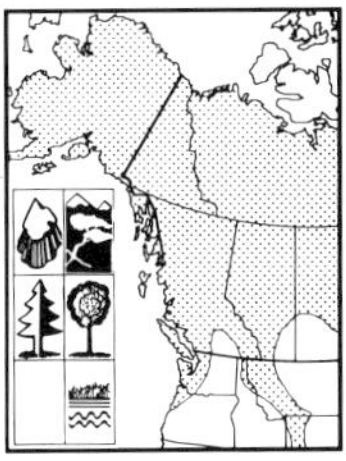

Climacium dendroides. The miniature tree look distinguishes this species. Underground stems produce erect stems about 2-10 cm high, these in turn produce branches in their upper portions, thus appearing as "trees". The leaf cells are long and smooth, and there is a strong costa. The margins are serrate and the leaves plicate. The stem leaves are altogether different. Capsules are rarely produced. This species usually grows on mesic organic soils in moist depressions and along streams and lake margins. It is common at the edges of fens, mostly in forested areas, but also in calcareous tundra habitats. Along the west coast it can become a yard weed, however east of the Rockies the yards are too dry!

x 2

Dendroalsia abietina is one of the spectacular mosses of the west coast. It forms mats on tree trunks and occasionally on calcareous cliffs. The individual plants are closely pinnately branched; when wet they produce elongate plumes that hang pendent or downward from the tree trunk. When dry they curl tightly downward, forming characteristic downcurled dry fronds, each with the branches pointed downward. The leaves are costate and capsules occur emergent from perichaetia arranged along the underside of the main stem. One must "feel" the undersides of the plants when wet to determine whether capsules are present or not.

x 1

Antitrichia curtipendula is coastal in distribution and occurs on tree branches and trunks, often festooning the larger branches in humid coniferous forests. It is a large moss (much larger than *Isothecium*) that has ovate, acute leaves and recurved margins. The costae are three in number, but indistinct. This is a robust, coarse moss that, when abundant, dominates the landscape. It really cannot be confused with any other large, epiphytic moss. When it occurs on logs and boulders, its large size might allow confusion with *Rhytidiadelphus* species, but the latter has an "unkempt" look. The recurved leaf margins and lack of a single, strong costa are good identifying field characteristics for *Antitrichia*.

x 1.5

Homalia trichomanoides, like its relatives in the genus *Neckera*, is complanate, has rather thick-walled rhombic leaf cells and no differentiated alar cells. However, in *Homalia*, the leaves are ovate, relatively broad and more or less obtuse, while in *Neckera* they are lanceolate to narrowly oblong and mostly acute. There is a single costa to midleaf. The complanate nature of the plants is very evident, so much so that the plants appear to have only two ranks of leaves, however, the leaf insertions are not on opposite sides of the stem, but all around it. Superficially, *Homalia* could be mistaken for a leafy hepatic, but its leaf cells are longer than wide and the presence of a costa should serve to differentiate it. A rare plant in western North America, it forms short pendent masses on basic to neutral, mesic cliff faces and on tree trunks near water courses. It has a peculiar lustre that immediately differentiates it from other complanate species such as *Hookeria* and *Plagiothecium*. It is not known east of the Rockies in our area.

x 2.5

Metaneckera menziesii is a beautiful moss, growing pendent from tree trunks and calcareous cliff faces. It has broadly oblong leaves with a costa, that are nearly rectangular and narrow quickly to a short point. They are strongly, transversely undulate and are arranged in a flattened or complanate pattern. The stems have paraphyllia and are irregularly branched, also in a complanate fashion. The capsules are immersed in the leaves. The robust (2-15 cm), flattened, glossy plants can only be mistaken for one of two species of *Neckera*; *N. douglasii* occurs on trees near the coast; *N. pennata* mostly on rocks in the interior and on trees near the coast. These two species have no costa and no paraphyllia. Also *Metaneckera* often has abundant, small, flagelliform branchlets, a feature neither of the two species of *Neckera* has.

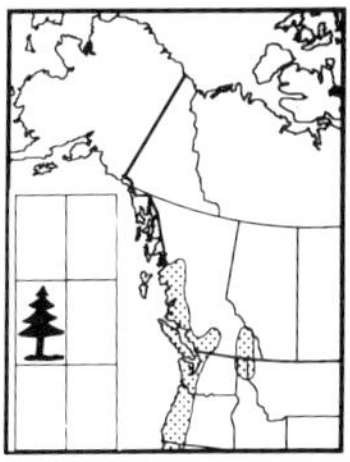

x 1

Neckera douglasii. This species is similar to *Metaneckera menziesii* in having large plants pendent from tree trunks and rock surfaces. The leaves of both species are complanate, undulate and somewhat shiny. Whereas the *Metaneckera* has paraphyllia, a single costa, immersed capsules and is a dark green colour, *Neckera douglasii* has no paraphyllia, no visible costa, shortly exserted capsules and is a light green colour. Both of these species are common in lowland rain forests, both extend inland to the western slopes of the Rockies, but only *Metaneckera* is found east of the divide. This species is named after David Douglas, a Scottish botanist, who in 1826 made the first recorded ascent of Mt. Hooker, a major peak in the Rocky Mountains. Unfortunately, in 1835 he was killed in Hawaii, trampled to death in a pit used to catch wild cattle.

x 2.5

Hookeria lucens belongs to a large genus of tropical mosses that is represented by two species in northwestern North America, both restricted to lowland temperate rainforests. Both are distinguished by having flaccid, ovate, complanate leaves with no costa and with large, thin-walled, hexagonal cells. The generally dark plants occur in wet, shaded areas, usually on soil, logs or at the edges of swampy areas. The individual leaf cells are large enough to see with a hand lens and the glossy plants easily identify the genus. The two species are distinguished by their leaf apex features: *H. lucens* has blunt, rounded leaf tips, while *H. acutifolia* has sharply acute ones. *Plagiothecium undulatum* can occur in similar habitats, but is much larger, yellow or whitish-green and has undulate leaves. The complanate leaves somewhat resemble those of liverworts, but the moss leaves are never in two or three distinct ranks.

Buxbaumia aphylla. The sporophytes of species of this genus are unique. The short papillose setae, very asymmetric capsules (each with a small mouth) and perfectly white, membranous peristome are distinctive. The gametophyte is reduced to a protonema and one or two small perichaetial leaves; thus only the sporophytes are readily seen. Although three species have been found in western Canada, *B. aphylla* is the most common. These all have been termed "bug on a stick moss". In the west, it is found on moist, acidic soil in the upper montane to alpine zones. Really a rare moss, it occurs as individual plants, each about a centimetre high on small soil patches on sparsely vegetated slopes. It has also been collected on acidic soil patches in mesic alpine tundra.

Bryobrittonia longipes. This is truly a beautiful moss. It was first described in 1864 from material collected by Thomas Drummond near Jasper town site in Alberta. The plants are relatively small, with fat, elliptic to ovate-obtuse leaves. Its nearest relative is the genus *Encalypta*. In that genus, all species have strongly papillose leaves, whereas *Bryobrittonia* has leaves wherein the cells are totally smooth but strongly convex. Thus when viewed closely the leaves glisten with many sparkling, golden points, each point representing a single cell. The sporophytes are similar to those of *Encalypta* (especially *E. procera*). *Bryobrittonia longipes* (the only species in the genus) occurs on moist calcareous soil along streams and occasionally on moist soil in crevices of rocks. Although not uncommon in the Yukon and Alaska, it is known from only a few localities in the Alberta-British Columbia Rockies.

x 3

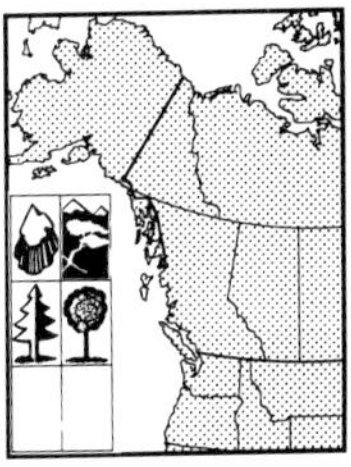

Encalypta procera is the largest species of the genus in western North America. It is distinguished by the spatulate, obtuse, crisped vegetative leaves. In the axils of the leaves are numerous, large, filamentous propagula; these alone will separate this species from most other acrocarpous mosses. When capsules are present, the large, delicate, red, double peristome is quite pretty. The outer layer curves outward and the inner one forms a cone, all on top of a slender, cylindric, spirally ribbed capsule. The calyptrae are typical (with a basal fringe) for *Encalypta* (see *E. brevicolla*). It occurs in crevices and on small ledges of calcareous rocks, particularly common in the Rocky Mountains. Often the plants have a white incrustation in the lower portions.

x 3.5

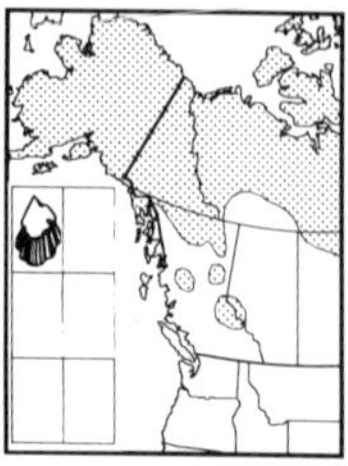

Encalypta brevicolla. Species of this genus are known as "candle snuffer mosses" due to the large, conspicuous, fringed, bell-shaped calyptrae that cover the young capsules. These are unique and readily identify species of this genus. Most species occur on calcareous rock; however a few species such as *E. brevicolla* and *E. ciliata* prefer acidic or neutral substrates and are found typically in rock crevices, usually growing on thin mats of soil. Both of these species have a delicate, fringed calyptra base. *Encalypta ciliata* has short calyptrae and leaves without hyaline hair points; *E. brevicolla* has long calyptrae and leaves with noticeable hair points. It is infrequent in the montane to lower alpine zones; probably more common northward. About 12 additional species occur in western Canada.

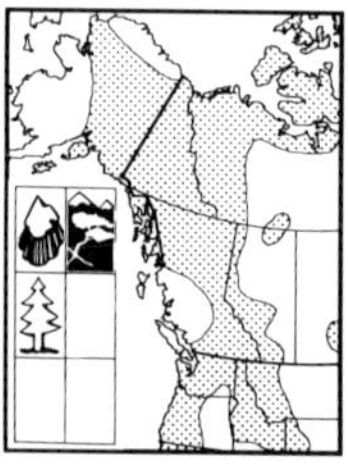

x 2

Encalypta rhaptocarpa. The oblong to oblong-ovate leaves, which terminate in a hyaline or yellow awn, are characteristic of this species. It often produces sporophytes, and when these are present, the erect, ribbed capsules with a single peristome and large warty spores are diagnostic. The calyptrae have no basal fringe. This species is common in crevices of calcareous rocks. The plants are smaller than those of *E. procera* and often occur on small soil covered ledges (with *Ditrichum flexicaule* and *Distichum capillaceum*).

x 3.5

Encalypta alpina. As the species name indicates, this is a species of higher elevations and latitudes where it is found on mesic, organic soil banks, associated with calcareous cliff faces. It is differentiated from all other species of the genus by gradually narrowed (lanceolate) leaves. The costa is shortly excurrent, but no hyaline awn is present. The capsules are smooth and lack a peristome. The calyptrae are unusually long and have a relatively inconspicuous fringe. This species occurs in mesic microhabitats and when compared to other *Encalypta* species, it is the least tolerant of xeric conditions.

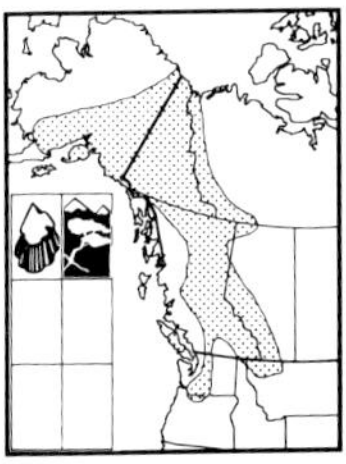

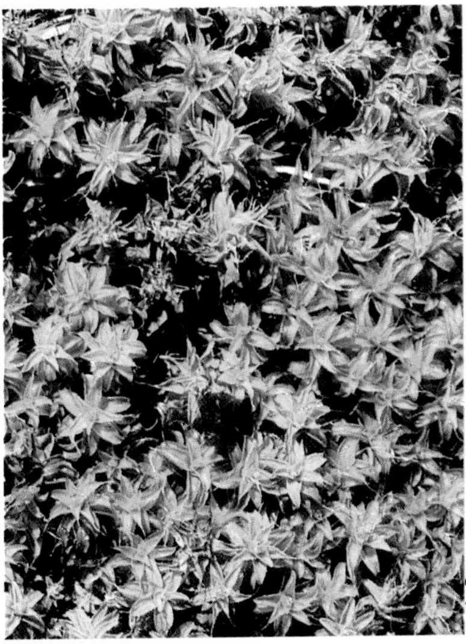

x 1.5

Tortula norvegica is somewhat smaller than *T. ruralis* and has a distinctive, clear red hair point. Some populations occur that have a reddish awn with the upper one third hyaline. We interpret these to be *T. ruralis*. The leaves of *T. ruralis* tend not to be as squarrose-recurved as those of *T. norvegica*. The striking difference between the leaves when wet and when dry is obvious in *T. norvegica* as well as in *T. ruralis*. *Tortula ruralis* occurs in a variety of habitats, but mostly on dry, calcareous soil from the prairies to xeric alpine and arctic tundra. *Tortula norvegica* is found only in late snow areas, often in lush meadows with *Cassiope* and other heaths. It is associated with *Lescuraea radicosa* and *Brachythecium groenlandicum*.

x 2

Tortula princeps. This species is similar to *T. ruralis*, except for its sexual condition. Whereas *T. ruralis* is dioicous and rarely with sporophytes, *T. princeps* is synoicous and often with capsules. We recommend distinguishing these species by "sexing" them. Whereas *T. ruralis* is common throughout our area, especially on calcareous cliff faces; *T. princeps* (or we should say plants that have been confirmed as being synoicous) seems most common in the coastal region of Vancouver Island northward to the Queen Charlotte Islands. We suggest that, except for plants in the extreme southwestern part of British Columbia and perhaps coastal Washington and Oregon, all other material is most likely to be *T. ruralis*, especially if sporophytes are not present. (See also the key for other useful features.)

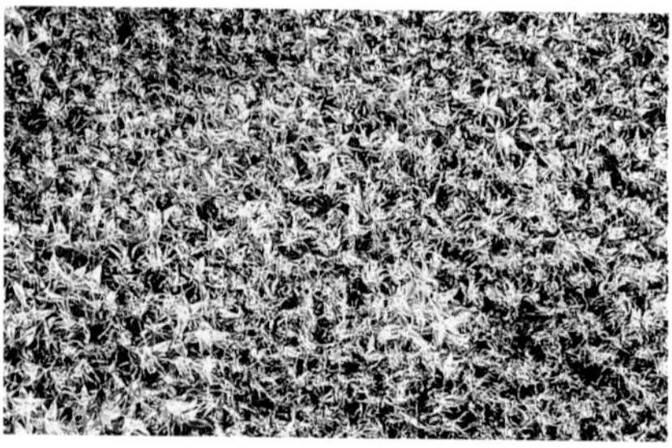

x .5

x 1

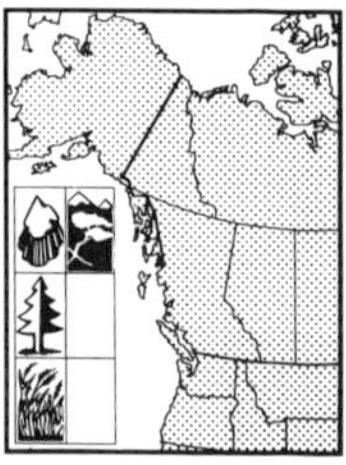

Tortula ruralis is most readily recognized by its leaves, which when moist are squarrose-recurved and when dry become folded, contorted and appressed. The leaves are dull (because of the large C-shaped papillae) and end in a long, spinulose, hyaline awn. The basal cells are lax and hyaline, but do not have the thickened cross walls of *Encalypta*. The leaves are abruptly narrowed to the awn and oblong in shape. The awn and leaf shape will distinguish it from species of *Barbula*, *Desmatodon* and *Didymodon*. The long, twisted peristome, consisting of 32 filiform teeth above a high basal membrane, is characteristic of *Tortula*; while species of *Barbula* have 32 twisted, filiform teeth but no basal membrane. *Tortella* species have much narrower leaves. It is common in a variety of habitats; most frequently in crevices and at the bases of calcareous rocks, but also on calcareous prairie soil and dry alpine tundra. Common associates are *Thuidium abietinum*, *Ditrichum flexicaule*, *Encalypta rhaptocarpa* and *Hypnum revolutum*.

x 4.5

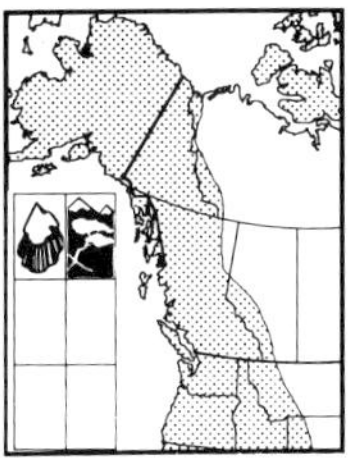

Desmatodon latifolius. Small, dull, acrocarpous plants with ovate-oblong, awned leaves characterize this species. The leaf awn is often yellowish instead of hyaline. Capsules are often produced; they are cylindric, smooth and terminate a relatively long seta. *Tortula* species are larger, *Tortella* species have narrower leaves, while *Barbula* species do not have awned leaves in our area. The papillose leaf cells and dull tone are distinctive. *Desmatodon latifolius* is the most common of three or four species of the genus. It is found on exposed soil patches in alpine and subalpine areas. The substrate is calcareous to neutral and it is most frequent in dry, cushion plant tundra.

x 3

Desmatodon obtusifolius is a rather rare and interesting species that occurs on calcareous prairie and dry montane rock outcrops. The small plants have densely papillose leaves and strongly revolute leaf margins. The rather broad, acute to obtuse (sometimes with an apiculus) leaves are widely spreading when moist, but the leaves become tightly twisted when dry, almost forming a knot of leaves. The capsules are erect and cylindric on a relatively long seta. The upper (adaxial) cells of the costa are papillose, somewhat enlarged and contain chloroplasts. They form a somewhat flattened pad of photosynthetic cells. Many mosses that live in dry habitats have shortened their life cycles (to an ephemeral style of life). Some of these mosses have photosynthetic filaments or lamellae on the upper costal surface. Perhaps this species shows the initial step in these, with its expanded costal surface. This species is widespread and southern in its distribution, known from Arizona and California, north to Alberta (Jasper area) and Alaska.

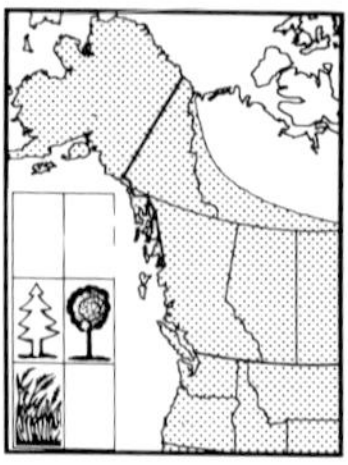

x 3

Barbula convoluta. This small butter-yellow moss is common on moist calcareous soil along roadsides, on disturbed soil in prairie and montane-boreal forests and near the coast it often invades garden and path margins. The leaves are blunt and widely spreading when moist. The upper leaf cells are densely papillose and these give the plants a dull appearance. The capsules are cylindric on relatively long yellow setae and the attractive *"Barbula"* peristome of 32 spirally arranged, reddish filaments is present. The yellow colour, blunt leaves and habitat are sufficient to recognize this moss. It is especially abundant along roadsides east of Jasper National Park in Alberta.

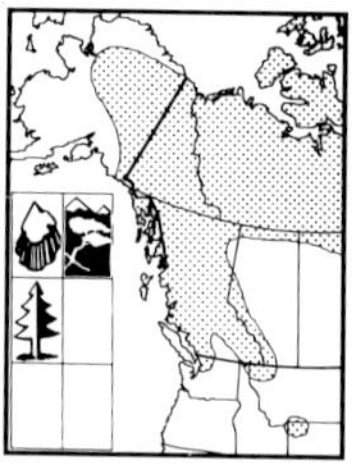

x 1.5

Gymnostomum recurvirostrum is characterized by the very small, acrocarpous, rich green plants with ligulate, obtuse leaves about 1.0 mm long. The leaves are erect and sometimes slightly incurved and the upper cells are slightly papillose with small conical papillae that are sometimes hard to observe. The margins are recurved below and the leaf insertion is not decurrent. *Amphidium lapponicum*, when depauperate, resembles this species but has oblong, cuticular bumps visible in the lower portion of the leaf. Neither of these ever has even a hint of a peristome. It is common and forms turfs, in moist crevices of limestone rock, especially near seeps and waterfalls. This species can be confused with a number of small, calcicolous species, including *Barbula*, *Didymodon* and *Seligeria*.

x 1

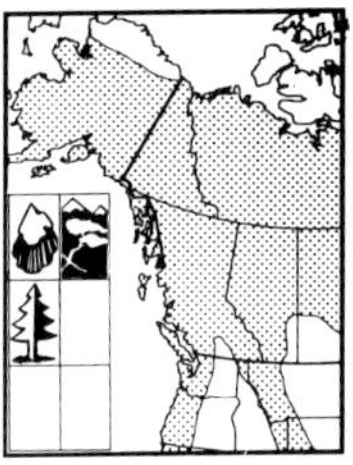

Tortella tortuosa has tortuose-crisped leaves that are lanceolate and not fragile. The upper laminae are dull while the strong, single costa is shiny. The basal cells are hyaline and much larger than the upper cells. They meet in a sharp transition, with the hyaline basal cells continuing farther up the leaf along the margin (thus a V-shaped transition). The leaves are much narrower than those of *Tortula* and *Desmatodon* and there are no hair points. No other genus has the V-shaped basal cell transition. In this genus, *T. fragilis* has stiff, fragile leaves. These two species sometimes occur together. *Tortella inclinata* is a calcareous gravel flat species with cucullate, bluntish leaf tips. *Tortella tortuosa* occurs on calcareous rock outcrops in montane forests. It is rare at high elevations and in the boreal forest where it sometimes is found on stream and lake banks.

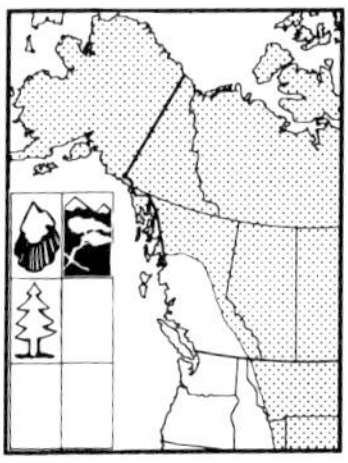

x 1.5

Tortella fragilis. The slightly curved, fragile leaves are diagnostic for this species. In addition, the yellow-green colour of the leaves along with the characteristic hyaline basal cells extending up the margins in a V are reliable identification features. The shiny, smooth costa contrasting sharply with the dull, papillose laminae are useful as well. In this species, the leaves are stiff and straight or at most curved, while *T. tortuosa* has mostly nonfragile, tortuose-crisped leaves. Rarely are capsules produced. *Tortella fragilis* is a frequent species of rock crevices in calcareous areas. It often occurs with *Encalypta rhaptocarpa*, *Hypnum revolutum* and *Ditrichum flexicaule* in montane and higher elevational areas.

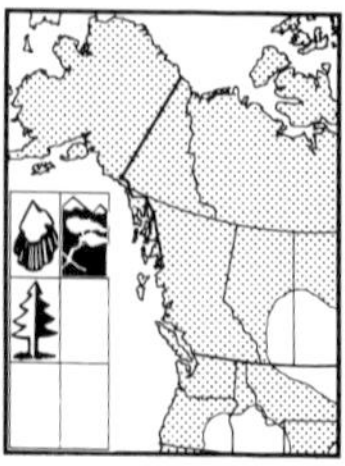

x 2

Dicranum scoparium. This species grows in loose mats, usually in sheltered areas and is most common in moist, spruce-fir subalpine forests. The leaves are erect to falcate-secund, ovate-lanceolate to lanceolate and toothed on the upper margins. The upper leaf cells are thin-walled, about 5-7:1 in length and slightly nodose. In cross section, the costa is thin, with several rows of large cells on the back side forming distinctive lamellae. The leaves are rarely squarrose (90°) from the stem in this species and can be told from *D. polysetum* by this feature, as well as the lack of undulating leaves.

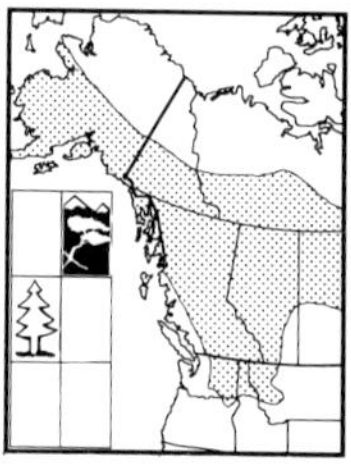

x 1

Dicranum polysetum. The large plants with abundant, whitish tomentum covering the stems, leaves strongly rugose and usually standing 90° from the stem (wet or dry), and production of two to six setae per plant are significant features. This species is abundant and typical of upland boreal and montane forests. There it forms mats 5-30 cm across. No other moss in this habitat has rugose leaves. *Dicranum undulatum* has undulate leaves that stand nearly erect. The latter species grows on organic soils. The stiffly divergent, rugose leaves appear as if the plants were hit with an electric shock, thus the common name "electric eels".

x 2

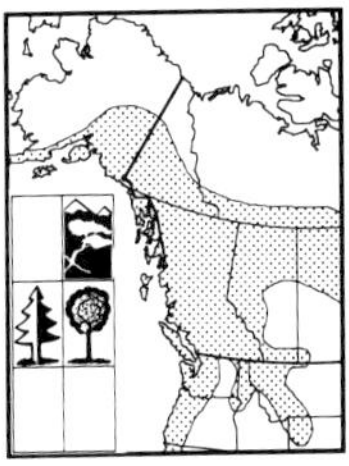

Dicranum fuscescens is hard to identify with certainty. Unfortunately, it is also common. Our interpretation of this species is one that restricts the name to those plants with falcate-secund leaves that have a distinctive keel in their upper portion (not tubular or rounded) and grow on wood - usually logs and stumps. *Dicranum brevifolium* grows on humus at higher elevations and has white tomentum and crisped leaves; while *D. sulcatum* is found in coastal British Columbia. Often found with *D. fuscescens* are *Pohlia nutans* and *Brachythecium salebrosum* or *B. campestre*.

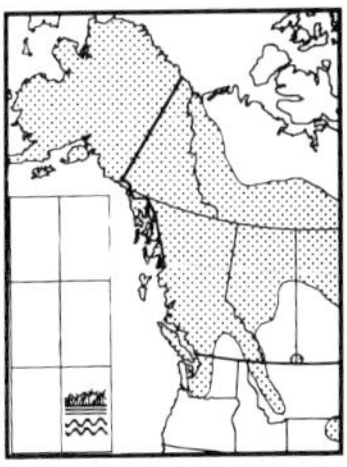

x 2

Dicranum undulatum. In some respects this species is similar to *D. polysetum*, however *D. undulatum* has erect leaves that are rather blunt and undulate. The upper cells are short and there are no ridges on the back of the costa. *Dicranum undulatum* grows on organic soils and is typical of "muskeg" habitats throughout the boreal forest. It often has some reddish tomentum on the stems, but never as much as *D. polysetum*. Plants with acute leaf apices and less undulate leaf surfaces are *D. acutifolium*, another upland species more common in the Yukon and Northwest Territories. *Dicranum undulatum* always produces a single seta per plant (see also *D. polysetum* for a comparison).

x 2

Dicranum tauricum. Only three mosses in western North America have fragile leaves; that is the upper one third to one half of normal vegetative leaves which break off leaving the lower portions blunt and stiffly erect. Other mosses have either fragile, specialized leaf tips; specialized branchlets (e.g. *D. flagellare*); or specialized, axillary propagula. *Tortella fragilis* has papillose upper leaf cells and grows on calcareous soil and *Dicranum tauricum (=Orthodicranum strictum)* is an epiphyte occurring west of the Rockies and has erect capsules. *Dicranum fragilifolium* occurs mostly north and east of the Rockies and has curved capsules. It is frequent along the eastern Rocky Mountain foothills on stumps, logs and tree bases in relatively dry montane and boreal forests; whereas *D. tauricum* occupies similar habitats in the wet west coast forests. The two Dicranums with fragile leaves overlap in distribution only in a small area in southwestern Alberta and southeastern British Columbia.

x 3.5

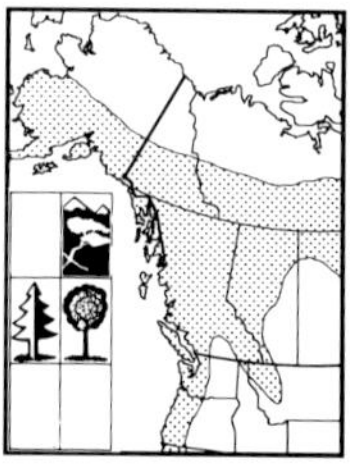

Dicranella varia. This is a genus of about 10-11 species. Most of these have slender stems with narrow, crisped or falcate-secund leaves. They are much smaller than species of *Dicranum*. They almost always have capsules; these are short (oblong), but variable in ribbing and curvature depending on species. Nearly all species of the genus grow on exposed, moist, inorganic soil. Such microhabitats as humus banks, ditch banks, overturned tree bases, roadsides, trail edges and sandy flats are all commonly inhabited. The leaves are always much more slender and often falcate, as opposed to species of *Barbula, Bryoerythrophyllum, Tortella* or *Didymodon* with broader leaves. Most of these have papillose leaf cells, *Dicranella* does not. *Oncophorus* is larger. *Dicranella varia* has falcate leaves, red setae and nonstrumose, inclined, smooth, short, ovoid capsules. Also common on the west coast is *D. heteromalla* with yellow setae and grooved capsules (when old) that are long and cylindric.

x 2.5

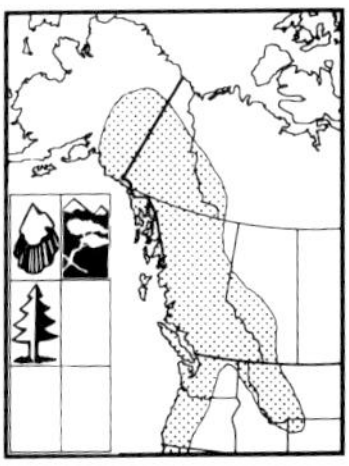

Dichodontium pellucidum. Few small, acrocarpous mosses have bulging-papillose (mamillose) leaf cells. Thus, microscopically, this species is quickly identified. However, it has little character at the macroscopic level. *Oncophorus* is similar, but larger with curved capsules and narrower, nonpapillose leaves. Barbulas are troublesome macroscopically; they generally have entire leaf margins, while *Dichodontium* has small teeth in the upper portions of leaves which can be seen with a hand lens. *Dichodontium pellucidum* can be described as a small acrocarpous moss with oblong leaves and erect capsules that are relatively common at least near the coast. It grows in wet places, especially on stream banks and seepy cliffs.

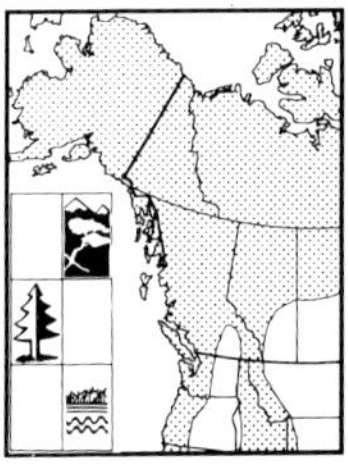

x 2.5

Oncophorus virens is a medium-sized, dark-coloured moss, differentiated by curled and contorted leaves, a sheathing leaf base and smooth, more or less quadrate upper leaf cells. The alar cells are slightly enlarged and the basal cells are linear to rectangular. The sheathing base is gradually narrowed to the subula. Capsules which are curved and strumose, with bright red peristome teeth are often present. This species resembles *Dicranoweisia crispula*, but is distinguished by the smooth leaf cells, more clasping leaf base, larger size and habitat. A second species of *Oncophorus*, *O. wahlenbergii*, is also common in our area. It is differentiated by having plane leaf margins and abruptly narrowed leaves (as opposed to plainly recurved margins and gradually narrowed leaves in *O. virens*). *Oncophorus wahlenbergii* grows on logs and rotting wood; while *O. virens* is a common species along calcareous streams and along the margins of transitional fens. It never grows on rock, as does *Dicranoweisia crispula*.

x 4

Dicranoweisia cirrata is a coastal species that is very common on roadside trees, fence posts, logs and roof-tops; but rarely on rock. The twisted-contorted, rich green, slender leaves; tufted plants and erect, cylindric capsules on elongate setae (5-10 mm long) distinguish it. It is very similar to *D. crispula*, however the latter grows almost exclusively on acidic alpine rocks and has plane leaf margins, while *D. cirrata* grows mainly on trees near the coast and has recurved leaf margins. Few other epiphytes are acrocarpous and form tight tufts. *Orthotrichum* species are much larger.

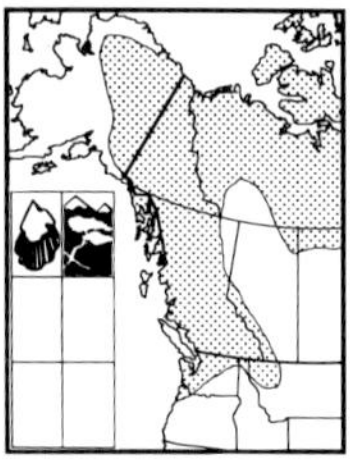

x 1

Dicranoweisia crispula. The light green tufts on granite rocks are characteristic of this moss. The leaves are contorted and twisted, with a large group of well-developed alar cells. The most diagnostic feature, however, is the longitudinal ridges of cuticular thickening of the leaves. Each ridge covers from two to several cells in length and usually only one cell in width. This is a species that occurs only on dry to mesic acidic rock faces, mostly in alpine and open subalpine habitats. Capsules are usually present and are erect, smooth and cylindric. Most other mosses occurring in this habitat have curved, asymmetric capsules.

Campylopus atrovirens. The genus *Campylopus* includes five species in western North America and is entirely coastal. The genus is closely related to *Dicranum* in having well defined alar cells and a typical *Dicranum*-like peristome. It differs in a very broad costa, about three quarters to five sixths the width. In fact, the entire upper two thirds of the leaves are in reality costa, not lamina. *Campylopus atrovirens* is characterized by hyaline leaf apices and reddish, inflated alar cells. It is often silvery-black in colour. The concave, lanceolate leaves with hyaline points and dense turfy mounds are nice features of this genus. It forms mounds and turfs in peatland areas often invading mud bottom habitats before *Sphagnum*.

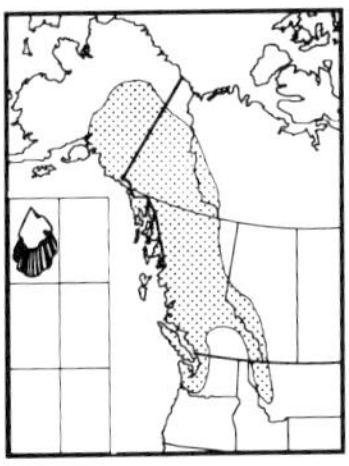

x 1.5

Paraleucobryum enerve. Almost all mosses have leaves composed of a single layered lamina. Many have a costa, while most Polytrichaceae have multi-layered leaves composed of lamellae arising from the costa and/or lamina. A few mosses have multi-layered leaves composed of an expanded costa, and since some cells of the costa are without chlorophyll, these mosses are whitish in colour. In eastern North America, *Leucobryum* is one such moss. It does not occur in the west; however, *Paraleucobryum*, with two species, does. It appears as a bleached out, stiff *Dicranum* (often looking dead), however the colour is due to the chlorophyll-containing cells being interspersed with dead, costal cells. Although not common, this species can be found (with *Conostomum*) in some abundance in mesic, acidic tundra depressions and at the top edge of montane rock outcrops with *Dicranum* species and *Ditrichum flexicaule*.

x .5

x 1

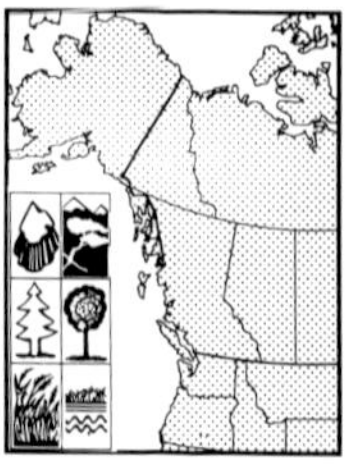

Ditrichum flexicaule is the most common moss on calcareous rock outcrops in western Canada. It can also occur in prairies, fens, meadows and on humus, but is rare in the boreal forest. The plants are slender and appear flexuose, with leaves arising from all sides of the stem. Microscopically, the lack of alar cells and the presence of a small border of pale, longer cells with oblique end walls in the lower portion of the leaves differentiates it from other species. Botanists unfamiliar with this species could confuse it with *Oncophorus wahlenbergii*, which has much more twisted-contorted leaves; *Dicranum* species, which have alar cells; and *Distichium* species, which have distichous leaves. *Distichium* is often found with *Ditrichum flexicaule*.

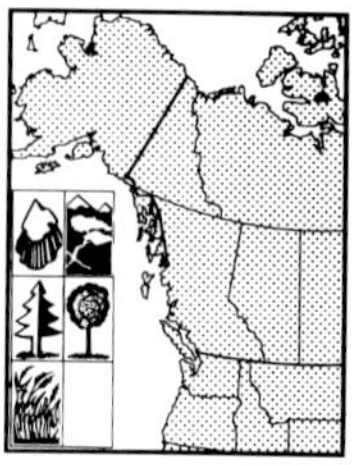

x 3

Ceratodon purpureus is easily recognized when sporophytes are present by the purple-red setae and capsules. The capsule is eight-ribbed, asymmetric and abruptly bent horizontal at the juncture of the seta as if it had been stepped upon. When sterile, it is identified with difficulty by the twisted, lanceolate leaves with recurved margins, which are irregularly dentate at the apex. The upper leaf cells are smooth and quadrate, while the lower ones are elongate. The strongly recurved leaf margins and absolutely smooth leaf cells help in identification in times of confusion. As a weed, occurring in association with disturbance, it is common on roof tops, in sidewalk cracks and on waste ground. In natural situations, it is common in montane and boreal forests on disturbed soil, while in more open areas it prefers sandy soils; rarely found in peatlands.

x 3

x 1

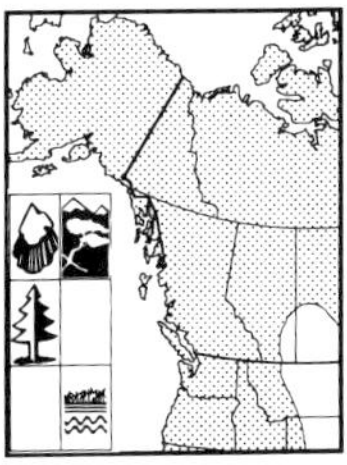

Distichium capillaceum. Species of *Distichium* are common in crevices of calcareous rocks throughout the western cordillera. The genus is easily known by the distichous leaves (like an *Iris*) that sheathe the stem. The leaf base is quickly narrowed to a stout, papillose awn which, in well-developed plants of *D. capillaceum*, is wide-spreading and flexuose. However, the less common *D. hagenii* (arctic) and *D. inclinatum* (fens and calcareous banks) as well as depauperate specimens of *D. capillaceum*, have stiff, erect leaves. *Distichium capillaceum* occurs commonly with sporophytes and can be distinguished by erect, cylindric capsules with spores 15-20 μm in diameter. Superficially similar to *Ditrichum flexicaule* and often growing together, these two genera are differentiated by the distichous versus "normal" leaf arrangement.

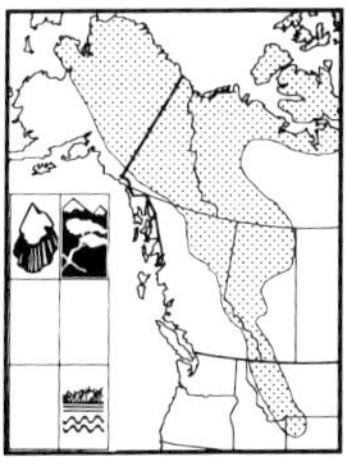

x 7

Distichium inclinatum is distinguished by inclined, oblong capsules with spores about 28-38 μm in diameter and a peristome of 16 irregularly divided teeth. The leaves are stiffly erect. (See also under *D. capillaceum*.) This species is much less common than *D. capillaceum*, which is most commonly found in calcareous rock crevices and overhanging bluffs. *Distichium inclinatum* is found in rich fens, wet depressions and on wet, calcareous, organic soil banks.

x 1.5

Fissidens grandifrons is a beautiful, large species (to 10-15 cm), that grows submerged in waterfalls and fast-running streams. It is also found around hot springs. It has nearly linear leaves that are rigid and coarse. It is shiny when wet and dull when dry. The habitat is sufficient to identify this species. *Fissidens* is a large genus (500 species) of mostly tropical species that is represented in western Canada by about 10 species. All species have distichous, equitant leaves (as *Iris*). In our area, except for *F. grandifrons*, the species are usually small (less than 1-2 cm long) and occur on exposed soil and on peaty banks, but nowhere in abundance.

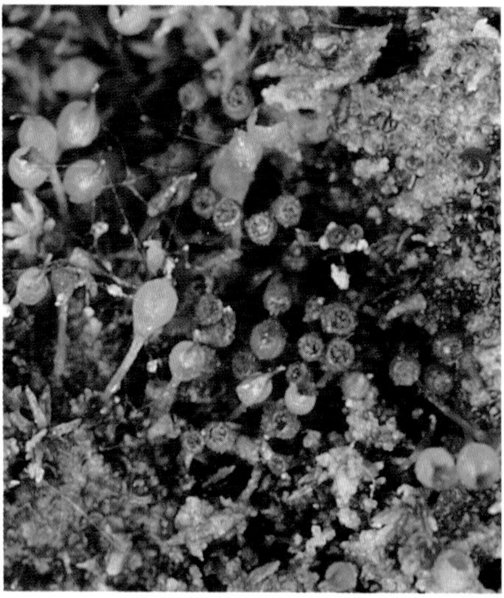

x 9

Seligeria donniana. Perhaps this genus of nine species in western North America contains the smallest of all mosses. The individual plants occur firmly attached on surfaces of limestone rock. They seldom are taller than 2 mm, and consist of unbranched leafy plants terminating in globose capsules on short setae. *Seligeria donniana* has no peristome and a straight seta, while the second most common species, *S. campylopoda*, has an obvious peristome and a cygneous setae (curved like a swan's neck); this is especially evident in moist material. The disjunct distribution pattern of this species is characteristic of all species of this genus. This is sometimes attributed to the lack of dispersal from small areas where the species weathered the last glaciation.

x 7

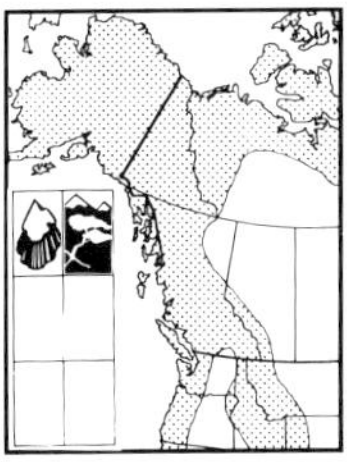

Amphidium lapponicum is distinguished by yellow-green, compact tufts or mats growing in crevices of acidic or neutral cliffs. The leaves are crisped, twisted and linear in shape when dry, but are wide-spreading and recurved when moist. When the plants are viewed from the side, the leaves appear to be in vertical files. The plants are often fertile and the emergent or shortly exserted, eight-ribbed capsules that lack a peristome are characteristic. Microscopically, the leaves have 5-8 papillae per cell. The papillae are often elliptic in surface view and toward the base of the leaf the cells are covered by small, elliptic, cuticular papillae that are sometimes hard to find but are diagnostic of the genus when present. This species is infrequent at higher elevations of the western cordillera. Two additional species of the genus occur near the coast of western North America. Typically, the crevices occupied by these three species become inundated by seepage during periods of rainfall and dry completely during dry periods.

x 1.5

x 2

Racomitrium aciculare. The broad, oblong leaves with obtuse apices are characteristic of this species. All other Racomitria have acute or awned leaves. As well, the leaves are erose with widely spaced, blunt teeth across the wide apex and upper portion of the leaf. The plants occur in cushions and tufts, attached to the substrate only at their base. When moist the widely-spreading leaves give an entirely different aspect than when they are dry and the leaves are tightly imbricate and erect. This species occurs on wet rocks, especially in sites where they are perennially splashed. It is most common along coastal British Columbia and Washington, but it also occurs inland to the Rockies. Although not easily confused with other common species of the genus, it is superficially similar to and occurs in similar habitats as *Scouleria* and *Schistidium rivulare*. The former has squarrose leaves when moist, while the latter has strongly revolute leaf margins. Both have immersed capsules, while *Racomitrium* has capsules exserted on relatively long setae.

x 2.5

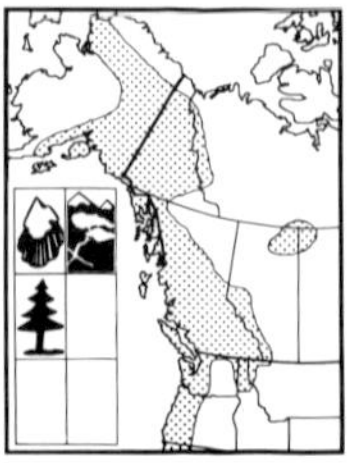

Racomitrium canescens. The highly papillose leaf cells, strongly recurved leaf margins and short hyaline awn, which does not extend down the leaf margin, are characters that can be used to distinguish *R. canescens*. It differs from *Hedwigia ciliata* by the presence of a costa, and from other Racomitria by the yellow-green colour and strong papillosity of nearly all leaf cells. Plants with numerous lateral branches are sometimes considered a separate species - *R. ericoides*. The leaf cells of *Racomitrium* have wavy walls (as does *Grimmia* to a lesser extent) and are unique to the genus. This species is very common west of the Rocky Mountains, but rare to the east. In British Columbia, it occurs on gravelly soil, sandy outwash and draping from cliff tops, especially on sterile, acidic substrates. It is a common roadside species along the Trans Canada Highway in that province and is frequent on acidic glacial outwash at higher elevations.

x 2

Racomitrium lanuginosum. The large cushions of whitish-green or grey-green moss which are conspicuous on acidic rocks are characteristic of this species. Microscopically, the smooth leaf cells and long hyaline awns of the leaf, which are coarsely papillose are distinctive features. The nonchlorophyllose, papillose cells of the awn extend down the upper margin of the leaf, giving the plants a hoary look. To distinguish it from other confusing species: Grimmias have hyaline points and form cushions, *Hedwigia ciliata* has no costa and *R. canescens* is white- or yellow-green. Racomitria have numerous branches and form spreading mats, or when densely packed, grow in erect turfs. *Racomitrium lanuginosum* is a common moss of drier acidic alpine habitats throughout the western cordillera extending into the Canadian arctic. It is not found at lower elevations east of the continental divide but is often abundant on coastal peatlands.

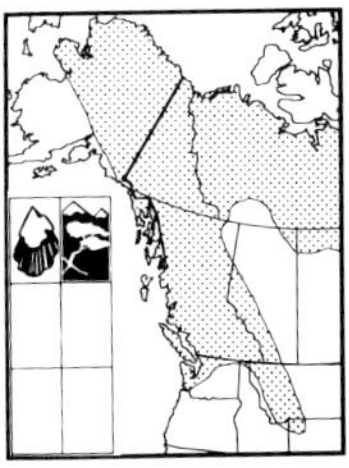

Grimmia affinis. Species of *Grimmia* are xerophytes, generally growing on dry rock surfaces. Most species have hyaline hair points and short capsules on short setae. The leaves become widely spreading upon wetting, but on drying they are erect and imbricate. *Grimmia donniana* is similar, but smaller, with plane leaf margins. Another xerophytic genus, *Orthotrichum*, is larger, produces looser cushions and never has hair points in our area. *Grimmia affinis* is distinguished by hair points and capsules exserted on short setae, and it differs from other closely related species by having recurved lower leaf margins. This species is common on dry acidic rocks at all elevations, but it is especially evident in the alpine of Jasper and northward.

Grimmia pulvinata has keeled, hyaline-pointed leaves and ribbed capsules exserted above the perichaetial leaves. The setae are strongly curved and flexuose, especially when moist. The exserted capsules and curved setae distinguish this species and *G. trichophylla* from all others in our area. This species is not easily distinguished from *G. trichophylla*; however, *G. pulvinata* is autoicous and *G. trichophylla* is dioicous. Neither species is common in our area, but they can be looked for on dry rocks in British Columbia and farther south. It is perhaps most common along coastal areas of Washington and southwestern British Columbia.

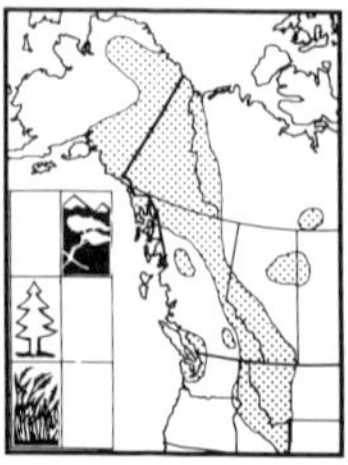

x 3

Grimmia anodon. These tiny plants have long hair points and perfectly hemispheric capsules immersed in the upper leaves. The capsules have no hint of peristome teeth. It often occurs with the larger *Orthotrichum pellucidum*. The hoary cushions are also much smaller and more compact than those of *Schistidium apocarpum*, which also occurs on calcareous rocks but has enlarged perichaetial leaves and much shorter hair points. This species is the most xerophytic of the *Grimmia* species in our area. It can be common on calcareous rocks in the Rockies.

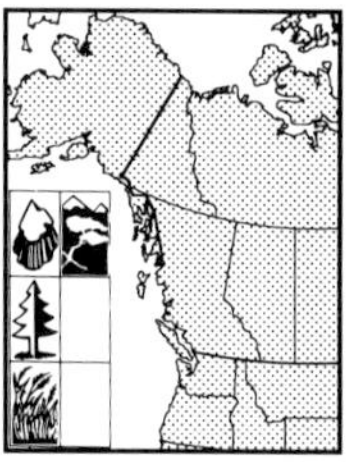

x 2

Schistidium apocarpum. The small, usually dark-brown plants with immersed, oblong-ovoid capsules and shortly hyaline awned (or rarely muticous) leaves distinguish this species. The perichaetial leaves are larger than the lower leaves and the capsules are positioned on very short (1.0 mm) setae. From *S. rivulare*, it is best distinguished by longer oblong-ovate capsules and smaller (9-15 μm) spores. The bright red peristome teeth of both of these species are especially attractive when viewed with a hand lens. *Schistidium strictum* is similar, but is reddish and has papillae on the back of the costa. *Grimmia* species generally have exserted capsules. *Schistidium apocarpum* occurs in small tufts on dry rocks; it is more delicate than *Orthotrichum* and *Racomitrium* species. Occasionally it is found in wetter sites on rocks near streams and in small depressions in rock outcrops; however, it never occurs submerged, as does *S. rivulare*.

x 2

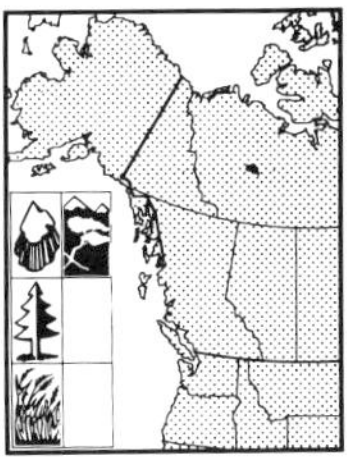

Schistidium rivulare (= **S. alpicolum** and **Grimmia alpicola**) has blackish plants and immersed capsules in somewhat enlarged perichaetial leaves. The leaves have a strong costa and do not have a hyaline point. *Schistidium apocarpum* has hair points and grows on dry rocks. *Scouleria aquatica* is much larger and coarser and its capsules are distinctive. Some *Racomitrium* species are black and occur on rocks along streams; these have coarsely toothed leaf apices. This species occurs on rocks subject to being splashed or inundated periodically by rapidly flowing water. Although it often appears to be aquatic, really it is only seasonally covered by water. It prefers calcareous substrates. These mosses, growing associated with rapidly flowing water, are really xerophytes, as they dry out completely at times of low water. They are best considered rheophytes for their constant association with running water.

x 3

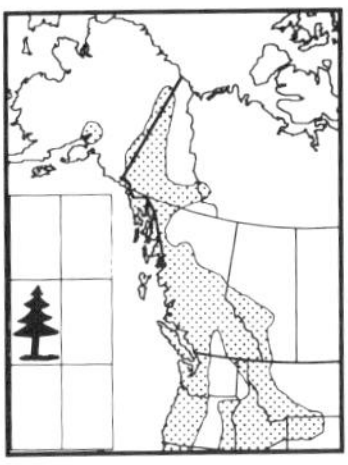

Scouleria aquatica is a characteristic moss of the splash zone of fast flowing montane streams. It forms black mats just at the high water level where, when well-developed, it constantly is wave washed and forms streams of branches 10-20 cm long. The large black plants can be confused only with the smaller ones of *Schistidium rivulare* or *Racomitrium aciculare. Scouleria* is often fertile and has immersed capsules with a very reduced peristome. The capsule opens and closes on wetting and drying by the operculum being raised and lowered on a thick central podium or columella. Large colonies of this moss can be seen at Hope, B.C., and at Marble Canyon, just west of Banff National Park.

Changes in Moss Names

BOOK	CHECKLIST*
Pogonatum alpinum	= *Polytrichastrum alpinum* (Hedw.) G.L. Sm.
Leucolepis menziesii	= *Leucolepis acanthoneuron* (Schwaegr.) Lindb.
Thuidium abietinum	= *Abietinella abietina* (Hedw.) Fleisch.
Haplocladium microphyllum	= *Bryohaplocladium microphyllum* (Hedw.) Wat. & Iwats.
Calliergon sarmentosum	= *Sarmenthypnum sarmentosum* (Wahlenb.) Tuom. & T. Kop.
Drepanocladus uncinatus	= *Sanionia uncinata* (Hedw.) Loeske
Cratoneuron commutatum	= *Palustriella commutata* (Brid.) Ochyra
Kindbergia praelonga	= *Eurhynchium praelongum* (Hedw.) Schimp.
Kingbergia oregana	= *Eurhynchium oreganum* (Sull.) Jaeg.
Brachythecium asperrimum	= *Brachythecium frigidum* (C. Muell.) Besch.
Isopterygium elegans	= *Pseudotaxiphyllum elegans* (Brid.) Iwats.
Lescuraea radicosa	= *Pseudoleskea radicosa* (Mitt.) Mac. & Kindb.
Gymnostomum recurvirostrum	= *Hymenostylium recurvirostre* (Hedw.) Dix.

* Anderson, L.E., H.A. Crum, and W.R. Buck. 1990. List of the mosses of North America, north of Mexico. *The Bryologist* 93: 448-499.

LIVERWORTS

Liverworts
Their Structure and Biology

Definition

Liverworts have many features in common with mosses and as a result they are classified as Bryophytes. Similarities of these two groups include sporophytes attached throughout their existance to the gametophyte; a general dominance of the gametophyte generation; leaves, when present, mostly with a lamina that is one cell thick; reproduction by single-celled spores; presence of rhizoids and occurrence of sperm in antheridia and eggs in archegonia. Neither group produces seeds, has roots, nor has a well-developed conducting system.

Technically, liverworts are defined by the nature of sporophyte development. In this group, the capsule is fully developed, meiosis occurs and then elongation of the seta takes place. Additionally, there are other differences. Listed below are ten of these differences:

1) Most liverworts have complex oil bodies in the leaf cells, mosses do not.
2) Most liverworts have the capsule ensheathed in a group of fused leaves - the perianth, mosses never have fused leaves.
3) Liverworts are either thalloid or leafy, mosses are always leafy.
4) Leafy liverworts usually have leaves in three ranks; two lateral and one ventral. The ventral rank of leaves is often reduced or absent. This is very rare in mosses.
5) The seta of liverworts is soft, hyaline and short-lived.
6) The capsule dehisces by four longitudinal slits; except for the granite mosses, mosses have an apical operculum. Liverworts never have a peristome.
7) Liverworts produce spirally twisted, hygroscopic threads termed elaters among their spores, mosses do not.
8) Liverworts have a complex chemistry, mosses much less so.
9) Lateral leaves in liverworts frequently have lobes; not so in mosses.
10) Rhizoids are unicellular in liverworts, multicellular in mosses.

Despite these differences, the life cycle and much of the structure is similar to that of mosses. So, what follows is a brief synopsis of the critical anomalies and differences from the moss section.

Life Cycle and Structural Features

The thalloid liverworts have a gametophyte consisting of a flattened, dorsi-ventral thallus, while the leafy liverworts possess three ranks of leaves. The apical cell of the leafy liverworts is used in the development of the archegonia (acrogynous), whereas in the thalloid ones, it is not (anacrogynous). Most leafy liverworts grow horizontally and the three ranks of leaves become complanate (flattened) with two lateral ones and one ventral rank. The erect growing species often are radially symmetric and have the three ranks of leaves of equal size.

Archegonia are developed terminally in leafy liverworts and look somewhat similar to those of mosses. However, the antheridia are globose and produced in the axils of the leaves. This situation is similar to that in *Sphagnum*, but in other mosses the antheridia are produced in groups (in perigonia if separate from the archegonia).

Many liverworts, especially the leafy ones, have the corners of the leaf cell walls thickened. When this occurs in vascular plants it is termed collenchymatous thickening of the walls; in liverworts, these corner thickenings are called trigones. These are very rare in mosses.

The Leaf

Leaf arrangement is critical to the identification of liverworts. Erect, radial liverworts have leaves transversely inserted; however, complanate species usually have obliquely inserted leaves. An oblique (45°) insertion can have two forms, one having the two lateral ranks inserted with the proximal edge up and the distal edge down thus resembling shingles of a roof when the tip of the stem is the apex of the roof. This is called succubous. The reverse, that is, with the proximal edge down and the distal edge up, is termed incubous. In both situations, the under leaves may be absent or reduced, or even full size in a few cases (and transversely inserted). The upper and under leaves (that is lateral and ventral leaves) are sometimes lobed with two, three or four points of each leaf. Our most common genus of leafy liverworts, *Lophozia*, has mostly bilobed (two-lobed) leaves. Other liverworts have their upper leaves complicate-bilobed where only the lateral leaves are folded to form an upper and under lobe, these attached at their base, usually through a keel. The upper lobes may be larger, completely hiding the smaller under lobes or the under lobes may be larger and seen surrounding the smaller upper lobes. Under leaves are never complicate-bilobed.

The Capsule

Liverwort capsules are four-valved (Fig. 14) and are elevated on a short-lived, flaccid, hyaline seta. In the *Marchantia*-like species, the capsules open very irregularly and are not four-valved. Liverwort capsules have neither a columella nor stomates, both present in

Fig. 14. Open capsule with four-valves of *Porella cordaeana*. Elaters and spores can be seen on open valves.

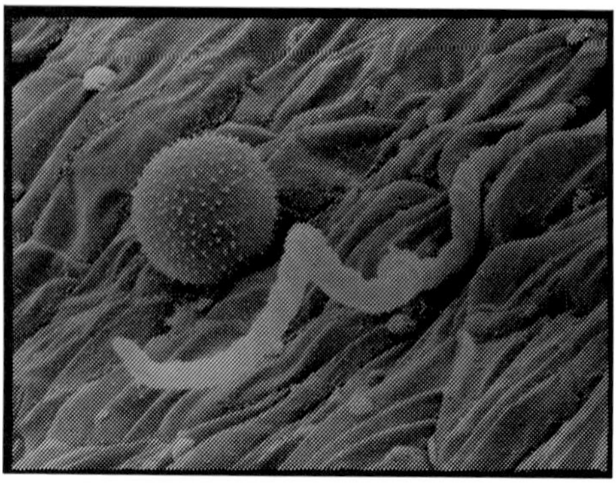

most mosses. Elaters are present among the spores of most liverworts (Fig. 15).

Fig. 15. Spore and elater lying on the inner capsule wall of *Porella cordaeana*.

Classification

There are about 6,000 species of liverworts, however, the greatest diversity is in the southern hemisphere. Two very small but distinctive groups are not included in this book even though both of these are found in our area, as they are very rare. Both are considered primitive members and are placed in their own orders (or even subclasses). These are *Takakia* (in the Takakiales) and *Haplomitrium* (in the Haplomitriales).

Additionally, three main groups can be recognized. The Marchantiales (with 500 species) are thalloid liverworts with complex internal gametophytic structure. They have surface pores on their thalli and various markings on the upper surface. They produce reduced sporophytes usually elevated on gametophytic stalks. The setae do not elongate.

The Metzgeriales (with 400 species) are also thalloid liverworts, but with little or no internal gametophytic differentiation. The thalli are smooth and do not have surface pores. They produce sporophytes from beneath a perianth-like flap of thallus tissue that are similar to those of the leafy liverworts and have capsules elevated on hyaline setae. There seem to be intermediates between this group and the leafy liverworts.

The Jungermanniales, or leafy liverworts with 5000 or so species are by far the largest group, with about 85% of our species belonging here. This group has ranked leaves and setae that elongate and terminate in round (or elliptic), four-valved capsules.

Key to the Recognition of Species*

* Names in parentheses are additional, common species not included in this book.

1. Plants consisting of a flat, dorsi-ventral thallus, without differentiated leaves and stem..2

1. Plants consisting of a stem and leaves arranged in 2 or 3 ranks...............6

2. Thalli covered with short cilia, these forming a fuzzy, pubescent covering; lamina 1 cell thick .... *Apometzgeria pubescens* (pg. 152)

2. Thalli without short cilia, shiny, reticulate or greasy; lamina more than 1 cell thick at least near midrib...3

3. Thallus with pores in upper surface, dull; female sex organs elevated on stalks . 4

3. Thallus without pores in upper surface, shiny to oily; female sex organs on upper thallus surface.....................................*Pellia neesiana* (pg. 153)

4. Upper thallus surface with conspicuous hexagonal pattern, pores easily seen with naked eye. Aromatic when crushed .... *Conocephalum conicum* (pg. 154)

4. Upper thallus surface without or with faint hexagonal pattern; pores evident only with a hand lens. Without aroma when crushed . . . 5

5. Thalli about 0.5 cm across, without flaring gemma cups on upper surface; male sex organs sessile on upper surface. On calcareous soil, especially common along river banks . . . *Preissia quadrata* (pg. 153)

5. Thalli about 1 cm across, often with round, flaring gemma cups on upper surface; male sex organs elevated on stalks. On moist organic soil, especially common after fire . . . *Marchantia polymorpha* (pg. 154)

6. Leaves complicate-bilobed, consisting of upper and lower lobes . . . 7

6. Leaves not complicate-bilobed, consisting of flat lamina . . . 14

7. Upper lobe smaller than lower one . . . 8

7. Upper lobe larger (and covering) lower one . . . 11

8. Lower lobe narrow, longer than broad, with a light, central group of elongate cells forming a costa-like band to 1/2 lobe length . . . *Diplophyllum albicans* (pg. 150)

8. Lower lobe broad, as long as broad, without differentiated central group of elongate cells, these round and similar to outer ones . . . 9

9. Leaves coarsely serrate. Common on coastal tree trunks and logs . . . *Scapania bolanderi* (pg. 149)

9. Leaves entire or with a few fine teeth. Common in fens or on rock outcrops . . 10

10. Large plants without gemmae; leaves with a highly arched ventral keel. In fens . . . (*Scapania paludicola*)

10. Small plants with conspicuous, brown, terminal gemmae; leaves with a straight (or nearly so) ventral keel. In calcareous rock crevices or on logs . . . *Scapania cuspiduligera* (pg. 149)

11. Under leaves absent . . . *Radula complanata* (pg. 150)

11. Under leaves present, large . . . 12

12. Lower lobes helmet shaped, with a central cavity, attached by a narrow constriction . . . *Frullania nisquallensis* (pg. 152)

12. Lower lobes tongue-shaped, without a central cavity (flat with recurved upper margins), attached directly along basal edge . . . 13

13. Lower lobes about half the width of the under leaves; under leaves markedly frilled and wavy along decurrent portion . . . *Porella cordaeana* (pg. 151)

13. Lower lobes about the same width as the under leaves; under leaves entire and straight along decurrent portion . . . *Porella navicularis* (pg. 151)

14. Leaves rounded, without any evidence of lobes, cilia, or points . . . 15

14. Leaves pointed, with either 2-4 lobes, numerous cilia, or shallow points . . 18

15. Leaf margins bordered by differentiated cells . . . 16

15. Leaf margins bordered by cells similar to those throughout leaf . . . 17

16. Plants blue-green; leaves opposite to one another. Found on calcareous rock outcrops . . . (*Arnellia fennica*)

16. Plants olive-green; leaves alternate to one another. Found on *Sphagnum* hummocks . . . *Mylia anomala* (pg. 148)

17. Plants purple-brown, odoriferous; leaves concave, nearly transverse. Emergent in seeps and streams. leaves concave, nearly transverse . . . (*Solenostoma cordifolium*)

17. Plants olive- to reddish-green, without distinctive odour; leaves flat, succubous. On mesic rocks or moist logs . . . (*Jamesoniella autumnalis**)

*Entire margined forms of *Plagiochila asplenioides* key here as well, these have both postical and antical leaf margins strongly reflexed downward).

18. Plants white-green; uppermost leaves frilly and undulate, not consistently 2, 3 or 4 lobed . . . . *Lophozia incisa* (pg. 146)

18. Plants yellow- to dark-green; uppermost leaves 2, 3 or 4 lobed, or ciliate . . 19

19. Leaves hand-shaped, divided into 3-many ciliate appendages 20

19. Leaves oval to tongue-shaped, divided into 2-4 broad lobes or with marginal teeth 22

20. Leaves with 3 lobes . . . . *Lepidozia reptans* (pg. 147)

20. Leaves with numerous cilia 21

21. Plants relatively large, loosely attached to their substrate; stems erect to ascending. Common in arctic and alpine tundra, and subarctic forest-tundra, frequent on boulder slopes . . . . *Ptilidium ciliare* (pg. 145)

21. Plants relatively small, firmly attached to their substrate; stems prostrate. Common in boreal forest on wood . . . . *Ptilidium pulcherrimum* (pg. 145)

22. Leaves with lower and upper margins strongly reflexed, margins with numerous teeth (or nearly entire) . . . . *Plagiochila asplenioides* (pg. 148)

22. Leaves with lower and upper margins erect to plane; margins entire (but leaves 2-4 lobed) 23

23. Leaves divided in upper portion into 4 lobes . . . . *Barbilophozia lycopodioides* (pg. 147)

23. Leaves divided in upper portion into 2 or 3 lobes 24

24. Leaves divided into 3 lobes, in this species the lowermost lobe larger than the 2 upper ones . . . . (*Tritomaria quinquedentata*)

24. Leaves divided into 2 shallow to deep equal lobes 25

25. Leaves 2-3 times as long as wide, divided 1/2-2/3 their length into 2 falcate-secund lobes. Large plants of coastal forests . . . . (*Herbertus aduncus*)

25. Leaves 1-1.5 times as long as wide, divided 1/5 to 1/3 their length into 2 erect to spreading lobes. Small plants of boreal forest, fens or tundra 26

26. Upper leaves with conspicuous yellow gemmae. Found on rotting logs in moist boreal-montane forests . . . . *Lophozia ventricosa* (pg. 146)

26. Upper leaves without gemmae. Found in seepages and tundra 27

27. Leaves succubous and obliquely inserted, loose, not over-lapping. Small plants of alpine seeps and lower elevation peatlands . . . . (*Gymnocolea inflata*)

27. Leaves transversely inserted, imbricate, erect. Small plants of alpine tundra . . 28

28. Plants silvery-gray, especially the leaf margins; worm-like, with leaf lobes imbricate . . . . (*Gymnomitrion corallioides*)

28. Plants black to reddish-black; leaf lobes somewhat spreading . . . . (*Marsupella sphacelata*)

x 2

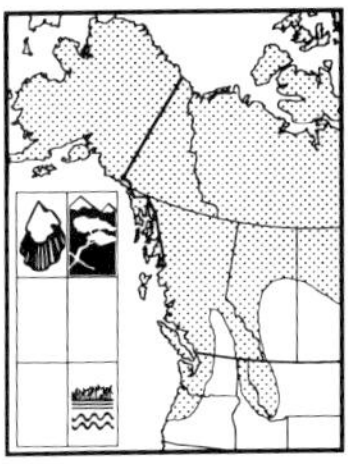

Ptilidium ciliare, like *P. pulcherrimum*, has leaves margined by numerous cilia. *Ptilidium ciliare* is more northern in distribution, common in arctic and alpine tundra and in subarctic treed tundra. It grows in loosely attached mats, with the stems ascending and easily removed from their substrate. It rarely occurs on logs like *P. pulcherrimum*. At higher elevations it occurs in depressions and in pockets between acidic boulders, often on rock slides that are not too dry. When wet, it is extremely slippery and we advise caution before jumping on to its rocks!

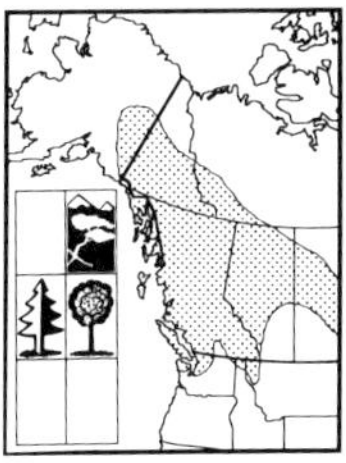

x 2

Ptilidium pulcherrimum forms flat mats on wood that are hard to remove with one's fingers. The plants are reddish-brown and appear as dense, fuzzy, spreading patches, usually on decorticated logs. The leaves are hand-shaped, that is, they have a round central area that is broken into several (four-six) ciliate lobes. These are diagnostic for the genus in our area. Near the coast and at higher elevations *P. californicum* is the common species. *Blepharostoma trichophyllum* is smaller and has three fingered leaves (divided to the base). *Ptilidium ciliare* is about twice the size, and forms loose, ascending mats in rock crevices and mesic tundra depressions.

x 4

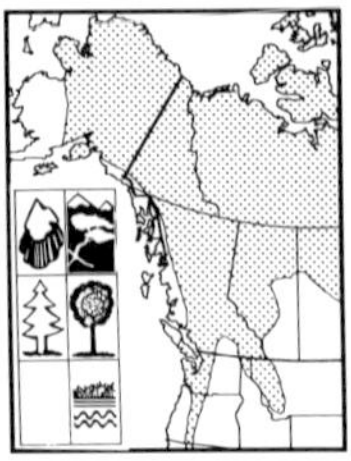

Lophozia ventricosa. *Lophozia* is the largest genus of hepatics in western North America, with about 25 species in our area. In general, the genus is characterized by two-lobed, obliquely to transversely inserted leaves. Most of the small species have very small or no under leaves and the rhizoids are scattered evenly along the stem. Gemmae are often present at the tips of the younger leaves and the plants vary around green and brown (rarely are they whitish or blackish). Several species of smaller Lophozias commonly occur on rotting logs in boreal, montane, and subalpine forests. *Lophozia ventricosa* has conspicuous yellowish gemmae; *L. longidens* has dark reddish-brown gemmae. *Lophozia excisa* is green, often has perianths and rarely produces gemmae, while *L. porphyroleuca* has dark reddish stems and commonly has perianths and no gemmae. *Tritomaria exsectiformis* is similar in producing dark red gemmae, but it has asymmetric, three-lobed leaves.

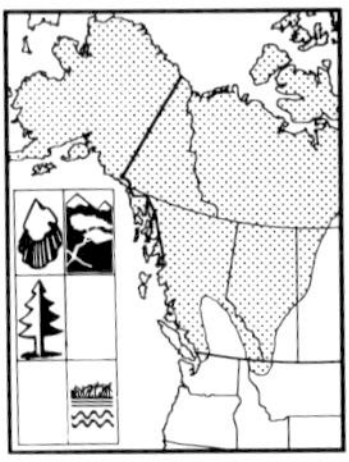

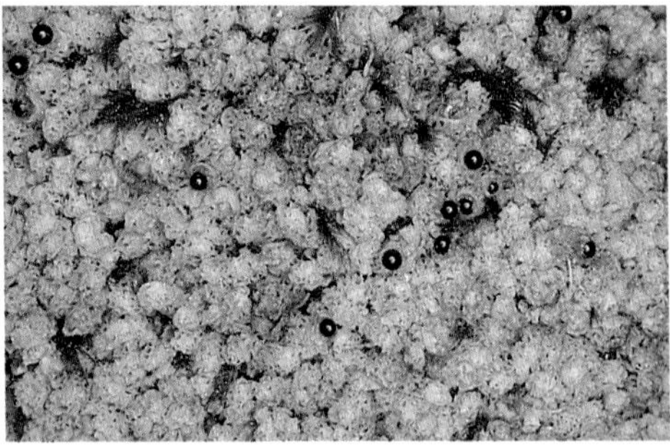

x 2

Lophozia incisa is a beautiful whitish-green hepatic with exceptionally frilly leaves. Lower on the stems, the leaves are two-lobed, but near the apices of the plants, they are variously lobed and undulate. The delicate appearance and light colour are due to extremely large, thin-walled leaf cells. Sporophytes are commonly produced. This species and *L. opacifolia* occur on decaying logs and organic soils in boreal and montane forests. The latter species appears to extend farther into the alpine. Another somewhat similar genus common in our area is *Tritomaria* which has three-lobed leaves. Most *Tritomaria* species (there are six in our area) have asymmetric leaves, with the upper lobe smallest, and the lower lobe the largest. Under leaves are lacking. *Tritomaria scitula* has three evenly lobed leaves and grows in calcareous rock crevices. *Tritomaria exsectiformis* has decidedly unevenly lobed leaves, brown gemmae and mostly occurs on logs, while *T. quinquedentata* has the lower lobe much larger, concave and it cups the two smaller upper ones.

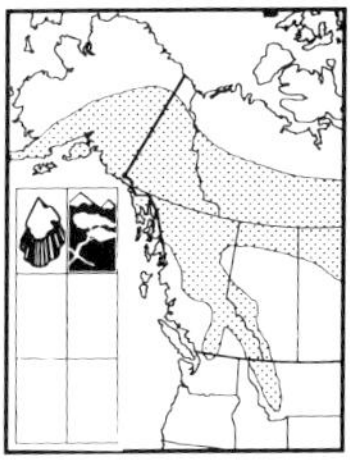

Barbilophozia lycopodioides. Few hepatics have four-lobed leaves as does this species. Here the leaves are frilly in appearance; each lobe terminated by a short apiculus. *Barbilophozia lycopodioides* is a large species (3-4 mm across) that is often very abundant in mesic subalpine forests. Several species can look like this species. Often growing with it or forming extensive carpets in similar habitats (especially in the Rockies) is *B. hatcheri*, which is slightly smaller, has less undulating leaves and reddish masses of gemmae. At higher elevations nearer the coast (eg. Glacier National Park and westward), *B. floerkii* with three-lobes is often very abundant and *B. kunzeana* with largely two-lobed leaves can look superficially similar. All these species are large, showy, have succubous leaves and well-developed under leaves. They are often considered in the genus *Lophozia*.

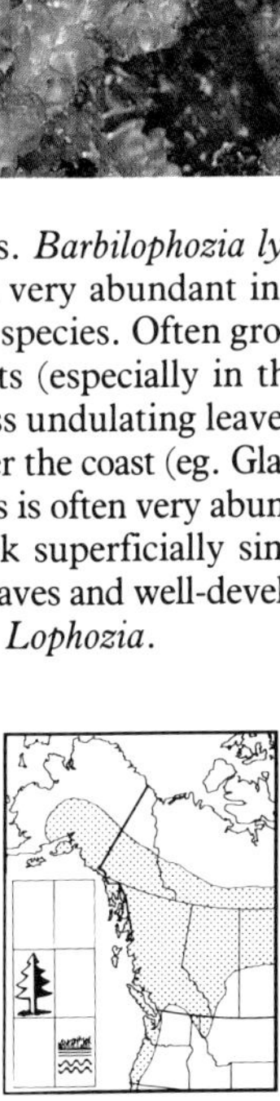

x 3

Lepidozia reptans is a small leafy hepatic with three-lobed, incubous leaves. The leaves are generally not close together and each appears as a small club-shaped hand (with three fingers curled downward). The leaves are dissected by the three lobes to about half way. *Bazzania* species, occurring only in wet coastal forests, have three-lobed incubous leaves, but the lobes are shallow and the plants much larger. *Calypogeia* species have incubous leaves that are often notched at the apex, whereas two very tiny species of *Kurzia* and *Blepharostoma trichophyllum* all have leaves divided to their base into three thread-like lobes. *Lepidozia reptans* is common throughout the area, occurring on rotten logs, stumps and wood; it often grows with *Tetraphis pellucida* and *Pohlia nutans*. These species all occupy rotting wood in an advanced stage of decay: if you can kick the stump and don't hurt your foot, *Lepidozia* will almost certainly be there!

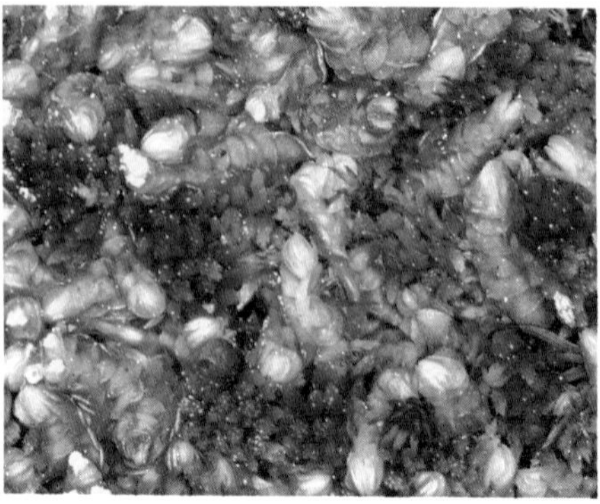

x 1.5

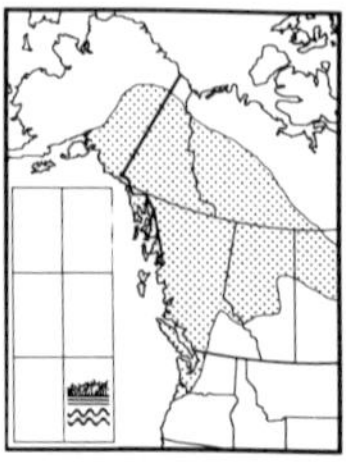

Mylia anomala has rounded (non-lobed) leaves with a distinctive border of larger cells. The leaves are concave, succubous and become erect-appressed when dry. The plants are brown-green and often have conspicuous, yellow gemmae on the leaf margins. No under leaves are present. This species occurs commonly on *Sphagnum fuscum* hummocks. No other hepatic with non-lobed, succubous leaves occurs here; it is rare elsewhere. In coastal forests, *M. taylorii* occurs on rotting logs. It is similar to *M. anomala* but is at least twice as large and has a carmine-red to purple-brown pigmentation. Microscopically, both these species have strong trigones.

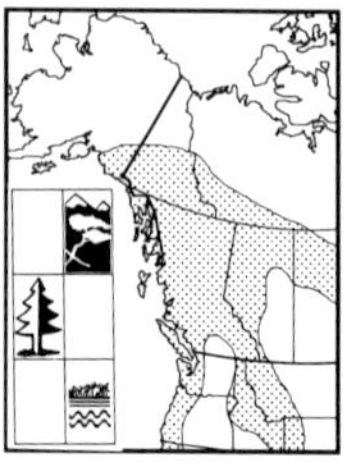

x 2

Plagiochila asplenioides (=*P. asplenioides* subsp. *porelloides* or *P. porelloides*). *Plagiochila* is one of the largest of the hepatic genera, with 500-600 species, that are almost entirely tropical in distribution. There they are large and beautiful plants. We have one (or maybe two) small, undistinguished species that are widespread and boreal in distribution, plus several larger (more distinguished) coastal rain forest species. *Plagiochila asplenioides* is in the former group. It has succubous, toothed, elliptic leaves. The upper and especially the lower leaf margins are reflexed backward, giving the plants a distinctive look. The leaves are antically (on the top) decurrent. Few hepatics have toothed leaf margins. This species occurs in fen depressions, calcareous rock crevices and associated humus and on soil covered banks. It has a wide tolerance for substrate chemistry. Arctic-alpine plants have nearly entire leaves.

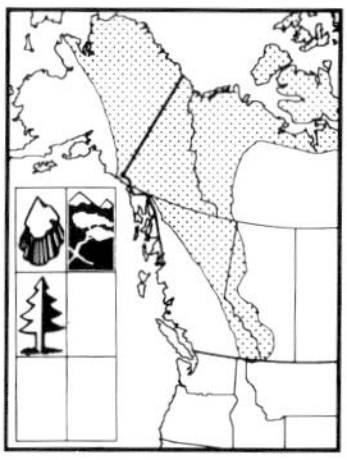

Scapania cuspiduligera is one of about 15-20 small species of *Scapania*. It is found infrequently, probably because of its small size, but is not uncommon in calcareous crevices of the Rockies and northward. The masses of dark-brown gemmae produced on the young terminal leaves, small size (stems 1-2.5 mm across), entire leaf margins, and upper lobes that spread stiffly away from the slightly larger lower lobes are characteristic features. These small Scapanias are difficult to name without use of a compound microscope and appropriate technical literature (see Schuster Vol. III as a source).

x 2.5

Scapania bolanderi ranks as one of the most common epiphytic liverworts of the lowland coastal rain forests. It has conspicuous serrations on both the smaller upper lobes and larger lower lobes and often forms extensive mats on tree trunks and logs. *Scapania americana* is similar and occurs on rock surfaces. There are many species of this genus, however *S. bolanderi* is usually easily recognized by distribution, habitat and toothed leaf margins. Farther north, several additional species occur that are superficially similar; these can be identified only with careful study.

x 5.5

Diplophyllum albicans. The complicate-bilobed leaves of this species, with the lower lobes larger than the upper ones, are features of this genus as well as of the genus *Scapania*. Whereas in the latter group of species the lobes are about as long as wide, in *Diplophyllum* they are two to four times longer than broad. *Diplophyllum albicans* has sharply pointed leaves and several rows of cells at the centre of the lobes, especially the lower ones, that are much longer than broad, of a light colour and form a differentiated costa-like area. No other liverwort in our area has this feature. Although several additional species of *Diplophyllum* occur in our area, *D. albicans* is the most common and is the only one with the differentiated cells. It is common on moist, non-calcareous rocks west of the Rockies, especially near the coast. A hand lens is needed to see the critical feature of this species.

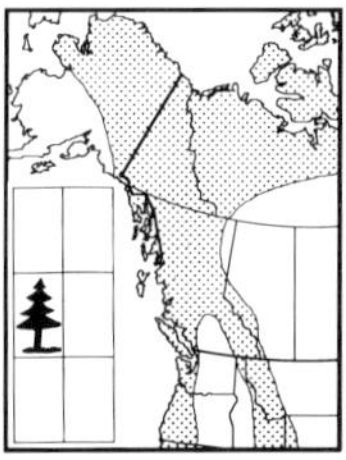

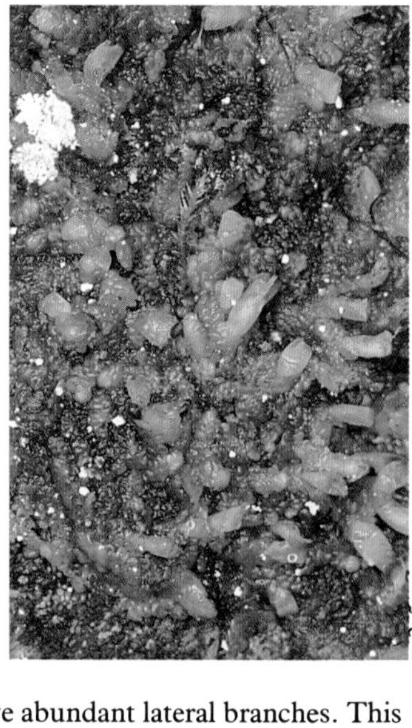

x 3.5

Radula complanata has incubous complicate-bilobed leaves with the upper lobe larger and shielding the under lobe. This lower lobe is attached to the upper lobe along the postical edge. Under leaves are absent and distinguish species of this genus from those of *Frullania* and *Porella*, as well as from the largely tropical Lejeuneaceae. *Radula complanata* has flattened perianths, which look like spades. The plants are a conspicuous yellow-green color and occur on mesic cliff faces, usually relatively tightly attached to the rock surface. Near the coast it is a common epiphyte. There are often gemmae present on the antical edge of the upper lobes and the plants often have abundant lateral branches. This species is found in northern tundra areas, southward in the Rockies and westward to the coast. It is most common west of the cordillera, especially in the humid interior forests of British Columbia.

Porella cordaeana has large, rounded, upper leaves in two ranks and tongue-shaped, smaller under leaves in one rank. The upper leaves have a large upper lobe and when viewed from the bottom side of the stem, have a small lower lobe. This lobed condition of the upper two ranks of leaves is termed complicate-bilobed; not to be confused with two, three or four-lobed leaves where the individual leaves terminate in two, three or four points. *Porella*, with about six local species, is largely restricted to the humid west coast rain forests. There it occurs on tree trunks, and farther inland on montane rock outcrops. Both the lower lobes and under leaves are tongue shaped and are obvious with the naked eye. *Frullania* has helmet-shaped lower lobes and notched under leaves. *Porella cordaeana* has the lower lobes long and decurrent and the under leaves about twice as wide as the under lobes.

x .5

Porella navicularis is quite similar to *P. cordaeana*, but is differentiated by having the lower lobes not or only shortly decurrent and under leaves about as wide as the lower lobes. Whereas *P. cordaeana* is found from the Rockies westward, *P. navicularis* occurs only as an epiphyte in coastal rain forests (one station is known from Idaho). As well, *P. cordaeana* has a few teeth along the basal margins of the under leaves while those of *P. navicularis* are entire. A third species, also fairly common on rocks and trees in coastal lowland rain forests from California to British Columbia, is *P. roellii*. It is similar to *P. navicularis* but it differs in having under leaves about twice as wide as the lower lobes and the cell walls of the leaves without their corners bulging into the cell lumens, whereas in *P. navicularis* the cell corners have the walls bulging inward. In interior British Columbia *P. cordaeana* is common.

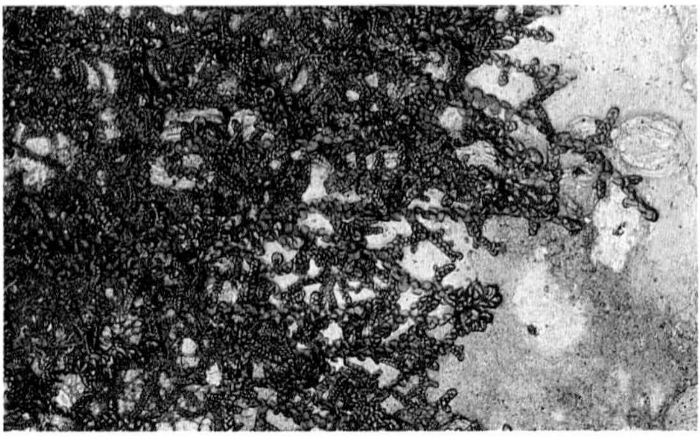

x 2

Frullania nisquallensis. Species of *Frullania*, like those of *Porella*, have complicate-bilobed leaves with the lower lobe much smaller, (and hidden) the upper one. *Frullania* has the lower lobe differentiated into a helmet, like a Roman soldier's, or a sac-shaped structure attached by a narrow constriction to the base of the upper lobe. This structure can fill with water during wet periods and perhaps functions as a mechanism for prolonged water storage. *Porella* has tongue shaped lower lobes as well as under leaves, whereas the under leaves of *Frullania* are notched at their apex. *F. nisquallensis* is the most common of several species that occur on the west coast in rain forests, mostly epiphytic on *Acer*, *Alnus* and *Betula* trunks. The dark reddish plants forming sparsely arranged, creeping stems are typical. *Porella* species are much larger and are not attached as firmly to their substrate along the entire stem. Although two additional species are known from east of the Rockies, they are very rare. *Frullania bolanderi*, of more southern distribution, has stems with most leaves broken off.

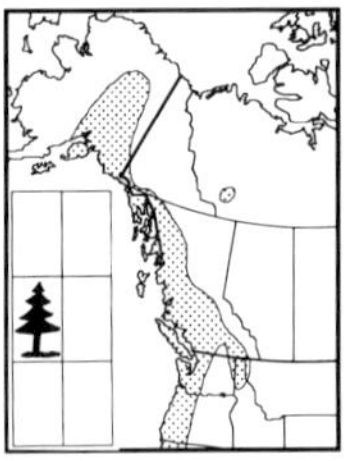

x 2

Apometzgeria pubescens is easily known by slender, delicate ribbon-like thalli occurring on mesic, usually somewhat acidic rock surfaces. It has short hairs (cilia) covering the entire thallus, thus the name *A. pubescens*. No other thalloid hepatic in our area has these hair-like structures. The thalli are light-green to almost whitish-green in colour. They have a strong, conspicuous midrib and the lamina of the thallus is one cell thick throughout. This species is known only from west of the Rockies, where it is not uncommon in mesic interior and humid coastal forests. *Metzgeria conjugata* is similar, but lacks the abundant surface cilia. It is frequent near the coast.

x 2.5

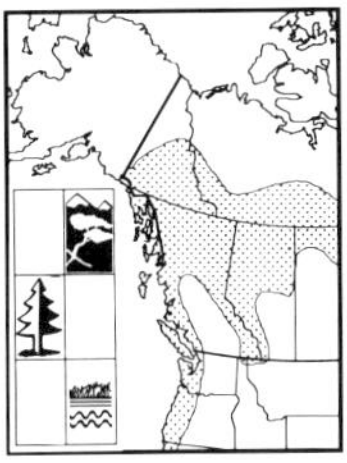

Pellia neesiana is a thallose liverwort. Unlike *Marchantia*, *Preissia* and relatives that are coarse and rough looking due to pores and internal differentiation of tissues, this genus is delicate and shiny, with no apparent pore structure or markings on the upper surfaces. The thallus has a central flattened midrib several cells thick which gradually thins to one cell thick margins. This species is unisexual; the antheridia (males) are produced in small blisters located along the midrib, while the archegonia (females) are produced beneath a terminal flap of tissue (the involucre). Capsules are spherical and are produced on hyaline, short-lived stalks; they open by four longitudinal valves. Only *Aneura pinguis* is similar; it has thalli several cells thick from centre to edge, has an oily look and the capsules are elongate. It grows in calcareous fen pools and on calcareous soil, while *Pellia* occurs on inorganic soil along streams, on lake margins and associated with sedge hummocks in swampy areas, often covered by dead leaves from the previous year. *P. endiviifolia*, with the involucre consisting of a complete, circular ring, is a second species more common east of the Rockies.

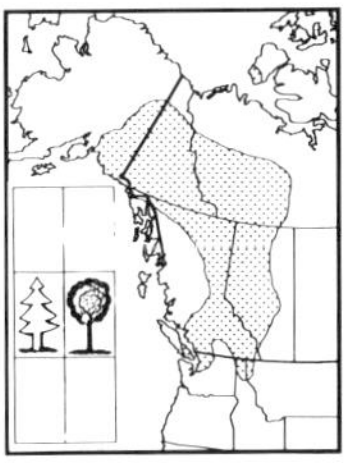

x 2.5

Preissia quadrata is similar to *Marchantia polymorpha*, but the thallus is smaller and has a grey tone versus the pure green of *Marchantia*. The pores in the upper surface have four cells that bulge into the hole - thus the name quadrata. These are characteristic of this species. The female portions of the plants (archegonia) are raised on short stalks (about 1-2 cm high). These are positioned under a round cap that usually has crossed ridges on top (thus quadrata as well). *Preissia* occurs on calcareous, mineral soil along river and stream banks, calcareous rock crevices and soil ledges under overhanging rock ledges.

x.3

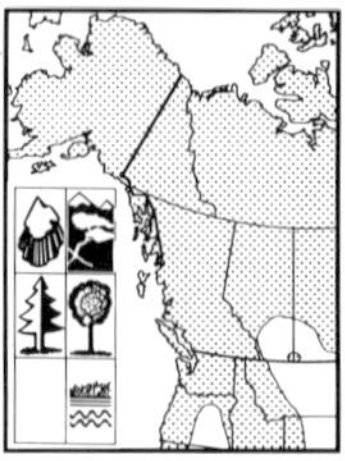

Marchantia polymorpha. This is one of our largest thalloid liverworts. Pores are obvious on the thallus and gemmae cups are often present near the edges of the thallus. The species is unisexual; male plants have lobed discs produced on stalks (about 1-3 cm high) and female plants have finger-like lobes extending outward from the tops of stalks. Sporophytes are produced from beneath these finger-like projections once fertilization takes place. *Conocephalum conicum*, with a distinctive hexagonal pattern surrounding each pore, is rare in our area except near the coast. In *Marchantia*, the hexagonal pattern is quite indistinct. *Preissia quadrata* is somewhat similar, but looks thicker, is overall smaller and has only female portions raised on stalks, these without finger-like projections. *Marchantia* grows in swampy areas or often can be very abundant after a fire (including old camp fires). In some areas it is a garden weed; it is a pernicious weed in greenhouses and tree nurseries.

x 1.5

Conocephalum conicum is the largest thalloid hepatic in our area, and when well-developed has a thallus up to 1 cm across and 9-10 cm long. When poorly developed, it is about the same size as *Marchantia* and *Preissia*. It is determined without difficulty by the presence of a well marked hexagonal pattern on the upper thallus surface. In the centre of each of these hexagons is a pore. The specialized branch that bears the sporangia is conic, hence the name of the hepatic. Both *Marchantia* and *Preissia*, as well as several additional less common species have these markings, but they are never very prominent. *Conocephalum* is a rich yellow-green colour, has a very nice aromatic odor when crushed, and has sessile antheridiophores. It is not as common as *Marchantia* in northwestern America, here occurring on constantly moist sandy substrates or on acidic rock surfaces; usually under overhanging rock cliffs near waterfalls and rushing streams. It is more abundant west of the Rockies. Perhaps the name "coneheads" will amuse only Saturday Night Live aficionados!

LICHENS

Lichens
Their Structure and Biology

Definition

Lichens are fungi that have established a symbiotic relationship with certain species of algae. In this type of relationship the fungus and alga live together and both generally benefit from the association. The fungus provides structural support to the alga by surrounding the algal cells with strands of hyphae. It also provides nutrients absorbed from the substrate and a relatively stable microenvironment for the algal cells to exist. The algae in turn provide carbohydrates produced in photosynthesis (the green pigment, chlorophyll, contained in the algal cells utilizes sunlight to produce carbohydrates from carbon dioxide and water). The fungus and alga have evolved together in such a way that an equilibrium exists, whereby the fungus does not utilize all of the carbohydrates made by the alga, while the alga derives structural integrity from the fungus. Most lichens derive their shape from the fungal component (often called the mycobiont), with the algal component (the photobiont) restricted to a single layer of cells. The process of the fungus and alga joining to form a lichen is called lichenization. When a lichen is separated in the laboratory into its fungal and algal components and these cultured separately, they grow perfectly well. Each forms its characteristic fungal or algal form. When these same components are placed together under a variety of conditions, the original lichen rarely reforms. Lichenization in nature has only been demonstrated a few times and still forms one of the great mysteries of biology. However, lichenization has often been demonstrated in the laboratory by culturing ascospores with their respective algae.

Some of the species of algae that exist as a photobiont can also be found as free-living organisms. About 30 genera of algae have been found in lichens, but the unicellular species of the green alga, *Trebouxia*, is by far the most common. Blue-green algae (cyanobacteria) such as *Nostoc* and *Stigonema* are also common algal partners in several lichens, including species of *Peltigera* and *Leptogium*. Within the lichen body (termed a thallus), algae reproduce mainly by mitotic cell division. Sexual reproduction of the photobiont may occur but has rarely been observed in the lichen thallus. Identification of the lichen alga is often difficult because the regular growth pattern is altered in the lichenized state. For example, chains of the filamentous green alga, *Trentepohlia*, may be separated into individual cells by hyphal branches of fungi and mistaken for unicellular algae.

There are about 15,000 to 20,000 species of lichens in the world, although many more names have been proposed. The names given to these lichens apply to their fungal symbionts and hence all lichens belong to the Kingdom Fungi. In almost all lichens the fungus is an ascomycete (like the cup fungi) with spores formed in sacs or asci. In a small number of species the fungus is a basidiomycete (a mushroom or shelf fungus), where the spores are formed on club-shaped basidia.

Lichens can grow almost everywhere in the world. Some species are able to colonize the very hot, harsh environments of deserts and others can survive in the cold, snowfree, alpine habitats where most other plants are not able to exist. In these extreme environments, crustose lichens may grow only a fraction of a millimetre a year and reach several hundred years in age, whereas foliose lichens growing in temperate or tropical areas may grow 1 centimetre or more per year. Moisture is essential for growth of lichens. Lichens act like a sponge and absorb water over their surface area. In the same way that they absorb water, they also dry out rapidly and become dormant. When dormant, the physiological process of photosynthesis stops while respiration is greatly arrested. Studies have shown that lichens that have been dormant for up to several years are capable of physiological function when again moistened. Dependence on moisture and humidity for optimum growth is one reason why lichens are abundant in mountain cloud forests and in areas influenced by fog and oceanic climates. The cooler temperatures of these areas are optimal for food producing lichen photosynthesis which may function best at temperatures less than 15°C, while food consuming respiration is limited at these temperatures.

Structural Features

The Thallus

A typical lichen thallus can be divided into three main layers - cortex, algal layer and medulla (Fig. 16). The cortex is specialized tissue composed of

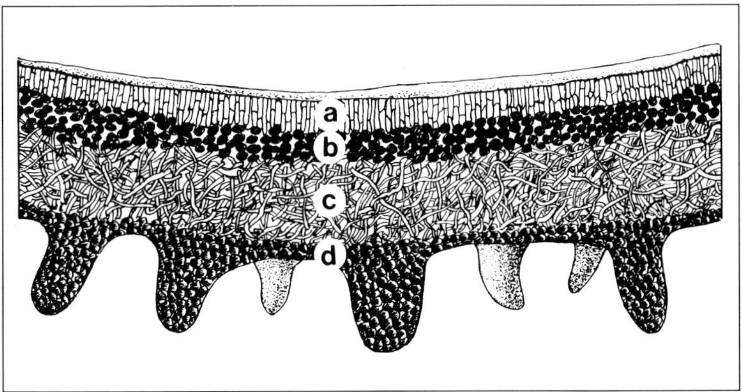

Fig. 16. The thallus structure a) upper cortex, b) algal layer, c) medulla and d) lower cortex.

compact fungal cells that forms a protective covering for the lichen. Fruticose lichens are enclosed by an outer cortex, while most foliose lichens have their outer surface covered by differentiated upper and lower cortices. Crustose and squamulose lichens have only an upper cortex.

The lower cortex, when present, usually produces rhizines (Fig. 17) or short hairs; these usually serve to attach the lichen to its substrate. Tomentum (Fig. 18), consisting of a felt-like mat of hyphae covers the lower surface of a few

Fig. 17. The simple rhizines of *Parmelia sulcata*.

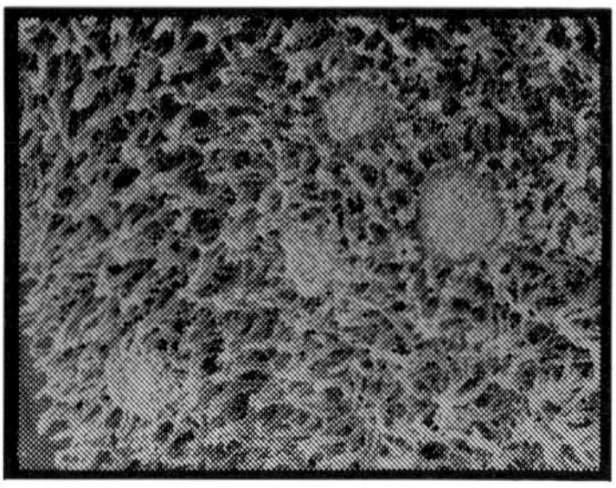

Fig. 18. The a) tomentum and b) papillae of *Nephroma resupinatum*.

foliose species (i.e. *Peltigera*, *Lobaria* and *Nephroma*). The algal layer is located just beneath the upper or outer cortex and contains algal cells and fungal hyphae. The algal cells may form a more or less continuous layer or occur in scattered clumps. In gelatinous lichens such as *Leptogium* species and in some filamentous fruticose lichens, the algae are not in a layer, but are distributed throughout the thallus and contribute significantly to the shape of the lichen. The medulla is composed only of fungal hyphae. It has been thought that these hyphae absorb and store most of the water and nutrients for the lichen. In some fruticose lichens, such as *Usnea*, the fungal hyphae of the medulla give support to the thallus. Several different structures can be found on the surface of lichens. These include cyphellae (Fig. 19) that

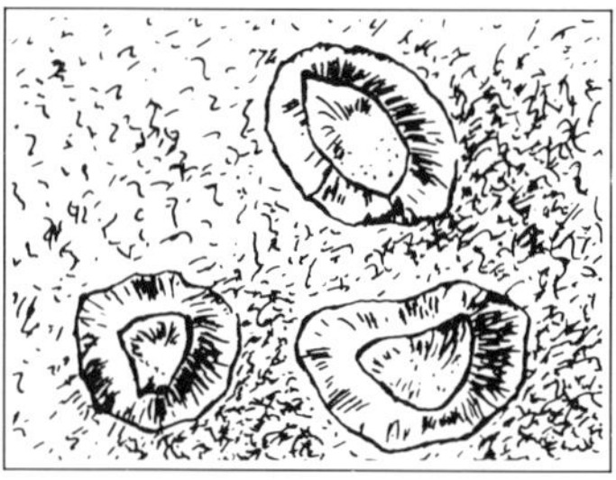

Fig. 19. The cyphellae of *Sticta fuliginosa*.

Fig. 20. The a) pseudocyphellae and b) marginal projections of *Cetraria islandica*.

are well structured pores, and pseudocyphellae (Fig. 20) that are simple breaks or depressions in the cortex. The lower cortex of species of *Sticta* have numerous cyphellae, while pseudocyphellae occur on the outer cortex of some species of *Bryoria*, the upper or lower cortex of *Cetraria* and the lower cortex of *Pseudocyphellaria*. Cephalodia are warts that contain a second algal species. Normally these warts contain a cyanobacterial species (e.g. *Nostoc*) that has the ability to change atmospheric nitrogen (N_2) to ammonium (NH_4^+) and occurs in species where the photobiont is a green alga (e.g. *Peltigera aphthosa*).

Growth Forms

Lichens are classified largely on the basis of the structure and development of the fruiting body (ascocarp) of the fungus. However, the form of the lichen thallus has been traditionally used to divide lichens into three major groups, namely crustose, foliose and fruticose.

Crustose Lichens

Crustose lichens are attached over their entire thallus to the substrate. They lack a lower cortex but most have an upper cortex, algal layer, and a medulla of fungal hyphae that penetrate the substrate. Many crustose species occur on rocks (saxicolous) and have a distinct, however, thin thallus. Endolithic lichens, as with some species of *Verrucaria*, have a thallus that exists just beneath the surface of the rock and only fruiting bodies are visible on the rock surface. Other crustose lichens produce a thin thallus on wood or bark (corticolous), while endophloic lichens have a thallus contained entirely within the surface layers of the bark. Some crustose species have a hypothallus, a thin layer of usually black, nonlichenized hyphae, that extends beyond the main thallus. The most active growth takes place along the margin of the lichen thallus, and in some crustose lichens a network of cracks develops in the older, central portion of the thallus; these thalli are termed rimose or rimose-areolate (Fig. 21). When the edges of the thallus are free from the substrate, the crustose lichen is termed squamulose. Many of these squamulose lichens tend to be composed of numerous small lobes and occur on bare soil.

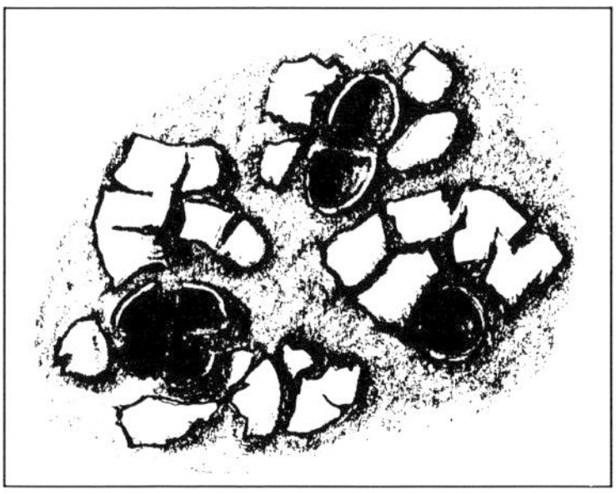

Fig. 21. The areolate thallus of *Rhizocarpon geographicum*.

Foliose Lichens

Foliose lichens, like crustose lichens, are bilaterally symmetric. As the name implies they may be leaf-like or they have distinct lobes. Unlike crustose lichens however, they are usually attached to their substrate by rhizines produced from a differentiated lower cortex. Although there are a few foliose lichens that do not have a lower cortex (e.g. *Peltigera*) or rhizines (e.g. *Hypogymnia*), this rule is generally true. In most foliose lichens, the layer of algal cells is located beneath the upper cortex. Below the algal layer is the medulla, which is composed only of fungal hyphae and this determines, to a large extent, the thickness of the lichen thallus. A lower cortex, similar to the upper cortex, but usually of a different colour, covers the lower surface of most foliose lichens. A few foliose lichens (e.g. *Collema*) are gelatinous when wet and lack an upper cortex and a distinct algal layer. In these species, the fungal hyphae and algae are intertwined throughout the thallus. Another variation of the foliose growth form is the umbilicate form where the thallus is attached to its substrate by a short stalk originating from a single central point on the lower cortex.

Fruticose Lichens

A fruticose lichen is radially symmetric and thus in transverse section the thallus is more or less round. An outer layer of fungal cells surrounds the algal layer that is usually comprised of clumps of algal cells interspersed among fungal hyphae. A layer consisting solely of fungal hyphae is to the inside of the algal layer. The centre of the thallus may be hollow, or filled with white, cottony fungal hyphae. In the genus *Cladonia*, the thallus is dimorphic with a primary thallus of flat, foliose squamules from which is produced a secondary thallus of fruiting stalks (podetia) that are erect and fruticose. Filamentous fruticose lichens such as *Ephebe* and *Spilonema* take the shape of their filamentous algal symbiont.

Reproduction

Lichens reproduce by producing small propagules or by fragmentation. If you step on a patch of dry *Cladonia* or *Cladina*, many fragments will be produced each of which has the potential to become a new lichen. However, many lichens also produce specialized structures which contain a few algal cells and some fungal hyphae. Two types can be described: soredia and isidia

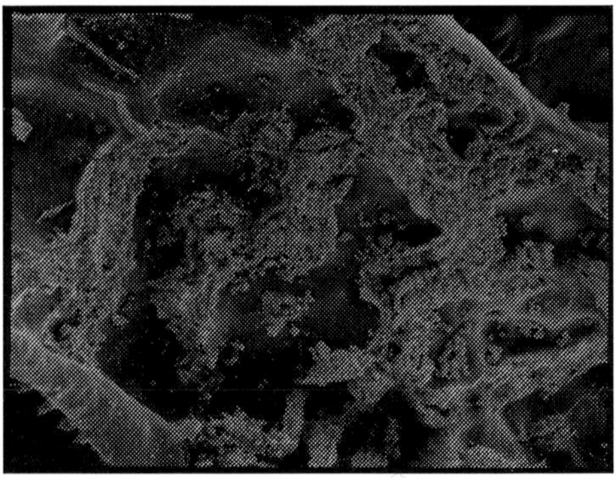

Fig. 22. The laminal soredia of *Parmelia sulcata*.

Fig. 23. Thie isidia of *Usnea hirta*.

(Fig. 22 & 23). Soredia are small granules originating in the algal layer from a crack or small hole in or on the margins of the upper cortex. These patches of soredia may be along the lobe margin (marginal), on the upper cortex (laminal), near the lobe tip (capitate) or in lip-shaped lobes (labrose). Each soredium contains both elements of the lichen and is produced by cell division of the fungal and algal cells. When soredia erupt in confined clumps or along distinct cracks, they form soralia. Isidia are thumb-shaped out-growths of the upper cortex that can occur anywhere on the surface of the thallus. They consist of protuberances of cortical, algal and medullary tissues and can be broken off and dispersed. Like soredia, the isidia arise solely by asexual reproduction. Hence, lichens reproduce as lichens only by asexual means. Sexual reproduction appears confined to the fungus when, in the fruiting body, fungal spores are produced by meiosis. Of course, in order for these to reproduce the lichen, the resultant fungus must be lichenized, a process that has been extremely difficult to demonstrate in nature. However, it probably occurs frequently, as ascospores germinate freely and lichenization is easy to demonstrate in the laboratory. Many crustose lichens must reproduce by this method.

Fungal Reproduction

All lichenized ascomycetes belong to three major groups, each of these producing a distinctive fruiting body or ascocarp. Most lichens produce apothecia, but a few have fruiting bodies that are either perithecia or in other cases pseudothecia. The apothecium is a cup shaped structure consisting of a fertile layer (the disc or hymenium) surrounded by a cup-like exciple. If the outer rim of the exciple forms a margin, termed the proper margin, the apothecium is called lecideine. Some lichen species have an additional layer of fungal hyphae that is associated with algal cells; this layer surrounds the exciple and is termed an amphithecium. The amphithecium together with any cortical tissue is called a thalline margin and forms an apothecium termed lecanorine. The thalline margin and amphithecium arise from and are continuous with the thallus and are the same colour as the thallus. The proper margin and exciple, composed only of fungal hyphae, are usually the same colour as the apothecial disc. Often the proper margin is obscured in older apothecia. The three main layers of the apothecial disc are the epithecium, hymenium and hypothecium (Fig. 24). The epithecium is the top layer of the disc and is formed by the expanded

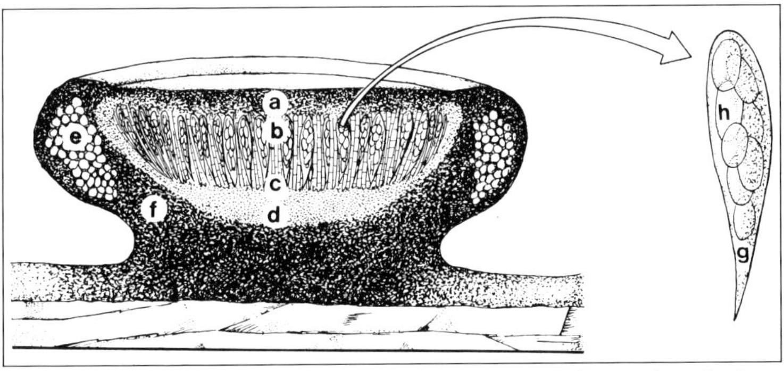

Fig. 24. The lecanorine apothecium a) epithecium, b) hymenium, c) hypothecium, d) exciple, e) algal cells, f) amphithecium, g) ascus and h) spore (ascospore).

tips of the paraphyses. It is often pigmented and gives the disc its colour. The hymenium is the layer of paraphyses and asci. Paraphyses are specialized fungal filaments that surround the asci. The asci are club-shaped sacs in which meiosis occurs and the ascospores develop. Usually each ascus contains eight spores, but the number may vary from one large spore (in *Pertusaria*) up to 100 minute spores (in *Acarospora*). Spores can be hyaline (clear) or brown. They may be

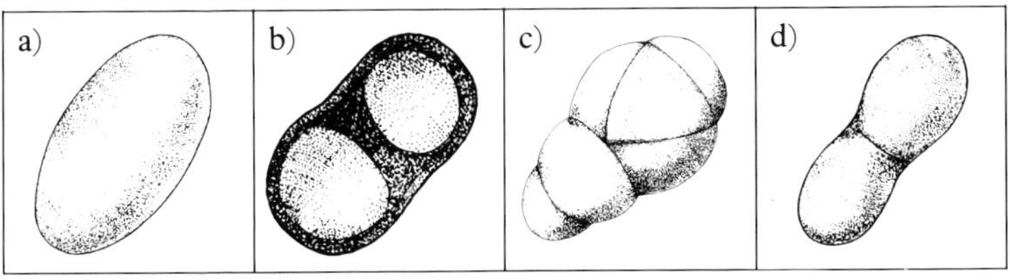

Fig. 25. Spores: a) simple, b) two-celled, c) muriform and d) two-celled asymmetric.

simple (unicellular) or have one to several horizontal septations, or be muriform (with both vertical and horizontal septations) (Fig. 25). The hypothecium is an area of fungal hyphae that gives rise to the hymenium which is directly above it. The colour of the hypothecium is an important diagnostic feature in identification. It can be hyaline, yellowish, red-brown or nearly black. In a few lichens (e.g. *Calicium, Sphaerophorus*), the asci disintegrate leaving a mass of loose spores, this type of apothecium is called a mazaedium. The perithecium is a tiny, pear- or sac-shaped fruiting body that appears as a black dot on the thallus surface. Inside and surrounding the perithecium is the exciple with the hymenial layer containing asci and paraphyses located at the bottom. Spores are released through the pore or ostiole (Fig. 26) at the top of the perithecium. An involucrellum, which is usually black and carbonaceous, is external to the

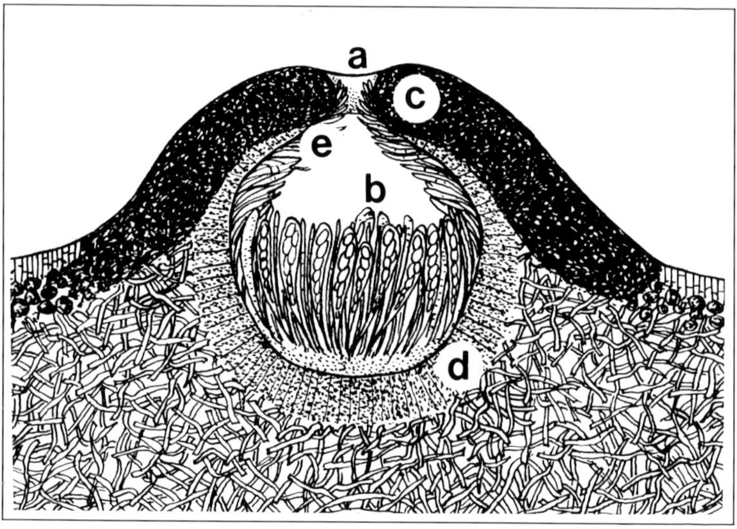

Fig. 26. Perithecium a) ostiole, b) ascus, c) involucrellum, d) exciple and e) periphyses.

exciple and often covers the perithecium. *Dermatocarpon, Verrucaria* and *Staurothele* are genera that have perithecia. Pseudothecia are fruiting bodies that lack a definite hymenium with asci produced in locules among branched hyphae (pseudoparaphyses). Pseudothecia found in species of our area are mostly irregular in shape, often having the shape of a cigar, or others resemble perithecia. Often they look like the irregular ascocarps (sometimes called lirellae) of the genus *Graphis*. However, in this genus a true hymenium is formed in an irregular, nearly linear ascocarp. Pseudothecia are mostly found in crustose genera, however they are also characteristic of *Roccella*, a beautiful fruticose genus. Superficially similar to perithecia are flask shaped structures called pycnidia. These occur immersed in the thallus of most lichens and open through a pore at the surface. Pycnidia do not contain asci, but only hyphae from which are produced numerous small, single-celled spores. These spores are termed conidia. It has been postulated that these may serve either as spermatia in sexual reproduction of the fungus or as propagules that have an asexual reproductive function.

Classification

In the classification of organisms, lichens are placed in the Kingdom Fungi. In the past the fungi were included in the Plant Kingdom, but in recent years the fungi have been classified as a separate Kingdom. The main reason for this change was based on cell wall chemistry. In fungi, chitin is the major component of the cell walls while in plants cellulose is predominant. Fungi have no chlorophyll and are heterotrophic, while plants have chlorophyll and are autotrophic. The Kingdom Fungi has six divisions. Since the fungi of most lichens belong in the Division Ascomycota or sac fungi with spores formed in sacs or asci, the vast majority of the 15,000 lichens known today are classified in this group. Within the Ascomycota, lichens have been separated into two major groups based on the development and structure of the hymenium. The first group, ascolocular lichens (Loculoascomycetidae) are those in which the asci are developed within locules in a specialized vegetative layer. The asci are bitunicate (double-walled) and surrounded by branched pseudoparaphyses. *Arthonia patellulata* is the only species of this group described in this book. The majority of lichens belong to the second group, the Ascomycetidae or ascohymenial lichens, in which the hymenial layer is developed directly from fungal hyphae, with the supporting hyphae differentiating to form true unbranched paraphyses and the tissue of the exciple. The asci are functionally unitunicate (single-walled). Within this group are the "Pyrenomycetes" that produce perithecia, as in the Verrucariales and the "Discomycetes" that produce apothecia like those of the Lecanorales. Most of our lichen species are classified in the Lecanorales. There are a small number of lichenized Basidomycetes or club fungi which have spores produced on club-shaped basidia. Here the lichen fungus resembles a mushroom or shelf fungus and the algae are concentrated in special tissues or lobes near the base of the fruiting body (Fig. 27). There are some lichens like *Lepraria* in which no sexual fruiting bodies have been observed.

Fig. 27. *Omphalina ericetorum*

Utilization

Lichens have been used to dye cloth, ferment beer and set the fragrance in French perfume; they have also been used in medicated lotions and toothpaste, and even as wolf poison and smoking tobacco. The Israelites fleeing from Egypt may have eaten a prairie-steppe species as their "Manna". This same species (*Lecanora esculenta*) is today important forage for sheep in Libya. Rock tripes (*Umbilicaria* species) are served as delicacies in Japan, and helped to keep John Franklin's first expedition alive for a month, although in this latter situation they were far from being thought of as a delicacy. Reindeer lichens (often incorrectly referred to as "reindeer mosses") are of considerable economic importance in northern Fennoscandia as a principle food for reindeer and are similarly essential for the Canadian caribou herds. During the Middle Ages, the Doctrine of Signatures held high regard for *Lobaria pulmonaria* in treating lung diseases, while *Parmelia sulcata* was used for cranial disorders. The use of lichens as dyestuffs has been important in the past because often no mordant is needed to set the colour. *Roccella* was a source of orchil dyes including "Royal Purple", so exclusive in the Middle Ages because of the high costs in producing the dyed cloth, that only the privileged few of the church and royalty could afford it. During these early times many lichens that were used to dye cloth were fermented with ammonia to develop a dye. As the source of ammonia was urine, there was always an abundant supply available! The rich brown dyes of *Parmelia omphalodes* and *Parmelia saxatilis* have been a favourite of Laplanders and Scots for over 200 years. The distinctive aroma of the Scottish Harris tweeds may be partly due to lichens. Today lichens are used as dyes by amateur dyers and craft groups. Because most species of lichens are sensitive to air pollution, they play an important role in monitoring air pollution around industrialized areas. In these areas, the distribution and health of lichen species can be mapped and any change in air pollution effects can be monitored.

Key to the Recognition of Species

1. Thallus bilaterally symmetric (leaflike or lobed), or a crust or composed of squamules 2

1. Thallus radially symmetric (± rounded), tufted, pendent or composed of erect stalks arising from a basal crust . . . . . Fruticose Lichens 105

  2. Thallus a crust or composed of squamules directly attached to the substrate; lower cortex absent . . . . . Crustose Lichens 3

  2. Thallus leaflike or lobed, ± loosely attached to the substrate; lower cortex generally present . . . . . Foliose Lichens 46

3. Thallus growing on rocks 4

3. Thallus growing on trees, wood, soil or mosses 23

  4. Thallus orange, yellow, yellow-green or copper coloured 5

  4. Thallus white, grey, brown or black 12

5. Thallus orange or rusty-orange 6

5. Thallus yellow, yellow-green or copper 7

  6. Apothecia large (1.0-1.5 mm), pruinose; thallus orange to pale orange, thick . . . . . *Porpidia flavocaerulescens* (pg. 180)

  6. Apothecia small (0.3-0.5 mm), epruinose; thallus rusty-orange, thin . . . . . *Tremolecia atrata* (pg. 180)

7. Apothecial discs black or lacking 8

7. Apothecial discs yellow or red 10

  8. Hypothallus present; thallus yellow-green or copper coloured 9

  8. Hypothallus absent; thallus yellow to yellow-green, edges black . . . . . *Dimelaena oriena* (pg. 185)

9. Thallus yellow-green, areolate, C- .... *Rhizocarpon geographicum* (pg. 184)
9. Thallus copper coloured, radiate, C+ red........ *Sporastatia testudinea* (pg. 184)

10. Discs blood-red .... *Haematomma lapponicum* (pg. 195)
10. Discs yellow 11

11. Thallus dispersed, areolate throughout, egg yolk colour; temperate and boreal . ... *Candelariella vitellina* (pg. 191)
11. Thallus radiate, areolate in centre, lemon-yellow; arctic-alpine .... *Acarospora chlorophana* (pg. 186)

12. Thallus white or grey 13
12. Thallus brown or black 19

13. Thallus with large, rust coloured, rosette-shaped cephalodia on upper cortex .... *Placopsis gelida* (pg. 192)
13. Thallus without large, rust coloured cephalodia on upper cortex 14

14. Apothecia lecanorine; margin with algae, smooth, same colour as thallus . 15
14. Apothecia lecideine; margin without algae, smooth or toothed, same colour as discs 18

15. Thallus white with pink to tan discs; on maritime rocks above salt spray zone .. .. *Coccotrema maritimum* (pg. 192)
15. Thallus grey with black or bluish pruinose discs; on sandstone, widespread .. 16

16. Discs bluish pruinose, C+ lemon-yellow; apothecia sessile on thallus .... *Lecanora rupicola* (pg. 196)
16. Discs black, smooth, C-; apothecia immersed in thallus 17

17. Medulla KOH- .... *Aspicilia caesiocinerea* (pg. 196)
17. Medulla KOH+ red .... *Aspicilia cinerea* (pg. 197)

18. Apothecial margin smooth, margin and disc level with surface of thallus; thallus thin to thick, C- .... *Lecidea tessellata* (pg. 179)
18. Apothecial margin toothed, margin and disc sunken in surface of thallus; thallus thick, C+ red .... *Diploschistes scruposus* (pg. 179)

19. Fruiting body a perithecium 20
19. Fruiting body an apothecium 21

20. Thallus black; on maritime rocks at high water mark .... *Verrucaria maura* (pg. 177)
20. Thallus brown; on calcareous rocks........... *Staurothele clopima* (pg. 177)

21. Marginal areoles radiate; thallus brown to black, C+ red .... *Sporastatia testudinea* (pg. 184)
21. Marginal areoles areolate; thallus brown, C- 22

22. Asci each with 2 muriform, brown spores; thallus thin.................. .... *Rhizocarpon geminatum* (pg. 184)
22. Asci each with 8 simple, hyaline spores; thallus thick.................. .... *Lecidea atrobrunnea* (pg. 183)

23. Thallus growing on the ground 24
23. Thallus growing on trees or wood 34

24. Thallus yellow or salmon coloured; squamulose; on calcareous soil or rocks 25
24. Thallus white, green or brown; crustose or squamulose; on soil, humus or peat 26

25. Thallus mustard yellow; lobe edges yellow; apothecia yellow, laminal .... *Fulgensia bracteata* (pg. 189)
25. Thallus salmon coloured; lobe edges white; apothecia black, marginal......... .... *Psora decipiens* (pg. 188)

26. Thallus with isidia, soredia or granulose 27
26. Thallus without isidia, soredia or granules 30

27. Thallus of columnar isidia, "finger-like", white; on soil or humus in arctic-alpine regions .... *Pertusaria dactylina* (pg. 194)
27. Thallus sorediate or granulose, white or grey-green; on soil, mosses or decaying wood; widespread 28

28. Thallus sterile, lacking apothecia, granulose, white or grey-white; on soil .... *Lepraria neglecta* (pg. 197)
28. Thallus fertile, with apothecia, smooth or granulose, pale green to grey-green; on soil, mosses or decaying wood 29

29. Apothecial discs brown-pink to lead-black; soredia granular, C+ pink; on soil or old wood .... *Trapeliopsis granulosa* (pg. 183)
29. Apothecial discs pink; soredia absent, C-; on soil, decaying wood or over mosses .... *Icmadophila ericetorum* (pg. 195)

30. Thallus verrucose, white; apothecial discs pink, pruinose; on soil, plant remains or mosses; arctic-alpine .... *Ochrolechia upsaliensis* (pg. 194)
30. Thallus squamulose or lobate, white or olive to grey-brown; apothecial discs black, tan or red-brown; on soil; widespread 31

31. Thallus growing on calcareous soil, in dry habitats 32
31. Thallus growing on soil or moss, in moist habitats 33

32. Thallus lobate, white; apothecia lecanorine with thalloid margins, discs tan .... *Squamarina lentigera* (pg. 189)
32. Thallus squamulate, olive to grey-brown, covered with silver pruina; apothecia lecideine, marginless, discs black .... *Toninia caeruleonigricans* (pg. 188)

33. Thallus pale grey to brown when moist or dry, with red-brown apothecial discs; apothecial margins entire to crenulate; appressed to soil or humus .... *Pannaria pezizoides* (pg. 227)
33. Thallus green when moist, brownish when dry, with orange to red-brown apothecial discs; apothecial margin granulate/squamulose; appressed to soil or moss .... *Psoroma hypnorum* (pg. 227)

34. Fruiting bodies on tiny black stalks (1.0 mm long, like pin heads); thallus granulose, bright green .... *Calicium viride* (pg. 176)
34. Fruiting bodies attached directly to or immersed in thallus; thallus smooth, grey to white or orange 35

35. Fruiting bodies irregular in shape, elongate 36
35. Fruiting bodies round in shape...37

36. Fruiting bodies elongate, sometimes branched, black, like hieroglyphics; thallus pale grey; on smooth barked trees; west coast .... *Graphis scripta* (pg. 178)
36. Fruiting bodies elliptic, never branched, brown, not like hieroglyphics; thallus grey to white; on rotting logs; widespread........ *Xylographa abietina* (pg. 178)

37. Thallus yellow to orange 38
37. Thallus white to grey 39

38. Thallus orange, usually not visible, KOH+ purple; apothecia always present; discs and margins orange; common on deciduous trees, especially *Populus* .... *Caloplaca holocarpa* (pg. 191)

38. Thallus egg yolk-yellow, composed of scattered flattened granules, KOH-; apothecia present or not; discs yellow; common on deciduous and evergreen trees, rocks and soil . . . . *Candelariella vitellina* (pg. 191)

39. Thallus sorediate 40

39. Thallus nonsorediate 41

40. Thallus crustose; discs red; soralia discrete on thallus, PD+ red; C-; on coniferous trees . . . . *Lecidea cinnabarina* (pg. 181)

40. Thallus squamulose; discs black; soredia on margins and underside of squamules, PD-, C+ red, on charred wood . . . . *Hypocenomyce scalaris* (pg. 181)

41. Apothecial discs pink or white, with thick thalloid margin; coastal 42

41. Apothecial discs black, without thick thalloid margin; widespread 43

42. Apothecia disc-shaped; discs pink; on deciduous trees; thallus C+ red . . . . *Ochrolechia laevigata* (pg. 193)

42. Apothecia volcano-like; discs white; on deciduous or coniferous trees; thallus C- . . . . *Thelotrema lepadinum* (pg. 193)

43. Discs large (1-3 mm in diameter); internal tissue of apothecia red under apothecial disc; in moist habitats . . . . *Mycoblastus sanguinarius* (pg. 182)

43. Discs small (up to 1 mm in diameter); internal tissue of apothecia not red; in moist and dry habitats 44

44. Apothecia without an exciplar margin; thallus only creating a stain on the bark; spores unequally 2-celled, hyaline; on bark of aspen . . . . *Arthonia patellulata* (pg. 176)

44. Apothecia with an exciplar margin; thallus superficial; spores 1-celled and hyaline or 2-celled and brown; on bark and wood 45

45. Spores 1-celled, hyaline; paraphyses free when squashed in water; epithecium blue-green; on bark and wood . . . . *Lecidella euphorea* (pg. 182)

45. Spores 2-celled, brown; paraphyses conglutinate when squashed in water; epithecium brown; on bark and wood, less commonly on rocks or soil . . . . *Buellia punctata* (pg. 185)

46. Thallus growing on rocks 47

46. Thallus growing on trees, wood, soil or mosses 62

47. Thallus yellow-green or orange 48

47. Thallus grey-green, brown or black 53

48. Thallus orange; on calcareous or neutral rock associated with bird perches . . . . *Xanthoria elegans* (pg. 239)

48. Thallus yellow-green; on acidic rock 49

49. Thallus attached at single centre point (umbilicate) 50

49. Thallus attached by rhizines on lower cortex 51

50. Apothecial discs salmon coloured, tan or orange . . . . *Rhizoplaca chrysoleuca* (pg. 190)

50. Apothecial discs green or dark purple . . *Rhizoplaca melanophthalma* (pg. 190)

51. Thallus closely attached to rock; lower cortex white or tan 52

51. Thallus loosely attached to rock; lower cortex tan . . . . *Xanthoparmelia taractica* (pg. 223)

52. Lower cortex white; medulla KOH-, UV+; thallus often forming concentric rings; apothecia rare . . . . *Arctoparmelia centrifuga* (pg. 221)

52. Lower cortex tan; medulla KOH+ yellow or yellow turning red, UV-; thallus forming rosettes on rock; apothecia common..... *Xanthoparmelia cumberlandia* (pg. 223)

53. Thallus grey-green; attached to rock by rhizines; cortex KOH+ yellow 54

53. Thallus grey, brown or black; attached to rock by rhizines or at a single centre point; cortex KOH- 55

54. Thallus with isidia; upper cortex with weak reticulate ridges, grey-green ....*Parmelia saxatilis* (pg. 219)

54. Thallus without isidia; upper cortex with strong reticulate ridges, often mottled brown .... *Parmelia omphalodes* (pg. 219)

55. Thallus dark brown, with rhizines on lower surface 56

55. Thallus grey, brown or black, with an umbilicus and rhizines ± present on lower surface..57

56. Pseudocyphellae and sunken pycnidia laminal; lobes flat, convex or channeled without thickened margins; apothecia laminal; medulla PD- or PD+ red .... *Melanelia stygia* (pg. 216)

56. Pseudocyphellae and sessile black pycnidia along margins; lobes channeled with thickened margins; apothecia at lobe tips; medulla PD+ orange .... *Cetraria hepatizon* (pg. 216)

57. Thallus brown or black; apothecia gyrose, like a 'cinnamon bun'...........58

57. Thallus grey; apothecia if present, smooth 59

58. Thallus brown, not pruniose toward centre; upper cortex rugose .... *Umbilicaria torrefacta* (pg. 241)

58. Thallus black, pruinose toward centre; upper cortex with a reticulate network around the umbilicus .... *Umbliciaria proboscidia* (pg. 242)

59. Fruiting bodies perithecia, seen as tiny black dots on upper cortex; lower surface tan; on calcareous rock .... *Dermatocarpon miniatum* (pg. 187)

59. Fruiting bodies apothecia or lacking; lower surface white or black; on calcareous or acidic rocks 60

60. Apothecial discs burgundy; lower surface white; on calcareous rocks .... *Glypholecia scabra* (pg. 187)

60. Apothecial discs black; lower surface pink or black; on acidic rocks 61

61. Lower surface pinkish, with brown-grey to pinkish simple rhizines thicker toward the thallus margin; thallus thin, leathery; apothecia present; growing on exposed rocks and pebbles.................................. *Umbilicaria virginis* (pg. 241)

61. Lower surface black, with black ball-tipped rhizines; thallus thick, brittle; apothecia absent; growing in humid habitats on vertical sides of rocks .... *Umbilicaria vellea* (pg. 240)

62. Thallus growing on soil or mosses 63

62. Thallus growing on trees, tree bases, logs or wood 76

63. Thallus with or without veins on the lower surface; lower cortex absent 64

63. Thallus without veins on the lower surface; lower cortex present 70

64. Thallus bright green when moist, pale green when dry (photobiont a green alga)...65

64. Thallus grey or blue-green when moist, grey or light brown when dry (photobiont a cyanobacterium).. 66

65. Thallus with brown cephalodia (warts) on upper cortex; apothecia on vertically, upturned lobe tips; lobes to 5 cm long; veins distinct or obscure; growing among and over mosses .... *Peltigera aphthosa* (pg. 229)

65. Thallus without cephalodia on upper cortex; apothecia on lobe margins, horizontal; lobes small to 2 cm long; veins distinct; growing on acidic soil .... *Peltigera venosa* (pg. 229)

66. Thallus surface with round sorediate patches ... *Peltigera didactyla* (pg. 231)

66. Thallus nonsorediate 67

67. Upper cortex shiny; apothecia longer than wide vertical; thallus grey .... *Peltigera neopolydactyla* (pg. 233)

67. Upper cortex dull,with tomentum on lobe tips; apothecia wider than long (horizontal); thallus dark grey or brown, dull when dry 68

68. Veins indistinct; lower surface covered with a dark felty mat of tomentum; thallus thick .... *Peltigera malacea* (pg. 231)

68. Veins distinct; lower surface with rhizines; thallus thin to thick 69

69. Thallus growing on soil in exposed habitats; lobe margins curled up .... *Peltigera rufescens* (pg. 230)

69. Thallus growing among mosses in sheltered habitats; lobe margins curled under .... *Peltigera canina* (pg. 230)

70. Thallus growing on soil 71

70. Thallus growing among mosses 73

71. Thallus unattached to soil, yellow-green; apothecia rare; found in prairie habitats .... *Xanthoparmelia chlorochroa* (pg. 224)

71. Thallus attached to soil, green to brown; apothecia sunken, always present; widespread 72

72. Lower surface of thallus reddish-orange; on acidic soils .... *Solorina crocea* (pg. 228)

72. Lower surface of thallus pale brown; on calcareous soils .... *Solorina saccata*

73. Apothecia on lower surface of lobe ends; thallus smooth 74

73. Apothecia laminal or marginal on upper cortex or absent; thallus smooth or with a reticulate network of pits and ridges 75

74. Thallus yellow-green when moist or dry; lobe tips curled under .... *Nephroma arcticum* (pg. 233)

74. Thallus green when moist or brown-grey when dry; lobe tips curled up .... *Nephroma expallidum* (pg. 234)

75. Thallus with network of pits and ridges, green to grey-brown; lower surface mottled brown and white with a felty tomentum and few rhizines ... *Lobaria linita* (pg. 234)

75. Thallus smooth, brown to grey, usually with white pruina covering the lobes; lower surface dark brown with black squarrose rhizines and no tomentum .... *Physconia muscigena* (pg. 237)

76. Thallus orange, yellow, or yellow-green 77

76. Thallus white to grey-green, or brown 86

77. Thallus orange 78

77. Thallus yellow or yellow-green 79

78. Thallus sorediate, usually without apothecia...... *Xanthoria fallax* (pg. 240)

78. Thallus nonsorediate, with apothecia .... *Xanthoria polycarpa* (pg. 239

79. Thallus sorediate or sorediate-isidiate 80

79. Thallus nonsorediate 83

80. Thallus with yellow soredia..81

80. Thallus with white soredia 82

81. Medulla yellow; soredia lemon-yellow, marginal; apothecia rare; lobe margins free . . . . *Cetraria pinastri* (pg. 212)

81. Medulla white; soredia pale yellow, laminal; apothecia often absent; lobe margins adnate . . . . *Parmeliopsis ambigua* (pg. 222)

82. Lobes narrow (under 4 mm), adnate, wrinkled; growth form orbicular; pseudocyphellae laminal; soredia laminal; lower surface tan with black rhizines; medulla C+ red . . . . *Flavopunctelia flaventior* (pg. 220)

82. Lobes broad (over 6 mm), loosely attached, with a reticulate network of pits and ridges; growth form irregular; pseudocyphellae absent; soredia marginal and laminal becoming mixed isidiate; lower surface mottled brown and white; medulla C- . . . . *Lobaria pulmonaria* (pg. 235)

83. Thallus lobes narrow (under 4 mm), yellow, usually with obvious apothecia 84

83. Thallus lobes broad (over 6 mm), yellow-green, usually lacking apothecia . . . 85

84. Thallus lemon-yellow, loosely attached; apothecial discs brown; on trees and shrubs below timberline . . . . *Cetraria canadensis* (pg. 212)

84. Thallus pale yellow, adnate; apothecial discs red-brown; on smooth-bark conifers at timberline . . . . *Ahtiana sphaerosporella* (pg. 221)

85. Lobe margins with tooth-like projections; medulla KOH+ yellow, PD+ orange; growing in moist forests . . . . *Lobaria oregana* (pg. 235)

85. Lobe margins smooth; medulla KOH-, PD-; growing in moss/heath communities . . . . *Lobaria linita* (pg. 234)

86. Thallus white to grey-green 87

86. Thallus brown 98

87. Thallus lobes hollow; rhizines or tomentum not present on lower surface; thallus loosely attached to substrate 88

87. Thallus lobes solid; rhizines or tomentum present on lower surface; thallus adnate to loosely attached to substrate 91

88. Thallus sorediate 89

88. Thallus nonsorediate 90

89. Soredia terminal under hooded lobes; upper cortex pale grey-green; medulla PD+ red . . . . *Hypogymnia physodes* (pg. 225)

89. Soredia laminal on straight lobes; upper cortex brownish-grey; medulla PD- . . . . *Hypogymnia austerodes* (pg. 224)

90. Thallus lobes narrow (to 2 mm wide); lobe tips imperforate; medulla white around central cavity . . . . *Hypogymnia imshaugii* (pg. 226)

90. Thallus lobes wide (to 5 mm), lobe tips perforate; medulla grey around central cavity . . . . *Hypogymnia metaphysodes* (pg. 225)

91. Thallus charcoal or slate-grey; cortex KOH- 92

91. Thallus light or mineral-grey (grey-green); cortex KOH+ yellow 93

92. Thallus grey, gelatinous and black when wet; isidia granular, laminal on upper cortex; soredia not present; lower cortex white, tomentose; infrequent on twigs of coniferous and deciduous trees and among mosses at tree bases . . . . *Leptogium saturninum* (pg. 226)

92. Thallus brown-grey, firm when wet; isidia not present; soredia laminal and capitate on upper cortex; lower cortex black, pale at the margins with black rhizines, not tomentose; common on trunks of deciduous trees . . . . *Phaeophyscia orbicularis* (pg. 237)

93. Soredia and isidia absent; upper cortex with white spots; apothecial discs often covered with white pruina; common on deciduous trees . . . . *Physcia aipolia* (pg. 238)

93. Soredia or isidia present; upper cortex without white spots; apothecial discs not covered with white pruina; frequent on deciduous and coniferous trees 94

94. Soredia absent; isidia marginal; thallus lobes narrow; west coast . . . . *Platismatia herrei* (pg. 218)

94. Soredia laminal or terminal; isidia absent; thallus lobes broad or narrow; widespread 95

95. Thallus adnate; soredia capitate and/or diffuse on upper cortex; common on coniferous tree bases, twigs and logs . . . . *Parmeliopsis hyperopta* (pg. 222)

95. Thallus loosely attached; soredia on underside of lobe tips or marginal; on deciduous and coniferous trees 96

96. Soredia on underside of helmet-shaped lobe tips; lobes narrow with marginal cilia; lower cortex white . . . . *Physcia adscendens* (pg. 238)

96. Soredia on lobe margins; lobes wide without marginal cilia; lower cortex black with pale edges 97

97. Soredia marginal and on ridges of reticulate network on upper cortex; lower cortex black with brown edges and black squarrose rhizines; on trees, wood and infrequently on rocks; widespread . . . . *Parmelia sulcata* (pg. 220)

97. Soredia and/or isidia marginal and in patches on upper cortex; lower cortex black to mottled white, brown and black; on trees in moist coastal and montane areas . . . . *Platismatia glauca* (pg. 218)

98. Soredia and isidia lacking 99

98. Soredia or isidia present. 100

99. Thallus grey-brown; apothecia on under side of lobe tips; lower cortex tan with white papillae and tan tomentum . . . . *Nephroma resupinatum* (pg. 232)

99. Thallus chestnut brown; apothecia on upper side of lobe tips; lower cortex light brown with few rhizines . . . . *Cetraria platyphylla* (pg. 215)

100. Thallus isidiate 101

100. Thallus sorediate. 102

101. Thallus brownish-grey to dark brown; isidia granular; lower cortex tan with cyphellae and long tan tomentum . . . . *Sticta fuliginosa* (pg. 236)

101. Thallus chestnut to olive-brown; isidia tall, inflated, and club-shaped; lower cortex brown with brown rhizines, lacking cyphellae . . . . . *Melanelia exasperatula* (pg. 217)

102. Thallus lobes with a reticulate network of ridges and depressions; soredia blue-grey on lobe margins and ridges; pseudocyphellae present on lower cortex; on trees in moist coniferous forests. . . . . *Pseudocyphellaria anomala* (pg. 236)

102. Thallus lobes smooth; soredia blue-grey or white on lobe margins; pseudocyphellae absent on lower cortex; on logs and trees in deciduous and coniferous forests 103

103. Soredia blue-grey, mostly on lobe margins; lower cortex tan, smooth . . . . *Nephroma parile* (pg. 232)

103. Soredia white to brown, on lobe margins or labriform; lower cortex brown or black, with rhizines 104

104. Soredia on lobe margins; thallus lobes long, channeled; lower cortex brown with few rhizines; medulla C-; on coniferous trees and wood . . . . *Cetraria chlorophylla* (pg. 215)

104. Soredia in marginal and labriform soralia; thallus lobes short, flat; lower cortex black with brown edges and rhizines; medulla C+ rose-red; on deciduous trees, especially *Populus* spp. and *Salix* spp. . . . . *Melanelia albertana* (pg. 217)

105. Thallus hair-like; found pendent or tufted on trees 106

105. Thallus of podetia or stalks or of fine branches, found on rocks, ground, logs, tree bases or among mosses 116

106. Thallus yellow-green 107

106. Thallus grey or brown 114

107. Central cord present (gently pull cortex apart) 108

107. Central cord absent 110

108. Soredia or isidia present; surface of main stems with or without papillae (small bumps); thallus tufted 109

108. Soredia and isidia absent; surface of main stems with papillae; thallus pendent . . . . . *Usnea alpina* (pg. 251)

109. Soralia present, especially on branch tips; isidia absent; papillae present . . . . . *Usnea lapponica* (pg. 250)

109. Soralia absent; isidia abundant on young branches; papillae absent . . . . . *Usnea hirta* (pg. 250)

110. Thallus bright chartreuse, tufted 111

110. Thallus yellow-green, tufted or pendent 112

111. Apothecia rare; thallus sorediate throughout . . . . . *Letharia vulpina* (pg. 253)

111. Apothecia common, with large brown discs; thallus nonsorediate . . . . . *Letharia columbiana* (pg. 253)

112. Thallus round in transverse-section, pendent, "hair-like", to 30 cm long; with white longitudinal pseudocyphellae . . . . . *Alectoria sarmentosa* (pg. 251)

112. Thallus flat or angular in transverse-section, tufted, to 6 cm long; with or without holes to medullary cavity 113

113. Thallus flat in transverse-section, up to 3 cm in length, soredia absent, with holes to medullary cavity . . . . . *Ramalina dilacerata* (pg. 252)

113. Thallus angular in transverse-section, to 6 cm in length, soredia present, without holes to medullary cavity . . . . . *Evernia mesomorpha* (pg. 252)

114. Thallus grey-brown, nonsorediate, KOH+ bright yellow . . . . . *Bryoria capillaris* (pg. 249)

114. Thallus brown, ± sorediate, KOH- 115

115. Thallus olive-brown; older thick branches even in diameter, shiny; soralia abundant to infrequent, white, cigar-shaped . . . . . *Bryoria glabra* (pg. 249)

115. Thallus chestnut-brown; older thick branches irregular in diameter, (pitted), dull to shiny; soralia rare, yellow, tuberculate . . . . . *Bryoria fremontii* (pg. 248)

116. Thallus growing on rocks 117

116. Thallus growing on the ground, logs, tree bases, mosses or on rocks . . . 119

117. Thallus of fine branches, "hair-like", forming a rosette; closely appressed to rock; arctic-alpine . . . . . *Pseudephebe pubescens* (pg. 248)

117. Thallus not of fine branches but of a basal crust with vertical stalks ending in apothecia; coastal, wet coniferous, and boreal forests 118

118. Apothecia pink-brown, flat, stalks to 5 mm tall; thallus greenish-grey; on rocks or soil . . . . . *Baeomyces rufus* (pg. 198)

118. Apothecia black, round, stalks to 30 mm tall; thallus pale grey; on rocks . . . . . *Pilophorus acicularis* (pg. 243)

119. Thallus a hollow vertical or horizontal stalk (podetium); stalks lined on the inside with cortical cells; primary thallus present or absent 120

119. Thallus a solid vertical stalk (pseudopodetium); stalks filled or lined with white, fungal hyphae; primary thallus absent 149

120. Podetia white, pointed, unbranched; growing on the ground; subalpine and arctic-alpine . . . . *Thamnolia subuliformis* (pg. 245)

120. Podetia yellow-green, grey-green or brown, pointed or ending in cups, unbranched to highly branched; widespread 121

121. Podetia highly branched, shrub-like ("reindeer lichens"), dull, yellow-green or grey; outer cortex lacking; growing on ground or among mosses 122

121. Podetia infrequently to highly branched, shiny, yellow-green or brown; outer cortex present; growing on the ground among mosses, on logs or tree bases 125

122. Thallus grey, with no hint of yellow-green, PD+ red . . . . *Cladina rangiferina* (pg. 210)

122. Thallus yellow-green to pale yellow-grey-green, PD- 123

123. Podetia forming definite rounded compact "heads", without a main stem . . . . *Cladina stellaris* (pg. 210)

123. Podetia not forming definite "heads", with a main stem 124

124. Podetia branching mainly in whorls of 3, upper portion spreading widely; west coast . . . . *Cladina portentosa* subsp. *pacifica* (pg. 209)

124. Podetia branching mainly in whorls of 4, upper portion narrow; widespread . . . . *Cladina mitis* (pg. 209)

125. Podetia highly branched, shiny, yellow-green; axils open, ... *Cladonia uncialis* (pg. 211)

125. Podetia with few branches, or ending in cups or points, dull or shiny, yellow-green, grey-green or brown; axils or insides of cups open or closed 126

126. Podetia ending in points or cups bearing red apothecia or pycnidia 127

126. Podetia ending in points or cups having tan or brown apothecia or pycnidia 130

127. Podetia sorediate 128

127. Podetia nonsorediate 129

128. Podetia stout, yellow-green, ending in cups, covered in yellow soredia . . . . *Cladonia deformis* (pg. 200)

128. Podetia slender, whitish, ending in blunt tips, covered in green soredia; . . . . *Cladonia bacillaris* (pg. 199)

129. Squamules usually abundant on podetia; cups narrow if present . . . . *Cladonia bellidiflora* (pg. 207)

129. Squamules absent on podetia; cups flaring . . . . *Cladonia coccifera* (pg. 201)

130. Podetia yellow-green; apothecia tan 131

130. Podetia grey-green, brown or grey; apothecia brown 132

131. Podetia without cups nonsorediate; apothecia large, at ends of slender podetia; . . . . *Cladonia botrytes* (pg. 198)

131. Podetia with cups sorediate; apothecia large, small or lacking on cup margins . . . . *Cladonia carneola* (pg. 200)

132. Podetia sorediate 133

132. Podetia nonsorediate 139

133. Podetia with cups 134

133. Podetia with points, blunt tips or apothecia 137

134. Soredia fine, powdery; cups narrow 135

134. Soredia coarse, granular; cups broad . . . . *Cladonia chlorophaea* (pg. 202)

135. Cups with inrolled edges; podetia UV+, PD- . . . . . . *Cladonia cenotea* (pg. 205)

135. Cups goblet-shaped; podetia UV-, PD+ red 136

136. Basal squamules mid-sized (4-8 mm long) to small and disappearing .... *Cladonia fimbriata* (pg. 202)

136. Basal squamules large (to 12 mm long), with podetia arising from the centres .... *Cladonia coniocraea* (pg. 199)

137. Soredia farinose; podetia short, slender, arising from the centres of large basal squamules .... *Cladonia coniocraea* (pg. 199)

137. Soredia granulose; podetia tall; basal squamules mid-sized to small and disappearing 138

138. Soredia present in patches on upper part of unbranched podetia; podetia brown or green-brown, usually with few squamules .... *Cladonia cornuta* (pg. 205)

138. Soredia and squamules uniformly present on upper part of branched podetia; podetia green, usually with abundant squamules . *Cladonia scabriuscula* (pg. 208)

139. Podetia with points or blunt tips 140

139. Podetia with cups 142

140. Podetia KOH+ yellow, pale grey-green, with yellow, black or brown bases 141

140. Podetia KOH-, brown, grey-green or brown-grey, with black bases....... .... *Cladonia gracilis* (pg. 206)

141. Podetia ending in large brown apothecia, split longitudinally, grey-green, PD-, with brown bases; widespread .... *Cladonia cariosa* (pg. 201)

141. Podetia ending in points or blunt tips, entire pale green or tan, PD+ red, with yellowish bases; subalpine to alpine .... *Cladonia ecmocyna* (pg. 206)

142. Cups in tiers, proliferating from cup centres; podetia brown .... *Cladonia cervicornis* subsp. *verticillata* (pg. 204)

142. Cups simple or if in tiers, then proliferating from cup margins; podetia grey-green or brown 143

143. Inside of cups continuous and not perforated, not opening into a hollow podetium 144

143. Inside of cups perforated with 2-several holes or a single hole opening into a hollow podetium 147

144 Podetia short (20 mm); cups with areoles or appressed squamules...... 145

144. Podetia tall (30+ mm); cups without squamules 146

145. Basal squamules with edges curled up to expose white lower surface; on acidic soil .... *Cladonia pyxidata* (pg. 203)

145. Basal squamules forming a rosette, edges not curled up; on calcareous soil.... .... *Cladonia pocillum* (pg. 203)

146. Podetia KOH+; podetial bases yellowish ..... *Cladonia ecmocyna* (pg. 206)

146. Podetia KOH-; podetial bases brown .... *Cladonia gracilis* (pg. 206)

147. Inside of cups with "slit" or "sieve-like" holes. Podetia hollow PD+ red, UV-; cups often proliferating from margins .... *Cladonia multiformis* (pg. 204)

147. Inside of cups with one gaping hole to interior of hollow podetia; podetia PD-, UV+; cups simple or proliferating from margins................................148

148. Cortex patchy; podetia covered with squamules less than 2 mm long; cups simple *Cladonia squamosa* (pg. 207)

148. Cortex continuous; podetia usually without squamules; cups often proliferating from margins .... *Cladonia crispata* (pg. 208)

149. Thallus white or greenish-grey 150

149. Thallus yellow-green or brown 154

150. Pseudopodetia tomentose, highly branched; branches covered with granular or squamulate phyllocladia (scales) 151

150. Pseudopodetia or thallus not tomentose, unbranched to highly branched; branches bare 152

151. Phyllocladia squamulate to granular; flattened pseudopodetia covered with grey tomentum; thallus PD+ red-orange; cephalodia hidden in tomentum on lower side of pseudopodetia . . . . *Stereocaulon tomentosum* (pg. 243)

151. Phyllocladia crenate, thick; pseudopodetia covered with white to rose coloured tomentum; thallus PD+ yellow; cephalodia obvious, on lower side of pseudopodetia . . . . *Stereocaulon alpinum* (pg. 242)

152. Thallus chalk-white with a white lower portion, pointed, unbranched or little branched; growing on ground or among mosses 153

152. Thallus cream-white with a brown lower portion, highly branched; growing on tree bark or on ground . . . . *Sphaerophorus globosus* (pg. 244)

153. Thallus hollow, pointed, smooth; in moist or dry habitats . . . . *Thamnolia subuliformis* (pg. 245)

153. Thallus solid, blunt tipped, longitudinally furrowed; in moist, especially peaty habitats . . . . *Siphula ceratites* (pg. 244)

154. Thallus yellow-green or yellow-brown 155

154. Thallus brown or red-brown 160

155. Thallus round in transverse-section 156

155. Thallus flat in transverse-section 158

156. Thallus "hair-like", 1-2 mm in diameter, with long white pseudocyphellae, growing on ground . . . . *Alectoria ochroleuca* (pg. 247)

156. Thallus finger-like, 3-12 mm in diameter, lacking pseudocyphellae; growing on ground or among mosses 157

157. Thallus tall (± 2 cm), unbranched or little branched, without pruina, hollow . . . . *Dactylina arctica* (pg. 245)

157. Thallus short (± 2 cm), branched, with blue pruina, filled with white cottony hyphae . . . . *Dactylina ramulosa* (pg. 246)

158. Thallus golden-yellow; on calcareous soil . . . . *Cetraria tilesii* (pg. 211)

158. Thallus pale yellow; on soil 159

159. Thallus lobes channeled, smooth, frilly along margins; decomposing bases red . . . . *Cetraria cucullata* (pg. 213)

159. Thallus lobes flat, reticulate, straight along margins; decomposing bases golden-yellow to brown . . . . *Cetraria nivalis* (pg. 213)

160. Thallus round in transverse-section, "hair-like" 161

160. Thallus flat in transverse-section, with marginal projections 162

161. Thallus with short, brittle, spine-like branches, dark brown; pseudocyphellae sunken; medulla C- . . . . *Coelocaulon aculeatum* (pg. 247)

161. Thallus with long branches, red-brown; pseudocyphellae raised; medulla C+ red . . . . *Bryocaulon divergens* (pg. 246)

162. Thallus lobes pale to dark brown, cucullate to flat; pseudocyphellae as white splotches, laminal and marginal on lower surface; medulla PD+ red . . . . *Cetraria islandica* (pg. 214)

162. Thallus lobes brown to dark brown, cucullate; pseudocyphellae mostly linear, marginal on lower surface; medulla PD- . . . . *Cetraria ericetorum* (pg. 214)

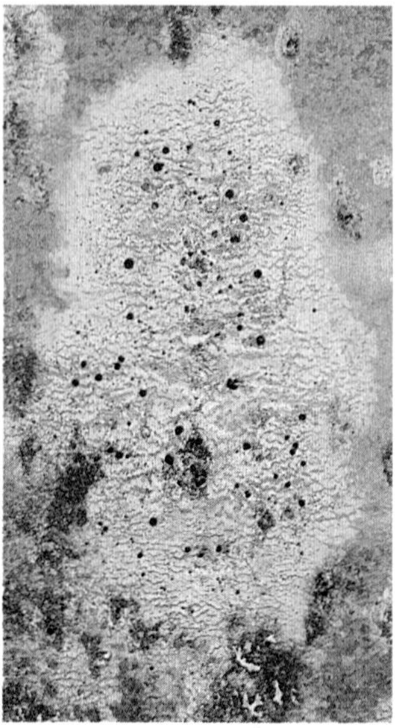

x 2.5

Arthonia patellulata. The thallus of this species is seen as a pale grey-white patch on the smooth bark of aspen trunks. The small black ascocarps look like those of *Lecidea*, however the spores are straight, two-celled and hyaline (Fig. 25d) with one cell larger than the other. A proper margin is absent, and technically the ascocarp is a pseudothecium. *Lecania dubitans (L. dimera)* resembles *Arthonia patellulata,* but the *Lecania* has a pure white thallus, smaller apothecia (up to 0.25 mm wide) and two evenly-sized cells in each hyaline, slightly curved spore. This species is common in the parkland areas of western Canada, and it often covers the north and west facing sides of tree trunks.

x 5

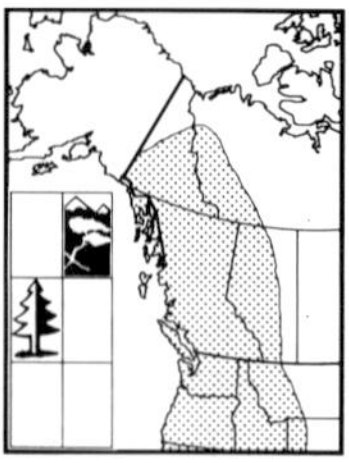

Calicium viride. This lichen is often overlooked because the fruiting stalks are small and inconspicuous, and one must look carefully to see the black, capitate masses of spores on tiny stalks. The heads of the black, pin-like fruiting stalks release brown, elliptic, two-celled spores. The fruiting structure is called a mazaedium, because when mature the asci disintegrate and the spores are liberated free in the hymenium. The crustose thallus is granular and green. This species is found growing on wood or bark of such trees as subalpine fir, englemann spruce, lodgepole pine, douglas fir and western red cedar.

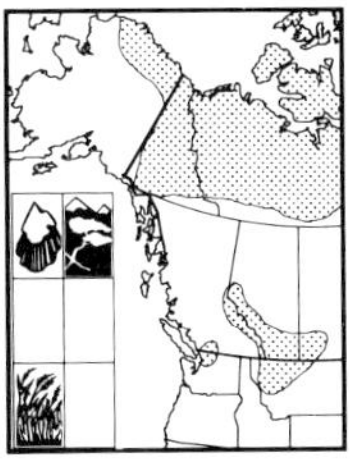

Staurothele clopima is a crustose, brown, areolate lichen that has immersed perithecia. The spores are large, brown, muriform and occur two per ascus. The hymenium is filled with cylindrical green algae. This lichen tends to be inconspicuous and is often only seen as a brown smudge on rocks. It has to be observed closely to see the perithecia. *Staurothele clopima* is widespread and common on sandstone and calcareous rocks, and is especially frequent on dolomite and limestone rock outcrops, on flat rocks, talus slopes and exposed arctic and alpine scree ridges.

x 2.5

Verrucaria maura is a thin, black, crustose species that is restricted to maritime rocks at the high water mark. A network of fine cracks can be detected on the dry thallus by using a hand lens. The thallus is gelatinous when wet. Perithecia are sometimes visible on the thallus as black bumps, but the black ostioles are always visible. The spores are elliptic, hyaline and eight per ascus. This species forms a black band at the high water mark on seashore rocks where it is periodically inundated by high tides. It can be associated with *Caloplaca marina* which has a crustose, orange and areolate thallus or *Coccotrema maritimum*, both of which occur in bands just above *V. maura*. There are other species of *Verrucaria* which are also found in maritime habitats.

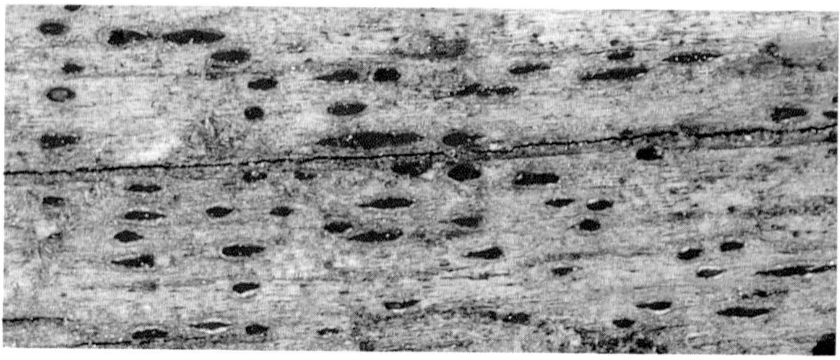

x 3.5

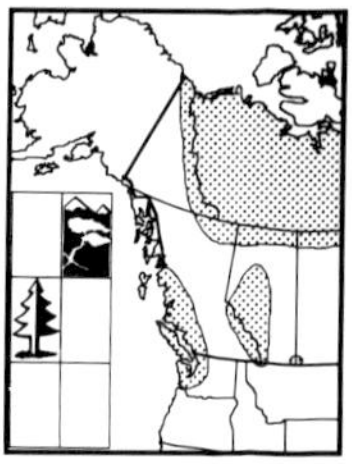

Xylographa abietina. This crustose species has brown to black, elliptic apothecia. The apothecia are formed parallel to the grain of the wood on which this species grows. The greyish-white thallus can be present or sometimes it is embedded in the substrate. Microchemical reactions are negative. The distinctive feature of this genus is the elliptic apothecia (sometimes termed lirellae). *Xylographa abietina* grows on decorticated and weathered wood, including the rotting deadfall of lodgepole pine, spruce or other coniferous species, in mature mesic forest stands. A similar species with sorediate patches is *Xylographa vitiligo*.

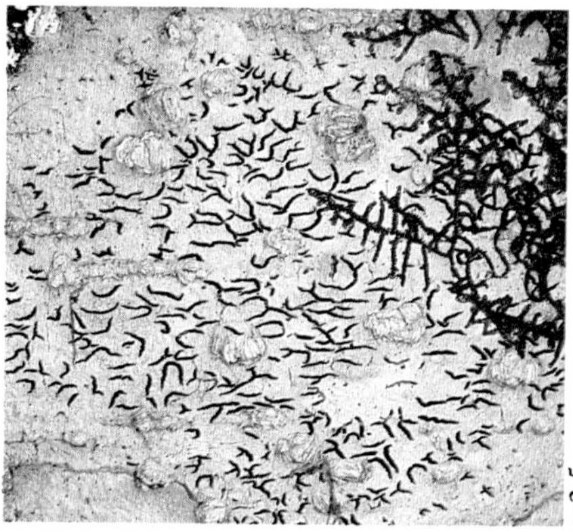

Graphis scripta. As the name implies, 'pencil marks' describes the narrow, elongate fruiting bodies (lirellae) that distinguish this crustose species. The thallus is white to grey, usually thin and smooth, but sometimes it can be thick and wrinkled. The fruiting bodies are simple or forked with distinct, black walls. The spores are hyaline to light brown, fusiform (cigar-shaped), multiseptate with lens-shaped cells and occur eight per ascus. *Graphis scripta* occurs on the smooth bark of deciduous trees in moist coastal forests, where it forms patterns that resemble hieroglyphic symbols.

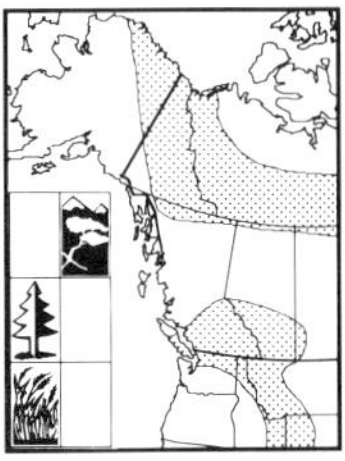

Diploschistes scruposus has a crustose thallus that is thick and areolate. The apothecia are sunken in the thallus with a thick, minutely-toothed margin around the black disc. Spores are brown and muriform and the thallus is C+ red. This is a widespread species, found on soil, mosses and rocks usually of a calcareous nature. The volcano-like sunken black discs surrounded by the minutely toothed grey margins are distinguishing features of this lichen.

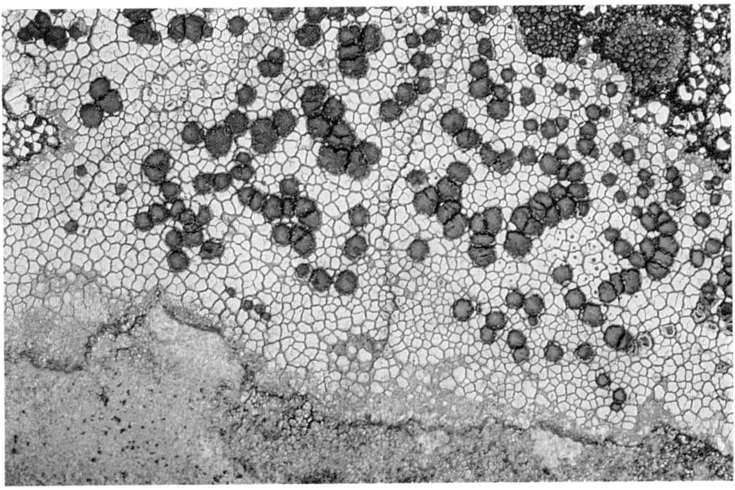

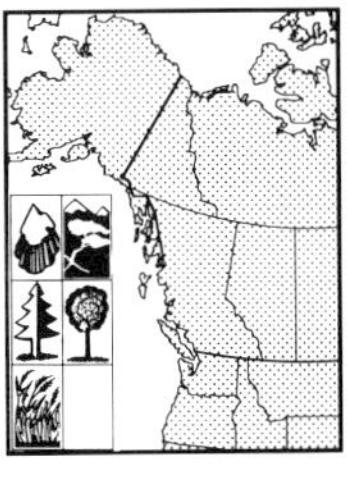

Lecidea tessellata has a grey to bluish-grey, areolate thallus, while the black hypothallus is sometimes visible. Black lecideine apothecia are located between the areoles, and are flush with the surface of the crust (thallus). The spores are hyaline, simple and eight per ascus, while the medulla is I+ blue. *Lecidea tessellata* occurs on exposed rocks, especially sandstone, in arid habitats from high alpine peaks to arctic tundra and from montane grasslands to the prairies. It is occasionally found in exposed maritime sites.

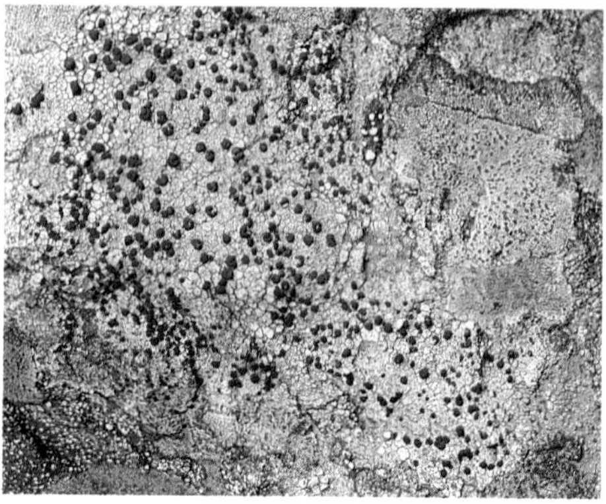

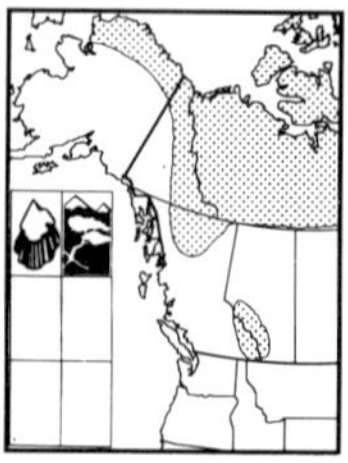

x 2.5

Porpidia flavocaerulescens (=**Huilia flavocaerulescens and Lecidea flavocaerulescens**). The areolate thallus has large, black, lecideine apothecia, up to 1.6 mm in diameter. Apothecia, especially young ones, are lightly pruinose. Spores are hyaline, simple and eight per ascus. A black hypothallus may be present, and if so it can be seen around the perimeter of the thallus. Occasionally *P. flavocaerulescens* will have grey soralia. This species occurs on sandstone boulders and is often found under ledges or on corners of rocks in somewhat shaded areas. Acidic rock outcrops in the arctic and alpine are substrates for this distinctive orange to pale orange lichen. *Porpidia (= Huilia) macrocarpa* has larger, black, usually convex apothecia about 0.5-2.5 mm in diameter. The ash coloured thallus is often very thin. This species prefers exposed acidic rocks in the alpine or rock slides and outcrops at lower elevations.

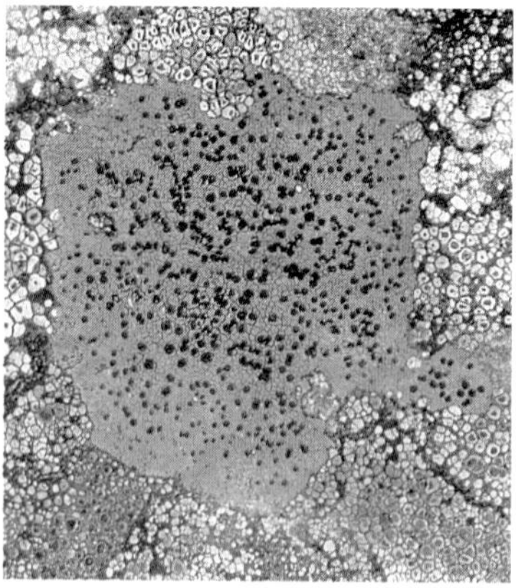

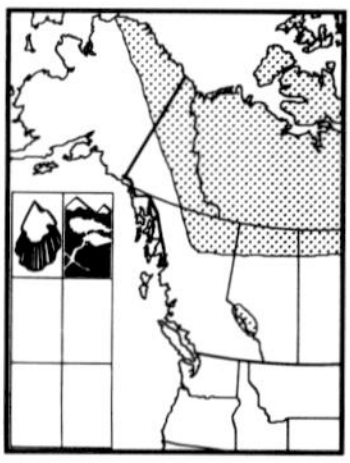

x 2.5

Tremolecia atrata (=**Lecidea atrata**). The bright rusty-red thallus over a black hypothallus is distinctive for this crustose lichen. The thin black lines of the hypothallus form a network between the thalli. The small, black, lecideine apothecia have simple, hyaline spores. This colourful species grows on acidic rocks with some iron content and full sun exposure in the arctic and alpine, as well as on rocks in exposed subalpine habitats.

Hypocenomyce scalaris (= **Lecidea scalaris**). The thallus is composed of tiny shell-like, overlapping squamules that have sorediate margins and are C+ red. Lecideine apothecia, if present, are black with flexuose margins. This species is found on burnt wood, usually of coniferous trees, and once recognized, this lichen is easily identified on the charred black substrate.

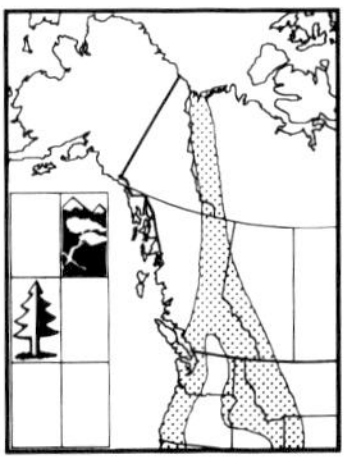

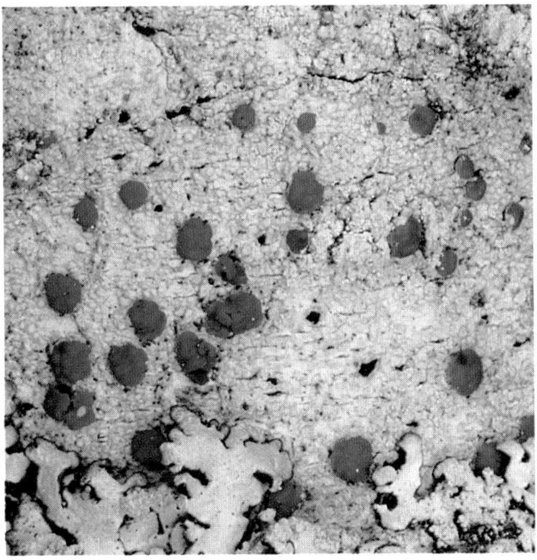

x 3.5

Lecidea cinnabarina has a thin, but continuous pale grey to white, crustose thallus with soralia in small patches. Bright red to orange lecideine apothecia dot the thallus of fertile specimens. Soralia are PD+ red. It often occurs sterile, and then can be confused with *Lecanora impudens*, which has a pale grey thallus and discrete granular sorediate patches that are PD-. Apothecia of *L. impudens* have red-brown discs, with white, partially sorediate, thalline margins. *Lecanora impudens* occurs on the bark of deciduous and coniferous trees and is KOH+ yellow. *Lecidea cinnabarina* is occasionally found on the bark of conifers, especially subalpine fir.

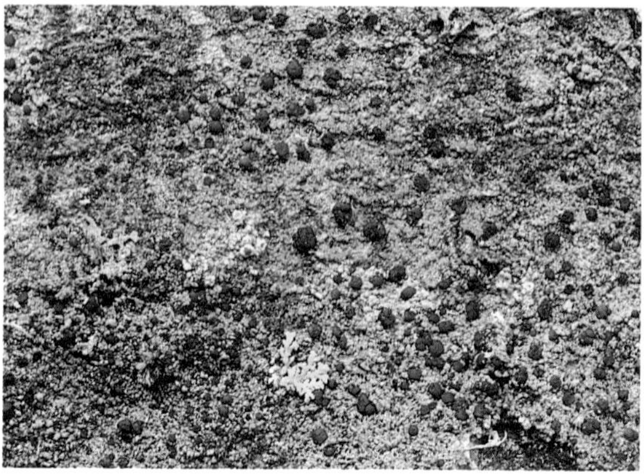

x 2.5

Lecidella euphorea (=**L. glomerulosa**). This common crustose lichen has black, lecideine apothecia on a granulose, grey-green thallus. The proper margin usually disappears in older apothecia. Spores are hyaline, simple and eight per ascus. *Lecidella euphorea* occurs on rotting tree stumps or logs. It may also be corticolous on bark of trunks, branches and twigs usually of conifer trees. Another corticolous species found on bark is *Buellia punctata* that also has lecideine apothecia with the proper margin lacking in older apothecia. In this latter species, the thallus is whitish and is often thin to obsolete and the spores are two-celled and brown.

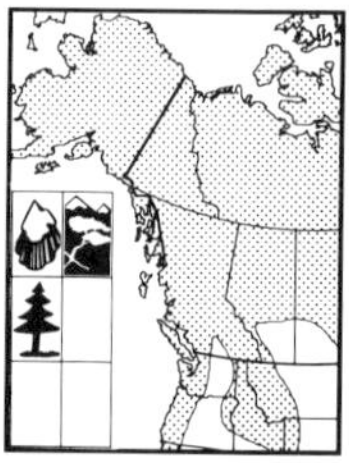

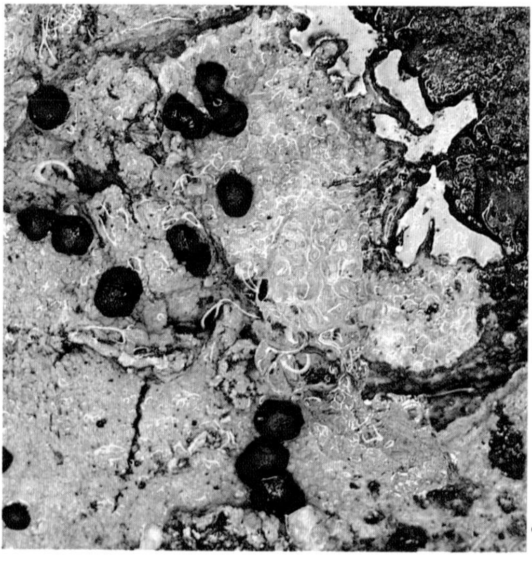

x 3

Mycoblastus sanguinarius has a crustose, greyish-green or whitish, warted thallus with large, shiny, black, hemispheric lecideine apothecia. The hypothecium is pigmented red (evident only when the apothecium is sliced). The spores are very large, thick-walled and occur one per ascus. This lichen is most common on the decaying bark of conifers, in moist forests. A similar species, *Mycoblastus affinis*, lacks the red pigmented hypothecium. Both of these species can be confused with *Lecidella euphorea* that has small, black apothecia with eight simple spores per ascus.

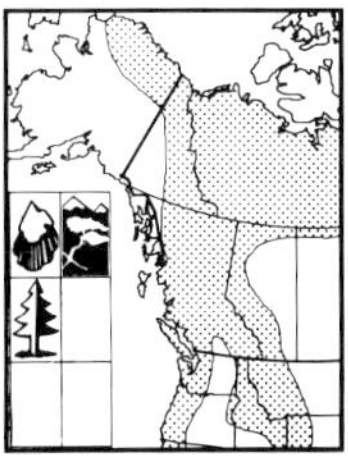

Lecidea atrobrunnea. This crustose species has a black hypothallus and black lecideine apothecia. The brown thallus areoles are scattered to contiguous on the black hypothallus. Usually the edges of the areoles are pale or more rarely the areoles are covered with white pruina. The black apothecia are convex or flat, with a thin margin. Spores are simple and hyaline, while the medulla is I+ blue. A similar species, *Lecanora badia*, has a shiny, chestnut-brown, thick thallus with lecanorine apothecia. *Lecidea atrobrunnea* is common on acidic rocks.

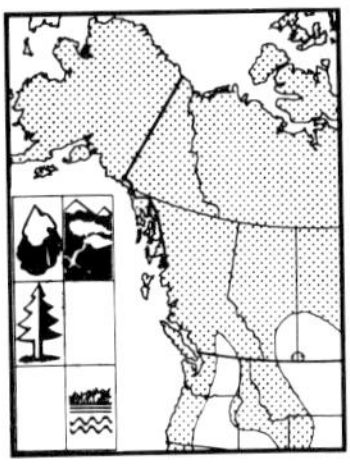

x 2.5

Trapeliopsis granulosa (= **Lecidea granulosa**). The thick, warty, crustose thallus has warts that break into brownish-pink, granular soredia. The thallus and soredia are C+ pink and PD-. Apothecia are brownish-pink to slate-grey and irregularly shaped. Non-fruiting thalli of *Baeomyces rufus* (PD+ orange) or *Icmadophila ericetorum*, (PD+ yellow to orange), may look like *T. granulosa*, but the thalli of these species have a positive reaction to PD. *Trapeliopsis granulosa* is found on soil, on peat hummocks and sometimes on rotting wood. This common lichen is an important soil stabilizer of roadbanks and trails, especially in burned areas.

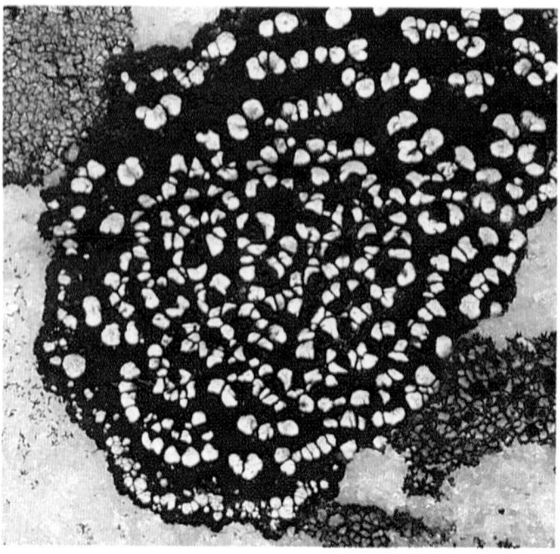

x 2

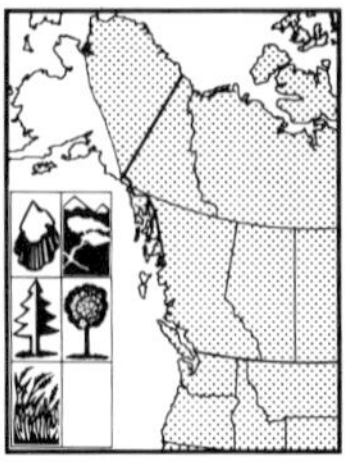

Rhizocarpon geographicum. The common name 'map lichen', is applied to a number of species, which are distinguished from each other on the basis of spore features, areole shape and microchemical tests. The most common 'map lichen' is *R. geographicum* which in the strict definition has eight, green to brown, few-celled muriform spores (Fig. 25c). The upper hymenium of the black apothecia is red tinted and KOH+ red and the thallus is I+ blue and PD+ yellow. A black hypothallus is present and black lecideine apothecia are found between the areoles. This common widespread lichen grows on acidic rocks throughout our area, but is most common in the alpine and arctic tundra. Studies of the glacial moraines at Mt. Edith Cavell in Jasper National Park have shown that *R. geographicum* has a growth rate of about 11 mm per century. Data from studies such as this, help to date other moraines and give valuable information about the movement of glaciers.

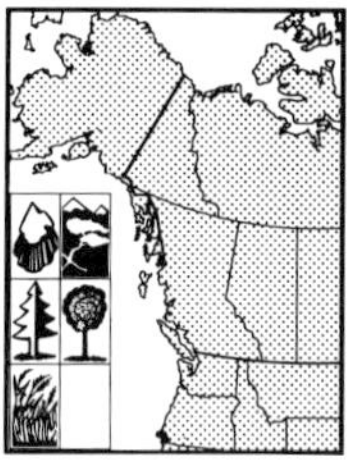

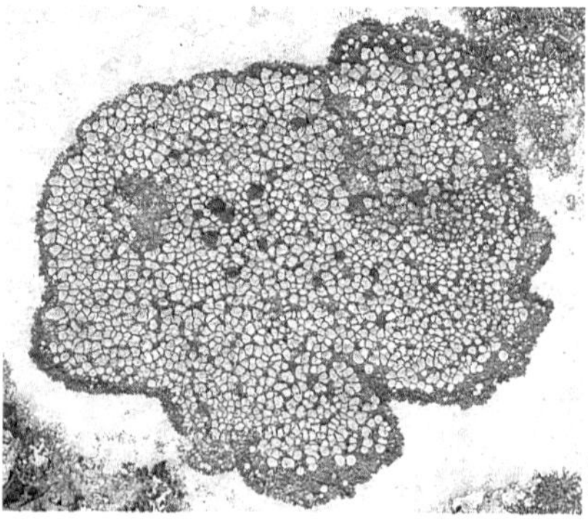

x 2.5

Rhizocarpon geminatum. The crustose thallus of this lichen has a black hypothallus, with brown or grey, convex, pruinose areoles. The black apothecia are lecideine and located between the areoles. As the name *geminatum* or twin spored implies, there are two large, brown, muriform spores contained in each ascus. Until recently *R. geminatum* was included with *R. disporum*, which has one brown, very large, muriform spore per ascus. *Rhizocarpon geminatum* (thallus C-, KOH+ red or KOH-) occurs on exposed acidic rocks throughout our area. Two other grey-brown Rhizocarpons, *R. grande* (thallus C+ red, KOH-) and *R. eupetraeum* (C-, KOH+ red) are also common in these habitats.

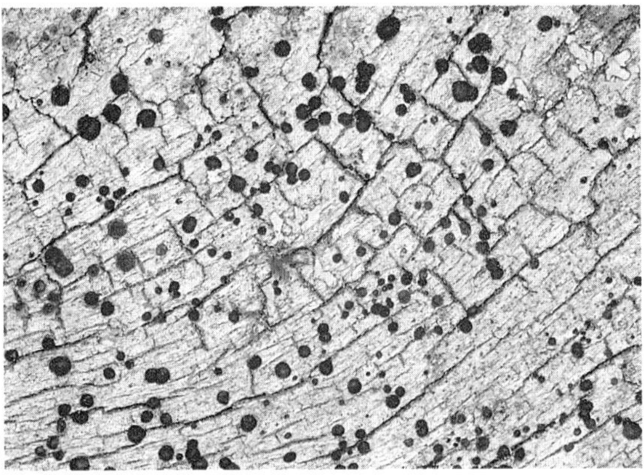

x 2.5

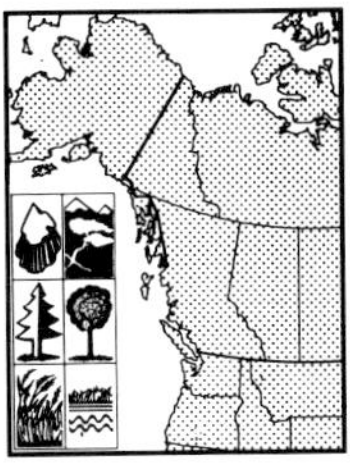

Buellia punctata is a variable, crustose species with a whitish, greenish or brownish thallus that can be areolate to very thin. The thallus is KOH+ yellow and PD-. Black lecideine apothecia are flat to convex with a thin margin. The spores are brown, elliptic, one-septate and eight per ascus. This species grows on twigs, bark and old wood of coniferous and deciduous trees. It less frequently occurs on rocks and soil. A similar species, *B. erubescens (= B. zahlbruckneri)*, with eight (sometimes four or six), larger (17 μm long on average), brown spores, occurs along the west coast. *Buellia papillata* has a white granulose thallus that is also KOH+ yellow, and occurs over mosses and soil. When sterile, these species can be mistaken for *Lepraria neglecta* that is also white granulose, but KOH-.

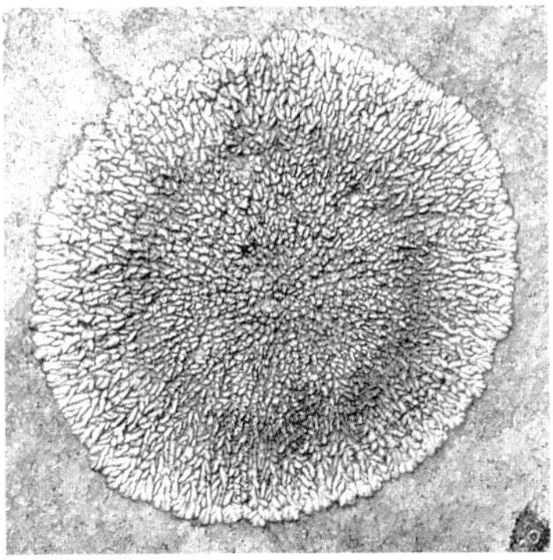

x 1

Dimelaena oreina (= Rinodina oreina) has a crustose thallus that is often circular in shape with distinct radiate-lobate margins. The lobes are thin and closely appressed to the rock while the centre is areolate. Lecanorine apothecia with black discs and two-celled, brown spores (Fig. 25b) are usually present. The yellow-green to grey-green thallus with distinct lobate margins and the apothecia with thin, concolorous margins and black discs, aid in field identification of this species. This widespread species is locally common on acidic rock, usually in dry, sunny areas from the montane to alpine and arctic zones. When it is placed in the genus *Rinodina*, the poetic scientific name is not easily forgotten.

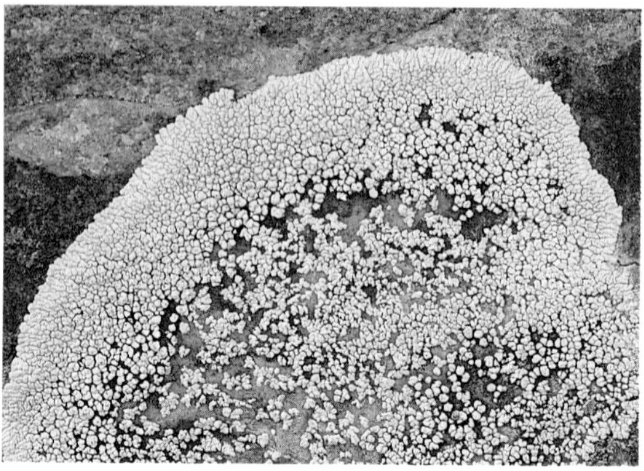

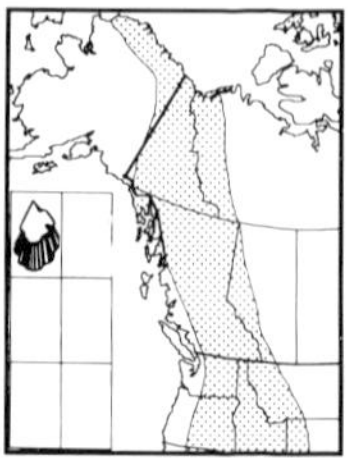

x 2.5

Acarospora chlorophana. The bright lemon-yellow colour of this crustose lichen is distinctive. Its circular thallus has lobes up to 1 mm wide and 1 mm thick, while the thallus can be several centimeters broad. Numerous lecanorine apothecia (to 1 mm) are found toward the centre of the thallus and several small, simple, hyaline spores are contained in each ascus. *Acarospora schleicheri*, also a bright lemon-yellow colour, has a thallus of ± separated areoles and nonlobed margins. This species grows on soil and infrequently on rocks in arid habitats. *Acarospora chlorophana* is found on dry arctic-alpine sandstone cliffs and boulders. It is not uncommon and most often occurs at higher elevations of the dry coniferous mountain regions. Perhaps it is one of our most colourful crustose lichen. The name of this species has recently been changed to *Pleosidium flavum.*

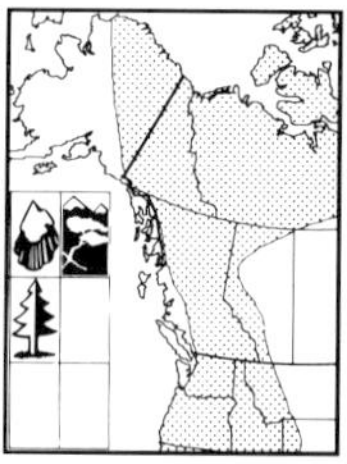

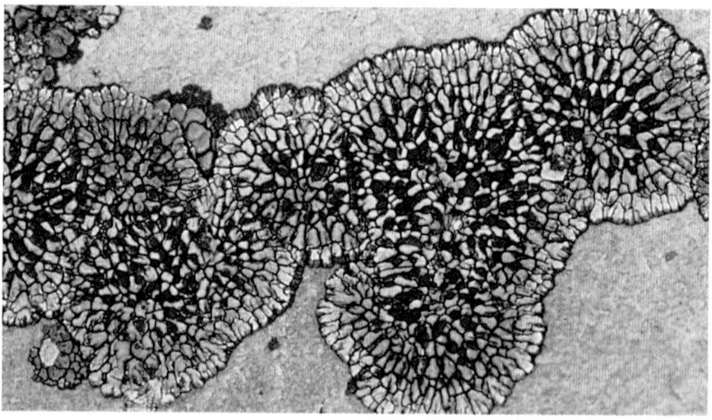

Sporastatia testudinea. The crustose, radiate thallus ranges in colour from copper to black on a distinct black hypothallus. Apothecia are black, lecideine, level with the thallus and appear located between the areoles. Spores are hyaline, with many per ascus. The hymenium is KOH+ blue-green, while the thallus is C+ red. This common widespread species grows on exposed siliceous rocks in the arctic and alpine, and on rock slides and outcrops in the subalpine.

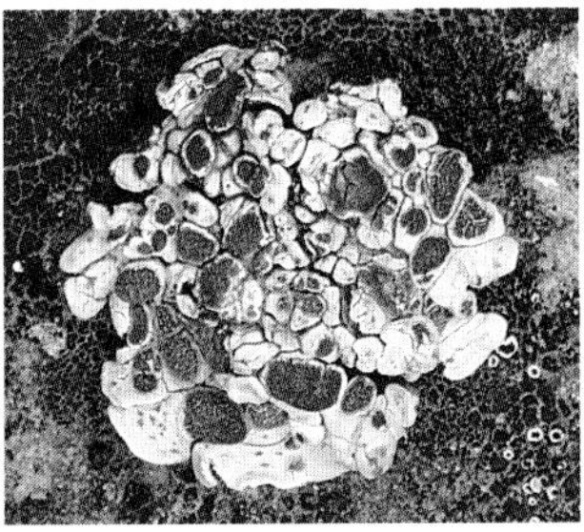

Glypholecia scabra has a foliose, umbilicate thallus with distinctive burgundy-coloured apothecia. The upper cortex is bluish-white pruinose. The apothecia are often compound (2-3 grouped together). Each ascus contains numerous, small, hyaline, spherical spores. The white lower surface lacks a cortex and has a broad point of attachment. This uncommon lichen grows on sheltered, calcareous rock faces such as under overhangs and between cracks in rock outcrops, as well as in crevices of large boulders. It tends to be found on softer rocks as limestone and large grain calcareous sandstone in dry habitats of the prairie and montane grasslands. The lichen is easily overlooked as it blends in well with its substrate, so there are few records of its distribution. It is distinctive as it resembles no other lichen.

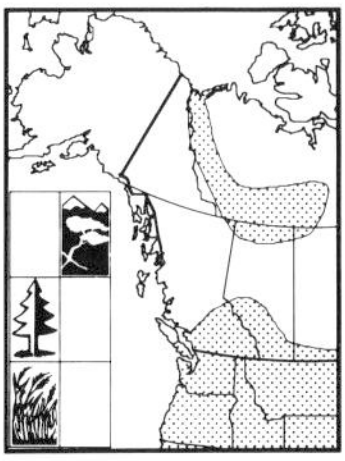

x 1.5

Dermatocarpon miniatum. This small, grey, foliose, umbilicate lichen is attached only at one point on the lower surface. It has tiny black dots, the ostioles of the perithecia, on the upper surface. Simple, hyaline spores are produced in the asci. The tan to brown lower surface is bare and finely papillate. In the photograph the thallus is many lobed, but this species commonly occurs singly lobed, and still has a single point of attachment. *Dermatocarpon reticulatum* has a reticulate, tan, lower surface and often grows with *D. miniatum*. Another similar species, *Dermatocarpon moulinsii*, is also found in these calcareous habitats. Its lower surface has many short, dark rhizines and appears tomentose. *Dermatocarpon luridum* (= *D. weberi*) grows on rocks inundated by water. The thallus is bright green when wet becoming brown upon drying, with a smooth to ridged lower surface. *Dermatocarpon miniatum* is a widespread species that occurs on calcareous rock outcrops either in cracks of rocks or on vertical ledges where there is intermittent water run-off.

x 2.5

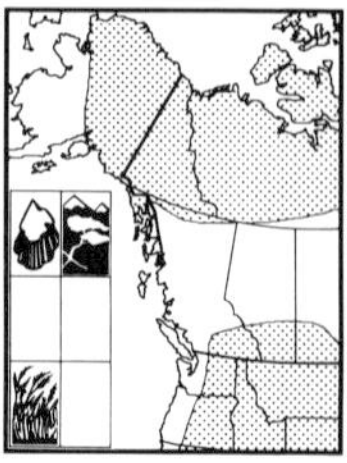

Psora decipiens (= **Lecidea decipiens**) has a squamulose thallus with a white margin around each squamule. It often produces black, convex, lecideine apothecia on the margins of the squamules. The distinctive salmon colour makes it easy to recognize. This common widespread lichen occurs on calcareous soils in such open areas as grasslands, rock outcrops and alpine tundra. It is also found in the same habitat as *Psora rubiformis*, which has a squamulose, brown thallus with a white margin, but the black apothecia are laminal.

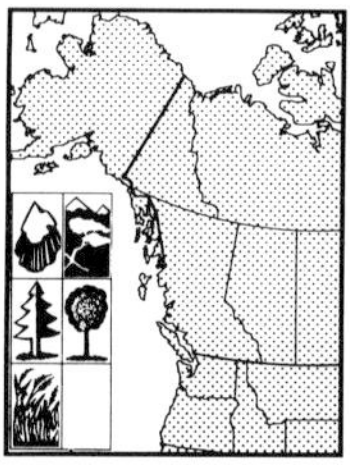

x 2

Toninia caeruleonigricans has a thallus of scattered, olive coloured, squamulose areoles that are blue-grey pruinose. Black lecideine apothecia are located between the areoles. This common soil lichen grows on calcareous, dry, exposed areas as prairies, montane grasslands and rock outcrops, and in calcareous arctic and alpine tundra, where it often occurs with *Psora decipiens*. The pronounciation of its cumbersome scientific name is exceeded only by the difficulty of spelling it correctly!

x 2

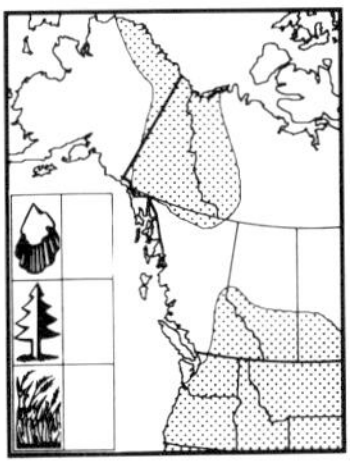

Squamarina lentigera has a squamulose thallus that is centrally areolate with marginal lobes that are linear. The upper cortex is greenish-white pruinose and the lecanorine apothecial discs are tan. The cortex is KOH+ yellow. This occasional species is widespread on dry, open calcareous soils in areas such as grasslands and sand dunes, and over mosses on calcareous rock outcrops. The lobate thallus margins and tan apothecial discs are the features that distinguish *S. lentigera*.

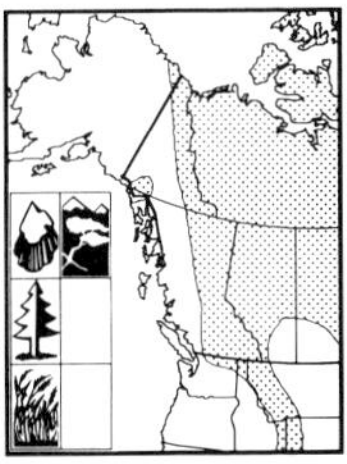

x 1.5

Fulgensia bracteata. The mustard-yellow thallus is areolate to squamulose over a white hypothallus that shows between the areoles. The thallus margins are not lobed. Apothecia, with orange-brown discs, are centrally located on the thallus. Spores are hyaline, simple and eight per ascus and the thallus is KOH+ purple. *Fulgensia fulgens* is a closely related species with radiate lobes and generally without apothecia. *Fulgensia bracteata* is common on wind-deposited calcareous soils of dry montane and prairie grasslands and it also occurs on calcareous soils in rocky, exposed habitats at elevations ranging from montane to alpine and in the arctic. It is often found with *Squamarina lentigera* and *Psora decipiens*.

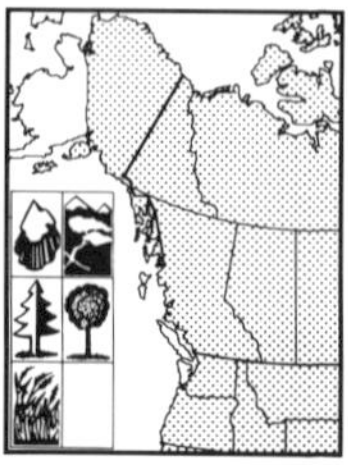

x 3

Rhizoplaca melanophthalma (= **Lecanora melanophthalma**). This foliose, umbilicate lichen has lecanorine apothecia with green to purple, pruinose discs on the upper cortex and a bare, tan, lower cortex with a thick, central holdfast that attaches the lichen to its substrate. This lichen is widespread and common on acidic sandstone boulders, and it is often found with *Rhizoplaca chrysoleuca*, which has tan to orange apothecia. Sometimes the parasitic lichen, *Caloplaca epithallina*, is associated with this *Rhizoplaca*. The parasite is visible only as tiny, bright red apothecia on the thallus surface of the *Rhizoplaca*.

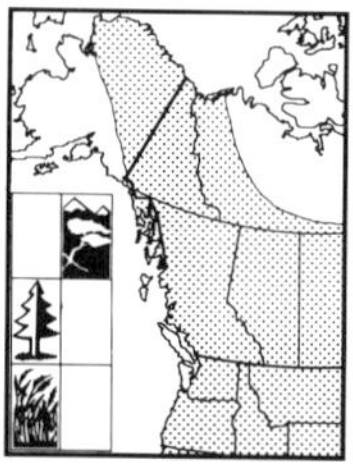

x 2.5

Rhizoplaca chrysoleuca (= **Lecanora chrysoleuca**). The foliose, umbilicate thallus with lecanorine, salmon, orange or tan apothecia characterizes this species; it is the only umbilicate lichen with apothecia of these colours. The lower cortex is tan and bare with a thick, central holdfast. This species is common on exposed acidic boulders (especially sandstone) in the prairies, montane grasslands, subalpine rock outcrops and arctic tundra.

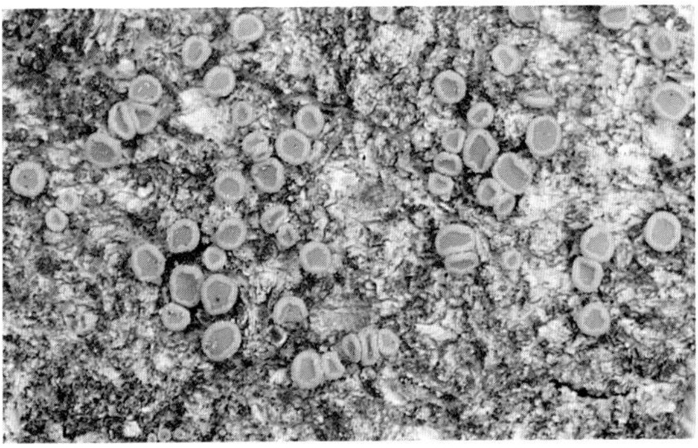

x 5

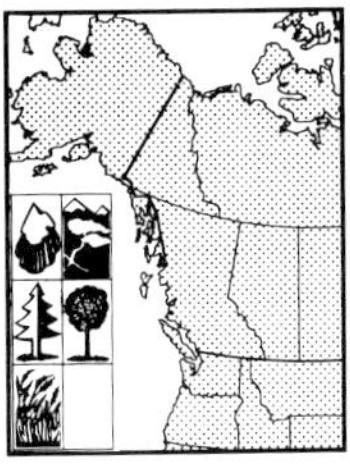

Caloplaca holocarpa is a corticolous, nonsorediate lichen that does not have a visible thallus. The spores are hyaline, polarilocular and eight per ascus. Generally only apothecia are present. It is KOH+ purple. The orange, thalline margin of the apothecia helps to separate this species from *C. cerina* that has a grey, thalline margin. *Caloplaca sinapisperma* has rusty-red apothecia in which the thalline margin disappears at maturity. This subalpine to arctic-alpine species is greyish-white and grows on mosses, humus and calcareous soil. *Caloplaca jungermanniae* occurs on arctic-alpine soil and humus with the apothecial margin the same colour as the thallus. *Caloplaca holocarpa* occurs on the bark of aspen, as well as on trunks and branches of other trees.

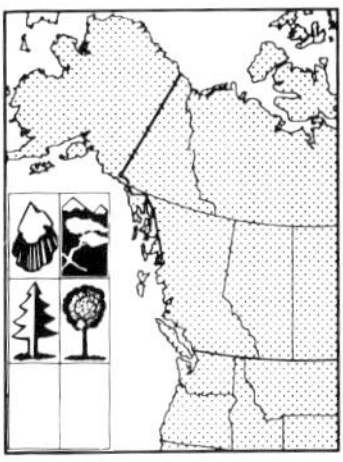

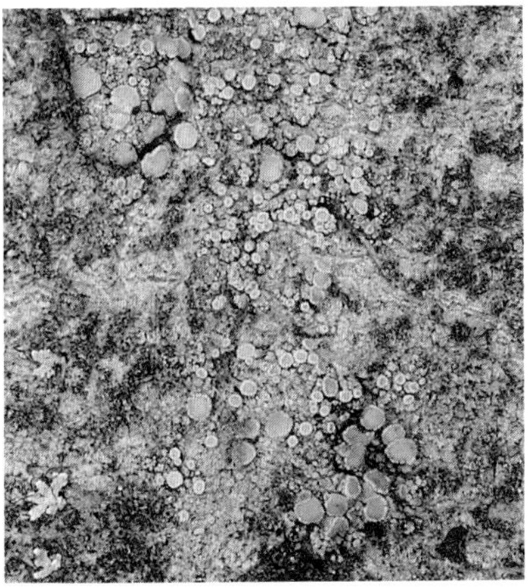

x 5

Candelariella vitellina. The egg-yolk coloured, scattered, flattened granules occurring on both acidic and calcareous rocks, tree bark and soil characterize this common species. Only the apothecia can be seen in some specimens and only the thallus in others. The apothecial margins are concolorous with the disc and thallus, and the thallus is KOH-. Whereas *Candelariella* species are egg-yolk yellow, *Caloplaca* species are usually orange. *Candelaria concolor*, a yellow foliose species, occurs on poplars and elms. Its thallus is KOH- and often is reduced to a yellow granular crust. Yellow granules or soredia are found along the margins of the tiny lobes of this latter species.

Coccotrema maritimum is a saxicolous crustose species of maritime rocks. The areolate, grey, yellow or white thallus has lecanorine apothecia with thick margins and small (up to 0.2 mm in diameter), sunken, pink to tan discs. The spores are hyaline and six to eight per ascus. The medulla is PD+ orange and KOH+ yellow to reddish. *Coccotrema maritimum* and the black *Verrucaria maura* form bands of contrasting colours on rocks in scattered locations on the west coast of the Queen Charlotte Islands, Vancouver Island and mainland British Columbia, where they occur at or just above the salt spray zone.

x 3

Placopsis gelida is a greenish-grey crustose species that forms circular thalli on rocks in open, moist habitats. Large, brown-pink cephalodia that form small rosettes on the upper cortex are characteristic of this species. The thallus margins are lobate and appressed to the substrate. Scattered soredia may be present. The medulla is C+ red. Lecanorine apothecia have thick margins with rose coloured discs. Spores are elliptic, hyaline, simple and eight per ascus. This species occurs on moist coastal rocks and inland on rocks near streams, rivers and moraines.

x 2.5

Ochrolechia laevigata has a pale grey to white, crustose thallus with lecanorine apothecia. The thin, smooth, continuous thallus is dotted with numerous apothecia (0.5-1.5 mm wide) that have thick, white thalline margins and pink discs. The thalline margins are almost devoid of algae when a horizontal slice is observed under a hand lens. In contrast, the apothecia of *O. subpallescens* have a continuous layer of algae in the thalline margins and *O. oregonensis* has apothecia which have double margins with numerous algae present. The thalli of *O. laevigata* and *O. subpallescens* form patches on the smooth bark of deciduous trees such as alder and maple in moist forests with *O. subpallescens* also rarely occurring on smooth conifer bark. *Ochrolechia oregonensis* occurs only on the rough bark of conifers. Microchemical spot tests on the thallus of these three species are KOH- and C+ red and the discs are C+ red. The distinctive pink apothecial discs are characteristic of this genus.

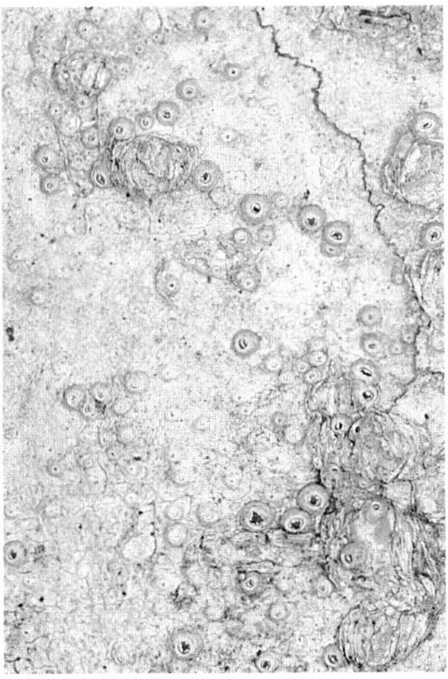

x 2

Thelotrema lepadinum is a crustose lichen with distinctive apothecia that are immersed in warts and look like two blisters, one within the other, with parchment-like edges. The thallus is smooth, wrinkled, thin to warty, membranous and whitish or yellow-grey. The apothecia have an outer thalline margin and an inner proper margin, both of which split open in the mature ascocarp. This species occurs on smooth-barked trees in moist coastal forests. The apothecia with double margins look like rock barnacles.

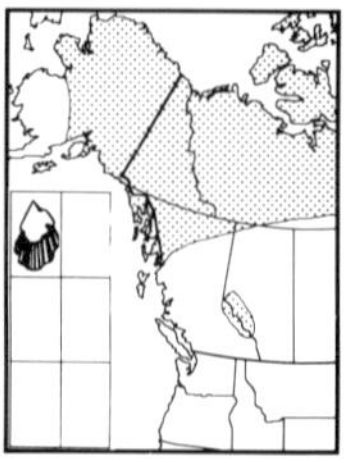

x 1.5

Pertusaria dactylina. The obvious parts of the thin thallus of this lichen are the finger-shaped, erect, thick isidia. It grows among mosses such as *Racomitrium* and *Tortula*, or on soil and humus. Apothecia, with pruinose black discs, are rare and immersed in the tips of the isidia. One, large, single, hyaline spore is in each ascus. The thallus is KOH + yellow to red-brown and PD + orange-red. This distinctive bone white lichen occurs in the arctic and alpine tundra, usually on exposed ridges. It is rare in the Rocky Mountains.

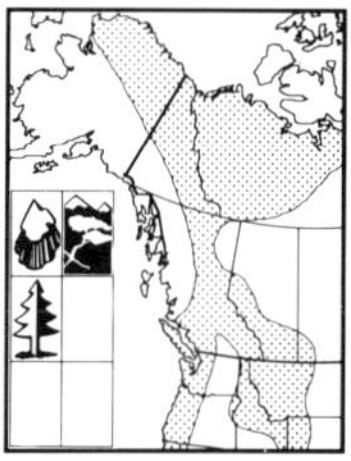

x 3

Ochrolechia upsaliensis. The crustose, nonsorediate, white thallus with pruinose, pink, apothecial discs characterize this species. Microchemical tests are C-, KOH- and PD-. *Orchrolechia upsaliensis* occurs on soil, mosses and over decaying plants in the alpine and arctic and infrequently at exposed maritime sites in southern British Columbia. There are other common terricolous or muscicolous *Ochrolechia* species which are sorediate. *Ochrolechia frigida*, a nonsorediate arctic lichen which grows on decaying plant material, has pink epruinose discs. The thallus is C + red. *Lecanora epibryon*, a common arctic-alpine terricolous and muscicolous species, has a white, warty, crustose thallus and bright red-brown lecanorine apothecia with thinner margins.

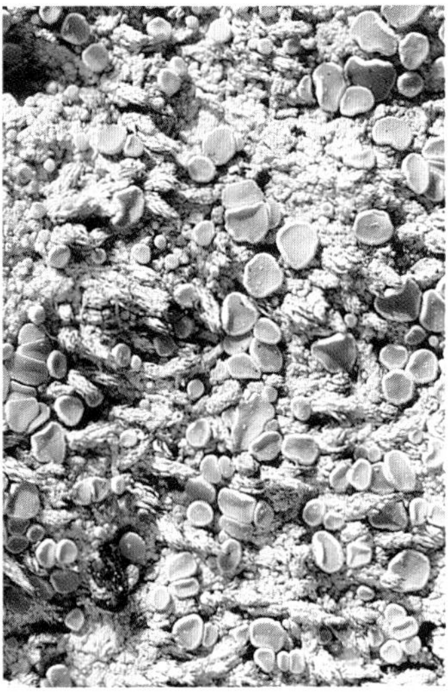

x 1

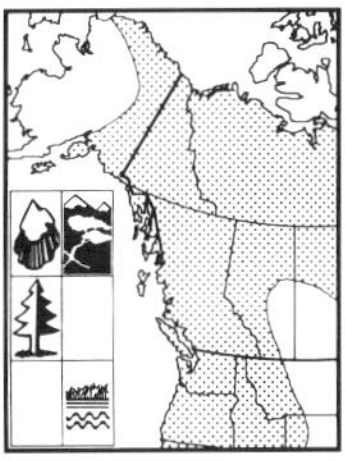

Icmadophila ericetorum. The pink lecanorine apothecia of this crustose lichen make it readily identified. The thallus is off-white when dry to bright pale green when moist. It can be smooth to granular or areolate and is KOH+ yellow to brown and PD+ yellow to orange. When non-fruiting, *I. ericetorum* can easily be confused with non-fruiting *Baeomyces rufus* that is KOH+ yellow and PD+ orange. The former species is common and widespread and occurs on rotting wood, humus and mosses, especially on *Sphagnum fuscum* hummocks and it is also abundant on trail banks. Whatever feelings the genus name may invoke, this is definitely a most beautiful lichen! The colour combination is striking.

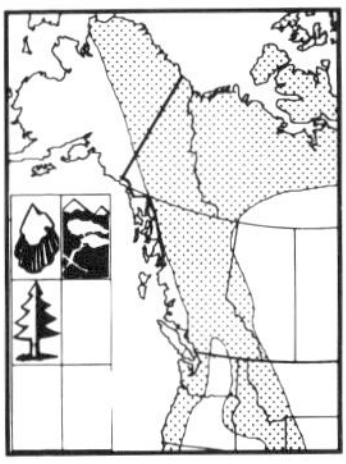

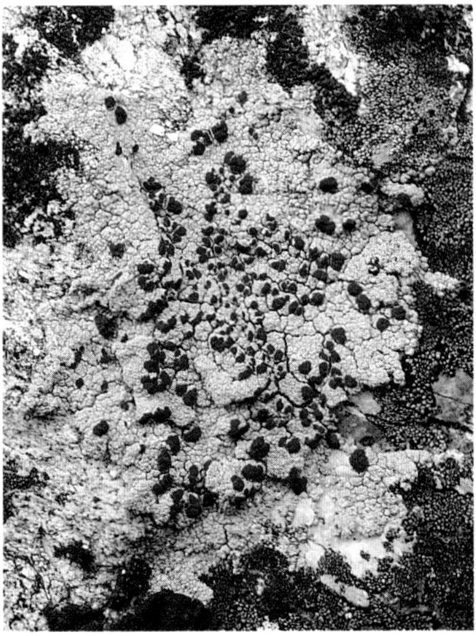

x 1.5

Haematomma lapponicum. The crustose, areolate thallus has large, distinctive blood-red apothecia, which are lecanorine with hyaline, three to seven septate spores. This is the only lichen genus that has large apothecia that are the colour of dried blood (the colour that gave the genus its scientific name and its common name "blood spot lichen"). *Haematomma lapponicum* grows on exposed, acidic rocks (quartzite or sandstone) in the subalpine, alpine and arctic and rarely at lower elevations near the coast. It can usually be found on the corners of large boulders on rock slides and rock walls on mountain sides or growing with grey Rhizocarpons on rock outcrops.

x 1.5

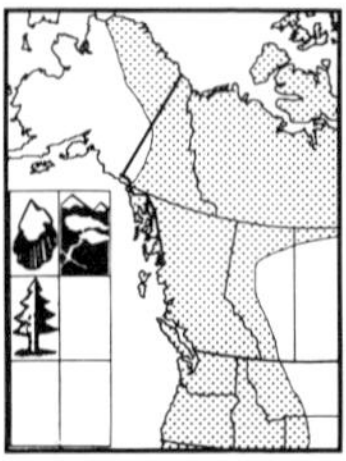

Lecanora rupicola is a crustose lichen that has lecanorine apothecia with blue pruinose discs. The areolate thallus usually grows in a circular pattern on the rock. The pruinose apothecial discs are C+ lemon-yellow. This common widespread species occurs on acidic rocks (especially sandstone), in arctic, alpine, subalpine and exposed coastal areas. The pale blue apothecial discs and grey-white thalli are distinctive features of this species.

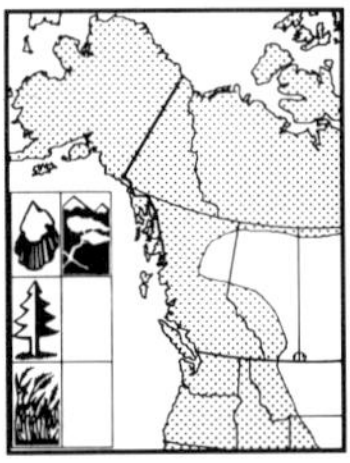

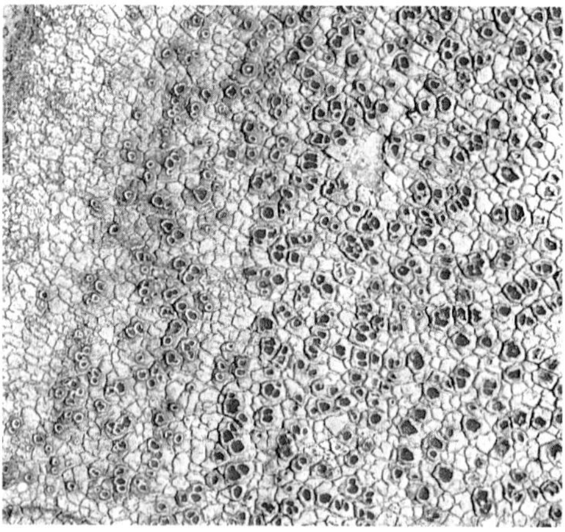

x 2

Aspicilia caesiocinerea (= **Lecanora caesiocinerea**). The thallus of this crustose lichen ranges in colour from whitish- to bluish-grey and often can be distinguished by a distinct margin. The areoles are angular and uneven. Apothecia are sunken, usually one per areole and have a black disc and grey thalline margin. Eight, simple, elliptic spores are contained in each ascus. The cortex and medulla are KOH-. This is a species of dry acidic rocks where it is often locally common. There are several other crustose, saxicolous, grey lichens that are species of *Aspicilia* and *Rhizocarpon*. Microchemical tests and microscopic examination of the spores are necessary in order to separate these species.

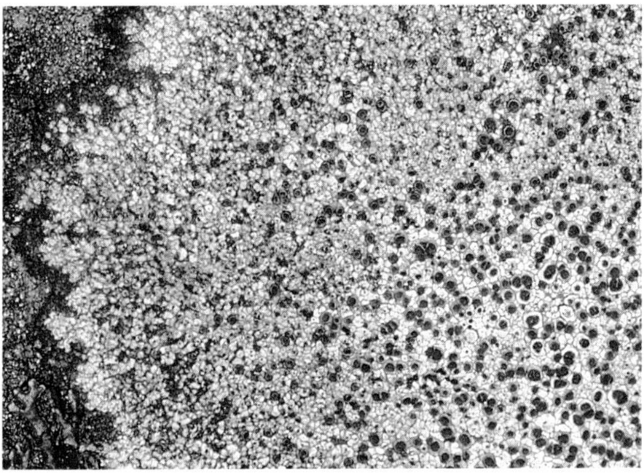

x 2.5

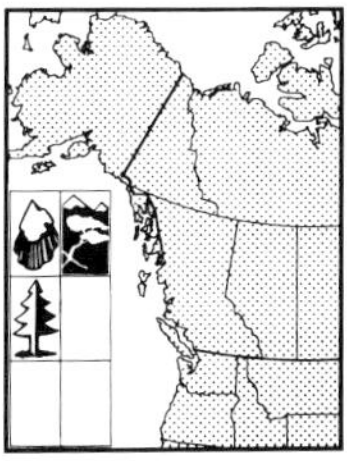

Aspicilia cinerea (= **Lecanora cinerea**). The crustose thallus is rimose-areolate with flat to slightly uneven areoles. The apothecia occur one to three per areole and have a darker margin around the black disc. Spores are simple, hyaline, elliptic and eight per ascus. The medulla is KOH+ red and I-. *Aspicilia verricugera* is similar in appearance and habitat but the medulla is KOH+ yellow. *Bellemerea alpina* (*Aspicilia alpina*) has a white thallus over a prominent black hypothallus. The medulla is KOH+ red, I+ blue; while the apothecia are reddish-brown (especially noticeable when wet). *Bellemerea cinereorufescens (= Aspicilia cinereorufescens)* has dark red-brown apothecial discs in a dark grey areolate thallus. The thin black lines of the hypothallus form a network throughout the thallus. The medulla is KOH- and I+ blue. *Aspicilia cinerea* is common on acid rocks, especially sandstone in the Rocky Mountains and along the west coast. It is a pioneer lichen species that often covers more than half the rock surface.

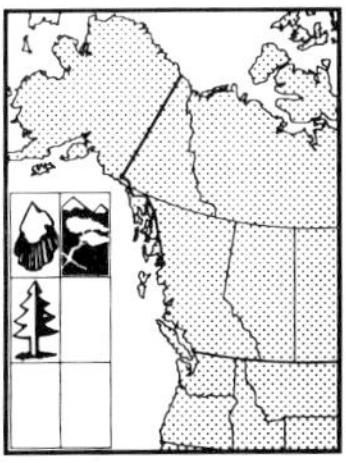

x 3

Lepraria neglecta has a white to grey, granular thallus with negative reactions to all microchemical tests; no ascocarps are known. *Lepraria neglecta* is common on calcareous soil and humus in the arctic, alpine and subalpine zones and it is occasional along the coast. It often grows with *Peltigera rufescens* and *Cladonia pocillum*. Another species of this sterile genus, *L. membranacea*, is found on a variety of substrates in forested areas and differs from *L. neglecta* by having the thallus comprised of pale green soredia and microchemical reactions of KOH+ yellow and PD+ orange.

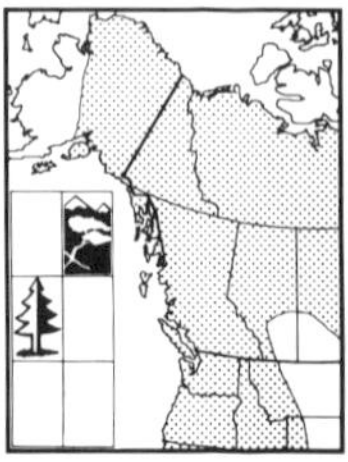

x 6

Baeomyces rufus. The finely granular, thin, green thallus is often seen growing on acidic soil of road- or cut banks and along trailsides, but it also grows on wood and on the surface of flat sandstone boulders along shorelines and coastlines. When *B. rufus* colonizes trail banks it stabilizes the soil and makes it less easily eroded by rain and snow melt and also the hiking trail aesthetics are enhanced by this lichen. The short (up to 3 mm), furrowed pseudopodetia (stalks), bearing light brown apothecia are an aid in identification. Microchemical reactions of *B. rufus* are KOH+ yellow and PD+ orange. When sterile this species may be confused with the sorediate *Trapeliopsis granulosa* (C+ red) and the granulose *Icmadophila ericetorum* (KOH+ yellow to brown and PD+ orange).

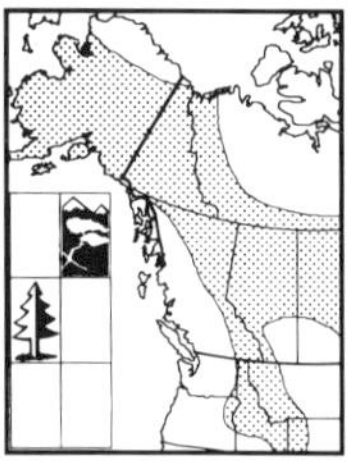

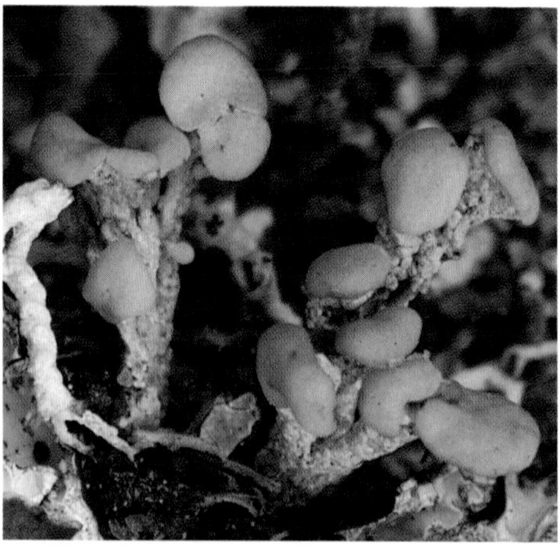

x 4

Cladonia botrytes is the only *Cladonia* which has large, tan to light-brown apothecia on top of slender, short (2-8 mm tall), yellow-green podetia. The thallus is nonsorediate and apothecia are always present. This fragile lichen can be found in dry coniferous forests growing on decaying logs and tree stumps where it is rare, but locally abundant.

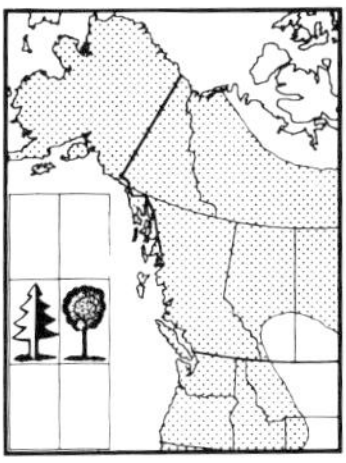

x 3

Cladonia bacillaris has grey-green to white, slender, tapered podetia that are covered with farinose soredia. Apothecia at the tips of the podetia are red, while the basal squamules are small and lobed or finely divided. The podetia are KOH-, PD- and UV+. Another sorediate, but also common, cupless species with red apothecia is *C. macilenta* which has podetia that are KOH+ deep yellow, PD+ orange and UV-. *Cladonia bacillaris* is infrequently found on soil, rotting logs or tree stumps in coniferous forests.

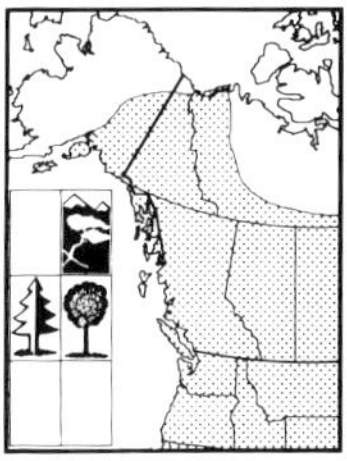

x 1.5

Cladonia coniocraea has simple podetia that arise from the centre of large, unlobed squamules (2-5 mm long). These squamules become granulose-sorediate along their margins and tend to curl up, showing white undersides. The podetia taper to a slightly bent point or have small, shallow cups at their tips, and for the most part are covered with farinose soredia. Microchemical spot tests include PD+ red. This common lichen is found on rotting wood and at the bases of trees, mainly in coniferous forests; it occurs also in stands of aspen and in dwarf birch fens. The large, conspicuous basal squamules with the podetia arising from their centres help to identify this lichen.

x 1

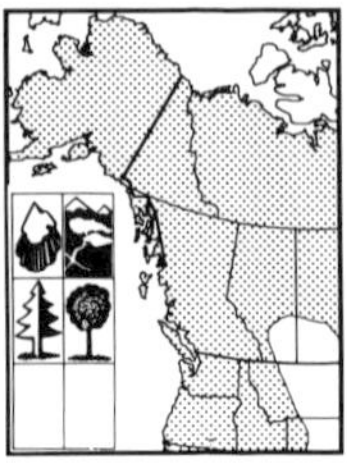

Cladonia carneola. Powdery soredia cover the short podetia of this cup lichen. Tan or pale brown apothecia and black pycnidia are located on the cup edges. The cups sometimes proliferate marginally. The distinctive yellow-green colour (usnic acid) and negative reactions to spot tests of KOH and PD separate this species from the similar-sized *Cladonia chlorophaea*, which is PD+ red and has a grey-greenish cast (no usnic acid). *Cladonia pleurota* differs from *C. carneola* in having red apothecia and coarser, granular soredia. *Cladonia carneola* is common in the Rocky Mountains where it occurs on humus and rotten wood.

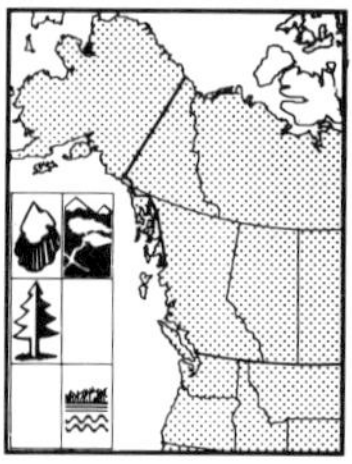

x 1

Cladonia deformis. The yellow-green podetia are covered with yellowish, farinose soredia. The podetia are funnel-shaped and tall (2-4 cm). Apothecia are red and occur on the cup margins. The medulla is UV-. *Cladonia sulphurina (= C. gonecha)*, is very similar to *C. deformis*, and is also sorediate but the cups are often irregularly formed and the podetia are longitudinally fissured and the medulla is UV+ white. Both of these common lichens are found on rotting logs and litter in coniferous forests.

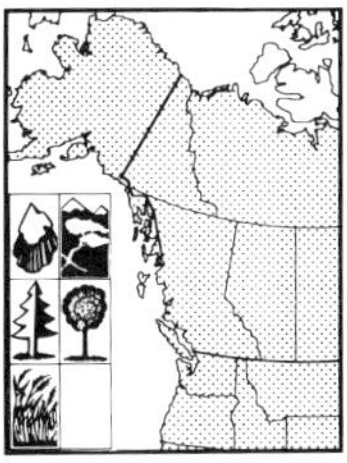

x 1

Cladonia cariosa has fissured podetia with large, terminal, dark brown apothecia. The cortex of large scattered areoles gives the podetia a warty appearance. The thallus is KOH+ yellow. This common woodland lichen occurs in mats on exposed soil and on humus over sand. The 'half-dead' look of the warty, longitudinally torn podetia and the large, dark brown apothecia distinguish this species from other Cladonias.

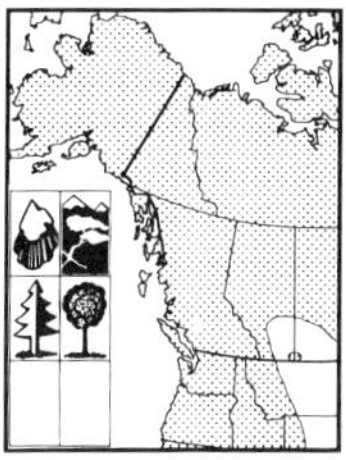

x 1

Cladonia coccifera has red apothecia that are usually present on the margins of wide funnel-shaped cups. The cortex of the short, nonsorediate podetia is warty to granulose. This common lichen is found on rotting logs and acidic soils. It can be confused with *C. pleurota* that is granular sorediate, or *C. carneola* that is farinose sorediate but with tan apothecia and/or black pycnidia on cup margins.

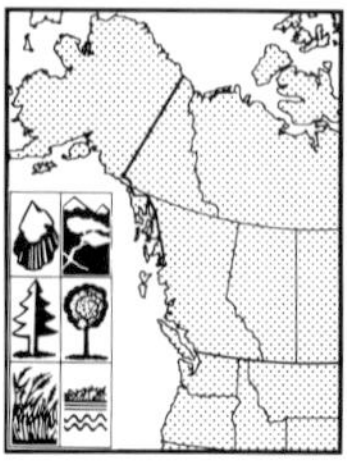

x 3

Cladonia chlorophaea. This common lichen has granular soredia that cover short podetia, including the inside of the wide funnel-shaped cups and hence the common name of mealy pixie cup lichen. The thallus tests PD+ red. It can be confused with *C. pyxidata* or *C. pocillum*, both of which are non-servediate. *Cladonia pleurota* has red apothecia on cup margins of sorediate, yellowish podetia. *Cladonia chlorophaea* has cups resembling wine glasses while *C. fimbriata* has trumpet-shaped cups. This species occurs throughout North America on soil, rotting logs and tree bases. Four chemical races of *C. chlorophaea* exist in North America; these are morphologically very similar.

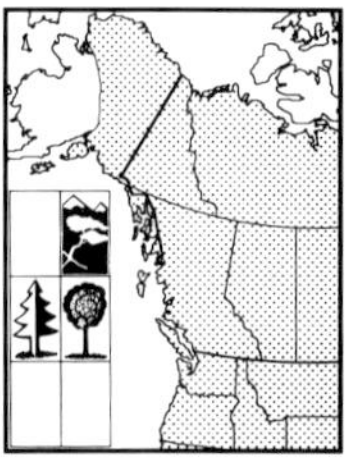

x 1.5

Cladonia fimbriata has podetia that are 1-3 cm tall and resemble golf tees covered with farinose soredia. Brown apothecia on the cup margins are only rarely present. The thallus is PD+ red. The podetia of the similar *C. chlorophaea* are 0.5-1.5 cm tall and are covered with granulose soredia and have wider, funnel-shaped cups. *Cladonia fimbriata* occurs on thin soil and decaying logs in deciduous and coniferous forests.

x 4

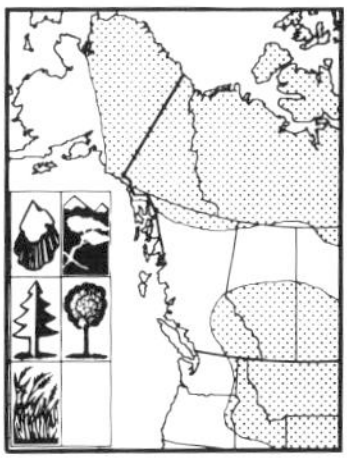

Cladonia pocillum. The short, goblet-shaped cups have peltate areoles covering their interior as well as their outer surface. Apothecia, although uncommon, are brown and produced on the margins of the cups. The thallus is PD+ red. The thick basal squamules form dense rosettes on soil. The similar *C. pyxidata* grows on mineral soils and has basal squamules upturned so the white undersides show, rather than flat in a rosette. *Cladonia pocillum* is found on calcareous soils in dry, open forests and meadows.

x 3.5

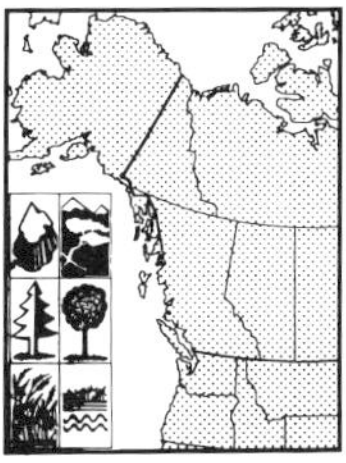

Cladonia pyxidata. Short, broad cups with peltate areoles on the inner and outer surfaces characterize this species. The primary thallus is of thick upturned scattered squamules. The podetial cortex consists of green areoles on a grey to black surface. Apothecia, although uncommon, are brown and occur on the margins of the cups. Brown pycnidia are common on cup margins. Squamules and podetia are PD+ red. *Cladonia pocillum* is similar, but has basal squamules forming dense, flat rosettes. *Cladonia pyxidata* is a species of mineral soils, but it also occurs on rotting logs, tree bases and on soil over rocks. It is widespread in open forests, shrub dominated communities and meadows.

x 1.5

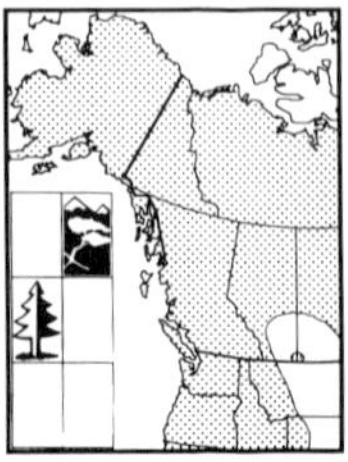

Cladonia cervicornis subsp. verticillata. The podetia are formed of cups tiered on top of one another, each cup proliferating from the centre of the cup below (giving it the name ladder lichen). The podetia are smooth, non-sorediate and PD+ red. *Cladonia stricta* also has cups that proliferate from the centre but this latter species has a thallus that is KOH+ yellow and PD+ red and the bases of the podetia are black beneath white areoles. The distinctive *C. cervicornis* subsp. *verticillata* is widespread on soil, decaying wood or thin soil over rocks in open localities of coniferous forests.

x .5

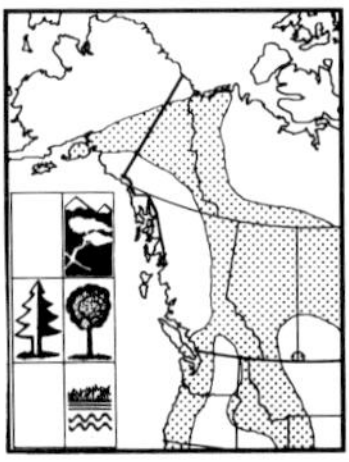

The perforated cups "sieve tubes" of *Cladonia multiformis.*

Cladonia multiformis. The sieve-like openings to the interior of the cups are the distinguishing features of this lichen. Cup formation is variable and the cups can be difficult to discern among the branching podetia. Brown pycnidia are often present on cup margins. The thallus is PD+ red. *Cladonia multiformis* can be confused with *C. phyllophora*, which also has cups that proliferate in successive tiers from the cup margins. In the latter species the cups are often irregular and the podetia split longitudinally, while the podetial bases are black with white areoles. The thallus is PD+ red. *Cladonia multiformis*, a species endemic to North America, is a common terricolous lichen found throughout the boreal forest in mesic areas. It is especially common on peaty hummocks in dry peatlands. It often grows in clumps on the ground intermixed with other Cladonias.

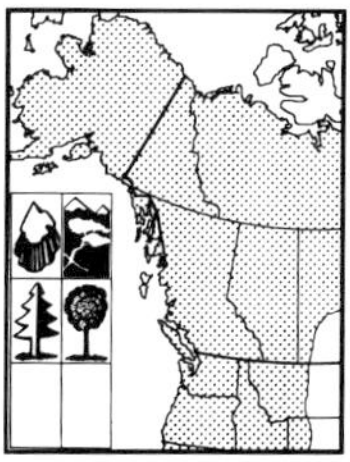

x 1.5

Cladonia cenotea has the interior of the cups open into hollow podetia. The cup margins are inrolled and lacerated, and the upper part of the podetia is covered with farinose soredia. The thallus is strongly UV+ white owing to the presence of squamatic acid. The podetia resemble the young velvet-covered antlers of deer. This common lichen usually grows in clumps on decaying logs or on humus in coniferous forests. The inrolled cups and powdery soredia that cover the podetia are key features.

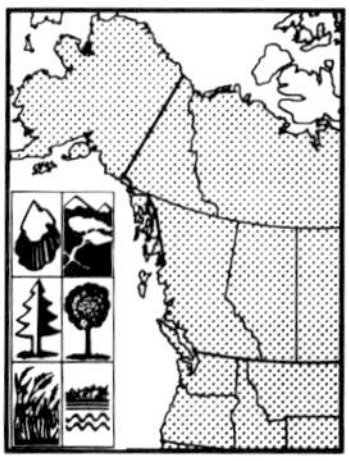

x 1

Cladonia cornuta. The long, tapered and pointed podetia have soredia (often in round patches) at their tips. The bases of the podetia are covered by a smooth cortex and are nonsorediate. This species may be confused with the tall, thin, pointed, brown podetia of *C. gracilis* that lack soredia; or with *C. subulata* which has podetia that are usually totally decorticate and covered with farinose soredia. *Cladonia cornuta* is often found growing in large mats on litter of open coniferous forests, especially those dominated by lodgepole pine or white spruce. As well as occurring on the ground, this species also grows on rotten wood and among mosses. Plants growing in full sunlight are darker brown than those in shaded habitats.

x .5

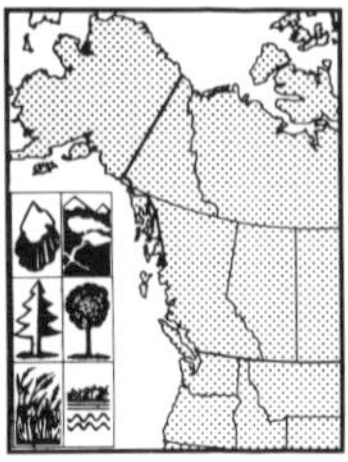

Cladonia gracilis. Some forms of this species have slender cups with the interior closed, while other forms are cupless with the podetia tapering to a point. The cortex is shiny, smooth and nonsorediate. Apothecia are brown on proliferations or cup margins. The podetial bases are dark brown to black. Microchemical tests are PD+ red and KOH-. *Cladonia ecmocyna* is similar but is lighter in colour and tests KOH+ yellow. Probably the most common species of *Cladonia* in the dry coniferous forest, *C. gracilis* is found growing in mats on humus in open forests, especially ones dominated by lodgepole pine. It also occurs on decaying logs, exposed or sandy soil, humus, soil over rocks or on peaty hummocks.

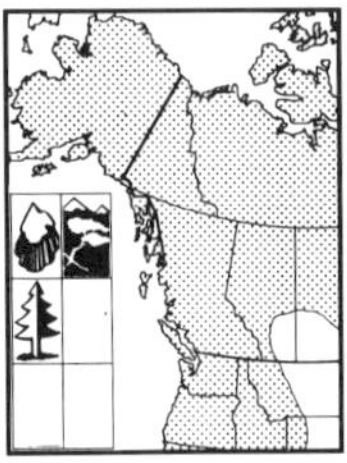

x .5

Cladonia ecmocyna. This nonsorediate lichen is somewhat variable in growth form, with the complex podetia either ending in cups or tapering to points. Apothecia are brown on the margins of cups. The podetial bases are yellow. Microchemical tests are KOH+ yellow and PD+ red. Mats of this species can be found in mesic, subalpine and montane forests of the Rocky Mountains. It is infrequent near the coast. This common species closely resembles *C. gracilis* in its growth form and habitat; however it differs in chemistry and in its thallus colour (grey-green, with yellowish bases versus green to brown *C. gracilis*).

x 1.5

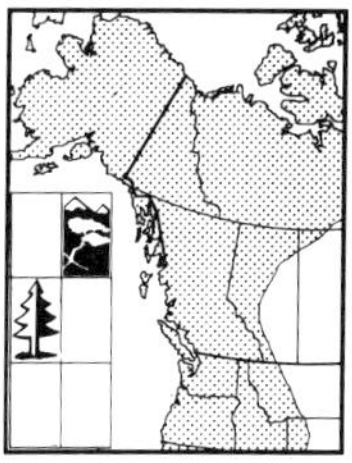

Cladonia bellidiflora has bright red apothecial discs that are found either on short, narrow cup edges or at the tapered ends of the podetia. Typically the whole podetia are squamulose; rarely are the squamules restricted to the apex. The medulla is UV + white. This lichen is similar to "british soldiers" *(C. cristatella)*, a species that is smaller, cupless, usually without squamules and rare in the western mountains. *Cladonia bellidiflora* grows on acidic soil, humus and among mosses in the mountains where it is rare, but sometimes locally common. It is relatively frequent near the coast and is an impressive sight with its bright red apothecia.

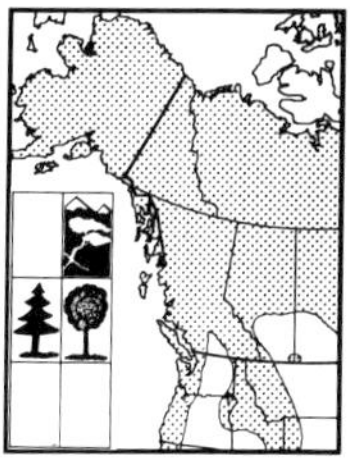

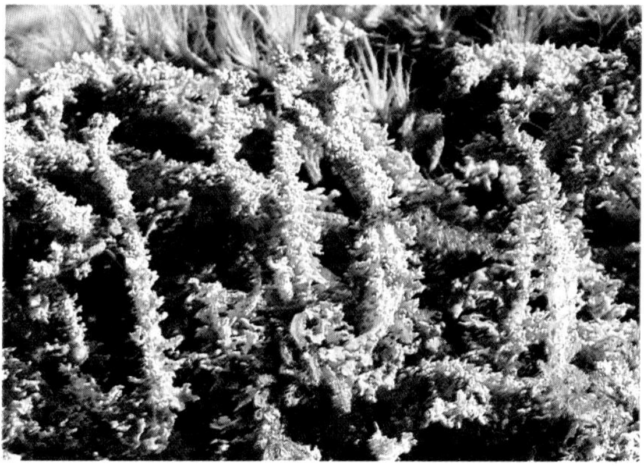

x 1

Cladonia squamosa. The podetia are covered in small squamules (2 mm long) and hence the podetial cortex is irregular or patchy. A single cup per podetium is formed. The thallus is UV+ white, PD- and KOH-. *Cladonia squamosa*, infrequent but locally common, occurs among mosses, on logs and on soil over rocks. It is more common in the boreal forest and along the west coast than in the Rocky Mountains. Aids to identification of this species are the totally squamulate podetia, the discontinuous cortex and the UV+ white (squamatic acid) reaction of the medulla.

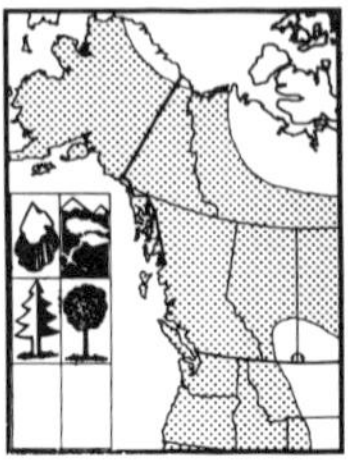

x 1.5

Cladonia crispata. This species grows in clusters on litter or logs in dry coniferous forests. The interior of the cups is open to the hollow podetium and the cup margin often proliferates in successive tiers of cups in this species. Apothecia and pycnidia are brown and usually present on the tips of the proliferations or on the margins of the cups. All microchemical tests are negative and the thallus is UV+ white. It is easily confused with *C. multiformis*, which has 'sieve-like' perforations in the cups, or *C. furcata*, which has divergent branching and is cupless. Both of these latter species are PD+ red.

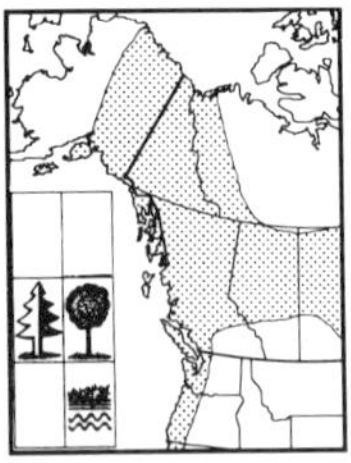

x .5

Cladonia scabriuscula has slim, sparsely branched podetia that are cupless. The branch axils are open to the interior of the podetia. Some squamules are present on the podetia, epecially near the base, while coarse soredia cover the upper portions. The thallus is PD+ red. *Cladonia furcata*, also PD+ red and cupless, is abundantly branched and nonsorediate. *Cladonia scabriuscula* grows on the ground or on logs in moist coniferous forests and in wetlands.

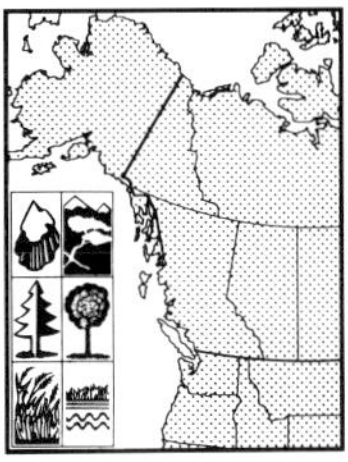

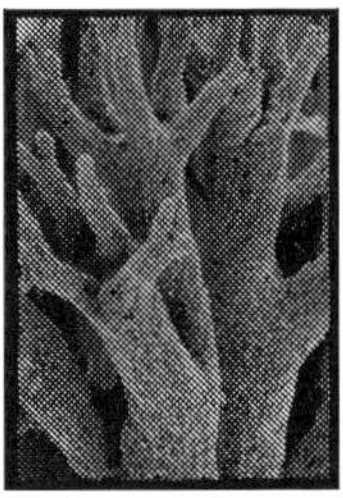

The podetial surface of *Cladina mitis*.

Cladina mitis whose common name is yellow reindeer lichen has yellow-green to yellow-grey, slender podetia, with the terminal branchlets in groups of ± four. Micro-chemical tests are PD- and KOH-. A cortex is lacking, causing the podetia to look cottony when viewed through a handlens. A closely related species of similar colour, *C. arbuscula*, has coarse branchlets that are more strongly curved in one direction. This species is PD+ red, and cannot be separated with certainty from *C. mitis* in the field. *Cladina mitis* is common in open lodgepole pine and jackpine forests, growing on soil or humus, in grasslands with sandy soils and in peatlands on the drier hummocks. It is the most common *Cladina* in the Rocky Mountains.

Cladina portentosa subsp. pacifica. The yellow-green podetia of this west coast 'reindeer lichen' are characterized by large main stems with smaller lateral branches. The podetia have a cottony appearance as the outer cortex is lacking, a feature common to all Cladinas. The algae are located in groups scattered on the surface of the podetia. Axils are open and the ultimate tips of ± three are often 'windswept' in one direction. This is a robust species that can attain heights of 15 cm. This species and the similar *C. mitis* are both PD-. The only definitive way to tell the two species apart is by the presence of perlatolic acid (requiring thin layer chromatography) in *C. portentosa* subsp. *pacifica*; *C. mitis*, however, is not common in coastal rain forests, while *C. portentosa* is restricted to coastal habitats where it occurs in mats or tufts on soil over rock outcrops along the Pacific coast or on humus, peat or mineral soil of coastal forests. A very pale grey form of this species occurs in the coastal wetlands of British Columbia.

x .5

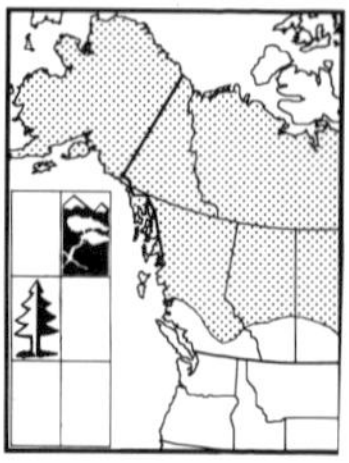

Cladina stellaris. The growth form in the shape of "cauliflower heads" distinguishes this yellow-green species from other Cladinas. The podetia are without a main central stem. Four or five terminal branchlets are in a star-shaped whorl around a central hole, hence the rounded top appearance. The thallus is PD-. This species grows on soil, humus and on thin soil over rocks in open coniferous forests, often in areas of late snow. It is widespread, but only locally common. This species is often dyed and sold as trees for model railways.

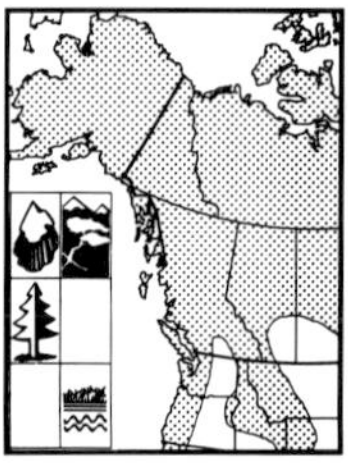

Cladina rangiferina known commonly as the true reindeer lichen is separated from other *Cladina* species by its grey-green colour. The podetia are robust and the terminal branchlets are swept aside in more or less one direction. As well, they are dark grey in the older portions, while the thallus is PD+ red and KOH+ yellow. *Cladina rangiferina* forms thick cushions on the ground in the boreal forest and subarctic forest-tundra. It is a source of food for woodland caribou in the winter, and is the largest and fastest growing species of the genus. Growth occurs as a new branch each year with successive lower branches elongating somewhat as well. Hence, the age of this species (and other Cladinas) can be estimated by dividing the total length of the podetia by the number of major branches; that is until the lower portions of the thallus begin to decompose, generally after 20 years. Traditionally in Finland this species was boiled in water and drunk as a laxative or boiled in milk and taken for coughs.

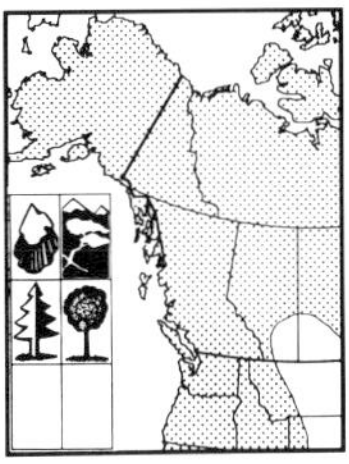

Cladonia uncialis. The presence of a smooth, shiny cortex separates this species from the *Cladina*-type lichens it resembles. No cups are ever present and holes are obvious in the upper axils of the branches. The podetia are 2-8 cm tall and the microchemical test is PD-. Taller but otherwise similar, *C. amaurocraea* has occasional cups and is a northern subarctic and northern boreal species. *Cladonia uncialis* is locally common in dry, well-lit, open forests on acidic, sandy soils and humus or over soil on rocks. It is often found growing with species of *Cladina*.

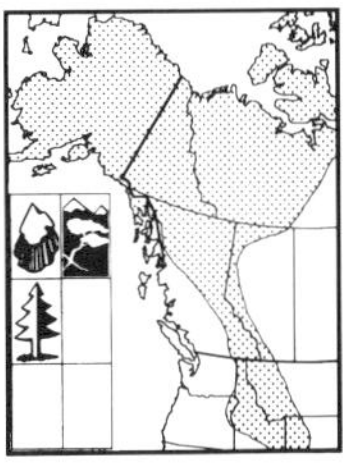

x .5

Cetraria tilesii has narrow lobes that are smooth and flat without marginal projections. The cortex and medulla are yellow due to the presence of vulpinic and pinastric acid. This fruticose, terricolous lichen occurs on calcareous soils and gravels in arctic-alpine tundra and on soil in calcareous rock outcrops at lower elevations. The deep lemon colour will distinguish this lichen from the terricolous, but ivory-yellow *C. nivalis* and *C. cucullata*. Although the thalli of many Cetraria's are flat, the terricolous species grow vertically and are usually considered fruticose.

x 1

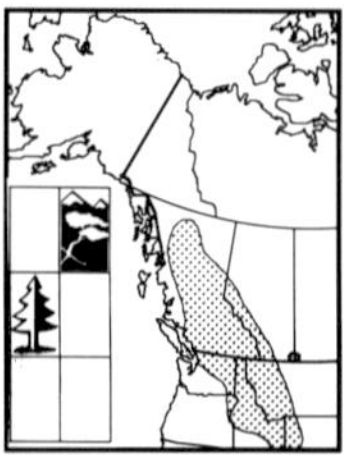

Cetraria canadensis. This bright yellow foliose lichen has a wrinkled, nonsorediate thallus and almost always bears conspicuous brown apothecia. The thallus and apothecial margins are finely divided. This corticolous species is found mostly in open, well-lit forests, but it also occurs on shrubs as *Shepherdia canadensis* and *Alnus crispa*. It is endemic to western North America, and is found more commonly west of the continental divide, (but can be found as far east as the Cypress Hills on the Alberta/Saskatchewan/Montana border). *Cetraria canadensis* could be confused with *C. pinastri*, which is common farther north, but the latter species is greenish-yellow with bright lemon-yellow sorediate margins and usually has no apothecia.

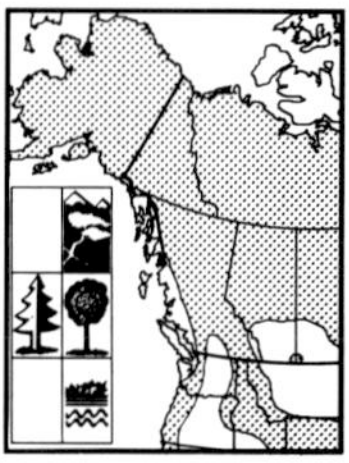

Cetraria pinastri has a greenish-yellow thallus with bright, lemon-yellow soredia along the lobe margins. The thallus lobes are flat and the medulla is yellow. Even though the thallus is yellow-green, when seen from a distance the abundant marginal yellow soredia make this species appear bright yellow. This corticolous lichen is found growing on branches of such shrubs as buffalo berry (*Shepherdia canadensis*), alder (*Alnus crispa*), willow (*Salix* spp.) and labrador tea (*Ledum groenlandicum*), as well as at the base of conifers, especially lodgepole pine. The foliose, closely adnate, sorediate lichens, *Parmeliopsis ambigua* and *P. hyperopta*, often occur on tree bases with *C. pinastri*, at or below maximum snow depth. This is the only yellow lichen with bright lemon-yellow soredia to grow on trees and shrubs.

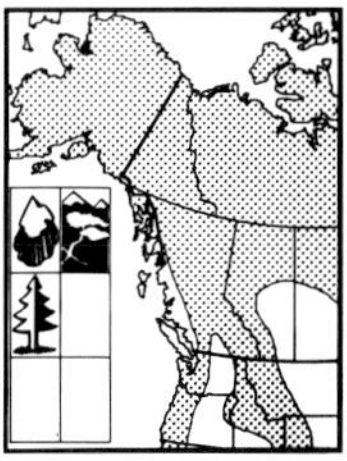

Cetraria cucullata. This erect, fruticose, terricolous lichen has channeled lobes with frilly margins. The lower surface has thin, white pseudocyphellae along the lobe margins; a hand lens is required to see these. The decomposing lower parts of the lobe bases turn red. *Cetraria cucullata* is found scattered in exposed sites or in clumps on soil or humus in sheltered sites. It occurs mainly on soil in arctic and alpine tundra, but also is found in open, well-lit, subalpine and subarctic forests. This species may be confused with the more common *C. nivalis* which has flat, wrinkled lobes.

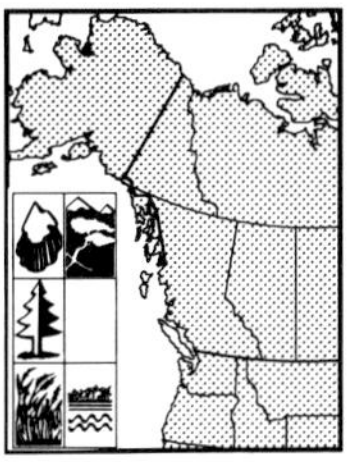

x 1.5

Cetraria nivalis has a wrinkled, flat, erect thallus with pitted lobes. The decomposing thallus bases are golden-yellow turning brown. The common name 'snow lichen' is indicative of the area of late snow melt in the tundra where this species is often found. It also occurs in terricolous habitats in subalpine forests, often with *C. islandica*, *C. ericetorum* and *C. cucullata*. *Cetraria cucullata* can be separated from *C. nivalis* by its channeled lobes. *Cetraria tilesii*, also an arctic-alpine, terricolous species, is bright lemon-yellow and has a yellow medulla.

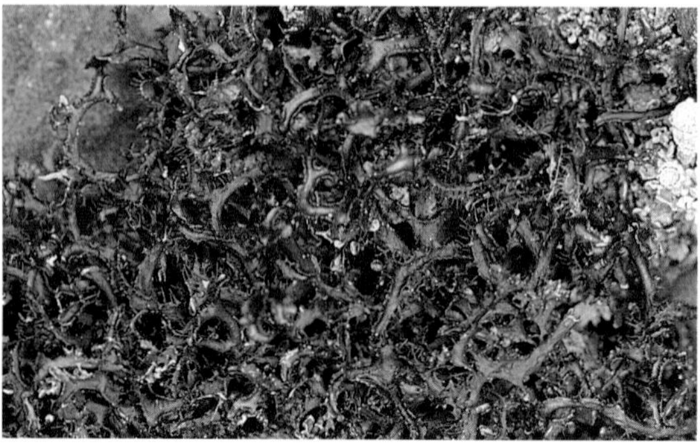

x 1.5

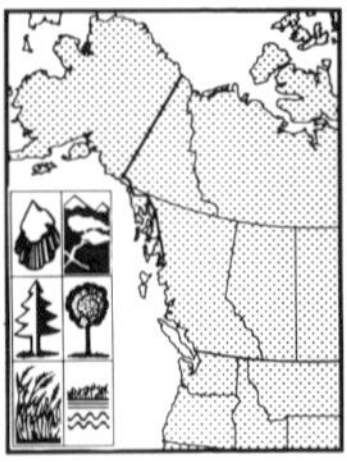

Cetraria ericetorum has erect, narrow, channeled lobes that often branch at their tips. The brown thallus has marginal projections (Fig. 20) occurring along the lobe edges. The lower surface is mottled brown, with narrow, marginal white lines (pseudocyphellae), while the basal parts of the thallus lobes are reddish. This species is found in tufts on soil or humus of tundra areas. It also occurs in open, dry, montane forests dominated by lodgepole pine, there occurring on bark at the base of trees. All microchemical tests are negative. *Cetraria ericetorum* is easily confused with *C. islandica*, which has wider lobes, a medulla that is PD+ red and scattered pseudocyphellae on the lower surface, especially at the base of the thallus. A tundra species, *C. deliseii*, is densely branched at the tips and has a medulla that is C+ rose and PD-. It grows in wet depressions or near late snowbanks.

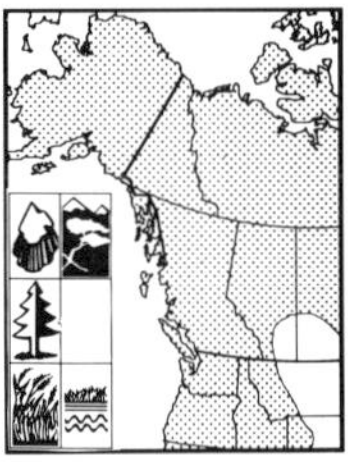

Cetraria islandica. This brown or sometimes tan lichen has a fruticose thallus that varies in shape and size. It usually has lobes that are channeled towards the tips and broader toward the reddish bases. Pseudocyphellae are marginal and laminal on the lower surface. Marginal projections (Fig. 20) are numerous. The medulla is PD+ red and KOH+ yellow to red-brown. *Cetraria islandica* grows in clumps on the ground in tundra communities and in open subalpine forests. Specimens of this species are sometimes difficult to distinguish from those of *C. ericetorum* without testing with PD. *Cetraria laevigata*, a northern boreal and arctic species, is light brown with wide, marginal, continuous pseudocyphellae; its medulla is also KOH+ yellow to red-brown and PD+ red. Historically, *C. islandica* or "Iceland moss" has been used in the manufacture of antibiotics to inhibit the causes of such diseases as tuberculosis and for treatment of athlete's foot and ringworm. Today it is still packaged and sold in stores in Iceland where it is added to soups and stews as thickeners.

x 1.5

Cetraria chlorophylla has a foliose, pale to olive-brown thallus that has narrow (to 5 mm wide), slightly channeled lobes with white to brown soredia along the margins. The paler lower surface has few rhizines that aid in the loose attachment of the thallus to the substrate. Apothecia are rarely produced and all microchemical tests are negative. *Cetraria chlorophylla* occurs on branches and twigs of conifers in open and mesic forests.

x 1.5

Cetraria platyphylla. This foliose, corticolous lichen is found growing on conifer branches and twigs in the Rocky Mountains and the Cascades where it occurs most commonly in open, pine-dominated forests. The thallus lobes are wrinkled and papillate, with apothecia located at the lobe ends. No marginal projections or cilia are present. Other corticolous Cetrarias include *C. halei*, which has narrower lobes, marginal cilia and is light brown in colour with a medulla that is KC+ pink and UV+ white. *Cetraria merrillii* has a dark olive-brown to black, narrow lobed thallus with a medualla that is KC- and UV-.

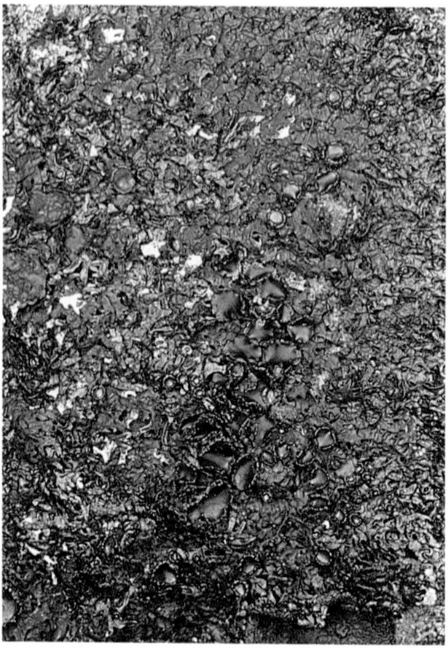

x 1.5

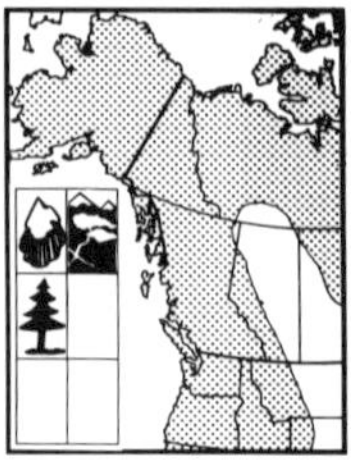

Cetraria hepatizon. This foliose lichen forms rosettes on rocks. The shiny lobes are concave and have pseudocyphellae and sessile black pycnidia along the lobe margins. Apothecia occur at the ends of the lobes. The lower surface has few rhizines and the medulla is PD+ orange. This occasional species grows on open, acidic rocks, especially on quartzite and sandstone in boreal and subalpine forests, in alpine and arctic tundra and infrequently near the seacoast at exposed sites. A similar species is *C. commixta* which has a medullar KOH- reaction. *Melanelia stygia*, also dark brown, has laminal pseudocyphellae and sunken pycnidia, while the medulla is PD- or PD+ red.

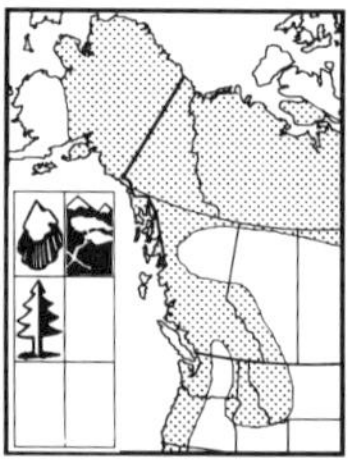

x 1

Melanelia stygia (= **Parmelia stygia**). The foliose thallus has scattered and laminal pseudocyphellae and sunken pycnidia. The lobes are narrow and tend to have shiny tips, while the centre of the thallus is dull. The lower surface of the lobes is dull black and has rhizines. Apothecia that are the same colour as the thallus are common on the upper cortex. Apothecial margins are crenate, and the medulla is PD- or PD+ red. *Melanelia stygia* grows on exposed, acidic, sandstone rocks and boulders. It can easily be confused with the dark brown *Cetraria hepatizon* or *C. commixta*, both of which have channeled lobes and marginal pseudocyphellae. *Melanelia substygia* has laminal and marginal soredia and the medulla is C+ rose.

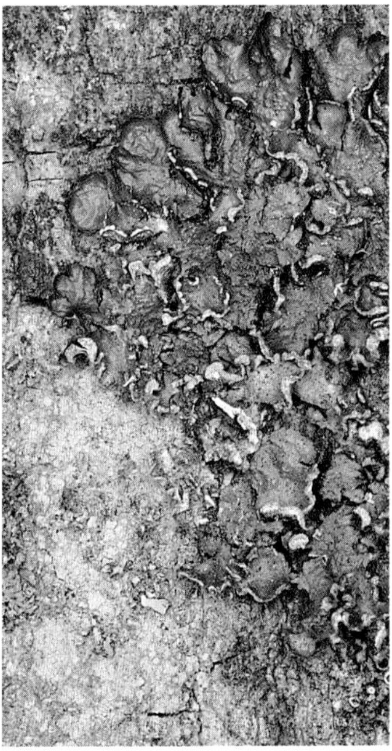

Melanelia albertana (= **Parmelia albertana**). The brown, foliose thallus has marginal and labriform soredia on the central lobes. The soredia are white to brown-grey and finely granulose. The lower cortex is dark brown becoming paler brown near the margins and rhizinate. Lobe margins that are sorediate appear silver when seen at a distance. The medulla is C+ red. *Melanelia albertana*, described in 1969, was named after the province of Alberta where it was first collected west of Edmonton. This species occurs on trunks and branches of such deciduous trees as poplar and willow in the aspen parkland zone of Alberta but is probably more common in the transition zone between parkland and boreal forest. A related species, *M. subargentifera* is pruinose, with laminal soredia and the lobe ends have tiny white hairs that are lacking in *M. albertana*. The medulla of *M. subargentifera* is also C+ red.

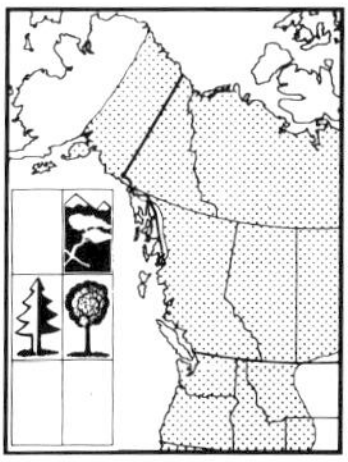

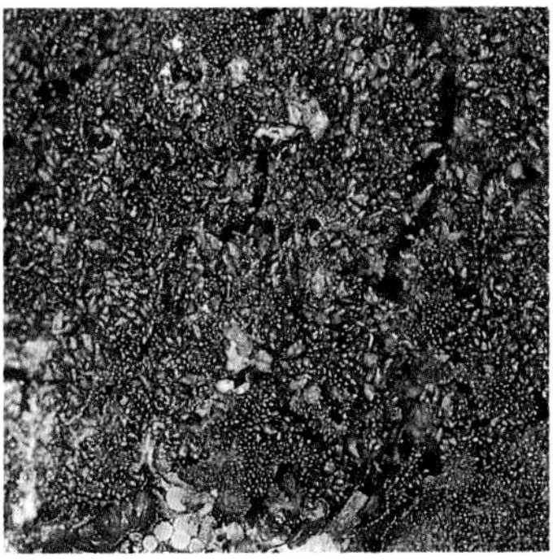

x 1

Melanelia exasperatula (= **Parmelia exasperatula**) has a thin, foliose thallus with hollow, club-shaped, inflated isidia on the upper cortex. The lower surface is dark brown with rhizines. Microchemical tests of the medulla are KOH-, PD- and C-. *Melanelia exasperatula* grows on bark of shrubs, conifers and deciduous trees as well as occasionally on boulders. This widespread species is the most common of the brown isidiate Melanelias. Other similar species include *M. infumata*, a saxicolous species with spherical isidia; *M. elegantula*, corticolous with cylindrical isidia; and *M. subolivacea* that lacks isidia and soredia, but has numerous apothecia and is corticolous.

x 1.5

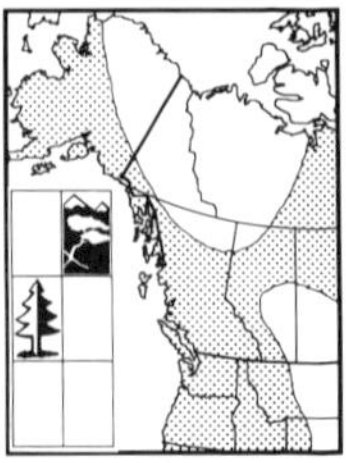

Platismatia glauca. The foliose thallus has upturned lobes that are frilly and servediate at the margins. The lower surface, brown on the outside and black towards the centre, is held loosely to the substrate by a few rhizines. This species may be confused with *Hypogymnia physodes* which has an inflated thallus and no rhizines on the lower surface. *Platismatia glauca* grows on the bark and wood of conifers, including douglas fir, white spruce and lodgepole pine in moist forests, as well as occasionally on boulders.

x 1

Platismatia herrei is a west coast foliose species that has narrow (2-6 mm wide) lobes with filigreed (isidiate) margins; richly branched isidia produce this effect. Few rhizines are present on the mottled white to brown or black lower cortex. The thallus is KOH+ yellow. A similar, but widespread species, *P. glauca*, has wider lobes (to 2 cm) and sorediate margins. *Platismatia lacunosa* has a distinctively sharp-ridged, reticulately-netted green-grey or whitish, broad lobed thallus with brown apothecia common at the lobe tips. This latter species has no isidia or soredia, while the medulla is PD+ red. It is found on exposed conifers. Another species, *P. norvegica*, otherwise similar to *P. lacunosa*, has isidiate ridges on the thallus. *Platismatia herrei* occurs on the branches and trunks of conifers and deciduous trees in moist forests. These species of *Platismatia* are among our most handsome lichens, especially on the west coast where they are all found. Only *P. glauca* reaches the dry coniferous forest zone.

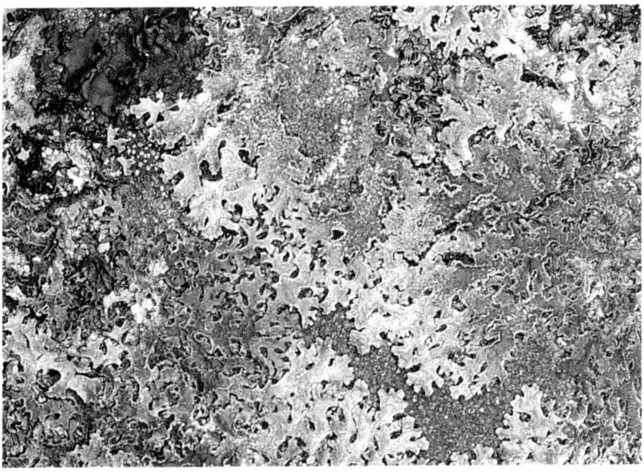

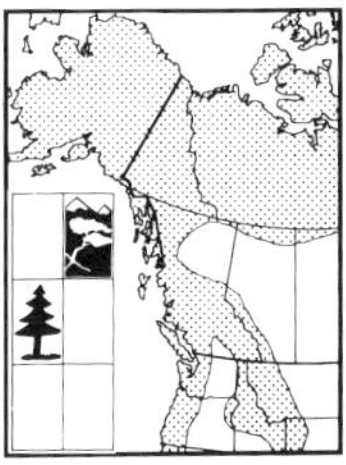

x 1

Parmelia omphalodes. This foliose nonsorediate lichen has a weakly reticulate pattern of ridges on the upper surface of the thallus. Black rhizines on the lower surface sometimes project beyond the lobe margins. The medulla is KOH+ yellow to red. It is widespread and common and occurs loosely attached to exposed boulders, especially in rock slides and on rock cliff faces in the arctic, alpine and subalpine. This lichen resembles *Parmelia sulcata*, however the latter species is sorediate.

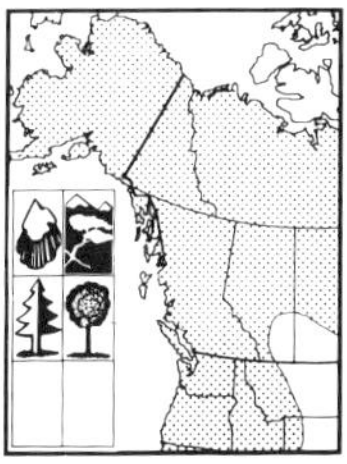

x 2.5

Parmelia saxatilis has abundant isidia located centrally on the foliose thallus. The upper cortex has a weak network of reticulate, white markings like those on *P. omphalodes*. The lower surface is black with simple or dichotomously branched rhizines and is loosely attached to the substrate. The cortex is KOH+ yellow, and the medulla is KOH+ yellow to red and PD+ orange. A similar species, *P. squarrosa*, has the rhizines on the lower surface squarrose (like a bottle brush) and can be found on rocks, among mosses or on trees. The widespread *P. saxatilis* occurs occasionally on acidic boulders on rock outcrops in open coniferous forests, on rock slides, talus slopes and commonly along the coast.

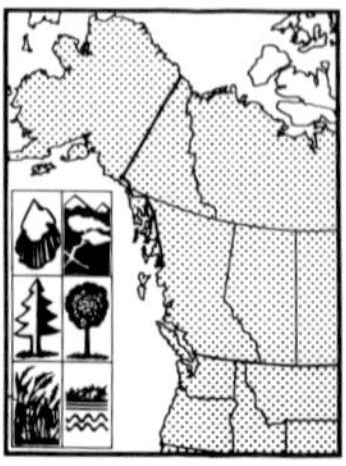

x 1.5

Parmelia sulcata has a grey-green thallus with a network of ridges that are mostly sorediate. The margins of the upper surface are generally sorediate as well; the lower surface is brown at the edges and black centrally. Squarrose rhizines are present. The medulla is KOH + red. This species is common and widespread on the bark of coniferous and deciduous trees and on shrubs; it is also sometimes found on rocks and mosses. It has been found as nesting material in hummingbirds' nests in Alberta. *Parmelia sulcata* and *Hypogymnia physodes* often grow together. At a glance they look alike, but *H. physodes* has inflated, hollow lobes and no rhizines, while *P. sulcata* has solid lobes. These two species are probably the two most common epiphytic species in the northern hemisphere.

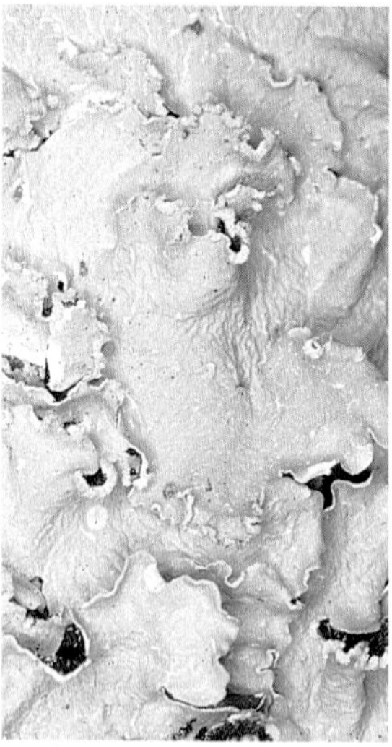

x 3

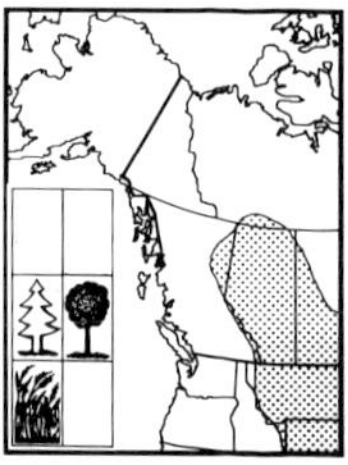

Flavopunctelia flaventior (= **Parmelia flaventior**) has a yellow-green, slightly wrinkled thallus with laminal soredia on the rounded lobes of the upper surface. Large, round to irregular, pseudocyphellae (white spots) are also present. The tan lower surface (darkening to black in the centre) has rhizines. The medulla is C+ bright red. This species forms circular thalli on tree trunks and branches of aspen, poplar, birch, willow and conifers. *Flavopunctelia soredica* = *Parmelia ulophyllodes*, a closely allied species, has no pseudocyphellae on the upper surface and its crescent shaped soredia are located on the lobe margins. The large thalli of these two yellow-green species will certainly catch your eye on your winter cross-country ski or snowshoe rambles.

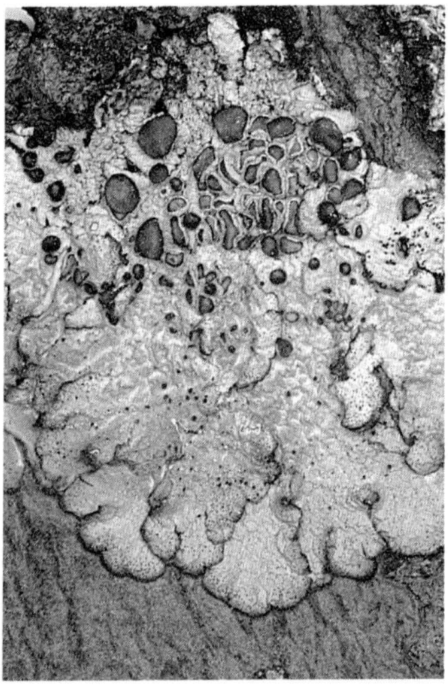

x 7

Ahtiana sphaerosporella (= **Parmelia sphaerosporella**) is characterized by the wrinkled upper cortex, the apothecia with brown discs and the buff-coloured and rhizinate lower cortex. This lichen grows closely appressed on the young bark of whitebark pine (*Pinus albicaulis*). It is common throughout the mountains at timberline where this pine occurs. The well-developed thalli of this pioneer species are also found on such smooth-bark conifers as *Abies lasiocarpa* and *Larix lyallii*. The yellowish, sorediate *Parmeliopsis ambigua* occurs on similar substrates just below timberline. *Ahtiana sphaerosporella* is only found in western North America.

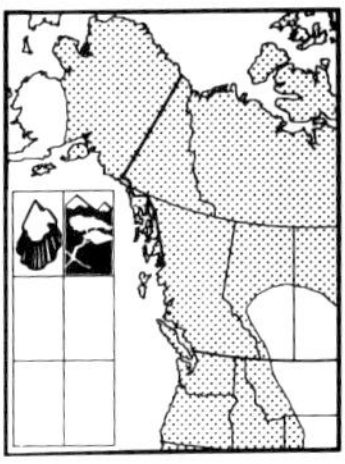

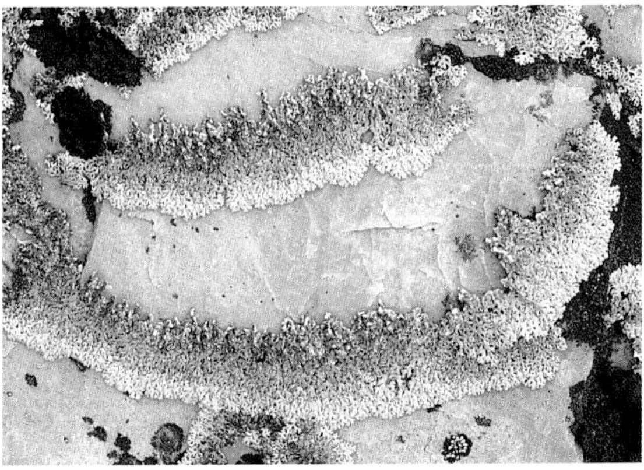

x .5

Arctoparmelia centrifuga (= **Parmelia centrifuga**). The foliose thallus grows in concentric rings recolonizing the inner portions as the centre of the thallus decays. The thallus is closely appressed to the substrate and the upper cortex is dull. The lower surface is white with few rhizines. Apothecia are rare. The medulla is UV+ blue-white, KC+ red and I-. *Arctoparmelia separata* (= *Parmelia separata*), also yellow-green, differs from *A. centrifuga* in having a thallus that is loosely appressed to the substrate, a lower surface that is grey and a thallus that does not form concentric rings. The medulla is I + blue. *Arctoparmelia centrifuga* is an occasional but locally common lichen species of acidic rocks. It grows on the vertical as well as the horizontal sides of rocks in rock slides, talus slopes and rock outcrops. The concentric growth pattern, when evident, is an aid to the identification of this lichen.

x 2

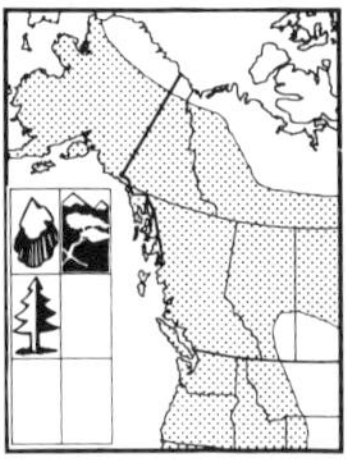

Left: Parmeliopsis hyperopta. Right: Parmeliopsis ambigua.

Parmeliopsis ambigua is closely adnate to the substrate, has yellow narrow lobes and is sorediate. The yellow soredia are abundant on the upper cortex and the thallus is centrally wrinkled. The black lower surface has shiny, brown, lobe tips and black rhizines. All microchemical tests are negative. This species occurs on smooth and rough conifer bark, but also on shrubs, old wood and rarely on rocks. It is a widely distributed species, often found growing at the base of coniferous trees, below the maximum snow line with *P. hyperopta* and *Cetraria pinastri*. *Parmeliopsis ambigua* is found in the alpine and arctic on rock, but is more common on trees and wood in boreal and subalpine forests.

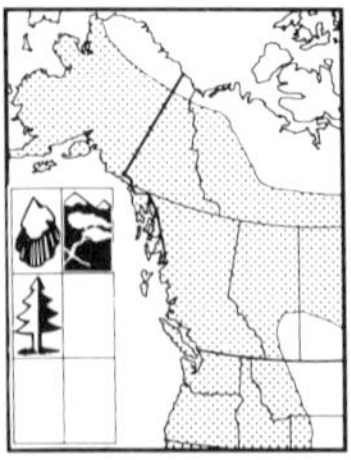

Parmeliopsis hyperopta. The grey-green to ash-grey, foliose thallus resembles that of *Parmelia* or *Physcia* species but the thallus lobes of this species are narrow and closely adnate to the substrate. Capitate soredia are abundant centrally and near lobe tips on the upper cortex. Apothecia with brown discs, are often common on the surface or margins. The underside is shiny-brown with light brown margins and dark rhizines. Microchemical tests are negative. This species is widespread on the base of conifer trunks and on logs; also occasionally on shrubs, humus and rocks. It often grows with *P. ambigua* (which is a coloured chemical variant of *P. hyperopta*). An infrequent, closely related species, *Imshaugia aleurites* (= *Parmeliopsis aleurites*), also has an ash-grey thallus, but has isidia instead of soredia. The cortex and medulla of *I. aleurites* are KOH+ orange and PD+ orange.

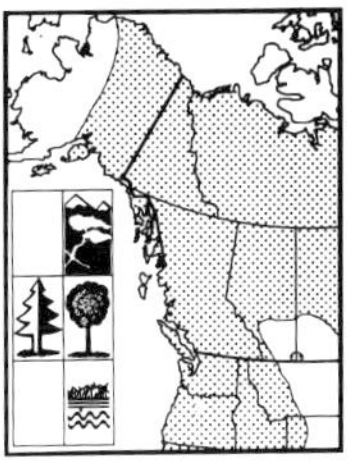

Xanthoparmelia taractica (= **Parmelia taractica**). The yellow-green thallus of this species occurs loosely attached to rock and is usually fertile, having several apothecia with brown discs. Thallus lobes are elongate, with the lower surface tan and rhizinate. Microchemical tests on the medulla are KOH + yellow to red and PD + orange. It is widespread but only occasionally found and occurs on exposed acidic rocks at higher elevations, where it occurs on rock slides, talus slopes and gravel of alpine ridges as well as exposed rocks in the boreal forest and arctic tundra.

x 1.5

Xanthoparmelia cumberlandia (= **Parmelia cumberlandia**) is a saxicolous, yellow-green, foliose lichen. The circular thallus is firmly attached to the rock surface. There are abundant dark brown apothecia present and the lower cortex is brown and rhizinate. Microchemical tests of the medulla are KOH + yellow to red and PD + orange to red-orange. This is a common species on exposed rocks south from southern British Columbia.

x 1

Xanthoparmelia chlorochroa (= **Parmelia chlorochroa**). The foliose, leathery thalli occur scattered loosely on soil. The thallus lobes have their margins curled under with the lower surface tan to dark brown, with few rhizines. This terricolous lichen is locally abundant on soil among grasses in dry calcareous grassland communities of the prairies and mountains. It is easily dispersed by wind when dry. Arid alpine grasslands of the Rocky Mountains will have *X. wyomingica*, a similar species that has narrower lobes, 1-2 mm wide. These two species rarely become attached to the soil and are blown from place to place by the wind. A similar migratory lichen of the arctic and subarctic is *Masonhalea richardsonii*. *Xanthoparmelia chlorochroa* may really be a highly modified version of some saxicolous *Xanthoparmelia* with similar chemistry. This needs study in our prairies, as sometimes one can find *X. chlorochroa* apparently growing from *X. taractica*.

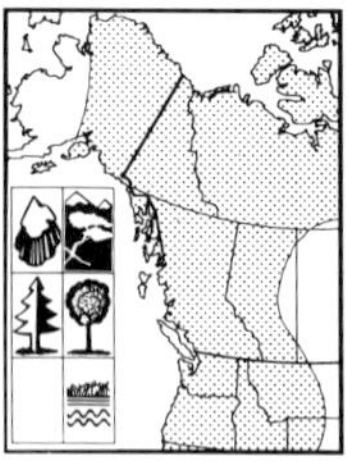

x 2

Hypogymnia austerodes. This foliose lichen forms rosettes on the substrate. The lobes are inflated, hollow and shiny and the upper surface has isidiose soredia toward the centre of the thallus. Thallus margins are black as is the lower surface. No rhizines are present. No other species of this genus has soredia near the centre of the thallus. *Hypogymnia austerodes* grows on wood, bark and mosses at tree bases (and more rarely on rock faces) in mesic forests. Thallus colour may vary from beige-green when growing in the shade to dark brown in sunny locations.

x 1.5

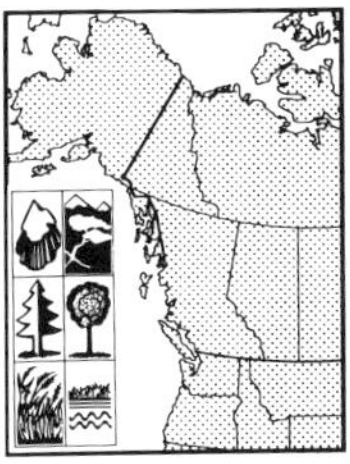

Hypogymnia physodes has inflated lobes with pale green, granular soredia occurring in soralia which are formed inside the lobe tips. The lobe tips then burst open. The upper surface lacks black dots while the lower surface is black and lacks rhizines. The medulla is PD+ red. This grey-green species is widespread and abundant in the mountains and boreal forest, growing on conifer branches, twigs and bark. It also occurs on birch, poplar and willow. *Hypogymnia tubulosa* differs by having capitate soralia at the lobe ends and the medulla PD-. Research has shown *Hypogymnia physodes* to be one of the most tolerant macrolichens to sulphur dioxide air pollution. Because it withstands higher pollution levels than other foliose or fruticose lichens, it is found closer to the pollution sources.

x 1

Hypogymnia metaphysodes has a foliose thallus with inflated lobes that are rarely perforate at their ends. Soredia are absent, but lecanorine apothecia are common and develop at the lobe tips. The large discs are brown, and black dots are often visible at the edge of the thallus lobes, while rhizines are not present. The small lobes, the flattened upper surface and the absence of marginal lobules distinguish this species from the more coastal *H. enteromorpha*. *H. metaphysodes* is a corticolous species that grows on twigs, branches and trunks of conifers, and occasionally on birch or poplar. It is a common lichen of mesic coniferous forests, west of the Rockies.

x 1

Hypogymnia imshaugii has a hollow, inflated thallus with narrow lobes (1-2 mm wide) that branch dichotomously and have nonperforated lobe tips. The upper cortex is light grey-green with black spots, while the lower surface is black without rhizines. The medullary hyphae surrounding the central cavity are white and PD+ orange-red. Lecanorine apothecia on short stalks are frequent. This species occurs on branches of conifers in moist forests. Another species, known from Oregon north to Alaska along the west coast, *H. duplicata*, has a long trailing thallus (to 2 dm), narrow lobes (±2 mm wide) and the medullar hyphae are uniformly dark. No holes are present in the lobe tips.

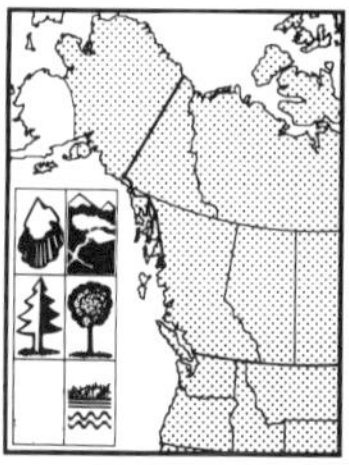

x 1

Leptogium saturninum. The dark, broad-lobed thallus has granular isidia on the upper surface. The lower surface is pale grey and covered with whitish tomentum. *Leptogium saturninum* grows on branches and trunks of white spruce, aspen, poplar, paper birch and willow, and on mosses on tree stumps. It is infrequent in the boreal forest and western mountains at low elevations. The algal symbiont of the genus *Leptogium* is the cyanobacterium, *Nostoc*, as is the case in the similar genus *Collema*. *Collema* species have no upper cortex, are usually black and are gelatinous when wet, whereas *Leptogium* species are dark grey and have an upper cortex. Collemas grow on calcareous rocks, soil and tree bark. *Leptogium corniculatum* (= *Leptogium palmatum*), a west coast species occurring among mosses and on soil and rocks, is lead-grey to brown and has narrow lobes that are wrinkled longitudinally and curl up. The lower surface is without tomentum.

x 1.5

Left: Psoroma hypnorum.
Right: Pannaria pezizoides.

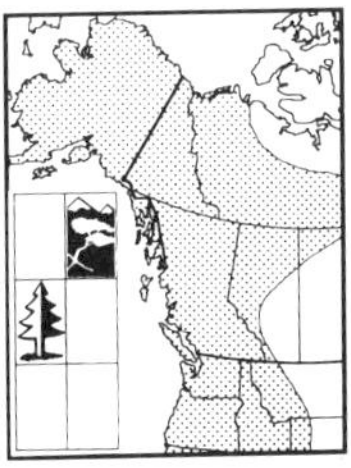

Pannaria pezizoides is a terricolous lichen with abundant flat, irregular red-brown or occasionally orange or black coloured apothecia. The thallus is composed of numerous overlapping squamules which are firmly attached to the soil or humus. The apothecial margin is entire to crenulate. The photobiont is the cyanobacterial genus *Nostoc*; hence the dark grey-brown thallus colour when this species is moist. This lichen grows over soil, mosses or humus, usually in moist forest habitats. It can be confused with *Psoroma hypnorum* that has raised, granular, squamulose to dentate apothecial margins, green algal photobiont and a bright green thallus when moist.

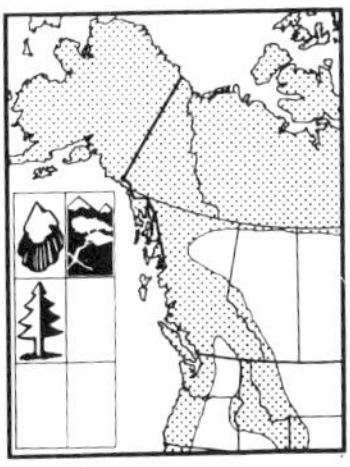

Psoroma hypnorum. The granular, squamulose thallus has large, flat to concave, orange to red-brown apothecia each with a granular, squamulate margin. The apothecia are slightly raised above the thallus. The thallus becomes bright green when moist, due to the presence of the green algal photobiont. *Psoroma hypnorum* grows on moist soil, humus and over mosses in subalpine forests where it is common, and in alpine and arctic tundra where it is rare. It is easily confused with *Pannaria pezizoides* that occupies a similar habitat but has blue-green algae and apothecia that have an entire margin and are at the same level as the thallus. Here, these two species were photographed growing side by side.

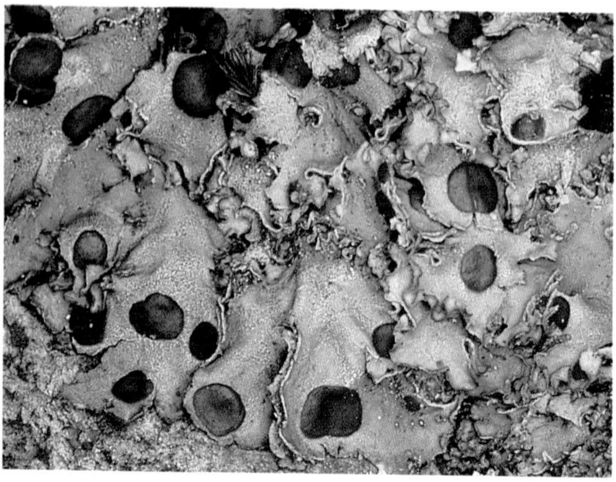

x 2.5

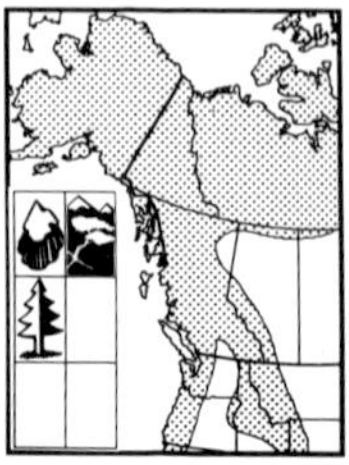

Solorina crocea. The foliose thallus often has large, flat, dark brown apothecia on the upper cortex. The medulla and lower surface are bright orange. This species grows on moist acidic soils along trails and river banks and also occurs on the sides of soil hummocks in the subalpine, alpine and arctic. The orange underside is absolutely distinctive.

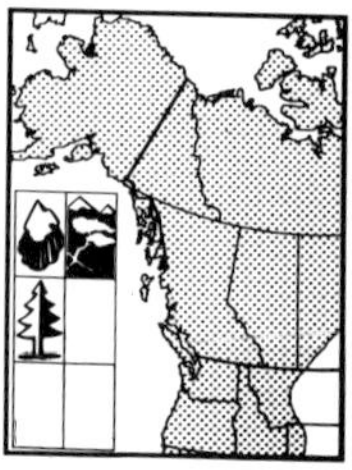

x 3

Solorina saccata. The foliose thallus has sunken, brown apothecia on the upper cortex. The lower surface is pale tan with white rhizines. Spores are two-celled, brown and four per ascus. The thallus is bright green when moist and becomes pale green when dry. *Solorina bispora* resembles this species, except that the thallus tends to be pruinose and the spores occur two per ascus. *Solorina octospora*, as one would guess, has eight spores per ascus; otherwise it is identical. *Solorina saccata* is found on moist calcareous soils, in such places as trail cuts, river banks, seepages, cliff sides and coniferous forests.

x.3

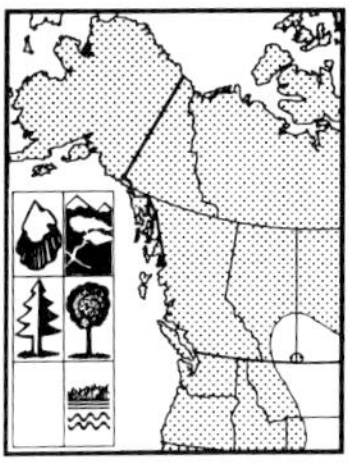

Peltigera aphthosa has a large, foliose thallus with brown warts (cephalodia) on the upper surface and thus the common name 'studded leather lichen'. The under surface of the thallus has broad veins, which may be indistinct and covered by tomentum. The apothecia are red-brown on the upper surface of erect lobe tips. The underside of the apothecium is corticate. When moist, this lichen is bright green but it dries to dull grey-green; this change in colour can be quite remarkable. This terricolous lichen grows over and among such boreal feather mosses as *Hylocomium splendens* and *Pleurozium schreberi* in coniferous forests. It is also found in low shrub communities of the arctic and alpine. In the winter, mountain caribou have been observed foraging for this lichen in the Maligne Lake area of Jasper National Park. *Peltigera leucophlebia*, with similar cephalodia, has distinct veins on the lower surface and the cortex on the underside of the apothecia is discontinuous. Both these species are widespread in our area and until recently have generally been regarded as one species - *P. aphthosa*.

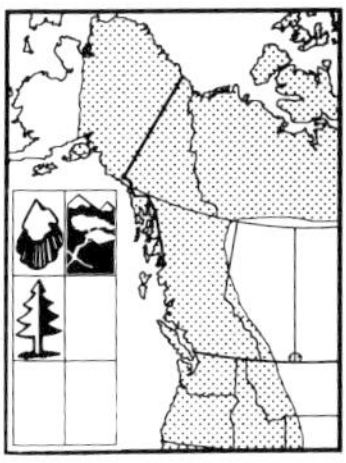

x 1

Peltigera venosa. This small *Peltigera* has dark brown apothecia on the upper cortex and distinct dark brown veins on the lower surface. The thallus is bright green when moist and becomes grey-green when dry. This lichen occurs infrequently on acidic soils, especially on moist banks along trails and rivers. Once recognized, this lichen is very distinctive, particularly the striking dark raised veins alternating with the white medulla of the lower surface.

x .5

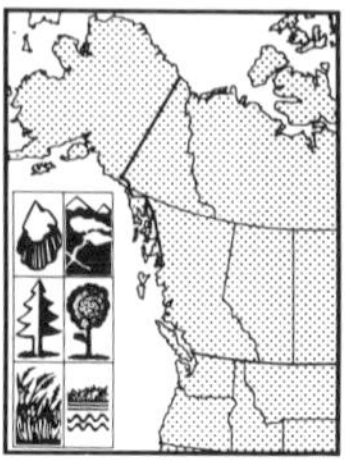

Peltigera canina has large lobes and conspicuous tomentum on almost all of the upper surface. The lobe margins are undulating and usually turned down toward the lower surface. Apothecia are large, dark brown and produced on erect lobes (appearing as raised dog ears). The thallus lower surface has central brown veins that become pale at the margins and rhizines; tomentum is sometimes present. The presence of veins, lack of cephalodia and dull upper cortex are useful features in identification. This foliose lichen grows on soil, humus, mosses and on decaying plant material in the forest. *Peltigera canina* was named 'dog lichen' in Europe where it was recommended as a cure for rabies. Others believed that if you put some of this lichen in your shoe, you would not be bitten by a dog!

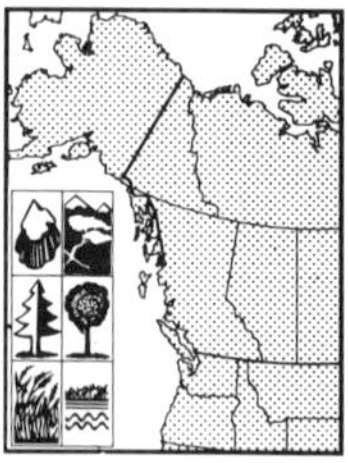

x 1.5

Peltigera rufescens. This terricolous, foliose lichen has medium to small-sized, crisped lobe margins and is frequently white pruinose on the upper surface. Tomentum is appressed to the upper surface. The underside has dark veins and rhizines. This common widespread lichen grows in exposed, dry, somewhat calcareous localities on soil, on soil over rocks and at tree bases in dry open forests, from the montane to the alpine.

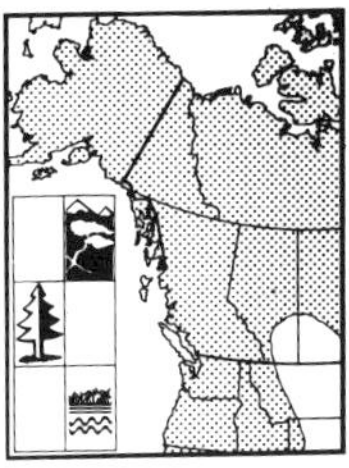

x .5

Peltigera malacea. The thallus of this foliose lichen is thick and when dry feels like cardboard. There are fine hairs on the upper cortex near the lobe margins. The lower surface is veinless and covered with thick, grey tomentum. When moist, this lichen is dark blue-green, but when dry it is grey and the upper surface is dull. This widespread terricolous lichen grows on acidic soils in coniferous forests. The dull upper surface and lack of veins on the lower surface distinguish this species.

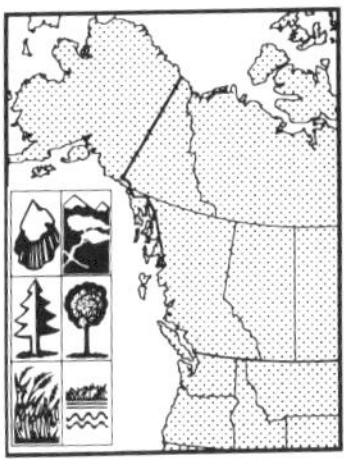

x 1.5

Peltigera didactyla (= **P. spuria**). When young, the greyish-brown foliose thallus has distinct round patches of grey soredia at the lobe tips on the upper cortex. Older thalli lose the sorediate patches as they develop apothecia on erect lobe tips. The lobes are deeply concave. The lower surface has conspicuous, brown, raised veins with white to tan interspaces and is rhizinate. This species occurs on soil beside trails and road-banks, over rocks and in open forests. The distinct round sorediate patches on the lobes of the young thalli are a distinguishing feature of the lichen.

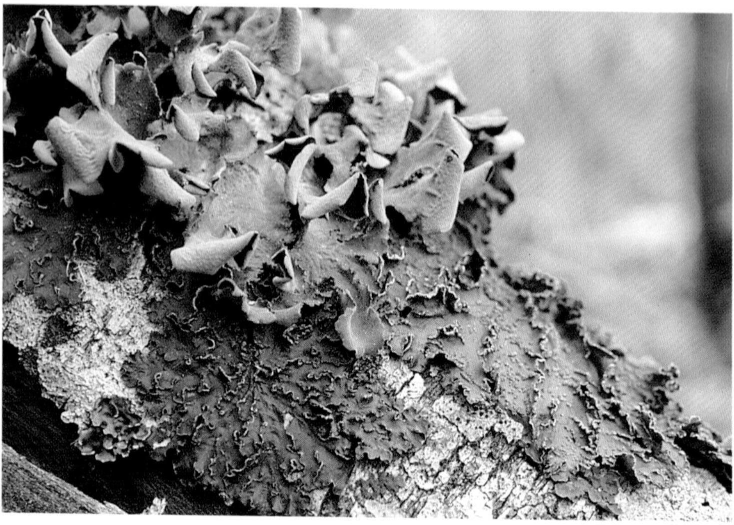

x 1.5

Top *Nephroma resupinatum* Bottom *Nephroma parile.*

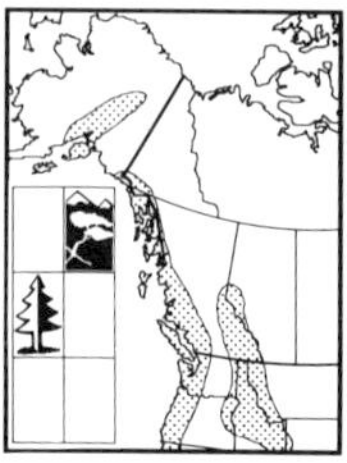

Nephroma resupinatum has large, brown apothecia located on the lower surface of the lobe tips. These lobes are ascending so the apothecia can easily be seen from above. The lower cortex is covered with thick beige tomentum that is interspersed with large white papillae - a hand lens is not required to see the papillae (Fig. 18. See page 158). The thallus is loosely attached to the substrate. This species is widespread and common in moist coniferous forests, occurring on tree trunks and branches and occasionally on rocks. The papillae on the lower cortex are a distinctive feature of this species.

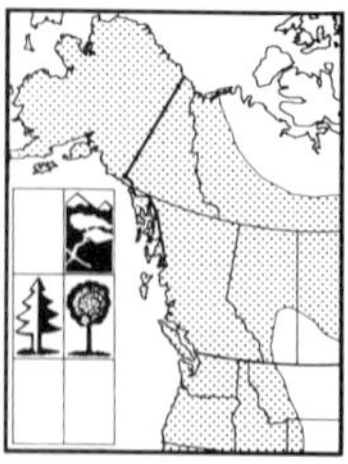

Nephroma parile. The thallus lobes of this foliose lichen have blue-grey marginal soredia. The lower cortex is tan and smooth. This species occurs on rocks, tree stumps and tree bark in moist coniferous and deciduous forests. It can be confused with *Peltigera collina* that also has blue-grey marginal soredia, but has a lower surface which lacks a cortex and has wide brown veins with white interspaces. The presence of soredia distinguishes *N. parile* from others in the genus.

x .5

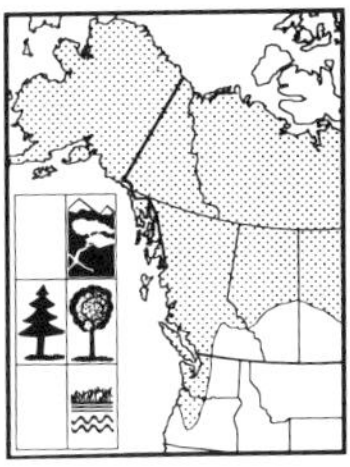

Peltigera neopolydactyla. The foliose, thin thallus has a glossy, billowed, grey upper surface with no hairs near the lobe margin. The brown and elongate apothecia are produced on erect narrow lobes. The lower surface bears pale to dark brown veins and long simple rhizines. This species is dark grey when moist and pale grey when dry. It grows predominently over mosses in mesic forests in the boreal and mountain zones. *Peltigera polydactyla*, which is rare east of the Rockies, differs by its crisped and narrow lobes. *Peltigera horizontalis* is similar to the latter but differs by its round, flat, horizontally orientated apothecia and the dimpled lobe margin. All of these species are easily told from *P. malacea* by the presence of distinct veins and the shiny upper surface. *Peltigera canina* and *P. rufescens* also have distinct veins but differ by the thick tomentum on the upper surface.

x .5

Nephroma arcticum. The bright whitish-green to yellow-green, smooth upper cortex of this large, very broad-lobed foliose lichen is distinctive. The lobe margins tend to curl under. The lower surface is light brown at the margins, becoming black toward the centre. Large brown apothecia are sometimes produced on the under surface of the lobe ends. Species of *Peltigera* are darker in colour and have apothecia produced on the upper surface of the lobes. *Nephroma arcticum* grows among mosses in moist subalpine coniferous forests and in moist moss/heath communities in the alpine. This attractive species is occasionally found in the arctic where it also grows in moss/heath areas.

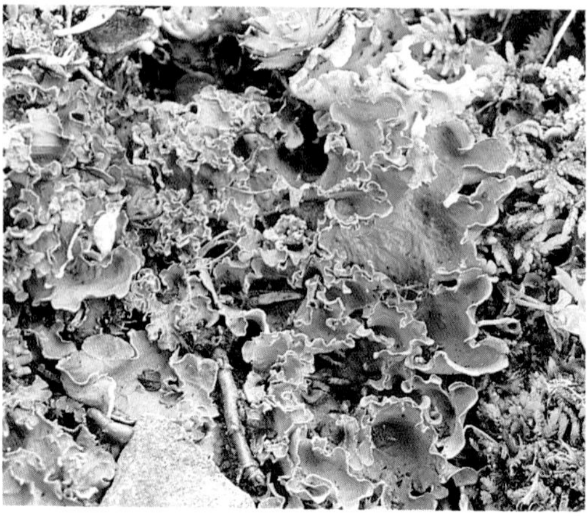

x 1

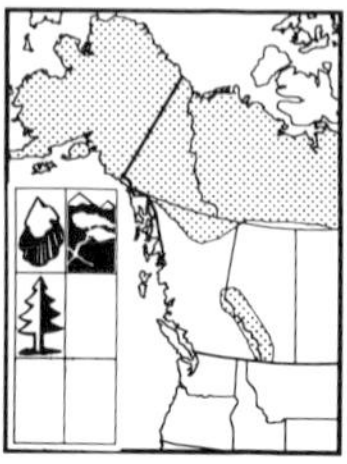

Nephroma expallidum. The thallus lobes are curly and turn up at the margins to show the tan lower surface. Brown apothecia are at the lobe tips of the lower surface. The thallus becomes bright green when wet and is brown-grey when dry. This species grows in moist, mossy, subalpine forests and arctic-alpine moss/heath communities often with *N. arcticum* or *Lobaria linita*. It can be confused with species of *Peltigera*, most of which have veins on the lower surface.

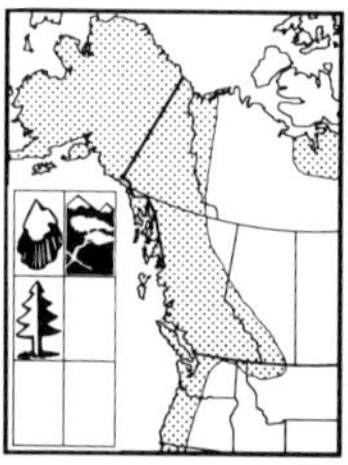

x .5

Lobaria linita. The foliose, broad-lobed thallus has a conspicuous pattern of hollows and ridges over the upper surface. The lower surface is finely tomentose and mottled white and brown. The thallus is bright green when moist, but brown when dry. This species grows on the ground over mosses and at the base of conifers such as subalpine fir and engelmann spruce. In mesic subalpine heath communities, *Nephroma expallidum* is often found growing with *L. linita* among mosses. *Lobaria linita* occurs infrequently in the mountains of Alberta, but is much more abundant in the moist forests of British Columbia.

x.3

Lobaria oregana. When dry the thallus is greenish-yellow to brown and is reticulately ridged with a network of ridges and depressions. The margins of the lobes are fringed with tooth-like lobules, and the thallus is nonsorediate. The brown and white mottled lower surface is covered by short tomentum. The medulla is KOH+ yellow and PD+ orange. This species occurs on conifers and moss covered rocks in open moist forests. As its specific name implies, it is common in Oregon, northward through the Cascades and in coastal forests where it can form large masses on tree trunks or branches. *Lobaria linita*, *L. oregana* and *L. pulmonaria* have a green photobiont and turn bright green when moist, whereas several other species of the genus have a cyanobacterial photobiont and turn dull green when moist.

x 1

Lobaria pulmonaria. The foliose, broad-lobed thallus has a patterned upper surface of hollows and ridges. The thallus margins and ridges have soredia and/or isidia. The lower surface is mottled white and brown and is finely tomentose on the ridges and smooth white in the hollows. The medulla is KOH+ yellow. *Lobaria pulmonaria* is rare on conifers, poplars, logs and mosses in moist forests of Alberta, but is common on trees in the moist forests of the Pacific Northwest. The abundant thalli of *L. pulmonaria* can cover large areas of branches and tree trunks. According to the Doctrine of Signatures, which was formulated in medieval times, this lichen was supposed to cure disorders of the lung, and certainly its large thalli look like limp flaccid lungs. Unfortunately for us, the cure does not seem to have had any foundation.

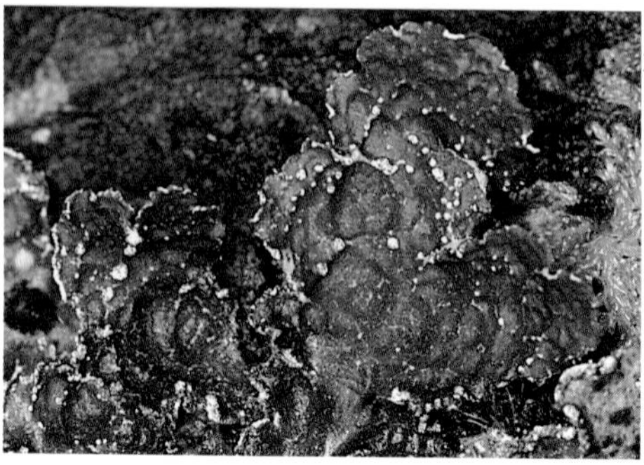

x 2.5

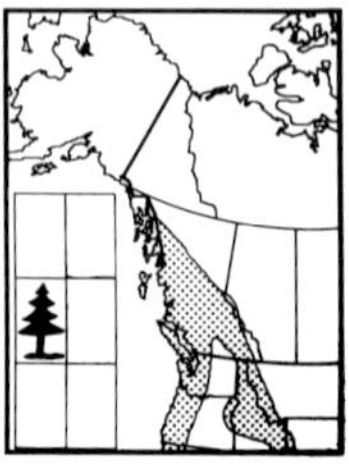

Pseudocyphellaria anomala. This broad lobed, foliose lichen is sorediate and has distinctive pseudocyphellae (white dots) on its lower surface. The upper cortex has white to blue-grey soredia that outline the network of ridges present on the thallus lobes. Soredia are also marginal and laminal on the lobes. The tan lower surface is wrinkled to smooth with short tomentum and numerous pseudocyphellae. The thallus occurs loosely attached to the branches and trunks of conifers and on logs in mature, moist, coniferous forests. Another species found in these same habitats is *P. anthraspis* which has a light brown-green thallus and also has white dots on the tan lower surface. Abundant red-brown to black apothecia are present on the upper strongly ridged surface. This species is nonsorediate. *Lobaria pulmonaria*, which is light brown-green when dry but bright green when moist, also occurs in these moist coniferous forest habitats. The lower surface of *L. pulmonaria* is mottled white and brown and the ridged upper surface is sorediate. *Pseudocyphellaria* is a spectacular genus of large southern hemisphere species.

x 1.5

Sticta fuliginosa (on the left) —here growing with *Peltigera collina* (on the right)—is characterized by cyphellae on the lower surface (Fig. 19. See page 158) while the upper cortex is covered by granular isidia. The thin thallus is loosely attached to the substrate, with the tan lower surface long tomentose. The cyphellae can be seen without the aid of a hand lens, as distinct indented white spots. This species is occasionally found on mosses and on tree branches and bases in moist coniferous forests on the west side of the continental divide, but is absent east of the divide. *Sticta,* like *Pseudocyphellaria,* is mainly a southern hemisphere genus, only poorly represented in our area.

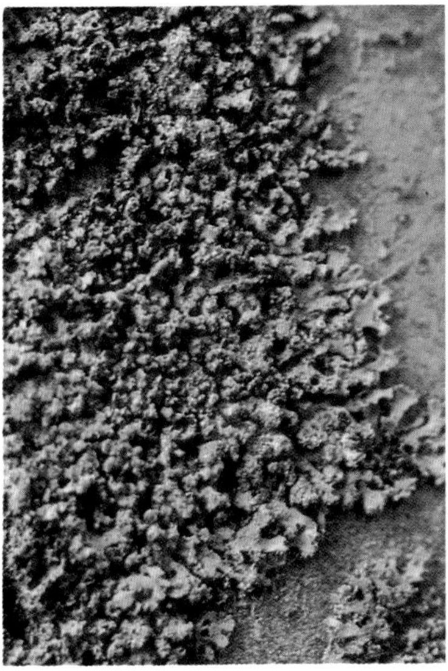

x 2

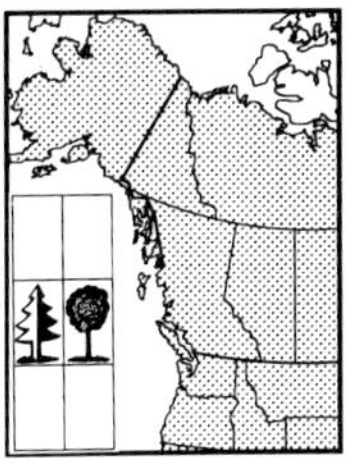

Phaeophyscia orbicularis (= **Physcia orbicularis**). This foliose, corticolous species has dark grey laminal soredia over much of the thallus as well as in capitate soralia at the lobe tips. The lower surface is black with short black rhizines. Microchemical tests are negative. This species grows closely appressed to tree bark, especially deciduous trees as poplar, aspen and elm, and occasionally grows over rocks, mosses and tree stumps. It is widespread in the aspen parkland of Alberta and in western and northern deciduous forests at lower elevations. It is resistant to pollution as witnessed by its ability to flourish on deciduous trees in urban areas.

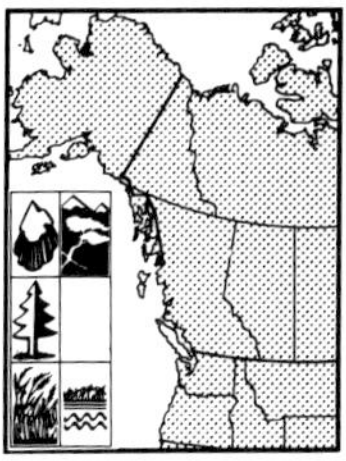

x .5

Physconia muscigena has a thallus with brown, pruinose lobes. The black lower surface has scattered, black, squarrose (like a bottle brush) rhizines. This lichen occurs on humus and soil, especially over moss mats and is widespread and common in grasslands, on peatland hummocks, arctic and alpine tundra and on rock outcrops. It is best distinguished by what it does not have (soredia, isidia, bright colour, rarely apothecia). The black squarrose rhizines, white pruinose lobes and exposed habitat are aids for identification of this lichen.

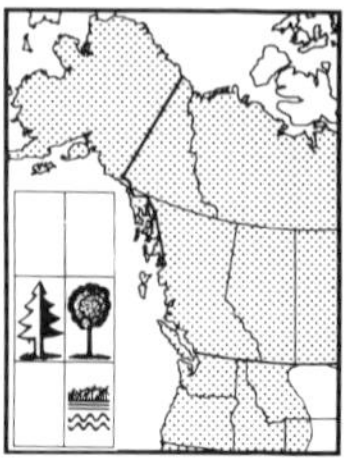

x 1

Physcia adscendens. The foliose thallus of *P. adscendens* has narrow lobes with projecting marginal cilia and ascending, inflated, helmet-shaped lobe ends containing soredia. The underside is white. This species is widespread and common on the bark of aspen, poplar, paper birch, white spruce and willow, as well as occasionally on rock. It is most common in the deciduous forest zone on aspen trunks. This is the only lichen species with helmet-shaped, ciliate lobe tips that contain granular soredia. It reminds one of a miniature snake with head raised and tongue out.

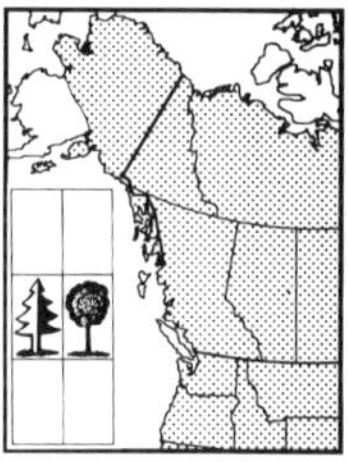

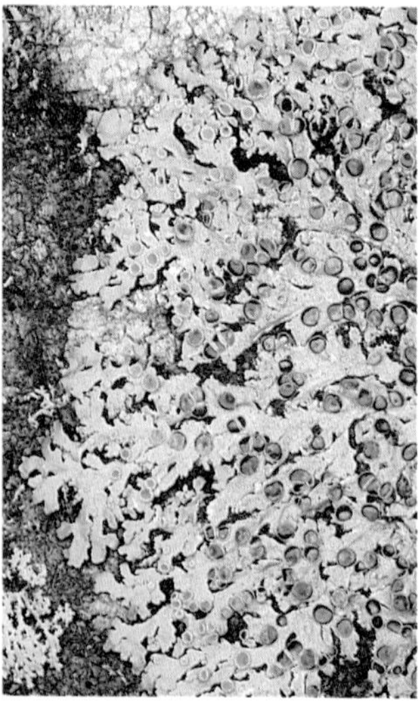

x 2

Physcia aipolia is a foliose, corticolous lichen that has pruinose, dark brown to black apothecial discs crowded toward the centre of the thallus. The upper cortex has small white spots (maculae). The lower cortex is white to pale brown, with brown rhizines. The medulla is KOH+ yellow. It is widespread and abundant on tree bark of deciduous trees, and also occurs on rocks. Although *P. aipolia* is fairly sensitive to air pollution, it does occur in urban areas. *Physcia stellaris* is closely allied to *P. aipolia*, but lacks white spots (maculae) on the upper surface, and the medulla is KOH-. These two species can be vertically stratified; *P. stellaris* occurs on canopy branches, while *P. aipolia* is found more on the main trunk nearer to the ground.

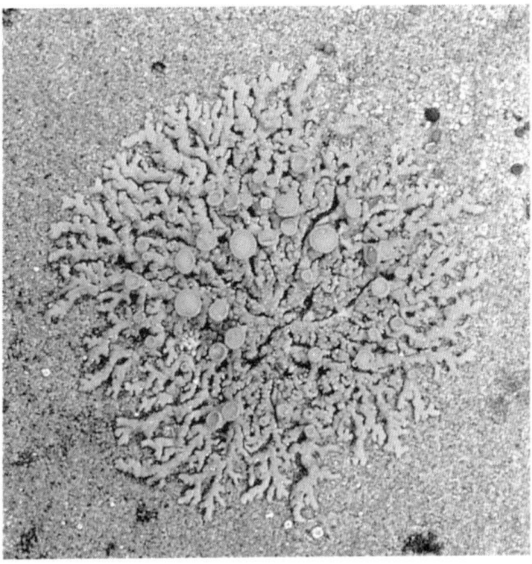

x 1.5

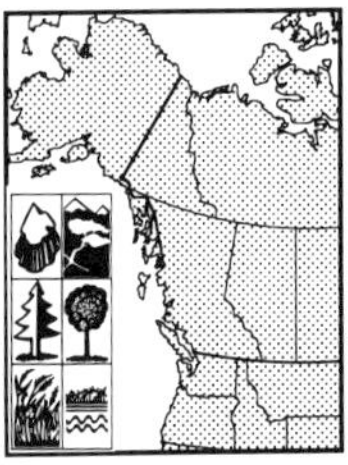

Xanthoria elegans. The orange, foliose thallus generally appears crustose, as it is closely appressed to its rock substrate, but it does have a lower cortex. The thallus lobes are often elongate and form rosettes. Lobe tips may be lightly pruinose and central apothecia are numerous. The cortex is KOH+ purple. This conspicuous species is abundant and widespread on exposed calcareous substrates including both limestone and dolomitic rocks. It is especially common on rocks that are frequented by birds as perches, where it seems to be associated with high nitrogen content. *Xanthoria elegans* is a cosmopolitan species occurring throughout the area at all elevations. Carbonate rich rocks can always be told from granitic and quartzitic ones by the presence of this species versus that of *Rhizocarpon geographicum* (bird perches excluded). *Xanthoria elegans* growing on the graves of the members of the ill-fated Sir John Franklin expedition enabled researchers to determine that this species has reached a diameter of 4.4 cm in the 102 years available for growth.

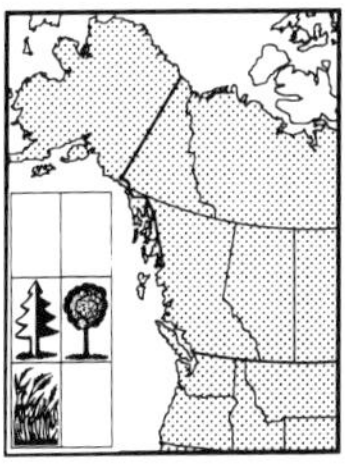

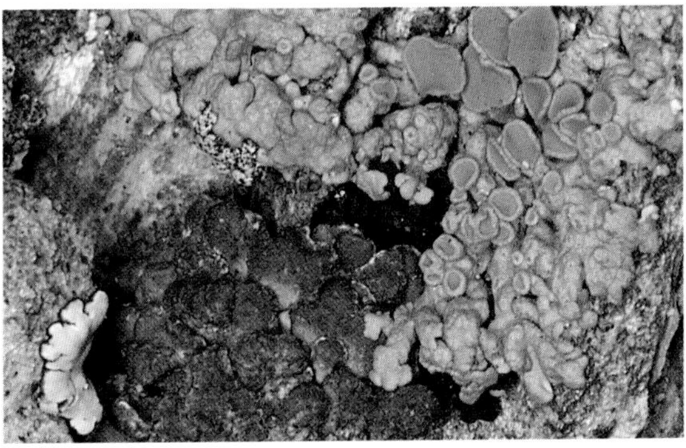

x 4

Xanthoria polycarpa has a bright orange, defined, roundish thallus with narrow imbricate lobes. The white lower cortex is sparsely rhizinate. Numerous lecanorine apothecia are present on the upper cortex. The thallus is KOH+ purple. It forms a species pair with the somewhat larger lobed *X. fallax*; one with apothecia, the other with soredia. This species is common and widespread, occurring on the twigs, branches and trunks of trees, especially aspen, elm and poplar.

x 3

Xanthoria fallax. The foliose thallus has small, appressed lobes (about 2 mm wide) that have raised sorediate margins and tips. Apothecia are absent. The thallus is KOH+ purple. *Xanthoria fallax* grows on the bark of such deciduous trees as poplar, aspen, paper birch and willow in the prairie and boreal forest. It is widespread and common on tree trunks along city streets often growing with *X. polycarpa*, that has apothecia and no soredia. Also common is the smaller, yellow *Candelaria concolor* that is KOH- and often has the centre of the thallus reduced to a granular crust, while its tiny lobes have marginal soredia or granules.

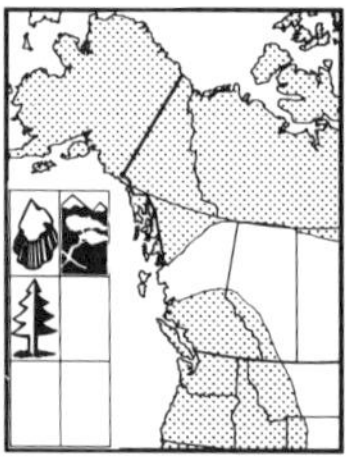

x 1

Umbilicaria vellea is an umbilicate lichen that has a heavily pruinose upper cortex; apothecia are absent. The lower surface is covered with a dense mat of black, ball-tipped rhizines. Sometimes these rhizines appear through cracks that have formed in the upper cortex. The thallus is thick and brittle resembling cardboard when dry. The thalli of this species are often quite large (to 15 cm) and grow on moist vertical cliffs or acidic boulders. This species occurs infrequently in the subarctic, alpine and subalpine, but may also be found on damp canyon walls and rock outcrops at lower elevations.

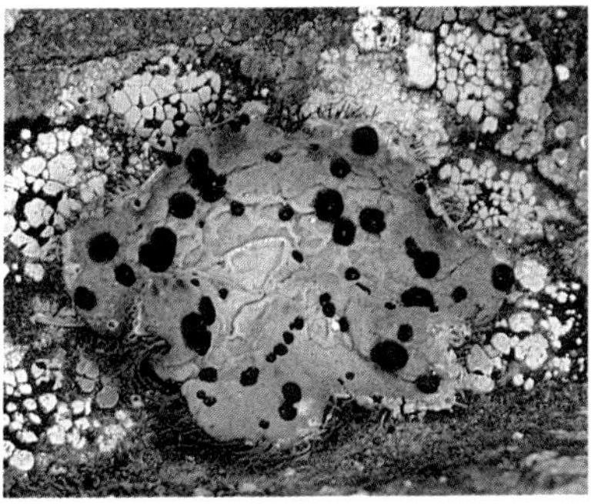

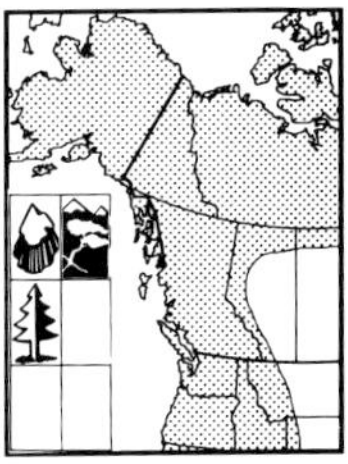

x 1.5

Umbilicaria virginis, an umbilicate lichen, has beige-pink rhizines on the lower surface. The upper cortex is lightly pruinose and apothecia are common; these have flat, black discs with a sterile central fissure. Brown-grey to pinkish rhizines showing from beneath the thallus and frequent apothecia make this lichen easy to distinguish from other *Umbilicaria* species. *Umbilicaria cylindrica*, also with projecting rhizines, is an attractive species with small, grey thalli having dark cilia protruding at the margins. The black apothecia are gyrose in this latter species. *Umbilicaria virginis* occurs infrequently on acidic rocks in the arctic, alpine and subalpine, especially on exposed boulders, rock slides, talus slopes and rock outcrops.

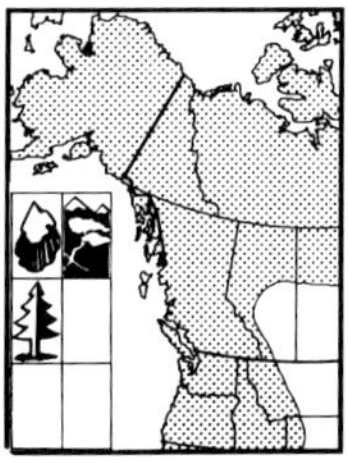

Gyrose apothecium

x 1.5

Umbilicaria torrefacta. The umbilicate thallus has a segmented, smooth upper surface and the lobes are fenestrate near the margin. The lower surface is pale to brown, smooth and without rhizines. The black apothecial surface is gyrose (contorted ridged). This species occurs on acidic rocks in the arctic, alpine and subalpine, usually in exposed areas such as rock outcrops and rock slides. It is widespread and among the most prevalent *Umbilicaria* in the mountains. *U. hyperborea* often occurs with *U. torrefacta,* but is easily distinguished by the ridged upper surface, the absence of marginal perforations and the brown to black lower surface. Rock stripes, a name given to all Umbilicarias, have been boiled and eaten as a survival food, but they do not provide much nourishment, at least to humans; however, they can be a winter food source for musk oxen in the arctic.

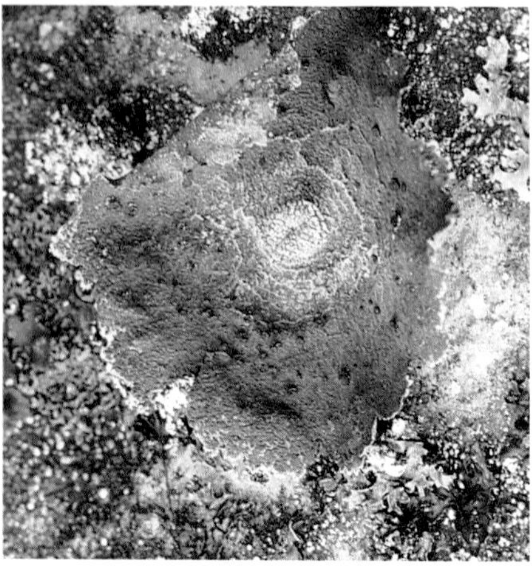

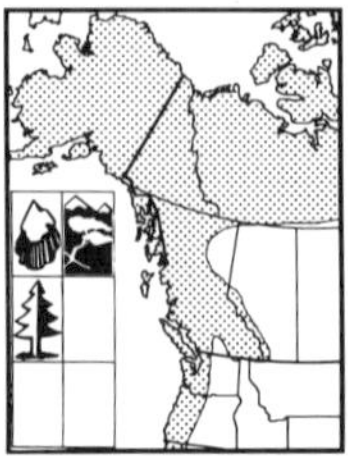

x 2

Umbilicaria proboscidea has white pruinose ridges on the upper cortex, encircling where the umbo, or point of attachment, is on the lower surface. The lower surface is dark grey, with few if any rhizines. Gyrose, black apothecia are common. Frequent on acidic sandstone in the arctic, alpine and subalpine, this species is found on rock slides, talus slopes and rock outcrops. The specific name '*proboscidea*' is also the generic name for the elephant and was given to the lichen because of its resemblance to elephant skin!

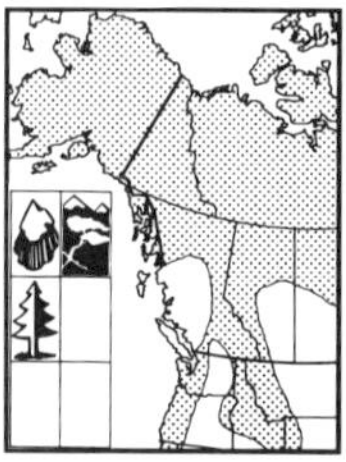

x .5

Stereocaulon alpinum is a lichen that has a small amount of rose to white coloured tomentum on the solid pseudopodetia which are usually widely separated and can be easily seen. The phyllocladia are granular, with the granules often united and flattened. The apothecia, without margins and with dark brown discs, are found at the ends of the branches or grouped on the upper branches. The thallus is PD+ yellow. Widespread and common, this species grows on soil or among mosses in subalpine forest communities and is less common in alpine tundra. It occurs occasionally in the arctic and boreal zones, where *S. tomentosum* is much more common.

x .5

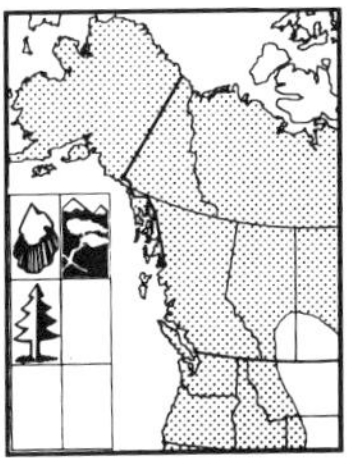

Phyllocladia

Stereocaulon tomentosum. This erect lichen has a conspicuous silver-grey tone and heavily tomentose pseudopodetia. The branches have a dorsal side that has abundant pale grey phyllocladia and a ventral side covered in tomentum. The phyllocladia are crenate, flattened and overlap each other. Small apothecia with pale margins and red-brown discs are often numerous along the length of the branches. The thallus is PD+ orange, but the reaction is often faint. This species is common on the ground where it forms cushions in open coniferous forests. It can be locally abundant on old river bed gravels. *Stereocaulon alpinum* differs from *S. tomentosum* by being white, having rose coloured tomentum and reacting PD+ yellow.

x 1.5

Pilophorus acicularis. The slender pseudopodetia (1-3 cm tall) of this species are terminated by round, black apothecia. They arise from a primary thallus that is granular to areolate (not squamules as in *Cladonia*). This quaint species is firmly attached to rocks in areas of moist coniferous forests that are especially humid such as along river banks, beside waterfalls and along the sea coast. A similar species, *P. clavatus* (= *P. hallii*), has elliptic apothecia and is often found with *P. acicularis* along the west coast.

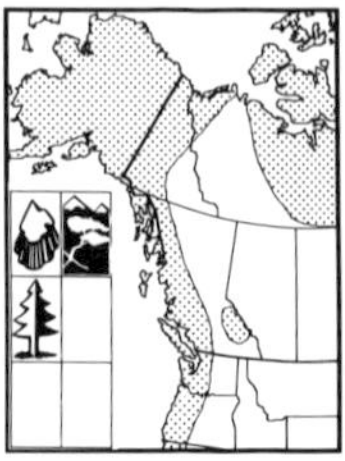

x .5

Sphaerophorus globosus var. gracilis has a highly branched thallus with distinct main stems and lateral branches, both of which are solid and round. The white to green-brown branches have white tips and the medulla is I+ blue. In the moist coniferous forest west of the continental divide, this lichen is commonly found growing on tree trunks. In the alpine and subalpine, *S. globosus* var. *globosus*, a chestnut brown, smaller, less branched variety grows on the ground or in rock crevices, where it is rare. It is more common in the arctic where it grows on humus, soil or gravel. Another arctic species, *Sphaerophorus fragilis* grows in dense cushions and has very fragile branches as the name implies.

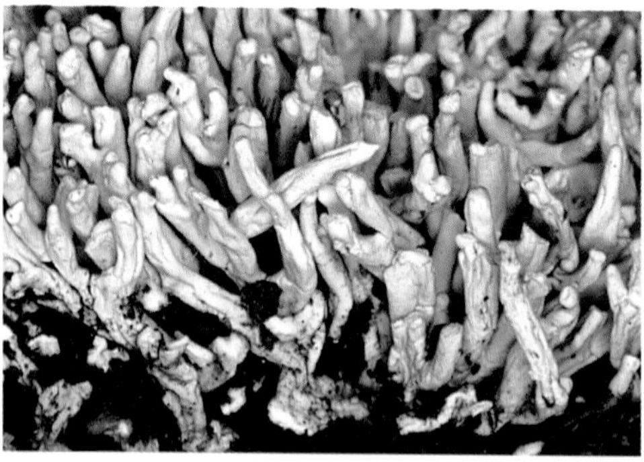

x 3

Siphula ceratites. The thalli consist of white, solid, erect, blunt-tipped, longitudinally wrinkled pseudopodetia (stalks). These pseudopodetia, which occur in tufts and mats, are usually 1-3 cm tall, but can grow to 5 cm. No fruiting bodies are known. This species occurs on peaty soil in minerotrophic peatlands of the west coast and on exposed outcrops in the wettest climatic zone, there forming mats ringing mud-bottoms of fens. It is also known from similar, predominately wet depressions in tundra and moist forests. *Thamnolia subuliformis*, a somewhat similar species, has a hollow thallus, is "worm-like" and grows in dry or moist arctic and alpine habitats.

x .5

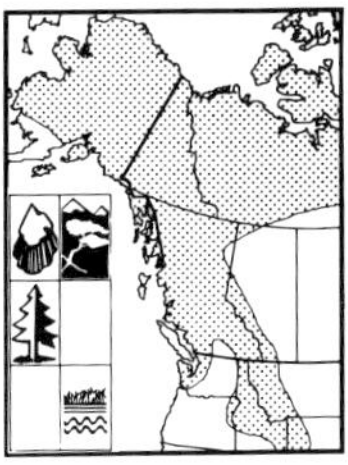

Thamnolia subuliformis. The thalli of unbranched; white, worm-like, hollow, pointed strands occur in tufts or singly. The thalli are UV+ orange, KOH+ pale yellow and PD+ orange. This species seems to reproduce only by thallus fragmentation as apothecia are unknown. This distinctive species is found on soil, humus and decaying vegetation in arctic-alpine areas, where it often grows on exposed, dry, gravelly ridges with other lichens such as *Cetraria nivalis* and *Alectoria ochroleuca*. *Thamnolia subuliformis* also occurs infrequently near sea level along the coast and on dry montane grasslands. *Thamnolia vermicularis* is morphologically identical to *T. subuliformis* but differs in its chemistry; it is characterized by UV-, KOH+ deep yellow or orange and PD+ orange to red. *Thamnolia vermicularis* is more common in the southern hemisphere, while *T. subuliformis* is more frequent in the northern hemisphere. The bone white colour of *Siphula*, *Thamnolia* and *Ochrolechia frigida*, all species of high light intensity, may suggest an adaptation for light reflectance, similar to hair points in xeric mosses. Those walking in tundra areas will quickly become familiar with *Thamnolia subuliformis*.

x .5

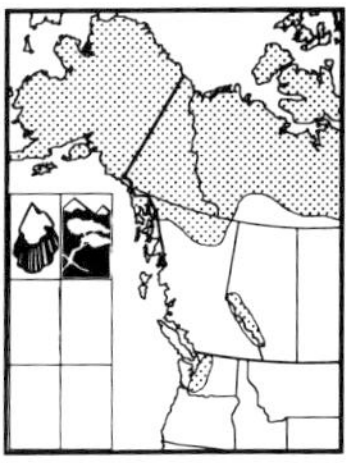

Dactylina arctica has yellow-brown, finger-like thalli that are inflated, hollow and little branched. The medulla of *D. arctica* is PD-, whereas *D. beringica* with an identical thallus is PD+ orange-red. *Dactylina arctica* grows on the ground among mosses or other lichens, or in mountain avens (*Dryas octopetala*) or white mountain heather (*Cassiope mertensiana*) communities in alpine and subalpine areas. In the arctic, this species is common in arctic heather (*Cassiope tetragona*) communities where other lichens such as *Cetraria nivalis* and *Thamnolia subuliformis* also occur. Species of *Dactylina* are distinctive in having an inflated, finger-like thallus structure and their unique growth form always makes them interesting to discover.

x 1.5

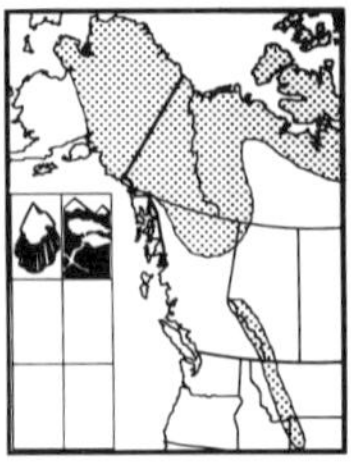

Dactylina ramulosa has short, erect, finger-like thalli with whitish pruina that gives a violet or pink hue to this lichen. The thalli are hollow, inflated and somewhat fragile, while the medulla is PD+ orange-red or PD-. *Dactylina madreporiformis*, a closely related species, which is soft and lacks pruina, has a PD- medulla reaction. The thalli are filled with cottony white hyphae. *Dactylina ramulosa* grows in tufts but also occurs scattered on soil in calcareous tundra habitats. It is frequent in the Rocky Mountains at high elevations and also in the arctic in calcareous habitats.

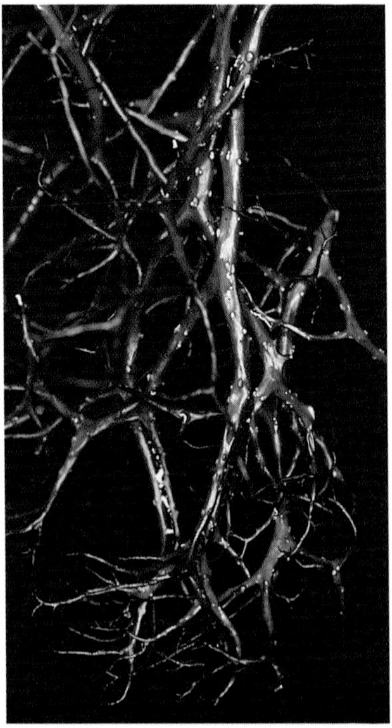

x 3

Bryocaulon divergens (= Cornicularia divergens) is a decumbent, terricolous lichen that has a distinctive, shiny, red-brown thallus. The long, white, furrowed pseudocyphellae react C+ red. *Bryocaulon divergens* is a rare component of windswept gravelly tundra. It occurs in a terricolous lichen association of *Alectoria ochroleuca*, *Thamnolia subuliformis*, *Cetraria ericetorum* and *C. nivalis*. It is the only fruticose terricolous lichen with a bright, shiny, red-brown thallus. *Alectoria nigricans* (also fruticose, decumbent and terricolous) has black tips mottled with grey and has pseudocyphellae that are C+ red. *Bryoria chalybeiformis* is brown to olivaceous-black and has soredia that are PD+ red although the rest of the thallus is PD-. *Bryoria nitidula* is a brown to black, nonsorediate, PD+ red, arctic species that is often associated with *Bryocaulon divergens*.

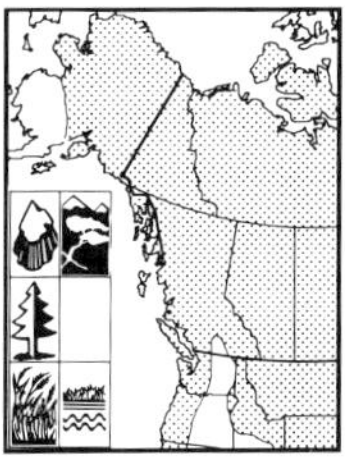

X 3

Coelocaulon aculeatum (= Cornicularia aculeata). Branches of this fruticose lichen are foveate with sunken, white pseudocyphellae occurring in the low areas. The shiny, delicate branch tips break off easily exposing the white inner hyphae. This lichen forms inconspicuous cushions on the ground in open, dry, gravelly or sandy areas such as river flats, forest edges, dry grassy meadows, sand dunes, prairie and tundra. Look for it among the vascular plants. *Coelocaulon muricatum* is very similar, but forms denser clumps with shorter branches and has fewer and less conspicuous pseudocyphellae in the pits.

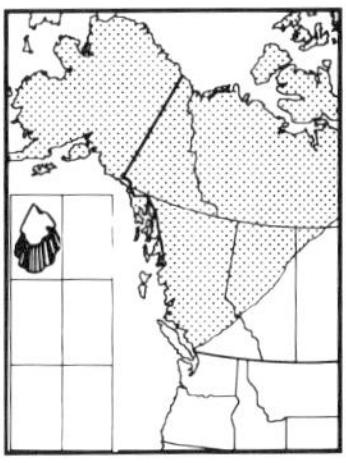

X 1

Alectoria ochroleuca. This yellow to yellow-green lichen grows on humus, soil and over pebbles with other terricolous lichens in open tundra habitats. Raised, white, elongate pseudocyphellae up to 1 mm are oriented longitudinally along the thallus branches. The thallus branches are round, stiff and erect, with pointed, blue-black tips. The fruticose thallus generally has ascending branches, which may be swept to one side in their apical portions. Exposure to solar radiation causes the upper surface to turn dark green while the lower surface remains paler yellow-green. Other terricolous lichens usually found with *Alectoria ochroleuca* are *Cetraria islandica, C. ericetorum, C. nivalis, C. tilesii* and *Thamnolia subuliformis*.

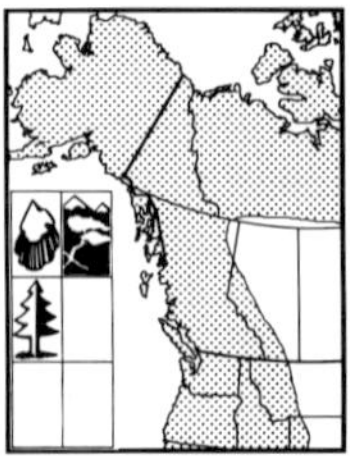

x 2

Pseudephebe pubescens is a fruticose lichen that grows closely attached to rocks, there forming rosettes of filamentous lobes with nodulose branches. It occurs on acidic rocks and stones in exposed subalpine rock outcrops and in alpine and arctic tundra. This species often covers extensive areas of rock surfaces. A closely related species, *P. minuscula*, has shorter internodes and filaments appressed to the substrate. Microchemical tests of both species are negative. *Pseudephebe* are the only 'hair-like' lichens whose whole thallus area, rather than just the base, is attached to the rock.

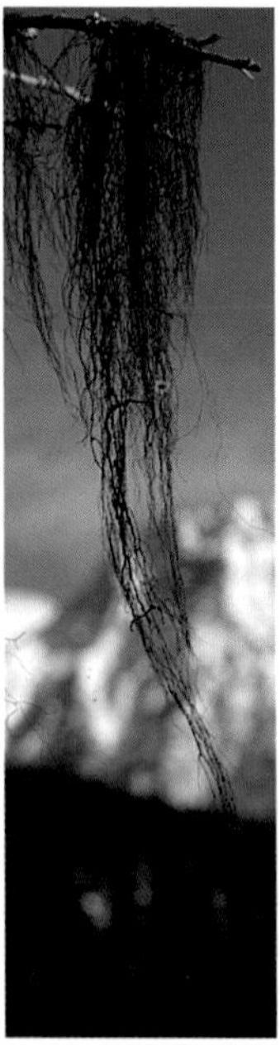

x .5

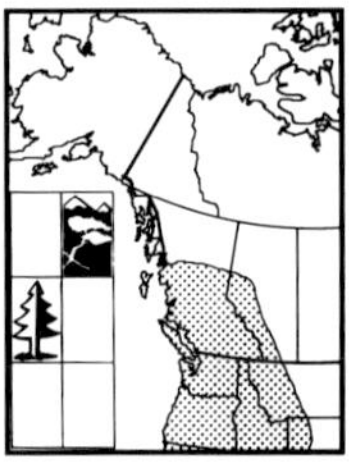

Bryoria fremontii. The long, chestnut-brown, shiny, pendent, usually nonsorediate thallus is often twisted and foveate, especially at the base where the branches are broader. A rare sorediate form has bright yellow soredia (vulpinic acid producing the same colour as *Letharia vulpina*). This lichen occurs mostly on conifer branches in open forests. The thicker basal branches and deep brown colour separate this lichen from the nonsorediate *B. oregana* that has longitudinally furrowed branches and is a dull red-brown colour. *Bryoria abbreviata*, a subalpine species, has a caespitose habit on trees and numerous ciliate apothecia. *Bryoria tortuosa*, a coastal species with twisted branches, is dull, dark red-brown to dusky yellow-brown and often has bright yellow (vulpinic acid), elongate pseudocyphellae that twist around the branches. Native peoples of inland British Columbia steamed these lichens in ground pits for 48 hours until they melted and formed a thick jelly-like substance that was then cooled, sliced and eaten, or dried for storage.

x 1

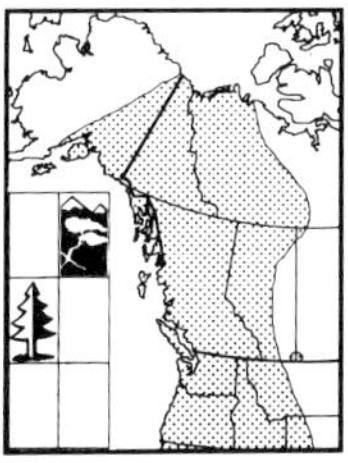

Bryoria glabra has branches of even diameter throughout the thallus. The pendent thallus is usually 10-15 cm long. Shiny, olive-green to black branches with regularly occurring fissural soredia characterize this species. Soredia test PD+ red. This lichen is found on coniferous trees, especially subalpine fir, engelmann spruce and white spruce of the subalpine zone. In coastal peatlands, *Bryoria glabra* is found on sitka spruce, shore lodgepole pine and western hemlock. *Bryoria fuscescens* is the most common species of the dry coniferous forests in the western mountain areas. It occurs pendent from such coniferous trees as lodgepole pine, ponderosa pine and douglas fir. The growing tips are fuscous brown, while the base is paler in colour. Black areas that fragment easily are often present. Soredia are usually numerous and test PD+ red. *Bryoria lanestris* is a common, pendent to sub-pendent species especially in wetland forests of black spruce and larch with brown-black, narrow, uneven, brittle branches. Soredia are often flecked with black or can be white. It resembles wool in texture. Often found intertwined with *B. lanestris* is *B. simplicior*, a tufted, brown to black species with abundant white to greenish-black soredia that are PD-.

x .5

Bryoria capillaris is a pendent epiphyte with a pale grey-brown to greenish-grey colour that distinguishes this species from the usual true brown tones of other *Bryoria* species. Soralia are absent on North American populations, but short white pseudocyphellae (shallow pits) are present. The thallus is persistently KOH+ bright yellow (colour does not fade if the KOH is applied to the lichen on filter paper). This species grows on such coniferous trees as spruce, douglas fir, subalpine fir and western and mountain hemlock in mature, well-lit, humid forests. *Bryoria capillaris* and *Alectoria sarmentosa* are often festooned from tree branches in especially humid areas such as near waterfalls, rivers and along the sea coast.

x.2

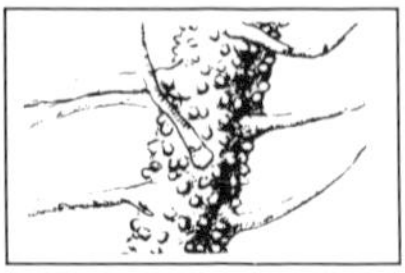

Papillae

Usnea lapponica (= U. sorediifera). The short, tufted thallus has a central cord and abundant papillae, especially near the bases of the main branches. Soralia are numerous near the ends of the branches, but no isidia are present. This species is widespread and abundant in the mountains from montane to subalpine elevations and less common in the boreal forest. It is the most common *Usnea* of the Rocky Mountains, where it is corticolous on conifers and deciduous trees. *Usnea subfloridana* resembles this species, but has isidia occurring in the soralia; it tends to be a boreal species, whereas *Usnea lapponica* is montane. It is often difficult to differentiate these two species as the isidia are sometimes not obvious.

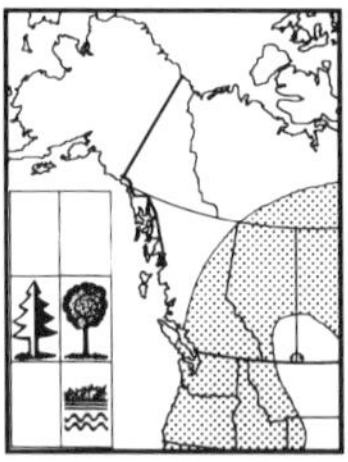

Usnea hirta has a short, tufted thallus with a central cord. No papillae are present at the basal area of the main branches, but peg-like isidia occur in dense masses on the main and side branches. This species is common on white spruce, black spruce and larch in the boreal forest, but is rare in the mountains.

x 1

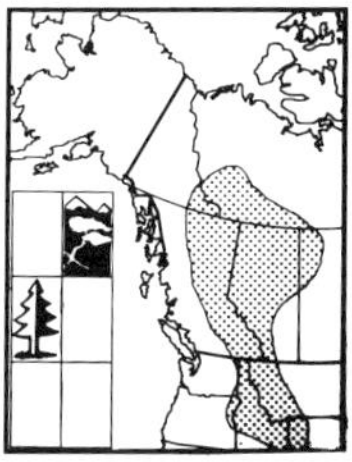

Central cord of Usnea

Usnea alpina. The pendent thallus has a central cord (a gentle pull on the branch will reveal this). Papillae (small bumps) are present at the base of the main branches. The thallus is nonsorediate and the branches slightly foveate. This lichen grows on conifers in the Rocky Mountains from the montane to the subalpine zone. It is common in moist forests. *Usnea scabrata* subsp. *nylanderiana* is pendent like the above species, but is strongly foveate and has numerous sharp pointed papillae and tubercles that are usually isidiate on the main branches. It occurs infrequently in the Rocky Mountains, boreal forest and along the west coast south of Vancouver.

Alectoria sarmentosa. Superficially, the yellow-green colour of this species is similar to that of all *Usnea* species. However, a central cord is lacking here. The basal area of attachment is rather stiff, while the hollow, shiny branches are flaccid and have raised, elongate, white pseudocyphellae about 1 mm in length. *Alectoria sarmentosa* is found in moist, coastal, montane and boreal areas, hanging from branches of conifers. It can easily be confused with *Usnea* species, which have a central cord; or *Ramalina thrausta,* whose branches are finer and have distinctive, curled, isidioid tips. Another similar species, *A. vancouverensis* is found along the west coast from southern British Columbia and Vancouver Island to northern California. This pendent, yellow-green lichen differs from *A. sarmentosa* in that the pseudocyphellae of *A. vancouverensis* twist around the branches and thus are conspicuous. The dense medulla of *A. vancouverensis* is C+ red, whereas the loose medulla of *A. sarmentosa* is C-. *Alectoria vancouverensis* grows in open coniferous forests near sea level, especially in humid zones.

x .5

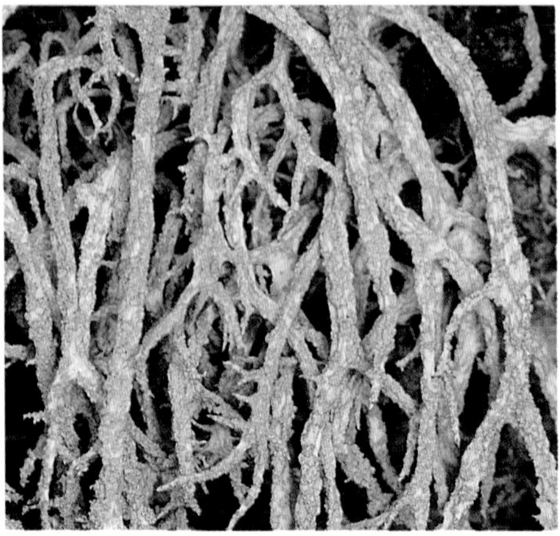

x 5

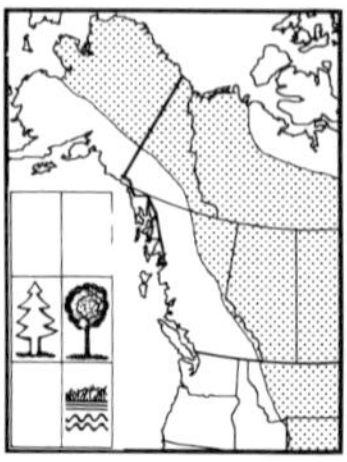

Evernia mesomorpha has a tufted thallus with angular, longitudinally wrinkled uneven branches that are yellow-green, soft and pliable. Granular soredia are scattered over most of the thallus surface. It is abundant in the boreal forest, growing on the branches and bark of black spruce, larch and birch, and is a dominant epiphyte of the boreal muskeg. In moist coniferous forests west of the Rockies, *E. prunastri* with flat sorediate branches (1-4 mm wide) and a lower surface paler than the upper, can be found. Other yellow-green lichens that may be confused with *Evernia* are *Usnea* which has a central cord, *Alectoria* which is round in cross section and *Ramalina* which has flattened branches.

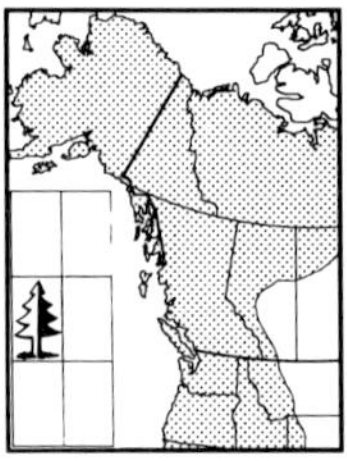

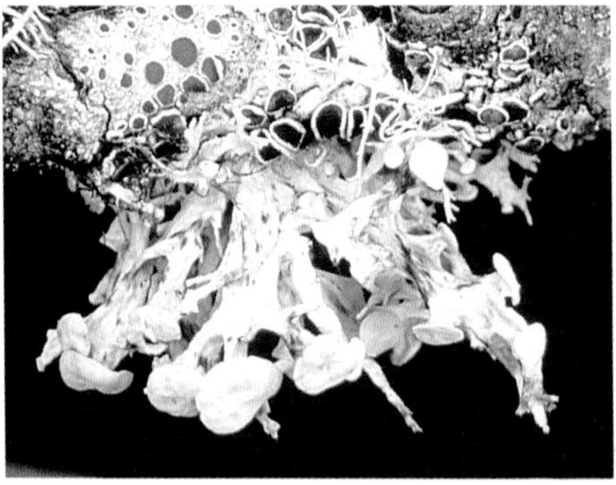

Ramalina dilacerata (= **Ramalina minuscula**). The short, tufted thallus has hollow, inflated, perforated branches. The branches are up to 3 mm wide and flattened only at their ends. Apothecia are often present at the ends of the branches. *Ramalina dilacerata* occurs on the stumps, trunks and branches of trees and shrubs. It is an occasional species and may be locally common. It is similar to some species of *Usnea* and *Evernia*, but does not have the central cord of *Usnea* and is not sorediate as is *Evernia mesomorpha*. *Ramalina thrausta* is a pendent species with round branches that have tiny, hooked-shaped isidia at their tips. This species is rare east of the Rocky Mountains, but common on conifers in the British Columbia mountains where it grows with *Alectoria sarmentosa*. *Ramalina menziesii* has a yellow-green, pendulous (to 40 cm), netlike thallus and festoons trees along the coast from Baja California, Mexico to British Columbia.

Letharia vulpina. The tufted, thallus has angular, pitted branches that are sorediate. This light-loving lichen is widespread and common on branches and trunks of conifers in open forests of the western mountains. Often it will form a prominent display, partially covering standing dead trees and snags, especially in northern Idaho and southeastern British Columbia. Skiers will notice this lichen in winter as its bright chartreuse colour contrasts sharply with the forest, snow and sky. This lichen is commonly called 'wolf lichen' because it was used in Europe to kill wolves by poisoning them with a rolled ball of *Letharia*, animal fat and nails. The prominent lichen acid present in the species, vulpinic acid, is in fact poisonous and perhaps added to the fate of the wolf - as much as the nails.

Letharia columbiana. The branches of this spectacular, chartreuse lichen are angular and wrinkled. Large, brown, apothecia are common, while soredia are never present. *Letharia columbiana* is found on the bark and wood of exposed branches and trunks of conifers at higher elevations, especially on *Larix lyallii*, *Pinus albicaulis* and *Abies lasiocarpa*. The eastern and northern limit for this species is close to the continental divide in Jasper National Park, Alberta. *Letharia columbiana* ranges south in the Rocky Mountains and west to the Pacific coast. *Letharia vulpina*, which lacks apothecia and is sorediate, is the most commonly observed species of the genus. Phytogeographically, sorediate lichens are more widespread than those with apothecia. This can be seen in species pairs as in *Letharia; L. vulpina* with soredia is widespread in Europe, Asia and North America, while *L. columbiana* with apothecia is endemic to a narrow area in western North America.

Changes in Lichen Names

BOOK	CHECKLIST*
Acarospora chlorophana	= *Pleopsidium flavum* (Bell.) Koer.
Haematomma lapponicum	= *Ophioparma lapponica* (Raes.) Haf. & Rogers
Cetraria canadenis	= *Vulpicida canadensis* (Raes.) Matts. & Lai
Cetraria chlorophylla	= *Tuckermaniopsis platyphylla* (Tuck.) Hale
Cetraria pinastri	= *Vulpicida pinastri* (Scop.) Matts. & Lai
Cetraria platyphylla	= *Tuckermaniopsis chlorophylla* (Willd. in Humb.) Hale
Cetraria tilesii	= *Vulpicida tilesii* (Ach.) Matts. & Lai
Xanthoparmelia taractica	= *Xanthoparmelia somloensis* (Gyel.) Hale

* Egan, R.S. 1989. Changes to "A fifth checklist of the lichen-forming, lichenicolous and allied fungi of the continental United States and Canada." Edition 1. *The Bryologist* 92: 68–72.
Mattsson, J.E. and Lai, M.J. 1993. *Vulpicida*, a new genus in the Parmeliaceae (Lichenized Ascomycetes). *Mycotaxon* 46: 425–428.

Ferns

Horsetails, Club Mosses & Ferns

Their Structure and Biology

Definition

The ferns, club mosses and horsetails have often been grouped together by botanists as pteridophytes, defined as those tracheophytes or vascular plants (see under "Definition of Mosses" as well), that reproduce by spores rather than seeds. In the mid 20th century however, considerable information was gathered that indicated that these three spore-bearing plant groups are not closely related. In fact, they represent three totally separate lines of evolution. They share only a common grade of evolution, that of reproduction by spores and the inability to increase in diametre by secondary growth (thus they do not produce "wood" as do conifers and flowering plants). All three groups also share a great antiquity and fossilized representatives of each can be found in rocks of Devonian age, a time when land was first being colonized. Even then, about 350 million years ago, the three groups were as distinct from one another as they are today.

There is only one genus of horsetails with about 15 species living on earth today. This genus, *Equisetum*, is characterized by having whorled, scale-like leaves and when branched, the branches arising in whorls as well. The stems and branches of most species have a partial coating of silicon dioxide, making them harsh to the touch and thus excellent scouring utensils or a substitute for sandpaper. The spores are produced in terminal cones, each cone consisting of numerous pads. Each pad has a stalk and on its inner surface are several sporangia containing spores of one size.

The club mosses consist of about four genera worldwide; in our area three of these occur: *Lycopodium* with 200-400 species worldwide, *Isoetes* with perhaps 75 species worldwide and *Selaginella* with about 500-700 species worldwide. In all three genera, the greatest diversity occurs in the tropics. These genera are similar, all having small leaves with single veins that are more or less spirally arranged, or sometimes in opposite pairs. They have sporangia in cones or in leaf axils. When in cones, the sporangia are located on the upper, or inner surface or in the axils of modified leaves called sporophylls. These lateral or axillary sporangia produce spores either all of one size (in *Lycopodium*), or of two sizes (in *Selaginella* and *Isoetes*). The latter two genera also have a tiny flap of tissue near the base of each leaf termed a ligule.

The ferns are a much larger group with over 150 genera and probably

10000-12000 species. About 24 genera and 100 species occur in our area. They all have large leaves often divided into several to many "leaflets" (pinnae) and possess numerous veins. The fern plant (Fig. 34) that one sees consists almost entirely of these leaves, with the stem apex hidden at the leaf bases. The stems usually grow horizontally at, or slightly below the ground surface and are termed rhizomes. The stems are often covered with scales. Spores are produced in sporangia; either eusporangia which are relatively large and produce numerous spores, and are found on special stalks in grape-like clusters or leptosporangia which are found in small clusters (the sori) produced on the undersurface or at the margins of leaves. Leptosporangia are small, produce a limited number of spores (32 or 64), are elevated on slender stalks and dehisce by an annulus. They often are covered and protected by a membranous tissue (an indusium) or are covered by a rolled-back leaf margin (a false indusium). Except for a few species of water ferns, all species produce spores of only one size.

Life Cycle and Structural Features

The Gametophyte

When a spore of a fern, a club moss or horsetail lands in a suitable habitat, it germinates and developes into a small, filamentous, heart-, carrot- or top-shaped gametophyte called the prothallus in some books. This gametophyte may be photosynthetic and short-lived as in most ferns, horsetails and a few club mosses, or it may be underground, have an associated symbiotic fungus, have little or no chlorophyll and be long-lived (up to 20 or more years) as found in most club mosses and some ferns. Eventually sex organs containing gametes are produced. Sperm are produced in antheridia; in ferns these are spherical structures consisting of several outer jacket cells and numerous internal spermatogenous cells. Eggs are produced in archegonia that are multicellular, flask-shaped structures, each with an enlarged venter (with the egg) and a short neck. Fertilization results in a zygote that when still contained in the venter begins to divide and develops into a several-celled embryo, with regions of foot, root, shoot and leaf.

When mature the gametophyte of most ferns is a heart-shaped green object less than 1 cm across. It is flattened and produces archegonia near the "V" of the heart and antheridia near the point or, antheridia may be produced separately on a different and usually smaller gametophyte nearby. This is the result of a system in which faster growing plants in a population produce a hormone which causes slower growing plants to produce antheridia, and thus assuring cross fertilization. Genetic analysis of fern populations indicate that the predominant mode of breeding in most species is cross fertilization. When the embryo begins to develop, it produces a young shoot (the sporophyte) that grows upward through the notch. Soon after the first leaves, roots and shoot are produced the gametophyte whithers and dies. Thus, the sporophyte becomes independent of the gametophyte.

The Sporophyte

The sporophyte of a fern consists of roots, leaves, a shoot or rhizome and sporangia (Fig. 34). Club mosses and horsetails, likewise, have these structures. As in all tracheophytes, these sporophytes will have well-developed conducting tissues - xylem and phloem - organized into a central stele in the stem, leaf traces through the cortex and into the leaf. Once in the leaf, these traces can be recognized as veins. The leaves are almost always more than

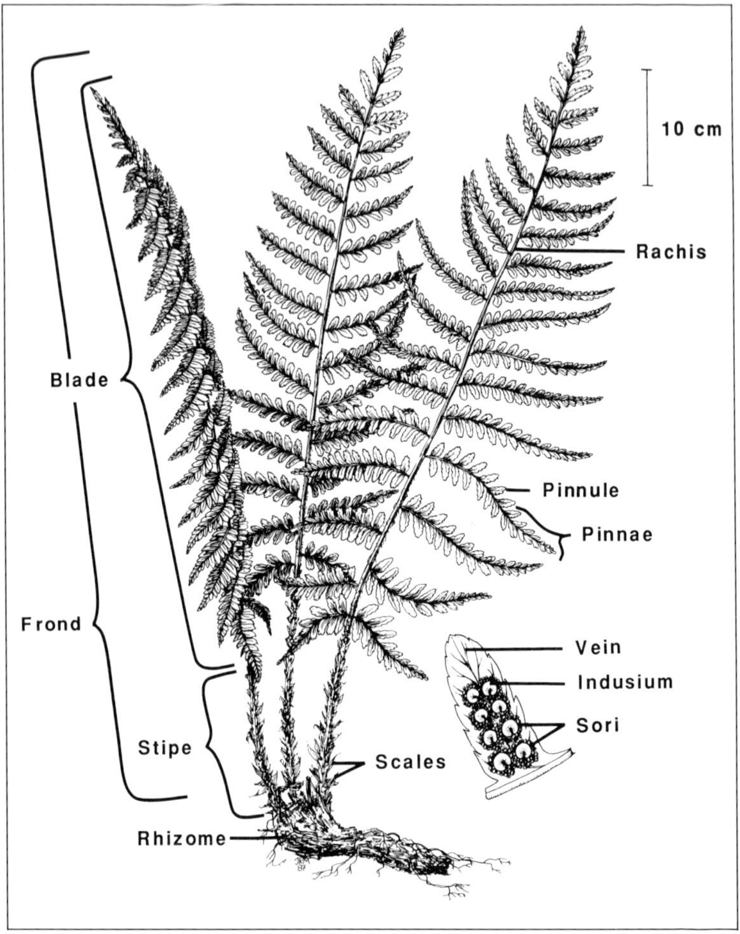

Fig. 34. A plant of *Dryopteris filix-max*.

one cell thick, however the filmy ferns of the family Hymenophyllaceae, represented in our area by *Hymenophyllum wrightii*, have leaves only one cell layer thick. Usually they have several photosynthetic layers of cells just beneath the upper surface and starch containing storage cells below these. The entire leaf is enclosed in a single layer of epidermis, with a cutinized, waterproof outer surface. Stomates provide regulated passages for gas exchange and evapotranspiration. As a result of this complex leaf structure, these plants must maintain turgor, and generally cannot dry up and become dormant as do many mosses and lichens.

Sporangia

Spores are produced in spherical, elliptic or reniform capsules called sporangia. Most ferns, *Lycopodium* and *Equisetum* have one type of sporangium that produces one size of spores (homospory); while *Selaginella*, a few water ferns and *Isoetes* have two types of sporangia (heterospory). One type produces a few large spores (megaspores-females), and the other contains numerous small ones (microspores-males). As a result, the gametophytes of most ferns are capable of producing both sexes, while in *Selaginella*, *Isoetes* and some water ferns the gametophytes are unisexual and quite different from one another. Sporangia can be single or organized into exposed clusters, in cones (=strobili) or in sori. Sori develop in most ferns on the back of the leaves. They consist of several sporangia (10-20) and are usually enclosed, over topped or surrounded by a membranous indusium. Each sporangium has a row of highly modified cells, the annulus, that because of the sudden rupture of the water column inside, disperses the spores in a catapult action as the sporangium dries out. The spores are produced by meiosis, and in most ferns the small sporangia hold only 32 to 64 spores. In club mosses and horsetails, the sporangia are larger and may hold thousands of spores. In horsetails, the spores have special hygroscopic bands (elaters) associated with them. When spores germinate, they develop into a free living gametophyte that at this stage is totally separate from the sporophyte. The sporophyte, of course will only develop at some future time if fertilization via sperm movement through water takes place. Since the gametophytes of these plants are small and inconspicuous, they are not frequently seen and collected, however, the existence of a sporophyte is always dependent on the initial success of the gametophyte.

Classification

Ferns and their allies are here classified in three separate classes. The horsetails are placed in the Equisetopsida with one family - the Equisetaceae. The club mosses are grouped together in the class - Lycopodopsida, with three families; the homosporous Lycopodiaceae, the heterosporous Selaginellaceae and Isoetaceae. Ferns are all placed in the class Pteropsida (or some authors use the name Filicopsida), and can be further divided into several families. Twelve families occur in our area, of which representatives of seven are treated here. The Ophioglossaceae with two genera have large Eusporangia, while the remaining families with 12 genera treated here have small Leptosporangia clustered in sori. Arrangement of these genera follows characteristics of the sorus. Basic to the arrangement is the presence or absence of true indusia and whether false indusia are present. Shape of the sori and indusia are also critical features. Our arrangement of ferns follows that proposed by Lellinger in 1985.

Key to the Recognition of Species

1. Leaves less than 1 cm long, simple, often inconspicuous and sometimes fused, with one unbranched midvein .... Fern Allies 2

1. Leaves from 5 cm to 1 m long, often divided into leaflets (pinnae), large and conspicuous, with numerous branched veins .... Ferns 13

2. Leaves whorled, sheathing the stem; stems conspicuously hollow and jointed .... Equisetaceae 4

2. Leaves spirally arranged or opposite one another, erect to spreading; stems solid, not jointed 3

3. Leafy shoots mostly 7-15 mm wide; cones rounded (terete); spores of one size (homosporous)... Lycopodiaceae 8

3. Leafy shoots mostly less than 6 mm wide; cones 4-sided; spores of two sizes (heterosporous) . . . . Selaginellaceae 12

4. Branches of stems rebranched (compound); stems rough to the touch due to 2 rows of sharply hooked spicules on each ridge . . *Equisetum sylvaticum* (pg. 263)

4. Branches of stems not branched (simple) or lacking; stems smooth to the touch, lacking rows of sharply hooked spicules 5

5. Stems simple or with only a few irregular branches; cones produced on stems similar to sterile ones. (present during most of growing season) 6

5. Sterile stems with regular whorls of branches; cones produced on simple, whitish, fertile stems produced in early spring, these soon withering (and not present during most of growing season) 7

6. Plants about 1 dm high; stems flexuose and ascending, evergreen; cones with an apiculus, about 2-5 mm long . . . . *Equisetum scirpoides* (pg. 264)

6. Plants about 2-10 dm high; stems straight and erect, annual; cones rounded at apex, about 6-10 mm long (or longer) . . . . *Equisetum fluviatile* (pg. 263)

7. Fertile stems (produced in early spring) with sheaths of 8-12 teeth; cones 2-3 cm long; sterile stems less that 0.5 m tall, with 6-14 furrows . . . . *Equisetum arvense* (pg. 262)

7. Fertile stems (produced in early spring) with sheaths of 20-30 teeth; cones 4-8 cm long; sterile stems 0.5-0.3 m tall, with 10-20 furrows . . . . *Equisetum telmateia* (pg. 262)

8. Stems simple or with equal, dichotomous branches 9

8. Stems with unequal branches, one of each division larger than the other 11

9. Leaves ending in a long slender hyaline awn; cones 1-6, elevated on stalks . . . . *Lycopodium clavatum* (pg. 265)

9. Leaves acute or apiculate, apex never hyaline; cones 1, sessile or sporangia in upper leaf axils 10

10. Sporangia in clearly differentiated, terminal cones; gemmae lacking . . . . *Lycopodium annotinum* (pg. 265)

10. Sporangia in axils of ordinary green leaves, not forming definate cones; gemmae often present in upper leaf axils, broad, flat . . . . . . *Lycopodium selago* (pg. 264)

11. Stems tree-like; leaves free, spirally arranged; branches rounded; cones sessile . . . . *Lycopodium dendroideum* (pg. 266)

11. Stems fan-like; leaves more or less fused and in 4-ranks; branches flattened; cones elevated on stalks . . . . *Lycopodium complanatum* (pg. 266)

12. Leaves decurrent, the stem covered by decurrencies when leaves not present. Forming dense mats, with closely spaced branches . . *Selaginella densa* (pg. 267)

12. Leaves abruptly attached, the stem easily seen when leaves not present. Forming loose mats with distantly spaced branches . . . . *Selaginella wallacei* (pg. 267)

13. Sporangia large, borne in terminal, grape-like clusters; rhizome producing a single leaf each year . . . . *Botrychium lunaria* (pg. 268)

13. Sporangia minute, borne in clusters (sori) on the back or near the margins of leaves or on modified fronds; rhizome producing several leaves (fronds) each year 14

14. Indusium present, at least on young fruiting fronds 15

14. Indusium wanting 25

15. Indusium formed entirely or in part by the revolute frond margin 16

15. Indusium formed on the lamina of the frond, or if marginal not formed by revolute margin 19

16. Sori clearly separate, formed on the underside of reflexed margins of fronds, segments of frond fan-shaped . . . . *Adiantum pedatum* (pg. 268)

16. Sori confluent, continuous along the margin of the reflexed frond segment; segments of frond oblong to lanceolate 17

17. Fronds taller than 3 dm; fronds individually scattered; occurring terrestrially in open forests . . . . *Pteridium aquilinum* (pg. 271)

17. Fronds shorter than 3 dm; fronds clustered; occurring in rock crevices 18

18. Stipes wiry, black and shiny; fertile fronds similar to sterile fronds, or nearly so . . . . *Cheilanthes feei* (pg. 269)

18. Stipes herbaceous, green and dull; fertile fronds conspicuously erect and different from spreading sterile fronds . . . . . . *Cryptogramma acrostichoides* (pg. 269)

19. Sporangia continuous along both sides of the midrib of the linear pinnae; fertile fronds conspicuously different from sterile fronds . . . . . . *Blechnum spicant* (pg. 275)

19. Sporangia discontinuous in decrete sori on the surface of pinnae, variable in shape; fertile fronds similar to sterile fronds 20

20. Indusium attached beneath the sorus, cup-like or dissected 21

20. Indusium spreading from above or from one side over the sorus 22

21. Indusium borne symmetrically under the sorus, splitting into filamentous segments; pinnae with numerous glands; veins not reaching the margins . . . . *Woodsia scopulina* (pg. 273)

21. Indusium borne asymmetrically, attached at one side of the sorus, hood-like and partially hidden by sporangia; pinnae glabrous; veins reaching the margins . . . . *Cystopteris fragilis* (pg. 272)

22. Indusium symmetric, centrally attached, ± peltate; fronds pinnate; pinnae asymmetric and auriculate at base . . . . *Polystichum munitum* (pg. 275)

22. Indusium asymmetric, laterally attached, kidney, horseshoe or crescent-shaped; fronds pinnate-pinnatifid to 3-pinnate; pinnae, except for lowest pair, symmetric, not auriculate 23

23. Lowest pair of pinnae asymmetric, having pinnules larger on lower side . . . . *Dryopteris expansa* (pg. 274)

23. Lowest pair of pinnae symmetric, having pinnules all of one size 24

24. Sori horseshoe to crescent-shaped, attached along one side; indusium toothed septate-ciliate; fronds deciduous. Coastal inland to Alberta . . . . *Athyrium filix-femina* (pg. 272)

24. Sori reniform, attached only near centre; indusium glandular-margined; fronds evergreen. Northern, southward to N.E. British Columbia and the Rockies of Alberta . . . . *Dryopteris fragrans* (pg. 274)

25. Fronds bipinnate, ternate, herbaceous, annual *Gymnocarpium dryopteris* (pg. 273)

25. Fronds pinnate (or with the pinna bases fused), coriaceous, evergreen 26

26. Pinnae acute to acuminate at apex, usually longer than 30 mm . . . . *Polypodium glycyrrhiza* (pg. 270)

26. Pinnae rounded (obtuse) at apex, usually shorter than 30 mm 27

27. Veins of pinnae anastomosing; fronds with less than 6 pinnae per side; found in coastal situations . . . . *Polypodium scouleri* (pg. 271)

27. Veins of pinnae branching but free; fronds with more than 6 pinnae per side; found in inland localities . . . . *Polypodium hesperium* (pg. 270)

x 0.05

Equisetum telmateia (giant horsetail) is the most handsome of our horsetails, with branched stems occasionally reaching a metre or even two metres high. The stems are annual, with the non-branched fertile (cone-bearing) stem present in early spring and only up to two decimetres in height. The sterile stems appear later and are present until fall. The branches are simple (not re-branched as in *E. sylvaticum*). Only large forms of *E. arvense* can be mistaken for this species, especially fertile stems in early spring. While *E. arvense* has three to four-angled branches, stems with between six to 14 furrows and cones about 2-3 cm long; *E. telmateia* has four to six-angled branches, stems with between 10 and 20 furrows and cones 4-8 cm long. This latter species is restricted to coastal western America, where it is found in moist forests, swampy areas and along streams.

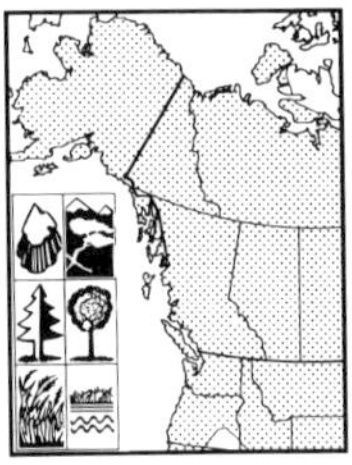

x .2

Equisetum arvense (common horsetail) is our most common species. It occurs in mesic woods, open fields, wet areas and along roadsides, where it often covers all of the road bank. It has been considered one of the 10 most common plants in the world! Although it can attain a height of 75 cm, generally it is much smaller. The stems are branched, with the branches always simple. The cone-bearing stems are unbranched and appear first, in early spring. These soon whither and are replaced by sterile stems that remain until fall. Only *E. pratense* is easily confused with this species, the former species has white tipped teeth and the first long internode of the branch sheath (leaves) shorter than the stem sheath, with flaring upper portions; while *E. arvense* has black tipped teeth and the first branch internodes as long or longer than the stem sheath and not flaring. Two varieties of *E. arvense* are fun to look for. The var. *boreale* has three angled branches and thus each node has three leaves, while the var. *arvense* has four angled branches and four leaves at each node. The former tends to be more northern in distribution.

x .2

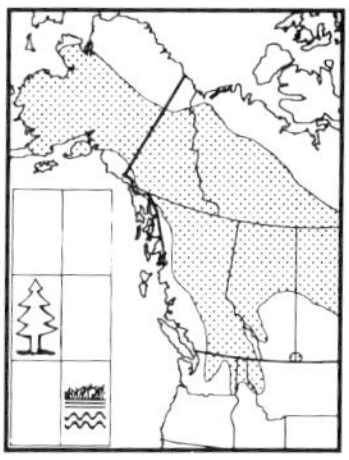

Equisetum sylvaticum (wood horsetail) is our only species with branches that branch several additional times. The stems are annual. The cone-bearing stems produced in the spring are at first unbranched, but later they produce whorls of compound branches. At this time the cones whither and drop off and and thus become identical to the sterile stems. The stems of this species are very rough to the touch, since each ridge has two rows of sharply hooked spicules. *Equisetum pratense* and *E. arvense* are of similar size, but have simple branches. While *E. arvense* has separate, unbranched cone-bearing stems, *E. pratense* is similar to *E. sylvaticum* in this respect. This species occurs in moist forests, away from the coast. It is often found with *E. pratense*.

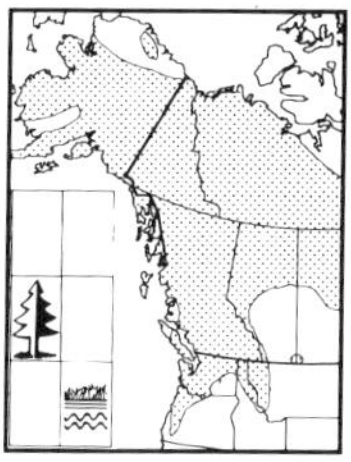

x .2

Equisetum fluviatile (swamp horsetail). The annual, largely unbranched stems are characteristic of this species. Occasional populations have a few irregular branches in the upper portions, but rarely are they regularly and profusely branched as the preceding species except in more southerly portions of the species' range. When broken, the stems are hollow, with the central cavity at least 4/5 the diametre. Cones are blunt. This is a species of eutrophic marshes, edges of calcareous lakes, wet ditches and is a characteristic species of extreme rich fens. *Equisetum palustre* is similar, but is easily distinguished by observing the broken stem, in this latter species the central cavity is small, (less than 1/2 the diametre) and the surrounding cavities (vallecular canals) are nearly as large (these are lacking in *E. fluviatile*). Other unbranched, rather large species of the genus include *E. laevigatum* and *E. hyemale*, the latter has apiculate cones. Usually the unfused, lanceolate, upper leaf sheaths are broken off in these two species; the former is yellow, green and smooth, while the latter is grey-green and rough to the touch.

x .3

Equisetum scirpoides (dwarf scouring-rush) is our smallest species, occurring in tangled mats in feather mosses. The stems are unbranched, flexuose-twisted, evergreen, and perennial. Cones are apiculate and the leaf sheaths fringed in white. *Equisetum variegatum* is similar, but larger and stiffer. The white fringe of the leaf sheath is more conspicuous. These two species are usually easily told by size alone, but in difficult cases - *E. variegatum* has a central cavity and five or more vallecular canals, while *E. scirpoides* has no central cavity and three vallecular canals. Both are common in the boreal forest; the former on sandy soils, the latter in peaty, mossy forests.

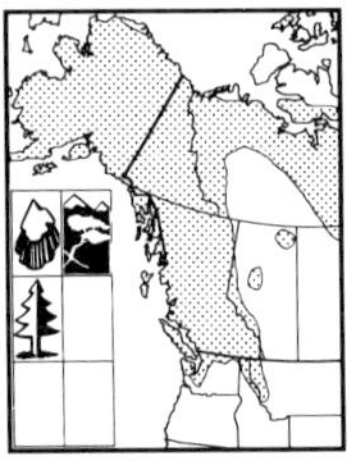

x .5

Lycopodium selago (mountain club-moss). The presence of sporangia in the upper leaf axils, leaves of one type and propagula occurring in the upper leaf axils, differentiate this species. The plants grow erect, without horizontal, spreading runners and all branching is dichotomous. Only the eastern *L. lucidulum* is similar; all other species in our area have distinct terminal cones. This species occurs in moist woods and in moist alpine and arctic tundra. It appears to prefer acidic substrates and is rare east of the Rockies and south of the subarctic.

x .4

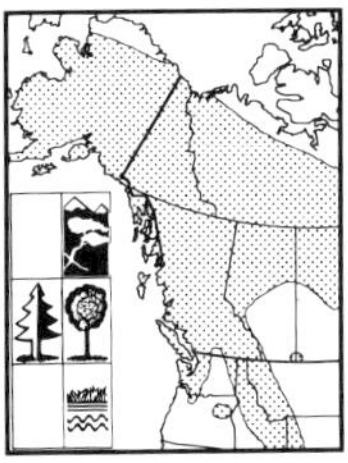

Lycopodium annotinum (stiff club-moss) has rather stiff dichotomous branches that arise from horizontal runners. The sporangia are in terminal, sessile cones, while the leaves are firm and divergent, each ending in a hard, stiff point. Perhaps our most common species, it is often abundant in moist woods and in acidic peatlands. It prefers acidic soils and is frequently found on sand dunes in moist depressions. It is generally fertile, but when sterile, the stout leaf points differentiate it from *L. clavatum*, while the dichotomous branches and spirally arranged leaves all of one size and shape differentiate it from other cone-bearing species of the genus. When sterile, this species could be mistaken for the moss *Polytrichum commune*, but the moss is much smaller and more delicate.

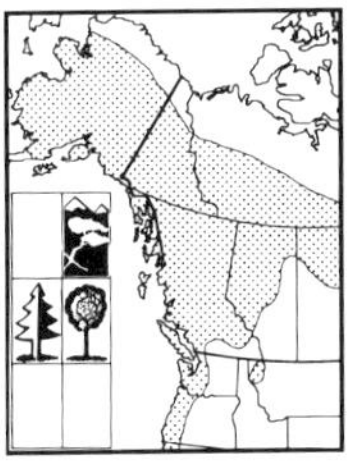

x .3

Lycopodium clavatum (running club-moss) forms extensive mats in dry open areas, mostly on sandy soils. In general, it occurs in drier situations than *L. annotinum*. The erect, dichotomously (sometimes asymmetric) branches arise from horizontal stems that lie on the surface of the ground; these often 1 metre or so in length. The leaves are ascending, soft and end in a long hyaline awn, a character that is definitive for this species. The sporangia are grouped into cones and terminate along stalks with reduced leaves. The cones generally number two to four on short dichotomous branches.

x .3

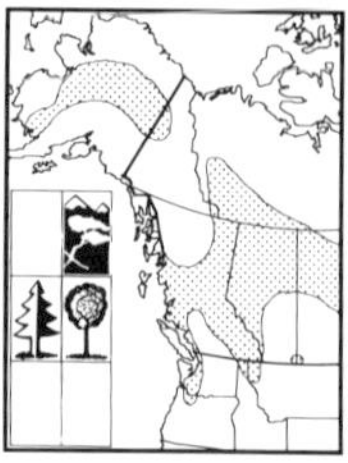

Lycopodium dendroideum (ground-pine) is the least frequent of the species of *Lycopodium* in our area. It has not been found as far north or south as the other species. East of the Rockies, it is often found with *L. annotinum* in moist, acidic woods along the margins of peatlands. The horizontal stems are deeply subterranean and difficult to collect. The branching is tree-like, with the main divisions having large and small branches originating at each division, however, the terminal branches are equally dichotomous. The leaves are six-ranked and small, but free, with the lower ranks appressed and the lateral ones spreading. Sessile cones terminate the upper-most branches. When well developed the distinctive branching patterns give the plants a nice layered appearance. It is closely related to the eastern North American *L. obscurum*.

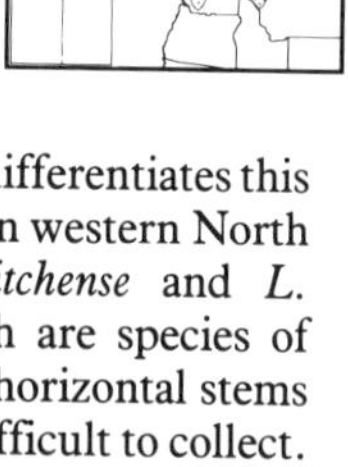

x .4

Lycopodium complanatum (ground-cedar) is a species of dry, sandy soils in open woods. The presence of four-ranked leaves, much like those of *Thuja plicata* (western red cedar), that are partially fused to the stem differentiates this species from all others in western North America except *L. sitchense* and *L. alpinum*, both of which are species of higher elevations. The horizontal stems are subterranean and difficult to collect. The cones are terminal on short dichotomous branches that arise on relatively long nearly leafless stalks. Careful study of the leaves shows that the ranks are different from one another, the lower one has leaves fused except for their tips, while the upper is nearly free. Another interesting feature of this and most other species of the genus is that they have yearly constrictions, making it possible to determine yearly growth patterns. All are evergreen and perennial.

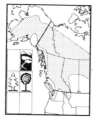

x .2

Selaginella wallacei (wallace's selaginella). This is a genus of seven species in our area. Four of these (*S. oregana, S. densa, S. rupestris* and *S. sibirica)* have decurrent leaves on all sides of the stem; *S. douglasii* has clearly differentiated leaves (in size and shape), while *S. selaginoides* has coarsely spinulose leaf margins. *S. wallacei* is a species of moist or sometimes dry cliffs and bluffs, often draping down from crevices. It is distinguished by occurring in loose mats, with distantly spaced branches and radially arranged leaves. The cones are terete in section and the leaves are not decurrent. It is restricted to areas west of the Rockies.

x .5

Selaginella densa (spike-moss) has dense, spreading plants with erect, sessile, 4-angled cones. The leaves end abruptly in a hyaline awn. The grey-green coloration, hyaline awns, thick (opaque) leaves and cones of numerous sporangia differentiate it from all mosses, especially *Polytrichum* species that superficially look similar. This species occurs on prairie soils or on dry, usually calcareous, rock outcrops. The leaves are decurrent along the stem and the hyaline awns broad at their base. *Selaginella densa*, together with *S. rupestris* (eastern) and *S. sibirica* (northern), form a group of closely related species not easily distinguished from each other.

x .6

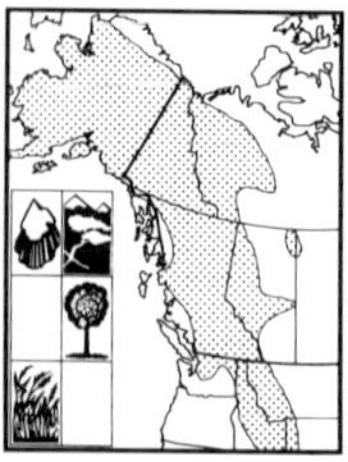

Botrychium lunaria (moonwort). About 13 species of this genus occur in northwestern America, ranging from those having large, highly dissected fronds (*B. virginianum*) to those with smaller, more simple ones (*B. lunaria*). All have large sporangia produced in grape-like clusters on a separate fertile frond. Each plant has one fertile and one sterile leaf. The individual sporangia are globose, sessile and open into two valves; they are never clustered into a sorus or protected by an indusium. This species of the genus is distinguished by having an oblong frond divided into 8-12, fan-shaped to semi-circular lobes. It is found in mountain meadows, grassy areas and moist parkland. Several other species resemble this one and need to be examined closely to make an accurate determination.

x .2

Adiantum pedatum (northern maidenhair) is a striking fern, known by its delicate fronds of stalked fan-shaped pinnae, with their blades borne on the distal sides of the midvein. The sori are interrupted, marginal and grouped into clusters covered by the distal edge of the reflexed pinnae. Although three species of the genus are found in the west, *A. pedatum* is the only one reaching our area, occurring on moist bluffs, rocky hillsides and mesic forests. It is not known from east of the continental divide in our area, but occurs disjunct in eastern North America.

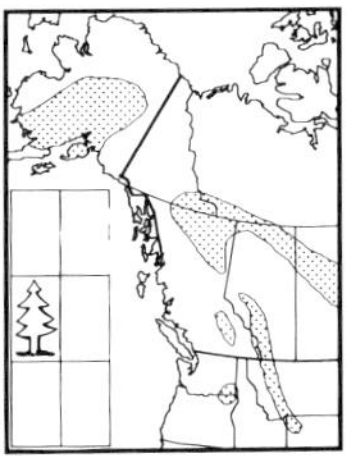

x .5

Cheilanthes feei (slender lip fern). This small fern of calcareous substrates has wiry, dark-brown to black stipes. This feature is shared by species of *Pellaea* and *Aspidotis*. Both of these genera have glabrous blades, while *Cheilanthes*, with two species in our area, has blades that are either hairy or scaly. *Cheilanthes feei* has leaf blades that lack scales, but is conspicuously long-pubescent. The stipes are hairy, while the blades are usually three-pinnate. This is the only species found in Canada, but *C. gracillima* is abundant in the northwestern states. The sori are found crowded beneath under rolled margins of the pinnae.

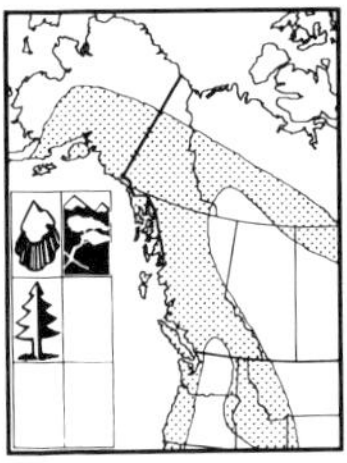

Photo: D.G. Horton

x .3

Cryptogramma acrostichoides (parsley fern) is a small, delicate fern of rocky crevices, talus slopes and rock ledges. The fronds are markedly dimorphic; sterile fronds are spreading, about 10-15 cm long, with ovate, crenate, twice pinnate blades. Stipes are delicate and green. The fertile fronds are erect with linear-oblong, simple, entire blades. Sori are produced near the margins and covered by the revolute margins. As in *Pellaea* (with blackish, wiry stipes), no true indusium is produced. This species superficially is similar to the less frequent *Aspidotis densa*, but the more complex vegetative frond of the *Aspidotis* is a good distinguishing feature. This is a beautiful genus with two species in northwestern America. It is a delight to find the remarkable fertile fronds protruding from alpine rock crevices.

x .2

Polypodium glycyrrhiza (licorice fern). This species has acute pinnae and acuminate to attenuate fronds. It is the largest of the genus in our area, and is restricted to habitats near the coast. Often found growing as an epiphyte on deciduous trees, this species can be recognized by its licorice taste (especially the rhizome). The genus *Polypodium* has pinnate to pinnatifid fronds with large, round, naked sori. No indusium is ever produced. Veins do not reach the margin. The fronds are evergreen and perennial. *Polypodium virginianum* is common on rock surfaces in eastern North America and is known from the Yukon and N.W. British Columbia, where it (and our west coast species as well) weathers periods of drought by curling and drying up, reviving when moisture returns. This poikilohydric ability is similar to that found commonly in mosses and lichens.

x .3

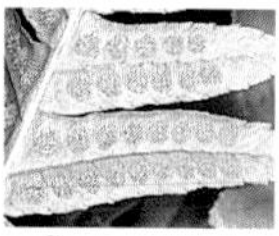

x 2

Polypodium hesperium (common polypody). The blunt pinnae distinguish this species of crevices and rocky slopes. Fronds rarely reach 35 cm in length and do not have sharply acute pinnae (as does *P. glycyrrhiza*). Some books would consider both *P. hesperium* and *P. glycyrrhiza* as varieties of the more widespread *P. vulgare*. In this case, then *P. glycyrrhiza* would be *P. vulgare* var. *occidentale*, while *P. hesperium* would be *P. vulgare* var. *columbianum*. However, in our area these varieties are readily recognized and have distinct geographic ranges and habitat preferences. We think they are sufficiently distinct to be recognized by their own species name. As well, *P. hesperium* is the allotetraploid hybrid of *P. glycyrrhiza* X *P. amorphum*. It is very common in the Fraser River Canyon, east of Vancouver.

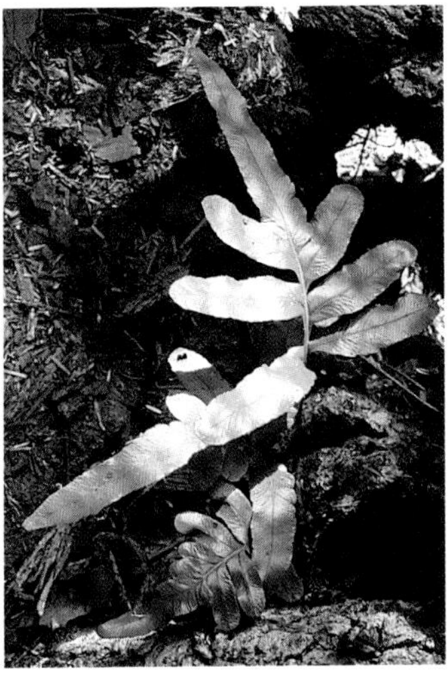

x .2

Polypodium scouleri (leathery polypody) is a coastal species distinguished by its unique frond shape as well as veins that fuse and form a series of areoles. The naked, round sori are unusually large and conspicuous, while the fronds are stout, stiff and leathery in texture. They may reach 50 cm in length. The pinnae are blunt and in this feature resemble those of *P. hesperium*, however that species has dichotomizing veins and occurs in inland habitats.

x .1

Pteridium aquilinum (bracken) is a large fern with fronds up to 5 metres high, but generally much less, about 1-1.5 m in height. The fronds occur individually, connected by a much branched subterranean rhizome. The fronds are annual with coarse, three pinnate blades (the pinnae are more or less opposite, while the pinnules are alternate). The stipes are without scales. Although mostly sterile, the sori, when present, are marginal, covered by an outer false indusium formed by the revolute margin and an inconspicuous, hyaline inner indusium. The revolute false indusium is present, even on sterile fronds. This genus, of one nearly cosmopolitan species, can be ranked as one of the most abundant plant species in the world. In our area, it occurs on acid, often sandy soils in open forests, mostly restricted to areas west of the Rockies.

Photo: D.G. Horton

x .1

Athyrium filix-femina (lady fern). This genus, represented by two species in our area has delicate, pale green fronds when compared to other rather large woodsy ferns as species of *Dryopteris*, *Thelypteris* and *Polystichum*. *Athyrium* is distinguished from these genera by having horseshoe to half moon-shaped indusia attached laterally along one side, while generally species of the other three genera have peltate or kidney shaped indusia, attached only at or near the centre. Whereas *A. alpestre* is largely an alpine species, *A. filix-femina* is a species of damp shady forests. It is common west of the cordillera in British Columbia and the northwestern states.

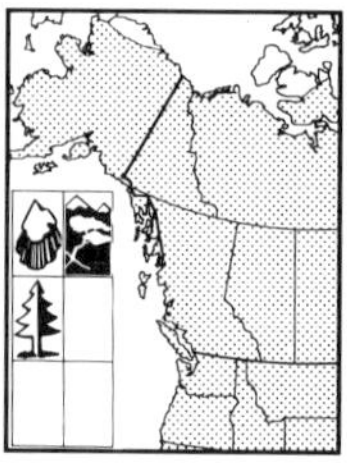

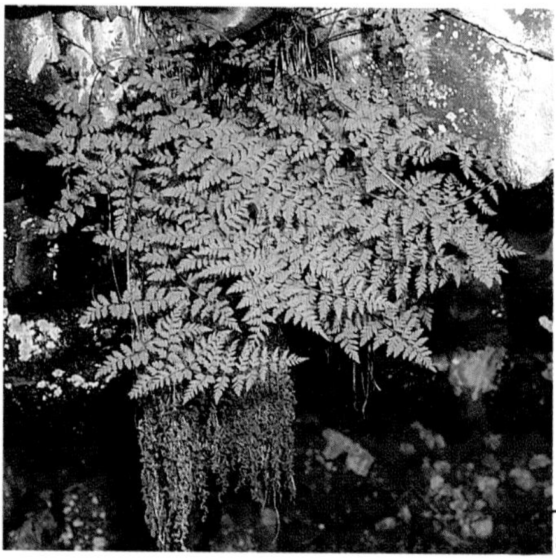

x .1

Cystopteris fragilis (fragile fern). This rather small fern (usually about 20-30 cm tall) is found in mesic rock crevices and among boulders on rocky slopes and in shady woods. The two, sometimes three, pinnate fronds are glabrous and lanceolate. *Cystopteris fragilis* has roundish sori with delicate, membranous, hooded indusia that are attached by a broad base on the side of the sorus. The attachment is partially under the sporangia and when mature the indusium is bent backward and becomes partially covered by the sporangia. Another, more northern species of the genus has deltoid-alternate leaves. Species of this genus and those of *Woodsia* are our only ferns with indusia attached beneath the sori. Other small, rock-growing ferns include *Cheilanthes* (two species) and *Aspidotis* (one species) with indusia formed from revolute, modified leaf margins and *Cryptogramma* (two species) with fertile fronds quite different than sterile ones.

Photo: D.G. Horton

x .2

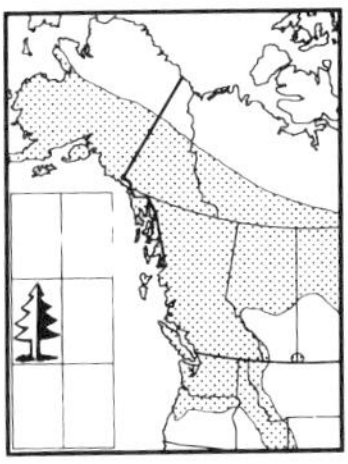

Gymnocarpium dryopteris (oak fern) is one of our most delicate ferns. It is often found in extensive yellow-green populations in moist woods and on rocky hillsides. The fronds are ternate-compound, that is, three pinnate-pinnatifid blades arise from one basal point. The two lateral blades are about half the length of the central one, with the entire frond being deltoid-triangular in shape. The sori are small, circular and without indusia. A second species, *G. robertianum*, is common farther north in Alaska and the Yukon; it is distinguished by densely glandular fronds.

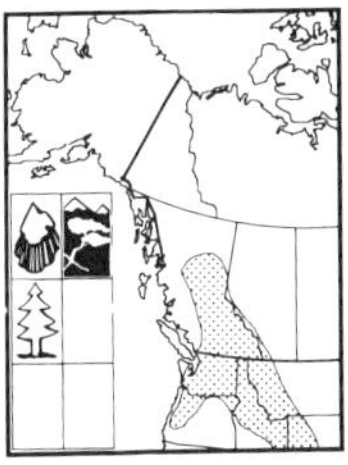

x .3

Woodsia scopulina (rocky mountain woodsia) is a small fern (10-20 cm tall) of mesic to dry rock crevices. The fronds are pinnate-pinnatifid, with the blades having numerous glands intermixed with whitish hairs. *Woodsia*, with five species in our area, is distinguished by round sori having thin indusia that arise from beneath the sporangia and surround them with numerous filamentous to linear lobes. When mature, the indusial lobes are mostly hidden by the dehiscing sporangia. Other species of the genus are distinguished by the presence or absence of hairs and glands.

Photo: D.G. Horton

x .2

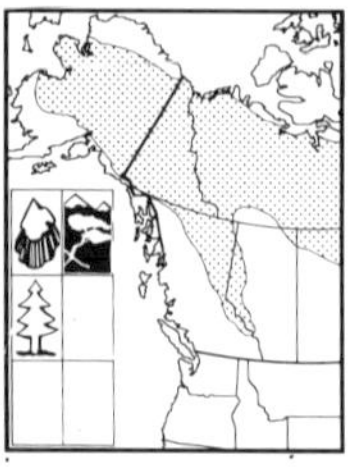

Dryopteris fragrans (fragrant wood fern). This northern fern is a beautiful rich dark green colour. The leaves persist for more than one year and are noticeably coriaceous in texture. The stipes and blades have numerous glands and scales. The sori are large, whitish and densely crowded toward the centre of the pinnae. The older fronds are grey and conspiciously curled. Some authors comment on the sickly sweet smell of the plants when fresh as an identifying feature. From other species of the genus, the glandular blades and indusia are distinctive. This fern is found in rock crevices or in shaded to exposed cliffs of neutral to basic rocks. Also it is found on talus slopes above tree line.

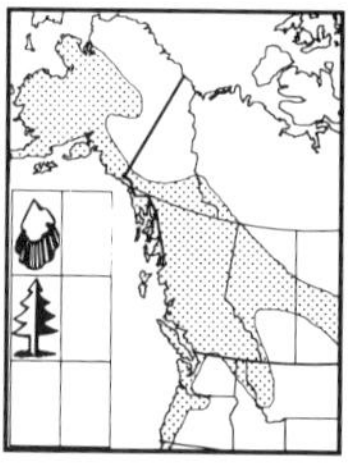

x .1

Dryopteris expansa (spreading wood fern) is a large fern reaching 1 metre in height that occurs in mesic forests. The fronds are three-pinnate, with broadly triangular blades, these broadest at their base. The lowest pinnae are broadly ovate and asymmetric; the pinnules on one side of the pinnae longer than those opposing them. The upper pinnae are symmetric and lanceolate. This species is also known as *D. austriaca*, *D. dilatata* and *D. assimilis*. Six species of *Dryopteris* are present in our area; all distinguished by round sori each with a large, persistent, reniform indusium attached at its sinus. The leaves are always pinnafid to two to three pinnate, and have scaly and chaffy lower portions. *Thelypteris*, with three species in our area, is somewhat similar in having reniform indusia, but it has softer, usually hairy leaves and veins that end at the pinna margins while species of *Dryopteris* have veins not reaching the margins. *Athyrium filix-femina* (lady fern) frequently grows at the same sites. It is distinguished by the half moon-shaped sori and the frond outline. The *Dryopteris* species inhabit mesic woodlands where they form large upright plants.

x .05

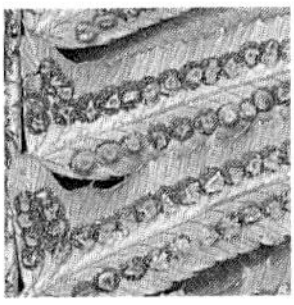

x .5

Polystichum munitum (western sword-fern) is a rather coarse (fronds to 1.8 m long), evergreen fern of rocky bluffs and moist forests, only occurring west of the Rockies. The fronds are pinnate, with each pinna two to four times as long as wide and having a prominant auricle at its distal base. The lower portions of the stipes are covered in reddish scales, and the pinnae are sharply serrate. Only *P. lonchitis* has somewhat similar once pinnate fronds with auriculate pinnae, this latter species having short pinnae, about one to two times as long as wide. Other species of the genus have pinnae deeply lobed or dissected. *Polystichum* is a large genus with at least 11 species in northwestern America. Although the fronds vary considerably among the species, all are large ferns with circular sori and round, centrally peltate indusia. The sori are always large, have persistent indusia and are conspicuous on the frond blades. None of the species has differentiated fertile fronds.

x .01

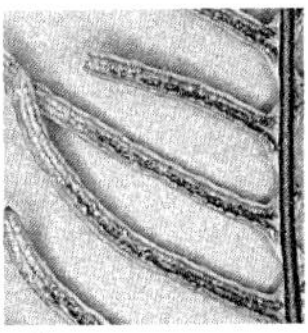

x 1

Blechnum spicant (deer fern). This genus of largely tropical and southern hemisphere species is represented in our area by only one species. It is easily recognized by dimorphic fronds, once pinnate (or pinnatifid) blades with entire margins and sori continuous and parallel to the midrib with membranous indusia attached to the margin and opening towards the midrib. Although superficially resembling a large *Polypodium*, it is easily identified by dimorphic fronds and elongate sori. This species is found in damp, coniferous forests on wet banks, usually near the coast; rare in interior British Columbia.

Additional Literature

MOSSES

Abramova, A.L., L.I. Savicz-Ljubitakaja, and Z.N. Smirnova. 1961. *Handbook of the Mosses of Arctic U.S.S.R.* Academy of Science, U.S.S.R. Moscow (In Russian). 714 pp. - comprehensive text, with line drawings of many species.

Conard, H.S. 1979. *How to Know the Mosses and Liverworts.* W.C. Brown. Dubuque, Iowa. 2nd ed. revised by P.L. Redfearn, Jr. 302 pp. - a pictured key to the bryophytes of North America; oriented to the east.

Crum, H.A. 1973. *Mosses of the Great Lakes Forest.* Contributions University of Michigan Herbarium. 10: 1-404. (3rd ed. 1983). - full of useful information, keys, descriptions and commentary on mosses of northern Michigan.

Crum, H.A. and L.E. Anderson. 1981. *Mosses of Eastern North America.* Volumes 1 and 2. Columbia University Press. New York. 1328 pp. - the most comprehensive treatment of mosses for the continent, fully usable in the west.

Flowers, S. 1973. *Mosses: Utah and the West.* Brigham Young University Press. Provo, Utah. 567 pp. (ed. A. Holmgren). - a book of beautiful drawings, detailed comments and descriptions of arid country mosses.

Frahm, J.-P. and W. Frey. 1983. *Moosflora.* Verlag Eugen Ulmer. Stuttgart, West Germany. (2nd ed. 1987. 525 pp.). - in german, a well done, condensed flora of central Europe.

Grout, A.J. 1931-1940. *Moss Flora of North America North of Mexico.* Volumes I - III. Published by the author. Newfane, Vermont and New York. 264, 285 and 275 pp. - an earlier, comprehensive revision of North American mosses.

Hallingbäck, T. and I. Holmåsen. 1982. *Mossor En fälthandbok.* Interpublishing. Stockholm, Sweden. 220 pp. - a book of beautiful coloured photographs, distribution maps and Swedish text for Scandanavian mosses and hepatics.

Inoue, H. 1986. *Field Guide for Bryophytes.* Tokai University Press. Tokyo, Japan. 194 pp. - a pocket book that includes about 375 colour photographs and 150 line drawings, with Japanese text of both mosses and liverworts of Japan.

Ireland, R.R. 1982. *Moss Flora of the Maritime Provinces.* National Museums of Canada Publications in Botany No. 13. Ottawa. 738 pp. - a comprehensive manual of the mosses of eastern Canada.

Iwatsuki, Z. and M. Mizutani. 1972. *Coloured Illustrations of Bryophytes of Japan.* Hoikusha Publishing Co. Osaka, Japan. 405 pp. - includes water-colours of the mosses and hepatics of Japan, with descriptions in Japanese.

Lawton, E. 1971. *Moss Flora of the Pacific Northwest.* Hattori Botanical Laboratory. Nichinan, Japan. 362 pp + 195 plates. - detailed descriptions and drawings of mosses of northwestern North America.

Nyholm, E. 1954-1969. *Illustrated Moss Flora of Fennoscandia.* II. Musci. Fasc. 1-6. CWK Gleerup, Lund and Natural Science Research Council. Stockholm, Sweden. 799 pp. – a most helpful treatment that is fully usable here in boreal America; with nice drawings.

Reese, W.D. 1984. *Mosses of the Gulf South from the Rio Grande to the Apalachicola.* Louisiana State University Press. Baton Rouge, La. 252 pp. – a regional flora with short descripions, line drawings and general comments on the mosses of southeastern North America.

Schofield, W.B. 1992 (2nd edition). *Some Common Mosses of British Columbia.* Royal British Columbia Museum Handbook. Victoria, B.C. 394 pp. – contains short descriptions, comments and line drawings of 120 common mosses of the west coast.

Schofield, W.B. 1985. *Introduction to Bryology.* Macmillan & Co. New York. 431 pp. – the latest book on bryology, with up-to-date chapters on distributions, morphology and physiology.

Schuster R.M. (editor). 1983-1984. *New Manual of Bryology.* Hattori Botanical Laboratory. Nichinan, Japan. 1295 pp. – full of the most recent ideas on all aspects of bryology including excellent reviews of most topics in bryology.

Smith, A.J.E. 1978. *The Moss Flora of Britain and Ireland.* Cambridge University Press. Cambridge, Great Britain. 706 pp. – a well written flora with keys, descriptions and critical drawings.

Smith, A.J.E. (editor). 1982. *Bryophyte Ecology.* Chapman and Hall. London. 511 pp. – contains 13 chapters that review the ecology of bryopytes.

Watson, E.V. 1968. *British Mosses and Liverworts.* Cambridge University Press. Cambridge, Great Britain. (2nd ed.) 493 pp. – a flora with easy to read, informative discussions of British mosses.

LIVERWORTS

Frye, T.C. and L. Clark. 1937-1947. *Hepaticae of North America.* University of Washington Publications in Biology. 6:1-1018. (Parts I-V). – a very comprehensive revision of the hepatics of the continent, but hard to use in its complexity.

MacVicar, S.M. 1926. *The Student's Handbook of British Hepatics.* (2nd ed.). Eastbourne: V.V. Sumfield. London. 464 pp. – although old, a very useful book on boreal-temperate species; however the outdated nomenclature may cause problems!

Schuster, R.M. 1953. *Boreal Hepaticae A Manual of the Liverworts of Minnesota and Adjacent Regions.* American Midland Naturalist 49: 257-684. – an early more regional treatment by Professor Schuster, still very useful for boreal America.

Schuster, R.M. 1966-1992. *The Hepaticae and Anthocerotae of North America East of the Hundredth Meridian.* Volumes 1-6. Columbia University Press. New York. 802, 1062, 880, 1334, 854, 937 pp. – the bible for hepatics of the Northern Hemisphere – extremely comprehensive and with beautiful detailed illustrations.

Scott, G.A.M. 1985. *Southern Australian Liverworts.* Australian Flora and Fauna Series Number 2. Australian Government Publishing Service. Canberra. 216 pp. – includes the most attractive black and white photographs of hepatics in print today.

LICHENS

Ahmadjian, V. and M.E. Hale. 1973. *The Lichens.* Academic Press, New York. 697 pp. – a comprehensive collection of papers on the biology of lichens.

Alvin, K.L. 1977. *The Observer's Book on Lichens.* Frederick Warne, London. 189 pp. – colour and black and white photographs and diagrams of common British lichens with an introduction to the biology of lichens and a key to the genera.

Brodo, I.M. 1989. *Lichens of the Ottawa Region, second edition.* National Museum of Natural Sciences, Ottawa. – this new edition will be available free from the National Museums of Canada. It is aimed at the interested amateur and is illustrated.

Culberson, C.F. 1969. *Chemical and Botanical Guide to Lichen Products*. University of North Carolina Press, Chapel Hill. 628 pp. - a comprehensive guide to the chemistry of lichen species and lichen substances.

Dahl, E. and H. Krog. 1973. *Macrolichens of Denmark, Finland, Norway, and Sweden*. Scandinavian University Books, Universitetsforlaget, Oslo. 185 pp. - keys with short species descriptions and some black and white illustrations of Scandinavian macrolichens; this book also contains a synopsis of lichen species chemistry.

Duncan, U.K. 1970. *Introduction to British Lichens*. T. Buncle & Co., Arbroath. 292 pp. - includes keys, species descriptions, black and white illustrations and text on biology and habitats of British lichens.

Hale, M.E. 1961. *Lichen Handbook, A Guide to the Lichens of Eastern North America*. Smithsonian Institution, Washington, D.C. 178 pp. - a good introduction to lichens and their genera, with keys.

Hale, M.E. 1974. *The Biology of Lichens, 2nd Edition*. Edward Arnold (Publishers) Ltd. London. 181 pp. - a readable book on lichenology in general.

Hale, M.E. 1979. *How to know the Lichens, 2nd Edition*. Wm. C. Brown Co., Dubuque, Iowa. 246 pp. - a pictured key to the macrolichens of North America.

Johns, H.M. 1983. *The Collins Guide to the Ferns, Mosses and Lichens of Britain and Northern and Central Europe*. William Collins and Co. Ltd., London. 272 pp. - over 600 colour photographs with species descriptions and keys to each group.

Kershaw, K.A. 1985. *Physiological Ecology of Lichens*. Cambridge University Press, Cambridge. 293 pp. - a review of recent studies of lichen physiological ecology.

Martin, W. and J. Child. 1972. *New Zealand Lichens*. A.H. and A.W. Reed Ltd., Wellington. 193 pp. - keys to identification, with colour and black and white photographs of common lichens of New Zealand.

McGrath, J.W. 1977. *Dyes from Lichens and Plants*. Van Nostrand Reinhold Ltd., Toronto. 144 pp. - a guide to dying natural fibers using various lichen species (mainly arctic).

Moberg, R. and I. Homåsen. 1982. *Lavar, En fälthandbok*. Interpublishing, Stockholm, Sweden. 237 pp. - a book of beautifully colour photographs, distribution maps and keys with Swedish text for Scandinavian lichens.

Noble, W.J., T. Ahti, G.F. Otto, and I.M. Brodo. 1987. *A Second Checklist and Bibliography of the Lichens and Allied Fungi of British Columbia*. Natural Museums of Canada. Syllogeus Series No. 61. 95 pp.

Ozenda, P. and G. Clauzade. 1970. *Les Lichens, Étude Biologique et Flore Illustrée*. Masson et Cie, Paris. 801 pp. - a comprehensive treatment of lichens, with black and white illustrations, photographs and line drawings of described species.

Richardson, D.H.S. 1975. *The Vanishing Lichens, Their History, Biology and Importance*. David & Charles Ltd., Vancouver. 231 pp. - a very interesting and readable book on lichens in general.

Seaward, M.R.D. 1977. *Lichen Ecology*. Academic Press. London. 550 pp. - a compilation of papers on the ecology of lichens.

Thomson, J.W. 1979. *Lichens of the Alaskan Arctic Slope*. University of Toronto Press, Toronto. 314 pp. - keys and detailed descriptions of arctic lichens.

Thomson, J.W. 1984. *American Arctic Lichens (The Macrolichens)*. Columbia University Press, New York. 504 pp. - a comprehensive manual including keys, distribution maps, detailed descriptions and black and white illustrations of arctic macrolichens.

Yoshimura, I. 1974. *Lichen Flora of Japan in Color*. Hoikusha Publishing Co., Osaka, Japan. 349 pp. - includes colour plates, black and white photographs, line drawings and descriptions for 528 lichen species; text in Japanese.

FERNS

Cobb, B. 1963. *A Field Guide to the Ferns*. Houghton Mifflin Co., Boston. 281 pp. - a useful, well illustrated guide.

Frye, T.C. 1934. *Ferns of the Northwest*. The Metropolitan Press. Portland, Oregon. 177 pp. - a useful, if dated, discussion of the ferns and allies with interesting observations unavailable elsewhere.

Hauke, R.L. 1963. *A Taxonomic monograph of the genus Equisetum subgenus Hippochaete*. Beihefte Nova Hedwigia 8:1-123. - a thorough revision of the group.

Hitchcock, C.L., A. Conquist and M. Ownbey. 1969. *Vascular Plants of the Pacific Northwest. Part I*. University of Washington Press, Seattle. Pages 22-102 cover the ferns and allies with beautiful line drawings, descriptions and keys to all taxa.

Hitchcock, C.L. and A. Cronquist. 1973. *Flora of the Pacific Northwest An Illustrated Manual*. University of Washington Press, Seattle. 730 pp. - an excellent flora for the northwestern U.S., very useable for southern British Columbia.

Hultén, E. 1968. *Flora of Alaska and Neighboring Territories. A Manual of the Vascular Plants*. Stanford University Press, Stanford, California. 1008 pp. - a beautifully done, comprehensive flora, recommended as the definitive treatment for the north.

Lellinger, D.B. 1985. *A Field Manual of the Ferns and Fern Allies of the United States and Canada*. Smithsonian Institution Press, Washington, D.C. 389 pp. - the most complete treatment of these plants, with keys, descriptions, up-to-date nomenclature and colour photographs of about 400 species.

Mickel, J.T. 1979. *How to Know the Ferns and Fern Allies*. W.C. Brown, Dubuque, Iowa. 229 pp. - an easy-to-use illustrated guide to ferns and fern allies of North America.

Moss, E.H. 1983. *Flora of Alberta. A Manual of Flowering Plants, Conifers, Ferns and Fern Allies Found Growing Without Cultivation in the Province of Alberta, Canada*. University of Toronto Press, Toronto. 2nd ed. revised by J.G. Packer. 687 pp. - an up-to-date revision of the vascular plants of the province; with distribution maps.

Porsild, A.E. and W.J. Cody. 1980. *Vascular Plants of Continental Northwest Territories, Canada*. National Museum of Natural Sciences, Ottawa. 667 pp. - a flora of the territory, complete with illustrations and continental scale distribution maps.

Scoggan, H.J. 1978. *The Flora of Canada Part 2 - Pterophyta Gymnospermae Monocotyledoneae*. National Museum of Natural Sciences Publications in Botany, No. 7(2). Ottawa. pp. 93-545. - a flora for all of Canada.

Taylor, T.M.C. 1963. *The Ferns and Fern-allies of British Columbia*. 2nd ed. British Columbia Provincial Museum Handbook No. 12. Victoria. 172 pp. - a nicely done treatment of the ferns of the province.

Taylor, T.M.C. 1970. *Pacific Northwest Ferns and Their Allies*. University of Toronto Press, Toronto. 247 pp. - the best fern treatment, with maps, illustrations and good discussions of each species. The best book on ferns for our area.

Tryon, R.M., Jr. 1955. *Selaginella rupestris and its allies*. Annuals Missouri Botanical Garden 42:1-99. - a detailed study of this species complex.

Weber, W.A. 1976. *Rocky Mountain Flora. A Field Guide for the Identification of the Ferns, Conifers, and Flowering Plants of the Southern Parkland From the Plains to the Continental Divide*. Colorado Associated University Press, Boulder. 479 pp. - a nicely illustrated field guide.

Glossary

[ ] denotes plural

Axial. Away from the stem or axis.
Acidic rock. Quartzite, granite, sandstone or other rocks that produce no bubbling when a strong acid is applied. Rocks with pH > 7.
Acidophile. A plant that occurs in acidic habitats.
Acrocarpous. Having the sporophyte at the apex of the main stem or terminating a well-developed branch in which the apical cell of the branch or stem is used in the production of the archegonia.
Acuminate. Tapering to a slender apex, at first curving inward and then reversing direction and narrowing gradually to a slender tip.
Acute. Used here in the context of sharply pointed and evenly tapered to the apex.
Adnate. Closely attached to substrate.
Alar cells. The cells at the basal angles of the leaf that attach the leaf to the stem.
Algal layer. Layer of photosynthetic algal cells in the lichen thallus.
Alluvial fan. The alluvial deposit of a stream where it issues from a gorge upon a plain.
Amphithecium. The portion of a lecanorine apothecium external to the proper exciple and usually containing algae, the edge of which forms the thalline margin.
Anastomose. To fuse together, as veins fusing to form a network.
Angiospermous. Pertaining to flowering plants (the Angiosperms).
Annulus. Any ringlike structure; special elastic ring in fern or moss sporangium by action of which the sporangium opens.
Antheridium [antheridia]. The male sex organ; in bryophytes a globose to shortly cylindric sac one cell layer thick in which sperm are developed by mitosis.
Antical. The upper surface or margin of a liverwort leaf.
Apex [apices]. The tip; the end opposite to the point of attachment.
Apical. Belonging to the apex or tip.
Apiculate. Ending in an abrupt, short, sharp point, but not stiff.
Apiculus. A short, abrupt point.
Apothecium [apothecia]. Disc shaped or elongate ascocarp found in most lichens.
Appressed. Adhering closely to the substrate as in lichens; or being closely applied to the stem as in mosses.
Arboreal. Living on trees.
Archegonium [archegonia]. The female sex organ, a flask-shaped structure producing an egg by mitosis.
Areolate. Broken up into small, irregular, usually angular patches, (areoles), often appearing tile-like.
Areole. An island formed by cracks in the thallus.
Ascocarp. The fruiting body of an ascomycete; the specialized structure in which asci are produced.
Ascomycetes. A class of fungi with septate hyphae and spores formed in asci.
Ascospore. A spore produced in an ascus, see spore.
Ascus [asci]. Club-shaped structure in the ascomycetes in which the ascospores are formed.
Asymmetric. Not symmetric.
Attenuate. Slenderly tapering; drawn out gradually to a point.
Auricle. A small, ear-like bulge or lobe at the basal margins of a leaf.
Autoicous. With archegonia and antheridia on the same plant but in separate sheaths of leaves.
Awn. A bristle at the tip of the leaf.

Axil. The upper angle between branches of fruticose lichens, either open or closed in lichens; or between leaf and stem in mosses.
Axillary. In the leaf axils.

Basal squamule. See primary thallus.
Bipinnate. Twice pinnate; each pinna being itself pinnate.
Bistratose. Having the cells in two layers, as in some leaves.
Blade. Expanded portion of leaf or frond.
Bog. A waterlogged, peat forming area, dominated by *Sphagnum*, poor in cations and nutrients because all water is derived from precipitation.
Bordered. Having margins differentiated from the rest of the leaf in shape, size, colour or thickness of cells.
Brood body. Detachable cells or organs which give rise vegetatively to new plants (= gemma).
Bulbiform. Bulb-shaped.

Caespitose. Growing in tufts.
Calcareous rock. Containing lime (calcium carbonate). Rocks with pH > 7 that vigorously bubble when treated by a strong acid.
Calciphile. A plant that occurs in calcareous habitats.
Calyptra [calyptrae]. The thin covering or hood fitted over the upper part of the capsule; it develops as an expansion of the upper part of the archegonium and thus is haploid.
Canaliculate. With a longitudinal groove.
Capitate. Shaped like a head, usually pertaining to apical, semi-globular soralia.
Capsule. The spore-containing sac which, with the seta and foot compose the sporophyte.
Cephalodium [cephalodia]. Warty growths within, or sessile on, the lichen thallus containing blue-green algae (cyanobacteria).
Chlorophyll. The green photosynthetic pigment of plants found in chloroplasts.
Cilium [cilia]. Hairlike outgrowths along margins of lobes or leaves or to the apothecial margin.
Columella. The axis of a capsule around which the spores develop.
Complanate. Flattened together or compressed in one plane.
Concave. Hollowed out or the cave half of a surface.
Concolourous. The same colour.
Conduplicate. Strongly folded along the middle.
Conglutinate. Glued together.
Contiguous. Touching or in close contact, as lobes.
Contorted. Bent into irregular curves, irregularly twisted.
Convex. Rounded on the upper surface.
Cordate. Heart-shaped.
Coriaceous. Leathery in texture.
Cortex. The outer layer of the thallus or stem, consisting of fungal hyphae in lichens; or the outermost row or rows of cells in the stem in mosses and liverworts.
Cortical cells. The outer layer or layers of stem or thallus cells.
Corticate. Having a distinct cortex.
Corticolous. Growing on bark.
Costa. The midrib or nerve in moss leaves.
Costate. Having a costa.
Crenate. With rounded teeth along the margin.
Crenulate. Finely crenate.
Crisped-contorted. Crisped as in a fried piece of bacon; contorted as a cork-screw.
Crustose. A lichen growth form with thalli growing in intimate contact with the substrate and lacking a lower cortex.
Cucullate. Forming a pocket opening on one side; of a calyptra, usually cone-shaped and slit on one side only.
Cuticular. Of or belonging to the cuticle (the non-cellular covering of such organs as leaves or capsules), often variously roughened.
Cyanobacterium. A group of organisms related to true bacteria and belonging to the Kingdom Monera. Classically considered as Cyanophyta or blue-green algae.
Cylindric. Relating to or having the form or properties of a cylinder, especially moss capsules with straight sides and much longer than wide.
Cyphella [cyphellae]. Recessed pores, such as on the undersurface of *Sticta*.

Deciduous. Used here to refer to trees belonging to the angiosperms.
Decorticate. Areas where the cortex has been lost, or in reference to log areas that have lost their bark.
Decumbent. Lying along the ground, usually with ascending apices.
Decurrent. Applied to leaves when the basal angles extend down the stem on each side in wing-like fashion.
Deltoid. Broadly triangular, especially like an equilateral triangle.
Dentate. Toothed, especially when the teeth are blunt and directed more or less outward from the leaves or lobes and other structures.
Depauperate. Poorly developed.
Dichotomous. Branching into two equal parts, as in the letter "Y".
Dimorphic. Occurring in two forms - ferns having sterile and fertile fronds.
Dioicous. With archegonia and antheridia on separate plants.
Disc. The central upper surface inside the margins of the apothecium.
Distichous. In two opposite rows, especially leaves inserted on opposite sides of the stem.
Divergent. Spreading from each other.
Dorsal. Upon, or relating to the back or lower surface of a frond; the surface away from the axis.

Ecostate. Without a costa.
Ecotonal. A transition area between two adjacent ecological communities.
Elater. Small, unicellular thread-like structures found among the spores of liverworts, usually spirally thickened and hygroscopic; also present in *Equisetum*.
Elliptic. Oblong with convex (rounded) ends and sides.
Elongate. Considerably longer than wide.
Embrown. Darken from exposure to the sun.
Emergent. Aquatic mosses partially extending out of water. Of capsules projecting partially above the perichaetial leaves.
Endemic. Confined to, or indigenous in, a certain region.
Endophloedal. Within bark.
Entire. Without teeth or lobing; with a continuous margin.
Epiphyte. A plant that derives its moisture and nutrients from the air and rain and occurs on another plant.
Epithecium [epithecia]. The layer on top of the hymenium formed by the tips of the paraphyses.
Epruinose. Without pruinia.
Equitant. Straddling, like a rider on horseback, referring to the conduplicate and strongly sheathing leaf bases of *Fissidens*.
Erose. Irregularly notched or ragged, as though gnawed.
Eutrophic. Originally referring to high levels of productivity, induced by high nutrient levels, as indicated by characteristic diatom assemblages; we use it to indicate nutrient-rich (nitrogen, phosphate) habitats.
Exciple. The portion of the apothecium that surrounds the hymenium and forms the proper margin of the apothecium.
Excurrent. Applied to a costa which extends beyond the lamina.
Exostome. Outer layer of peristome in those mosses with two peristome layers, technically the peristome layer with teeth having two tiers of cells when viewed from the outside.
Exserted. Extending beyond; of capsules when the perichaetial leaves do not reach as high as the base.

Falcate. Curved like the blade of a sickle.
Falcate-secund. Strongly curved and turned to one side.
Farinose. Very fine, powdery soredia.
Fen. A peat-forming area receiving nutrients from ground water and precipitation, hence more ionically-rich than a bog.
Festooning. Hanging or draping from.
Fibril. Thickening of the hyaline cells of *Sphagnum* that projects into the cell and forms an oblique to transverse bar across the cell.
Filamentous. Very slender or thread-like; applied to divisions of peristome teeth or to paraphyllia.
Filiform. See filamentous.
Fissure. Narrow opening or crack.
Flagelliform. Like the lash of a whip.

Flark. The elongate pools of water that form perpendicular to the direction of water flow and alternate with the drier strings in patterned fens.
Flexuose. Slightly and irregularly bent, twisted or wavy.
Foliose. A lichen growth form, bilaterally symmetric, leaflike with an upper and usually a lower cortex.
Foveate. Pitted, with grooves or depressions.
Frond. A much divided leaf, as that of a fern.
Fruticose. A lichen growth form that is radially symmetric; tufted, stalked or pendent and surrounded by a cortex.
Fuscous. A smoky dark colour, dark brown.

Gametophyte. The dominant, sexual generation; in mosses - the green, leafy plant; in liverworts - the gametophyte may be leafy or thallose. Haploid.
Gemma. Small, globose, elliptic or cylindric body of a few cells serving in vegetative reproduction.
Glabrous. Smooth; without any pubescence or hairs.
Glaucous. With a whitish, greyish or bluish overcast (resembling the waxy bloom on a plum).
Globose. Spherical.
Granulose. Pertaining to soredia; granules or particles seen under a dissecting microscope - not powdery as farinose.
Gyrose. Convolutedly ridged, folded as the top of a cinnamon bun.

Hoary. Whitish or greyish.
Hollow. The low, wet portion of the undulating surface of a peatland.
Hummock. The raised, usually circular mounds in bogs and fens.
Hyaline. Colourless, transparent or clear.
Hyalodermus. In *Sphagnum*, a cortex of large, empty, colourless cells.
Hygroscopic. Changing position with a change in humidity.
Hymenium. The fertile layer of an ascocarp containing the asci and paraphyses.
Hypha [hyphae]. Microscopic multicellular fungal thread that gives shape to the lichen thallus.
Hypothallus [hypothalli]. A layer of fungal tissue (usually black) next to the substrate and below the thallus proper often appearing between areoles of a crustose lichen or forming a marginal zone around the thallus.
Hypothecium [hypothecia]. The tissue layer immediately below the hymenium, usually expanded into a cone between the exciple and hymenium (as seen in a medial apothecial section).

Imarginate. Lacking a clearly defined margin.
Imbricate. Closely appressed and overlapping.
Incubous. Opposite of succubous: with leaves overlapping like shingles on a roof if base of plant is at the ridge of the roof and the apex at the eaves.
Indusium. Membrane covering or surrounding a sorus in ferns.
Internode. Portion of a stem between adjacent nodes.
Involucre. In hepatics, a protective covering around the calyptra (hood of capsule).
Involucrellum. A cap or covering over the perithecium and its exciple.
Isidiate. With isidia.
Isidium [isidia]. Minute thalline outgrowth which is corticate and contains algae; functions as a vegetative propagule.
Isodiametric. Having equal diameters in all directions.

Julaceous. Shoots rendered smoothly cylindrical by the closely and evenly imbricate leaves.

Keel. A sharp ridge as when a leaf is folded along the midrib or main division.
Krummholz. Stunted forest characteristic of alpine timberline.

Labriform. Lip shaped (= labrose).
Lacerate. With irregularly cut or torn margins.

Lamella. Green ridge or plate on the costa or lamina of some moss leaves or the undersurface of some species of the lichen genus *Umbilicaria*.
Lamina [laminae]. The blade of the leaf as distinguished from the costa.
Laminal. Superficial on the surface of the thallus as in soredia or apothecia of lichens.
Lanceolate. Shaped like the head of a lance, broadest at the base and narrowed to the apex.
Lax. Soft or loose, usually referring to large thin-walled cells.
Lecanorine. Apothecium having a thalline margin, in which both algae and fungi are present.
Lecideine. Apothecium with a proper margin; in which no algal cells are present.
Lignicolous. Growing on decorticated wood, not on living bark.
Ligulate. Strap-shaped with margins parallel.
Linear. Very narrow, with parallel sides.
Lirella. Ascocarp with an elongate disc.
Lobate. Lobed.
Lobe. A rounded or strap-shaped division of the thallus of lichens; or a division of a leaf in liverworts.
Lower lobe. In a folded, complicate-bilobed leaf (see *Porella cordaeana*); the part lying nearest the substratum.
Lumen. The cavity of a cell.

Macula [maculae]. White area, blotch or spot on a thallus surface caused by an absence of algae just below the cortex.
Mamillose. Applied to cells that are bulging with a central nipple.
Mazaedium. An ascocarp in which a mass of spores and paraphyses is formed by the disintegration of the asci as in *Calicium*.
Medulla [medullae]. The inner part of the thallus that lacks algae, usually of loosely packed fungal hyphae.
Mesic. Of moist habitat, neither very wet nor very dry.
Minerotrophic. Influenced by ground water, often areas with highly ionic water.
Mire. A peatland; an area with a deposition of organic soil.
Multistratose. Having the cells in many layers.
Muriform. Describes spores divided into many chambers by transverse and longitudinal walls.
Musicolous. Growing on moss.
Muticous. Without a point; blunt or rounded at the apex.
Mycobiont. Fungal symbiont of a lichen.

Nodose. With rounded thickenings at intervals.
Nonsorediate. Lacking soredia.
Nostoc. A genus of blue-green algae (cyanobacteria) that grows in bead-like chains when free living but sometimes occurs singly or in small groups when lichenized.

Obliquely. An angle of leaf insertion between 0° and 90° to the stem, between transverse (90° to stem) and flat (0° to stem).
Oblong. Rectangular.
Obtuse. Blunt or rounded.
Ombrotrophic. Receiving water and nutrients only from precipitation.
Operculum [opercula]. The lid or cover of the capsule.
Orbicular. Round and flat.
Ostiole. Small, round, apical pore in various types of ascocarps, especially in perithecia of the Verrucariaceae.
Ovate. Egg-shaped (with the base broader than the apex).
Ovoid. Usually of solid objects, like capsules, ovate or oval in outline.

Papilla [papillae]. Minute, wart-like protuberance.
Papillate. With papillae.
Papillose. With one or more small projections from cells, usually solid and confined to the cell lumen.
Paraphyllium. Minute leaflike or filamentous structure borne on the stems and branches among the leaves of pleurocarpous mosses.
Paraphysis [paraphyses]. Sterile hair growing between the asci in the hymenium of an Ascomycete or between sex organs of mosses and liverworts.
Pellucid. Clear, translucent or transparent.

Peltate. Attached at the centre of the lower surface, edges are free in an umbrella-shape.
Pendent. Hanging down, forming a long, slender thallus.
Percurrent. Reaching to the apex but not beyond; percurrent costa.
Perennial. Lasting or growing for several years.
Perforate. With holes.
Perianth. A tube, apparently derived from two or three fused leaves, surrounding the developing sporophyte of liverworts.
Perichaetial leaf. The special leaf or bract surrounding the archegonium and base of the seta.
Perichaetium [perichaetia]. See perichaetial leaf.
Periphyses. Sterile hyphae located inside the ostiole of the Verrucariaceae.
Peristome. The fringe of teeth around the mouth of a capsule of mosses.
Perithecium. A flask-shaped fruiting body (ascocarp) immersed in the thallus, with a terminal, dark and often protruding opening.
Photobiont. Algal symbiont of a lichen.
Phyllocladium. Tiny granular or lobed structure on branches of *Stereocaulon*.
Pinna. Primary division of a pinnately compound blade.
Pinnate. With numerous, spreading branches on two sides of the axis and thus resembling a feather.
Pinnatifid. Pinnately cut; the divisions extending deeply but not all the way to the rachis or midrib.
Pinnule. Primary division of a pinna; the secondary segment of a compound blade.
Pleuripapillose. With more than one papilla per cell cavity.
Pleurocarpous. Producing the sporophytes laterally from a perichaetial bud or a short, specialized branch, thus not using the apical cell of the stem in archegonial production.
Plicate. Of leaves and capsules when they are folded longitudinally in pleats, or with ridges and furrows.
Plume. Feathery.
Podetium [podetia]. A stalk-like thalline elevation supporting an apothecium or apothecia in the genera *Cladina*, *Cladonia* and *Baeomyces*.
Podium. A platform.
Poikilohydric. The physiological ability to resist drought, reviving and green when moist, dry and brown when water is lacking.
Polarilocular. Two-celled spores separated by a thick septum through which a narrow canal or isthmus passes, e.g. in *Caloplaca*.
Polysetous. With more than one seta per perichaetium.
Porose. Walls of cells indented or perforated with pores.
Postical. The lower surface of the plant or lower margin of a leaf in liverworts.
Primary thallus. The thallus of *Cladonia* species exclusive of the podetia; the basal squamules.
Proliferate. To produce parts in succession, as cups in some *Cladonia* species.
Proliferating. Having small offshoots or outgrowths.
Propagulum [propagula]. A reduced bud, branch or leaf serving in asexual reproduction.
Proper margin. The edge of the apothecial exciple containing fungal, but not algal cells; usually the same colour as the disc.
Prostrate. Lying flat on the substrate.
Protonema [protonemata]. Branched filaments or plate-like growths arising from spores on which the leafy parts of mosses develop.
Pruina. A fine, white, wooly or granular covering on the upper cortex or on the disc of apothecia.
Pruinose. Having a frosted appearance.
Pseudocyphellum. White patch, dot and line on the upper and/or lower cortex of some foliose and fruticose lichens caused by a break in the cortex and extension of the medulla to the surface.
Pseudopodetium. Podetium-like stalk formed by upward growth of the thalline tissue supporting the apothecia in *Stereocaulon*.
Pseudopodium. A gametophytic stalk that functions as a seta in *Andreaea* and *Sphagnum*.

Pseudothecium. A fruiting body that lacks a hymenium. Asci are produced in locules among branched hyphae.

Pycnidium. Small flask-shaped structure in which pycnoconidia (spore-like conidia) are produced; having an ostiole and resembling a perithecium.

Rachis. Main axis of a compound frond or leaf.

Radiate. To spread outwards from a central point.

Rank. Row.

Recurved. Curved downward or backward, referring to leaf margins or tips, marginal teeth or peristome teeth.

Reflexed. Bent backward.

Relict. A persistent remnant of an otherwise extinct flora or fauna or kind of organism.

Reniform. Kidney-shaped.

Reticulate. With a network of ridges, grooves, lines or pigmentation on the surface.

Revolute. Rolled backward and under, as the margins of leaves.

Rheophyte. A plant that is associated with swiftly flowing water.

Rhizine. Threadlike branched, unbranched, tufted, or brush-like organ of attachment that is composed of fungal hyphae.

Rhizoid. A thread-like growth, simple or branched, which serves for absorption and anchorage, never with chlorophyll in mosses and liverworts.

Rhizome. An underground stem from which fronds or upright stems arise.

Rhombic. Diamond-shaped.

Rimose. Marked with numerous cracks.

Rimose-areolate. Spaces (areoles) separated by cracks (rimae).

Robust. Large, both in overall size and in coarseness.

Rosette. A roughly circular cluster of leaves (lobes) (areoles) radiating from a central point.

Rugose. Wrinkled as crumpled paper.

Saxicolous. Growing on rocks.

Secund. Curved to one side.

Sedge. Any of a family of tufted marsh plants differing from grasses in having achenes and solid stems. (Cyperaceae, the sedge family).

Septate. Divided into two or more parts by a septum or wall, in septate spores composed of more than one cell.

Serrate. Saw-toothed, having sharp teeth directed forward.

Serrulate. Finely or weakly serrate.

Sessile. Without a stalk or seta.

Seta [setae]. The stalk of the capsule in the sporophyte of mosses and liverworts.

Setaceous. Bristle-like.

Sheath. The leaves or bases of leaves that surround or clasp the stem or base of the seta.

Siliceous. Applied to quartzite, sandstone, granite or other acidic substrate.

Simple. With one part.

Sinuose. Wavy, bending from side to side.

Soralium (soralia). Localized clump of soredia on the surface or margin of a lichen thallus.

Soredium [soredia]. Small powdery propagule that contains several algal cells and fungal hyphae, originating in the algal layer and breaking through the cortex of a lichen.

Sorediate. Having soredia.

Sorus. Cluster of sporangia in ferns.

Spathulate. Narrow at the base and broadened to a rounded apex, like a spathula.

Spicule. A small, curved to straight spine.

Spinulose. Beset with small spines or sharp points.

Sporangium. A sac or container in which spores are produced as the result of meiosis.

Spore. Produced in an ascus (lichens), capsule (mosses and liverworts) or sporangium (ferns); capable of giving rise to a new plant; can be single-celled, two-celled or multi-celled; hyaline greenish or brown; always haploid and the result of meiosis.

Sporophyll. Spore-bearing leaf.

Sporophyte. The spore-bearing part or phase, in bryophytes composed of foot, seta (stalk) and capsule, in ferns the leafy plant. Diploid.

Squamulose. Scaly, a thallus made up of squamules.
Squamule. A small scale-like lobe or areole, which lacks a lower cortex and generally is at least partially ascending.
Squarrose. Spreading at right angles.
Squarrose-recurved. Spreading at right angles, with the tips curved downward.
Stipe. Stem or stalk.
Striate. Marked with fine parallel ridges.
Strobilus [strobili]. Group of sporophylls forming a conelike structure.
Strumose. Having a struma (a goiter-like swelling).
Subula. A long, evenly tapering point.
Subulate. Slenderly long-acuminate, shaped like a needle or awl.
Succubous. With leaves overlapping like shingles on a roof if base of plant is at "eaves" and apex at "ridge".

Taxon. A taxonomic group of any rank.
Taxonomy. The theory and practice of describing organisms and ordering them into a system of classification.
Terete. Circular in transverse section.
Ternate. Arranged in threes, or divided into three segments.
Terricolous. Growing on soil.
Thalline. Resembling the thallus; the edge of the amphithecium that when present surrounds the proper margin and contains both algal and fungal cells.
Thallose. Having a thallus; thallus-like in appearance.
Thallus [thalli]. The lichen body, consisting of both fungus and alga; or a plant body not differentiated into stem and leaf in liverworts.
Tomentum. A covering of fine densely matted hairs, rhizoids or paraphyllia.
Tristichous. With three ranks.
Tubercle. Warty, knob-like structure found in *Usnea*.
Tubular. In leaves, when margins are inrolled and overlapping to form a tube.
Tufted. Referring to fruticose lichens whose short (<10 cm long), branches are clustered at the base to a round or angular clump.

Umbilicate. Attached to the substrate by a single, central point on the lower surface of the thallus.
Umbilicus. A depression or 'belly button' seen on the upper surface of a thallus that coincides with the point of attachment on the lower surface of umbilicate lichens, especially species of *Umbilicaria*.
Undulate. With wavy margin or surface. The waves oriented across the leaves, as opposed to plicate, where the waves are longitudinally oriented.
Unipapillate. Having one papilla per cell surface.
Unistratose. Having cells in one layer.
Upper lobe. In a folded, complicate-bilobed leaf, the part lying on top.

Vallecular. Pertaining to the region in the stem of *Equisetum* opposite a groove.
Valve. Sections (usually four) into which the capsule wall splits to release spores in liverworts.
Vein. On the lower surface of some species of *Peltigera*, thickenings of hyphae which form ridges, often pigmented.
Ventral. Upper or inner face of a leaf; opposite side to dorsal.
Verruca. Wart-like elevation on the surface of the thallus.

Whorl. Several structures arising at the same level on an axis.

Xeric. Very dry.
Xerophyte. A plant occurring in dry habitats.

Zonate. Ringed (particularly at the margin of the thallus), in circular lines.

Index to Scientific and Common Names

This is an index to names used in this book. Species treated in this book have their authority names and are in bold face; synonymous scientific names are in italics and generic and species names mentioned in the discussions and common names are in regular face. Vascular plants other than ferns and their allies and species mentioned in the introduction are not included.